Dicks Out 2

You're not Singing Any More ?

by

Rob Merrills

Red Card Publishing

Written by
Rob Merrills

Edited by
David Jenkins & Judi Holly

© Red Card Publishing Ltd
First Impression August 1997

Published in Great Britain by
Red Card Publishing Ltd.
4 Bowater Place
Blackheath
London   SE3 8ST
England

Film output by
Scantech Limited
Heathfield
East Sussex

Printed by
D C Graphics
Bexhill on Sea
East Sussex
and
Longridge Print
Crowborough
East Sussex

Paper supplied by
Fenner Paper Ltd
Tonbridge
Kent

Bound by
Independent Binders
Tunbridge Wells
Kent

A catalogue record for this book
is available from the British Library

ISBN 0 952661020

For Dad

For Dad

Contents

Preface   ix

Introduction   xi

The South & South East   A F C Bournemouth   3
                              Brighton & Hove Albion   5
                              Gillingham   9
                              Portsmouth   11
                              Southampton   14
                              Southend United   17

The Thames Valley   Oxford United   23
                              Reading   24
                              Swindon Town   27
                              Wycombe Wanderers   28

London   Arsenal   33
                              Barnet   36
                              Brentford   37
                              Charlton Athletic   39
                              Chelsea   41
                              Crystal Palace   47
                              Fulham   49
                              Leyton Orient   51
                              Millwall   54
                              Tottenham Hotspur   55
                              Watford   58
                              West Ham United   60

East Anglia   Cambridge United   67
                              Ipswich Town   69
                              Northampton Town   73
                              Norwich City   76
                              Peterborough United   78

East Midlands   Chesterfield   83
                              Derby County   84
                              Leicester City   87
                              Mansfield Town   89
                              Nottingham Forest   91
                              Notts County   94

Humberside   Grimsby Town   99
                              Hull City   102
                              Lincoln City   107
                              Scunthorpe United   109

Yorkshire   Barnsley   115
                              Bradford City   117
                              Doncaster Rovers   119
                              Huddersfield Town   123
                              Leeds United   125
                              Rotherham United   129
                              Scarborough   131
                              Sheffield United   132
                              Sheffield Wednesday   135
                              York City   139

The North East	Darlington	143
	Hartlepool	144
	Middlesbrough	147
	Newcastle United	150
	Sunderland	155

The North West	Blackburn Rovers	161
	Bolton Wanderers	163
	Burnley	165
	Everton	168
	Liverpool	172
	Manchester City	175
	Manchester United	181
	Oldham Athletic	188
	Preston North End	190
	Stockport County	192
	Wigan Athletic	194

Potteries & Marches	Crewe Alexandra	199
	Hereford United	201
	Port Vale	205
	Shrewsbury Town	208
	Stoke City	210
	Tranmere Rovers	211

The West Midlands	Aston Villa	217
	Birmingham City	218
	Coventry City	221
	West Bromwich Albion	223
	Wolverhampton Wanderers	227

Wales & West Country	Bristol City	237
	Bristol Rovers	239
	Cardiff City	241
	Exeter City	243
	Plymouth Argyle	244
	Swansea City	247
	Torquay United	250
	Wrexham	252

Scotland	Aberdeen	257
	Celtic	260
	East Fife	267
	Heart of Midlothian	270
	Kilmarnock	276
	Rangers	279

Northern Ireland	Cliftonville	291
	Coleraine	294
	Glentoran	296
	Larne	299
	Linfield	301

| Appendix | | 305 |

| Index | | 309 |

Preface

Five years on from the original *Dicks Out!* it is a pleasure to report that the grim scenario which then faced domestic football and its supporters has ultimately not come to pass. The footballing public of the U K have - after a brief period of grudging acceptance - refused to be silenced by the strictures of the Taylor Report. Its recommendations threatened to sanitise the game to such an extent that the reason for its very existence - the entertainment of the people - was on the brink of being relegated to little more than an afterthought to be afforded cursory consideration by the money men who run the game after balance sheets had been reconciled, share dividends calculated and profits maximised.

In 1992 the historic terraces from which much of the driving passion behind the game had come for so many years were being swept away under an avalanche of plastic seats. With the authorities loftily claiming that this was all for the good of the spectators in the light of Bradford, Heysel and Hillsborough, it took a while for their genuine, hidden agenda to become clear. It was all down to simple economics - pile seats on to the terraces, reduce the capacities, but charge those that were still able to get in more than enough to compensate for the smaller attendances. Demand for the reduced number of spaces was sure to be high, as the same number of people would still want to attend matches - and here the real beauty of the scheme came in to its own - having created a shortfall in the number of available places under the pretence of looking after supporters' interests, you could charge those same supporters vastly inflated prices claiming that it was merely a case of supply and demand - brilliant! This all worked very well for two or three seasons, but slowly a feeling developed that something was missing from the game. Fair enough, multi-million pound players were cavorting about in multi-million pound stadiums while multi-million pound deals were rubber-stamped by disinterested corporate hospitality guests in soundproofed executive boxes - but did anybody really care any more?

With the once-boisterous terracing now filled with regimented ranks of muted family groups, and the disenfranchised supporters preferring to stay in the pubs on match days and watch what was once their team on satellite and cable, the game as an occasion, as a passion play was threatening to die on its feet. It was decided that the forgotten supporters had to be wooed back into the grounds, and all manner of feeble Americanisms were initiated in an attempt to resurrect the old atmosphere - inflatable sumo wrestlers, firework displays, laser shows and stunt-driving police dogs suddenly became the order of the day. Certain clubs even stooped so low as to enlist supporters to participate in orchestrated singalongs to try and bring back the vibrancy on which the game had thrived, but these insulting and condescending schemes were given the reception they deserved and were soon forgotten.

Then came the European Championships in 1996.

Throughout June of that year, the country revelled in the competition which was enlivened by each participating nation's fans bringing their own particular brand of exuberance to the matches. Even the England supporters - so often morose and eager to criticise their team - were caught up in the excitement of the run to the semi-finals. More importantly they rediscovered their voices, almost entirely by way of the ludicrously popular *Three Lions* song. There was a feeling that the nation's football fans had been reminded that it was both possible and acceptable to enjoy themselves while watching the game, and the following domestic season saw this renaissance extend to matches in the Premiership and Nationwide League. *Three Lions* could be heard everywhere in any number of different guises, as could *Daydream Believer* which had been introduced to the footballing community by Sunderland supporters towards the end of the 95/6 season. The European influence was also to the fore, with the Sheffield Wednesday band popularising a Dutch tune from Euro '96 which was instantly picked up on by supporters across the length and breadth of the United Kingdom. At grounds everywhere supporters who had spent the previous few seasons sullenly squeezed into their seats decided that they were going to stand up again (a movement which engendered many songs in its own right) and reclaim what amounted to their birthright to let their hair down on a Saturday afternoon. Singing was very much back on the agenda and, with a new government sweeping to power in May '97, there was even a glimmer of hope that some of the hated seats might be ripped out and the terraces opened up again.

It is against this background of renewed optimism that this book is now being released. No longer having to fulfil the role of an epitaph to a dying art, but rather as a catalogue, a source book from which inspiration can be taken. Find your favourite songs from the pages which follow, adapt the words to suit your team, stand up on your bloody seat and sing, and don't let any po-faced steward tell you that you can't!

Rob Merrills
July 1997

x

Introduction

Full of excuses and apologies this bit, but there are a few matters that need clearing up before we get down to business! In the first instance - swearing. There are, at a conservative estimate, four or five naughty swearwords which appear in the pages that follow, but these have been left "unasterisked" as it were, as one of the few recurring complaints received after the first edition was along the lines of "why have the rude words been blotted out when everyone knows full well what they are anyway, and when they are so integral to some of the songs?" This seemed to be a fair comment, so the songs and chants which follow have been reproduced in all their Anglo Saxon glory - sorry if anyone is offended!

On the subject of offending people, another point borne in mind in the aftermath of the first coming of *Dicks Out!* is that the decision not to include one particular category of song met with universal approval. We all know what these songs are - the Munich chants, the Hillsborough and Bradford songs, anything about the death of someone particularly associated with a certain club - all the tactless crap which was sung with the sole intention of provoking some sort of violent reaction from the supporters to whom it was directed. None of these songs have been included this time round as they simply have no place alongside the other material which is - for the most part - all about the wit and humour of football supporters from across the United Kingdom (apart from most of the Hartlepool United songs which are a law entirely unto themselves!).

One of the most glaring omissions from this edition is anything from the incomparable collection of vocal lunacy authored by the supporters of Meadowbank Thistle which provided many of the high points of the original publication. Thistle, sadly, are no more, and the songs have died with the old club (as it would appear that barely a handful of supporters have bothered to follow the new outfit to Livingston). For a similar reason, Halifax Town and Maidstone United have both lost their places in these hallowed pages, but with indecision as to their respective futures very much the order of the day as we go to press, both Hereford United and Brighton & Hove Albion have been included.

With regard to the words to the songs which follow, remember that in the majority of cases these have been sent in by individual contributors who - if you know the songs yourself - may not have heard exactly the same version. Please don't feel obliged to write in and point out that the song *you* know about Scunthorpe United's kit or whatever actually says "to" in the fourth line when it's got "of" in the book! If, however, you know some substantially different version of a particular song, or perhaps something of the story behind why a song has developed, then feel free to drop us a line - future generations may then get to read some more accurate and worthwhile information. Equally, there are a dozen or so songs contained herein which have been submitted along with a note to the effect of "me and my mate Dave heard this in the pub after an away game at Colchester in 1992" - everything has been reproduced in good faith, and just because you've been to every Port Vale game since 1904 and have never heard something that has been attributed to your club, bear in mind that you may not be party to absolutely everything which goes on!

Less contentiously, where there are no songs at all listed for a particular club, this is not as a result of deep-seated editorial bias (I've always had a sneaking affection for Rochdale and Wimbledon, as it happens) but purely because not one - not a single one - of their supporters could be bothered to put pen to paper and send anything in at any time over the last five years. I suggest that scorn and derision is the order of the day next time you find yourself in the vicinity of a supporter of any of the clubs thus excluded. See if you can provoke them into some sort of reaction by way of some cruel taunting - experience would dictate that they will silently shrug their shoulders and remain utterly impassive!

As far as tunes go, I have tried to give as good an idea of what each song sounds like by simply noting the title of whatever tune it takes. In some cases, no idea at all of tune or rhythm has been given by contributors, and while it has been possible to make an educated guess in some cases, others have utterly defied comprehension and must sadly remain a mystery. As with lyrics, any additional information on this subject in cases where nothing has been put forward would be gratefully received.

Finally, just a note to say that it would be impossible to have given a true reflection of the nature of the UK's football songs without including many of the contributions which might appear to be less than complementary toward a particular club or player. It goes without saying that publication of such material does not in any way endorse the sentiments contained therein. So, if you happen to be a retired ex-pro who finally finds out the horrific truth of exactly what the Carlisle supporters were singing at you during that Full Members Cup tie back in 1983, please don't take it to heart - they were probably all drunk anyway!

Section One

The South & South East

A F C Bournemouth

Brighton & Hove Albion

Gillingham

Portsmouth

Southampton

Southend United

The South & South East

Never really an area of the country renowned for the passion of its supporters, there are still some notable songs which have gone on to greater things having first been heard down on the South Coast. Brighton & Hove Albion have provided both of the region's seminal songs with *The Quartermaster's Stores* establishing itself throughout the country, and *Celery* proving equally as popular while not managing to gain a real foothold more than a mile or so north of the River Thames (by way of its appearance at Stamford Bridge).

None of the clubs covered in this section can really have been said to have enjoyed a prolonged spell of league success - which is seemingly a prerequisite for the development of a reasonable repertoire of songs. Since terrace songs became fashionable in the 1960's, only Southampton have enjoyed more than a fleeting acquaintance with the top division, and their supporters have had their efforts curtailed by having to "perform" at The Dell, which has never been one of the best grounds for generating atmosphere. Before redevelopment, Fratton Park was perhaps the region's venue most conducive to singing, but Pompey have only briefly flirted with the sort of league status which guarantees large and vocal crowds, and have fallen as far as the old Fourth Division in the not too distant past. As a result of these failings, it has been occasional cup runs which have provided the best opportunity for the supporters of the South of England to show their true colours - and all have risen to the occasion. Bournemouth can look to their epic encounters with Manchester United for inspiration, Pompey have managed a couple of excursions to the latter stages of the F A Cup, Southampton can number two Wembley appearances amongst their achievements and even Brighton have been able to console themselves during their recent woes with the memories of 1983. However, fleeting glory in knock-out competitions only tends to leave a legacy of one or two songs which refer to specific matches, and when the "part time supporters" have disappeared from the scene, the terraces of the Southern counties swiftly return to their more usual rather sedate state.

Where even cup success has failed to materialise, some interesting alternatives have cropped up by way of subject matter. Southend United supporters, for instance, have travelled the country for many a year extolling the virtues of their pier which juts into the Thames Estuary - particularly when they find themselves playing in another seaside town which cannot boast so impressive a structure. Gillingham, lacking a pier, cup glory, sustained league success and even a local rival since the demise of Maidstone United, have only a fat goalkeeper to inspire them - but even this has proved enough to generate a bit of interest, which shows some resourcefulness if nothing else!

A F C Bournemouth

A very welcome debut for The Cherries given their non-appearance in the first edition of this book, and especially so as they managed to survive a succession of winding up orders during 1997 and football now seems assured under the innovative community lead scheme which is in place. From a singing point of view, a bit of a hotch potch from Dean Court with a great many standard reworking of well worn themes but also a couple of more worthy efforts. The first of these serves up probably the most substantial adaptation of the oft-used *Tennessee Wig Walk* (by Bonnie Lou), which was a very popular tune on the terraces during the late 1960's and early 1970's (witness surviving efforts at Scunthorpe, Northampton and others). Unusually, there is also a degree of background information to the Bournemouth version which, incidentally, is....

> *Bertie Mee said to Bill Shankley*
> *"Have you heard of the North Bank, Highbury?"*
> *Shanks said "No, I don't think so,*
> *But I've heard of the Bournemouth Boot Boys"*
> *Laaaa - la, la, la, la, la, la, la, la, la, la, la, la, la, la, laaaa;*
> *Laaaa - la, la, la, la, la, la, la,*
> *Doing the Bournemouth Boot Walk.*
>
> *I'm a knock kneed chicken, I'm a bow-legged hen,*
> *I ain't had a fuck since I don't know when,*
> *I walk with a wiggle and a squiggle and a squawk,*
> *Doing the Bournemouth Boot Walk!*
> *Laaaa - la, la, la, la, la, la, la, la, la, la, la, la, la, la, laaaa;*
> *Laaaa - la, la, la, la, la, la, la,*
> *Doing the Bournemouth Boot Walk!*

Utterly incomprehensible unless you know the tune, or unless you are a Fulham supporter, as they also have a version of the above which extends beyond the bounds of the less ambitious performances from Glandford Park and Sixfields, but which is not as complete a reproduction of the original as the Dean Court opus. Anyway, the point which makes the song particularly pertinent to The Cherries is the mention of the Bournemouth Boot Walk, which was formerly the popular name of the wooden section at the top of the South End terrace at Dean Court. Now closed as a result of Justice Taylor's strictures, this evidently used to be the area of the ground inhabited by those who were not averse to slapping a few heads in the name of A F C Bournemouth - which was, of course, thoroughly reprehensible behaviour.

With regard to the somewhat less original fare on offer, *You Are My Sunshine* makes an appearance in its usual format (as set out under the Leicester City

section), and The Beatles' peculiarly-hued mode of underwater transport becomes
a red and black submarine" when it is given voice in the Bournemouth cause.
Of a more event-specific nature than these general songs, the club's famous
1983/84 F A Cup win over Manchester United was immortalised through the
use of....

> *A F C, we'll score three,*
> *Bryan Robson's hurt his knee,*
> *With a nick nack paddy whack,*
> *Give a dog a bone,*
> *Man United, fuck off home*

....to the traditional tune (*cf* Lincoln City), though containing a rather bizarre
reference to the result of the match in the first line - Bournemouth actually
beat United 2-0! The exclusively Southern-based *Celery* chant (*cf* Brighton,
Gillingham and Chelsea) has been known to get an airing or two at Cherries'
games, particularly during the 1986/87 Third Division championship-winning
season and with the "original" lyrics intact apart from the small but nonetheless
significant fact that the apocryphal young lady is actually tickled *on* the bum
by her Bournemouth suitors, whereas everyone else just tickles her bum!
Another song, the like of which only tends to be heard south of an imaginary
line between Bristol and London, is one which is prone to crop up during less
enthralling passages of play when alternative entertainment is required. To
no particular tune, and to be repeated as many times as is possible, we
have....

> *We're from Bournemouth - sunny, sunny Bournemouth,*
> *And if you can't hear us, we'll sing a little louder....*
> *We're from Bournemouth - sunny, sunny Bournemouth,*
> *And if you can't hear us, we'll sing a little louder....*

The theory with this is that each repetition is supposed to be that little bit
louder than the previous one so that the song builds up to a crescendo over
the course of a few minutes, but everyone generally ends up shouting as
loudly as possible after just two or three rounds, and it then continues at an
even volume until the singers get fed up. Rumour has it that this was initially
a Plymouth Argyle composition (though obviously having been *"We're from
Plymouth...."* in its original format), which was copied from the green and white
hordes after Bournemouth's game at Swindon in November 1987. It transpires
that there were a good many Argyle supporters in attendance as they were
looking to exact revenge after one of their number had been stabbed during
their visit to the County Ground a fortnight earlier - history unfortunately does
not record the outcome of this vengeful excursion.

Lastly - passing over such staple fare as *"Walking in a Machin Wonderland"* (in
praise of manager Mel who engineered an extraordinary escape from relegation

during the second half of 94/5) and something about having the arse of a crow and flying over Southampton (*cf* Sheffield United) - we come to the second of the more laudable Bournemouth songs. A simple, straightforward and utterly impressive variation on the Simon & Garfunkel ditty from *The Graduate* (although perhaps more likely to have been inspired by The Lemonheads version released in 1992) we have the following, in praise of Steve Robinson who was rescued from the obscurity of a loan period at Leyton Orient when The Cherries signed him from Spurs in October 1994....

> *Just score a goal, Stevie Robinson,*
> *And we will love you more than you will know,*
> *Woah-oh-oh, woah-oh-oh!*

Suitably inspired, Steve was to register twelve league goals in seventy three appearances up to the end of the 95/6 season. A similar effort subsequently made an appearance a few miles up the coast at The Dell, with Neil Shipperley being the player thus feted by the Southampton fans, but the song does not then appear to have continued its eastward migration and followed Shipperley to Crystal Palace. If, as is reputedly the case, a similar sort of thing made an appearance at The Goldstone Ground directed at Michael Robinson, this would seem to have become another common theme peculiar to the counties bordering the English Channel in the same way as *Celery* has now found itself established in the region.

Brighton & Hove Albion

Much loved by the media, much loathed by the supporters of other clubs at the foot of Division Three as 96/7 drew to a close and much relieved to have stuck around long enough for anyone to care, Albion will take a rich singing heritage with them as they decamp to Hove Greyhound Stadium, Toads Hole Valley or wherever else fate may propel them in the future. Never really acknowledged as being the most passionate of crowds, the Goldstone faithful have still managed to bequeath three particularly noteworthy songs to footballing history, two of which have slowly but surely spread throughout the game and must now be recognised as being amongst the most well known examples of their ilk. First up is the renowned *Celery* chant which - dating from the mid 1980's - seems to have had its roots in a clandestine group known mysteriously as The Caveman Crew. It is not even certain if this select bunch of Brighton residents were football supporters or not, but it seems that in order to be initiated into the organisation, it was necessary to creep onto Brighton's

Palace Pier in the dead of night and, in simple terms, have a stick of celery poked up your backside! Whatever the footballing connections of this bizarre group of rectal deviants, the verbal element of their strange rite ended up on the terraces of the Goldstone Ground in the following format....

> Celery, celery,
> If she don't come,
> I'll tickle her bum,
> With stick of celery!

....the rhythm to which is very similar to the ubiquitous *"Wembley, Wembley, we're the famous Shrewsbury Town and we're going to Wembley"* type of thing. As mentioned, since first having appeared at the Goldstone, the chant has cropped up at several other grounds throughout, for the most part, the southern counties - with subtle variations at both Bournemouth and Chelsea, and whilst retaining its original form in the most recent reappearance at Gillingham's Priestfield Stadium. The Chelsea version has become far and away the most well known, if only because of the four teams who have adopted the chant, they are on T V far more frequently than the others, but the next time the West Stand are in full cry, it might be appropriate to remember the less than wholesome circumstance in which the chant was first saw the light of day (or night, to be entirely accurate)!

The second Brighton song - although again it is more of a chant - which has gone on to wider acclaim predates *Celery* by a decade or so, and was initially used to celebrate the goalscoring prowess of one Peter Ward, later of Nottingham Forest fame. Taking its tune from a traditional song, *The Quartermaster's Stores*, the Goldstone forerunner of innumerable variations was....

> He shot, he scored,
> It must be Peter Ward,
> Peter Ward,
> Peter Ward!

....these four lines being repeated any number of times. Although this has been adapted to apply to literally hundreds of different players during the two decades since it was first heard, there are perhaps two variants which became more well known than any of the others - probably due to the high profile of the clubs at which they were heard. In the first instance, the less than sylph-like Liverpool midfielder Sammy Lee was honoured with *"He's fat, he's round, he bounces on the ground, Sammy Lee...."*, and secondly, Manchester United's durable striker Brian McClair has played out his entire career at Old Trafford to the accompaniment of *"He's here, he's there, he's every fucking where, Brian McClair...."*. In addition to these two, many other versions of one of the games most easily adaptable chants have come and gone over the years, and virtually every ground from Pittodrie in the far North to Home Park in the South West will have heard at least one of these, if not more. It's a fair bet that this one chant has spawned more different descendents than has any other, and for this reason alone it must be considered as one of the games' truly seminal efforts.

Now, from two chants which have become extremely well known after first seeing the light of day on the south coast to a Brighton song which should be noted for an entirely different reason in that it dates from the First World War and is, therefore, one of the oldest songs which is still doing the rounds. Prior to being shipped out to the Western Front and certain death in the trenches, the soldiers of the Royal Sussex Regiment were billeted at the Goldstone Ground, and the Regimental Song was a traditional county anthem entitled *Sussex By The Sea*. Having no doubt been heard on numerous occasions whilst the troops were encamped at the ground, the song became attached to the football club itself and has remained so ever since. It has also retained its military links in spite of the original Sussex Regiment having amalgamated with half a dozen or so other local corps to form the Home Counties Battalion in 1958, and thence being redesignated as 1st-4th Battalion Queen's Regiment eight years later. The song can still be heard on Regimental Days of 3rd Bttn Queen's Regiment, who are the direct descendants of the original outfit who paraded up and down the Goldstone some eighty odd years ago. Anyway, setting the interminable history of the British Army to one side for a moment, the song actually goes....

> Good old Sussex by the sea,
> Good old Sussex by the sea,
> For we're going up,
> And we'll win the Cup,
> For Sussex by the sea.

....obviously, these are the words to the footy version of the song - those to the original have unfortunately proved unobtainable - but it's a fair bet that essentially only lines three and four are much different from those that the troops of 1915 would have been familiar with.

Other than Peter Ward, few Albion players seem to have been favoured with their own songs over the years. It has been suggested that Ward's latter day contemporary, Michael Robinson, may have benefited from the *Mrs Robinson* treatment as has his 1990's namesake Steve at Bournemouth, but apart from Spain's premier television football pundit only Kurt Nogan seems to have proved efficient enough to merit some sort of vocal worship from the North Stand. During his three year stint on the South coast during the early 90's *No Limits* by 2 Unlimited found itself effortlessly amended to *"No, No, No No No*

No, No No No No, No No No No-Nogan!", which is not wholly dissimilar to the treatment given to Bobby Bowry at Selhurst Park (*cf* Crystal Palace), and which followed Nogan northwards when he moved to Burnley in 1994.

Now to a subject briefly touched on already, in that The Seagulls have endured some particularly well documented lean times in recent years, which culminated in the near extinction of the club towards the end of the 1996/7 season. These struggles - so popular opinion would have it - have been brought about almost entirely by the devious machinations of chairman Bill Archer and his minion David Bellotti, who are naturally somewhat less than popular with the clubs' remaining supporters. From a singing point of view, actions have tended to speak louder than words with all manner of demonstrations and pitch invasions being staged to illustrate the depth of feeling which exists against the culpable regime - but none of these have really been enlivened with any protest songs worthy of the name. The only enduring effort to have emerged from the months of anguish - apart from some rather lacklustre personal abuse for the despised duo - has been a straightforward rehash of the Wigan Athletic version of *My Darling Clementine*, with name checks being given to the relevant parties....

> *Build a bonfire, build a bonfire,*
> *Put Bellotti on the top,*
> *Put Bill Archer in the middle,*
> *And burn the fucking lot!*

The one other recognisable theme to come out of the months of turmoil during which Brighton have languished at the foot of the Third Division was the *Blue Moon* derivative *"Brazil - it's just like watching Brazil, it's just like watching Brazil...."*, the thinking behind which was similar to that which gave rise to the Barnsley version of the same song: in simple terms, the Albion team of late 1996 had been abjectly shite, but the appointment of Steve Gritt as manager signalled the start of the revival which would ultimately lead to the dramatic last-day-of-the-season salvation at Hereford. Gritt's first game in charge was a 3-0 win over Hull City (only the second victory in twenty games!), and so incomparably superb was this performance when set alongside the dross which had preceded it that drawing parallels with Brazil suddenly became appropriate. On the subject of the fateful encounter at Edgar Street which saw Brighton send Hereford United down to the Conference in their place there was - amidst the justifiable jubilation of the visiting supporters - time for a bit of wonderfully cruel taunting. Notable also for being one of the quickest ever importations of a song onto the terraces, *Love Is Law* by The Seahorses was used to remind United's supporters of the fate which had befallen them. The song had received just a handful of pre-release plays on the radio before the day of the game, and it was some really swift rewriting which has bequeathed the following to football....

Now we all know where you're going,
So fuck off, enjoy the ride,
Morecambe and Southport and Dover,
Stalybridge, Welling and Hyde.

This lists a few venues at which Hereford were going to find themselves playing after their return to the non-league ranks, but also includes a healthy dose of artistic license through the mention of Hyde United (a Northern Premier League team rather than a Conference outfit, but one of the very few teams whose name happens to rhyme with *"ride"*!). One possible explanation behind the rapid adoption and adaptation of the tune has come to light in that it appears that the video for the song was shot at least in part on Brighton seafront and, presuming that this was done well in advance of the release date, it might just have given a few attendant Albion supporters an early chance to appreciate the tune's potential for subsequent development - possible rather than probable methinks! Anyway, with that piece of thoroughly unsubstantiated speculation, Brighton's section draws to a close having shown the club's beleaguered supporters to be responsible for two of football's most enduring chants, one of its oldest songs and a bit of particularly spiteful inventiveness - a more than reasonable return from what may have at first been considered one of the least innovative of the nation's footballing venues.

Gillingham

Although now cast as the County of Kent's solitary footballing outpost since the tragic demise of Maidstone United, Priestfield Stadium does not provide a beacon of singing splendidness in its isolation. Very few worthy efforts from the Medway Towns have been brought to our attention, but one which does perhaps deserve some comment is the following adaptation of *Just One Of Those Songs*. Though not a particularly astonishing composition in its own right, the song should be noted as being the first in a long line of similarly motivated efforts which have taken children's television programmes as their inspiration. Unlike Cambridge United and Huddersfield, however, the Gillingham song is very much rooted in the early 1970's - as can be seen from the programmes which get a mention....

We ain't Jack and Jill and we ain't Bill and Ben,
We ain't Ken Dodd or his Diddy Men,
We ain't Looby Loo with all her toys,
We are the Gillingham boot boys!

....Looby Loo - for the benefit of our younger readers - was one of the triumvirate of characters that went to make up the cult show that was Andy Pandy (along with Teddy and Andy himself, of course!).

The Rainham End terrace of the early seventies must have been swarming with depilated thugs, as this next offering again mentions one of the archetypal pre-casual football hooligan groups....

> *Walking down the high street swinging my chain,*
> *Along came a copper and he asked me my name,*
> *So I kicked him in the bollocks and stabbed him in the head,*
> *We are the Gillingham Skinheads*
> *Gillingham Skinheads; Skinheads, Skinheads, ooh!*
> *Gillingham Skinheads, Skinheads, Skinheads., ooh!*

This noble effort is to the tune of *The Teddy Boy Boogie* by Crazy Cavan - a rockabilly band of some renown (so we've been told!).

And that paltry selection is about the extent of football songs in Kent, apart from a couple which are directed at particular players and which are far more recent than either of the two detailed above - both referring to members of the playing staff who were with the club at the end of the 96/7 campaign.

The first is the chorus to *She'll Be Coming Round The Mountain*, and it doesn't take too much thought to work out how it goes when you know that the player at whom it is directed is Iffy Onuora - the ex Huddersfield and Mansfield striker who enjoyed the most prolific spell of his career having moved to Priestfield. Quite simply, anything remotely impressive from Onuora will prompt a chorus of....

> *Singing aye, aye, Iffy, Iffy, aye,*
> *Singing aye, aye, Iffy, Iffy, aye,*
> *Singing aye, aye, Iffy, aye, aye, Iffy,*
> *Aye, aye, Iffy, Iffy, aye!*

The second effort sees the appearance of the *Celery* chant - with the words exactly the same as for the Chelsea version - but unlike its manifestation at Stamford Bridge, Bournemouth and Brighton, the Kentish incarnation of the song cropped up for a specific reason. It is basically a chorus of devotion to goalkeeper Jim Stannard who, according to the succinct terms of reference so frequently applied by supporters of clubs other than Gillingham, is fat, round, bounces on the ground, and possesses all the other qualities associated with a player who is probably a few pounds over his ideal fighting weight (in fact, a full two stone heavier now that when he started his career at Fulham!). At some point either late in 95/6 or early the following season, some sort of official comment must have been forthcoming from the club that Stannard really ought to lose a bit of weight - basically an enforced diet - and the following match saw the first sporadic outbursts of *Celery* as an obvious reference to the sort of food that was now very much on the menu *chez Stannard*. A natural progression then saw the appearance of sticks of celery at matches as the chant grew in popularity, then a predilection for lobbing said sticks into Stannard's penalty area, then - most predictably of all - a pathetic edict from the club threatening anyone found bringing celery to matches with a life ban - isn't it marvellous how the cretins who run football take so much pleasure in putting a stop to anything which constitutes a bit of fun nowadays?

Portsmouth

Passionate but limited best sums up the contributions from Fratton Park, as Pompey supporters seem eager to sing the praises of their team, but have failed to come up with any means of real substance by which they can best do it. The club does, however, have a well known "theme tune" by way of The Pompey Chimes which consists of the chant *"Play up Pompey, Pompey play up"* sung to an instantly recognisable tune which is supposed to approximate the sound of the city's Guildhall clock striking the hour. These words are repeated only twice, apparently, and not for an indefinite number of times as was originally thought to be the case.   Showing a similar inclination to amend their own song as do West Ham supporters with *Bubbles*, Portsmouth followers can generally be relied upon to punctuate the visit of any West County team to Fratton by intoning *"oooh arr, oooh arr - oooh arr, oooh arr!"* to the same tune as the original - Hampshire wit at its finest, eh?

Illustrating a rather better developed sense of humour is this next offering, dedicated to Joey Beauchamp, now returned to Oxford United after a spell at Swindon and crucially, after signing for West Ham but leaving the club without playing a game because he was homesick. Beauchamp turned out for Swindon at Fratton Park shortly after making his much publicised departure from Upton Park, and Gene Pitney's *Twenty Four Hours From Tulsa* became....

> *Only seventy miles from Oxford,*
> *Only seventy miles from home.*
> *And you miss your mummy like mad,*
> *So you have to go home to your dad.*

The far more common chant of *"Does your mummy know you're here"* to the *Bread Of Heaven* tune made a rather more pertinent appearance than usual at

...ame game, being directed at Beauchamp instead of appearing in its regular role in which it is sung at any particularly irritating group of schoolboys who are annoying their elders and betters during the course of a game (in this context it is invariably paired with *"Back to school on Monday"* - another comment on the tender age of the aggravating brats in question).

Next, one of the few appearances of *The Wild Rover* in southern latitudes (the song is usually the preserve of teams in the North West of England). Although the Portsmouth version does not extend beyond the standard adaptation of the chorus, the words are a little odd....

> *And it's Portsmouth City,*
> *Portsmouth City F C,*
> *We're by far the greatest City,*
> *The World has ever seen.*

....out of the ordinary for two reasons, this: first and foremost the club are not (and never have been) called Portsmouth City, and secondly, this apparent error is compounded by the third line being *"by far the greatest City"* instead of the far more usual *"by far the greatest team"*, which appears in every other version of the song. The reason for this deviation from the norm was not forthcoming, but it may be a reference to the fact that Portsmouth has been granted the civic status of being designated a Cathedral City whereas Southampton (home of the club's much despised local rivals) has not - a straightforward case of one-upmanship perhaps? By the way, this information was gleaned from a rather old source, so if Southampton has since been elevated to a similar constitutional standing as Portsmouth, the song would now simply reflect that Pompey had been afforded the higher status first! On the subject of the Portsmouth - Southampton rivalry, it is perhaps surprising that such virulent hatred as exists between the clubs has not produced any decent songs, but neither camp has managed to come up with anything of note with which to abuse their hated foe. Pompey's contribution to the atmosphere at the infrequent derby matches seems to extend no further than shrieking *"Scummers, Scummers, Scummers!"* at anything of a red and white persuasion, this being a peculiarly abusive nickname for Saints' players or supporters, although it seems to be a regional favourite (also used at Bournemouth) rather than being exclusive to Pompey. Why the term "Scummer" is used, and what it might mean, has proved impossible to establish thus far.

Of rather wider relevance, we come to the Pompey supporter's claim to fame on the singing front (other than as having sole rights to the Pompey Chimes), in that they have proclaimed themselves as having been the first to have sung the now widespread social dissertation which is *"In your Liverpool slums...."*. In common with all the songs recorded in this book, there does of course actually have to be one group of supporters who are the originators, and as with Scarborough and their circumstantial evidence for being the progenitors of the *Three Lions* and *Daydream Believer* derivatives, Pompey do have some evidence on which to call to back up their case. It would seem that the story goes back to a Tuesday night in October 1980, with Pompey facing a League Cup tie at Anfield. Reputedly, fifteen thousand (!) travelled up from the South Coast and, in common with other visitors who arrived by train, the majority of these supporters were escorted along the three quarter of a mile route from Lime Street Station to the ground. Having made this walk myself on occasion, I can vouch for the fact that during the 1980's the area was not one of the foremost examples of architectural splendour and a thriving local economy. It was, in fact, a desolate scene with burned out houses lining the road, rubbish everywhere and little or no sign of life - the archetypal scene of inner city decay. Things were evidently the same when Pompey had been in town, as *My Liverpool Home* was rehashed as....

> *In your Liverpool slums,*
> *In your Liverpool slums,*
> *You look in the dustbin for something to eat,*
> *You find a dead cat and you think it's a treat,*
> *In your Liverpool slums.*

This song has since gone on to far wider acclaim, and it is easily altered to make reference to any other town or city, with a few finer adjustments occasionally being made to give it added relevance (the Scunthorpe United version for instance, when directed at Doncaster Rovers, sees line five as *"You find Arthur Scargill and think it's a treat"* !). Perhaps the most earnest acolytes of the song have been the supporters of Manchester United who, having a particular affection for their chums from Merseyside, have added a second verse (see United's section for details), which has itself slowly become more widespread. As for the Pompey claims to have been the originators of this particular song, these have subsequently been found to be patently untrue, due to its appearance at the Manor Ground, Oxford, at least a couple of years prior to the match mentioned above. There is, however, probably some justification in listing Portsmouth supporters as the fans who popularised the song - in a similar way to which Manchester City brought the Crewe original *Blue Moon* to the attention of a much wider audience than would have been the case had it remained the exclusive preserve of those who were the first to bring it onto the terraces.

And with that, the Portsmouth songbook has run its course - not a publication of inordinate length it has to be said, but one which has provided a couple of staple tunes from which the supporters of other clubs have been able to work over the years. As Pompey are a club with the ability to draw more than ample crowds when times are good, however, there is surely plenty of room for improvement should the team ever achieve any sort of consistent success.

Southampton

Only one possible contender for the opening song in the Southampton section, it must be *When The Saints Go Marching In*! Having now been inextricably linked with the club for over thirty five years, this is one of the few songs that have come about purely and simply as a result of a team's name. With consternation and incomprehension now rife amongst the *Dicks Out 2* readership, it's time to remind you that Southampton started life back in the 1880's as Southampton St. Mary's F C, their first president being the curate of St. Mary's Church - hence the ecclesiastical link! The song itself had been doing the rounds as a hymn for many years prior to its arrival at The Dell, which can be traced to the 1960/61 season when The Albion Brass Band were invited to entertain spectators before kick off. Some bright spark noted the saintly connection 'twixt song and club, added it to the band's repertoire, and soon would have noted that it had become a firm favourite with the supporters. It took a couple of years to really take a hold, but after numerous lusty renditions during the 1963 F A Cup semi-final which were noted by the press of the day, the song was set in stone as the Southampton club anthem and has remained so to this day. As is more often the case than not for such an enduring tune, their is a fairly extensive array of derivations which have developed over the years. Straightforward substitution of any number of other club's names and nicknames (or more usually their shirt colour) for that of Southampton has proved to be the standard fare, but their have also been a couple of subsequent developments substantially different from the original, which was....

> *Oh when the Saints, go marching in,*
> *Oh when the Saints go marching in,*
> *I wanna be in that number,*
> *When the Saints go marching in.*

One alternative rendition follows exactly the same tune and structure, and is invariably used to assert that a particular town (home to the opposition of the day) is not, perhaps, the nicest place to visit with the basic theme being *"Oh Shrewsbury, is full of shit, Oh Shrewsbury is full of shit, It's full of shit, shit and more shit....."*. Obviously - number of syllables permitting - virtually any town/club in the league can find itself the recipient of this treatment. For details of other songs which have taken their lead from the Saints' theme tune, turn to Southend United and Birmingham City's entries for a brief sortie into the bizarre parallel universe of sizeable seaside structures and garden sheds!

At about the same time that *When The Saints....* was becoming established at The Dell, a bizarre effort going by the name of *The Old Brown Cow* was also popular with the club's supporters. I am genuinely disappointed to disclose that it has proved impossible to ascertain the full words to this particular song, as the only concrete fact that has come to light is that it included a passage during which everyone would rattle their rattles (!) to approximate the sound of an old brown cow, err, passing waste matter noisily and copiously. The lyrics were for the most part obscene, which make the song a real one off for the mid 1960's, and it is to my eternal shame that I am unable to shed any more light on what was no doubt a particularly fine effort. In passing, it should also be noted that the sixties saw *We Shall Overcome* form part of the Saints repertoire, no doubt inspired by the 1965 release of Joan Baez' recording of the Black American hymn. Whether it was this initial exposure that lead to Middlesbrough adopting the song (both football versions retaining the traditional words) is open to conjecture.

Leaving bovine lavatorial excesses behind for a moment, it's time to consider Southampton F C's finest hour - their 1976 F A Cup victory. Several songs were created to celebrate the triumph, the first to the popular tune of *Macnamara's Band* which has since cropped up at one or two other venues with predominantly similar words and in similar circumstances. Anyway, the Saints version is....

> *'twas back in 1976, upon the first of May,*
> *We all went up to Wembley to see Southampton play,*
> *We showed 'em how to drink the beer,*
> *We showed 'em how to sup,*
> *We even showed United how to win the F A Cup.*

To an equally common tune, this time *The Wild Rover*, the next effort extends to a second section, but does not include a chorus, as does the more traditional versions which are popular at Burnley and Blackburn....

> *'twas back in '76 in the fine month of May,*
> *The crowd were all roaring and roaring away,*
> *And when it was over and when it was done,*
> *We'd beaten United by one goal to none.*
>
> *There stood Lawrie Mac, with the cup in his hand,*
> *Southampton F C, the pride of the land,*
> *The team to remember, the team to recall,*
> *Southampton F C, the pride of football.*

....a rather contrived version, particularly over the last couple of lines, and not perhaps one of the more impressive of the original's many descendents. *"Lawrie Mac"*, of course, is none other than Lawrie McMenemy, the then Saints' manager who has since gone on to far greater things with Sunderland and as part of the England set up (!). Still on the subject of the late Bobby Stokes' finest hour, there is a rather odd import from the East End of London when *Me And My*

Girl travels across the city and down the A3 to Hampshire. A couple of alterations are necessarily made from the West Ham ditty, most importantly by way of the appearance of the colours of Southampton's change strip....

> *The bells are ringing for the yellow and blue,*
> *The bells are ringing for the yellow and blue,*
> *Everybody's been knowing,*
> *It's up to Wembley we are going,*
> *And there's no way of knowing,*
> *What we're going to go through.*
> *No relegation for the yellow and blue,*
> *Just celebration for the yellow and blue,*
> *And one day we'll win the Cup,*
> *One day it'll just come true,*
> *For The Saints,*
> *For the yellow and blue.*

The goalscorer on that famous day beneath the twin towers unsurprisingly found himself the subject of a song, with *Viva Bobby Joe* by The Equals being fairly predictably changed to *"Viva Bobby Stokes"* - the words are exactly as per the original song, but with *"Stokes"* inserted in place of *"Joe"* throughout. Mention of songs dedicated to particular players brings us to two far more recent efforts and to The Dell's adaptation of a Bournemouth and Brighton song, which sees Neil Shipperley being given the *Mrs Robinson* treatment (see Bournemouth for the gory details). Of a far more inspirational nature comes the hymnal in praise of Israeli striker Eyal Berkovic, who proved thoroughly popular in Hampshire before his move to West Ham in June '97 (presumably as a belated exchange for the rights to sing *Me And My Girl*). To the tune of a Christmas carol which may or may not have been called simply *Noel Noel*, Berkovic was rarely able to set foot outside the dressing room without hearing a few choruses of....

> *Eyal, Eyal, Eyal, Eyal,*
> *Born is the king of Israel!*

...which, in my humble estimation, is rather good if rather short. This must just about qualify as a Saints original, as it was one of the very few Christmas carols to have escaped the attention of the festive choristers at Grimsby, and there haven't been all that many players called Noel who could have featured in a more lyrically correct version (well, I've heard nothing from Ewood Park about any Noel Brotherstone songs, anyway).

Lastly, another inexplicable migrant from the East End (similar to Iain Dowie, really, but he has now been repatriated to the verdant sod of Upton Park). The Lambeth Walk was another cup final song, but this time referring to the

1979 excursion for the League Cup decider against Nottingham Forest. With a commendably uncomplicated message, the song was....

> *When you walk down Wembley Way,*
> *You will hear the Saints fans say,*
> *Just who are we going to stuff?*
> *It's Notts Forest and Brian Clough!*

This, with its cup final flavour, was an unwitting and partial resurrection of Wolverhampton's *Westcott Walk* song, which had surfaced for the F A Cup denouement exactly forty years earlier. Having therefore spanned four decades, it must qualify as one of most enduring football songs ever to have seen the light of day, and also rounds of what has been a rather impressive selection of Saints' songs

Southend United

Strangely similar to the aura that surrounds Cambridge United, there is an air at Roots Hall that something vaguely interesting is always on the verge of happening - relegation had very definitely been pending for a couple of seasons before it ultimately happened at the end of 96/7 and prior to that, successive promotion seasons had ensured that their was never a dull moment on the Essex coast. Rumours of vast super stadia have come and gone, numerous Anfield cast-offs have drifted onto the scene (and very nearly off again), and any amount of players who always threatened to make the grade at a higher level without actually doing so have arrived at the club promising much but have generally failed to deliver. To the outsider, United have the look of a "nearly" club, one full of bright ideas but which is never really able to come up with the goods when it matters, and whilst this atmosphere of impending but unfulfilled greatness might seem to provide a fertile breeding ground for songs, typically, this has never quite happened. Instead, there are very few Shrimpers anthems worthy of the name, and Roots Hall is for the most part home to little more than the bog standard fare of name and colour related chants which can be found virtually anywhere. One or two submissions, however, have ensured that United have been afforded their own section. Firstly, one of the aforementioned grandiose plans (a vast new footballing amphitheatre to be built just down the road at Basildon) gave rise to something a little more substantial than the norm, with a popular tune given a new lease of life by way of....

> *Oh we do like to be beside the seaside,*
> *Oh we do like to be beside the sea,*
> *With our buckets and spades,*
> *And our fucking hand grenades,*
> *Beside the seaside, beside the sea.*

....this, in the period when the move to Basildon was being mooted, was coined by the Roots Hall traditionalists in order to assert that they were perfectly happy to stay put at the old ground, and would be less than delighted with any sort of relocation. The strange reference to hand grenades (having been queried in the first edition of this book) can now be confirmed as a reference to the regular discovery on Southend beach of various wartime armaments, usually washed ashore from sunken munitions ships in the Thames Estuary and which occasionally enliven family picnics on the sea front. Again on the subject of the town's status as a noted coastal resort, Southend's famous pier was deemed worthy of song, with *When The Saints Go Marching In* given a sort of Birmingham City-esque reworking to leave us with....

> *Oh Southend Pier (oh Southend Pier!)*
> *Is longer than yours (is longer than yours!)*
> *Oh Southend Pier is longer than yours,*
> *It's got some shops and a railway,*
> *Oh Southend Pier is longer than yours!*

The *"longer than yours"* section of this classic example of a "repetition" type song (the bracketed sections being sung alternately by different sections of the crowd) indicate that this was reserved for the occasion of trips to other seaside towns which also possessed piers, all of which must have been far less impressive than the one at Southend which was, in fact, the longest in the world (at least it was before a ship carved it in half during a storm at some point in the not too distant past). There was indeed a train which used to carry visitors the full length of the structure, and it no doubt boasted a few suitably tawdry shops selling candy floss, plastic troll keyrings and printing amusing slogans on shoddily made tee shirts. Still, in the murky world of pier-related competitiveness, these were all things which proved invaluable when asserting the superiority of one such littoral protruberance over another.

With the relative merits of architectural developments still to the fore, Colchester United's Layer Road ground was assured of some abuse - both actual and metaphorical - whenever the two Essex giants clashed in their local derby. Travelling Southend supporters would invariably be housed in the away section on the covered terrace, complete with its splendidly bouncy wooden terracing (which was rather unsportingly ripped out in 1992 after providing endless amusement for thousands of spectators over the course of some fifty odd years). Towards the end of its working life, this terracing naturally became a bit unstable, and a few well placed kicks would usually managed to dislodge fair sized chunks of timber which could then be lobbed at the Colchester supporters in the adjoining Cow Shed to the right. These energetic attempts at amateur structural engineering would generally be accompanied by a chorus or two of....

> *Layer Road is falling down, falling down, falling down,*
> *Layer Road is falling down, poor old Col U.*
> *Shall we kick it down some more, down some more, down some more?*
> *Shall we kick it down some more? Poor old Col U.*

....obviously to the *London Bridge Is Falling Down* tune. Maximum damage was usually inflicted to the wooden edifice during the *"Shall we kick it down..."* section, which was posed as a rhetorical question whilst earnest acts of vandalism were actually taking place.

And that - common chants excluded - is the Southend United vocal archive in its entirety; not outstanding but certainly worthy of some bonus points for originality of subject matter!

Section Two

The Thames Valley

Oxford United

Reading

Swindon Town

Wycombe Wanderers

The Thames Valley

This region has been elevated to having a section in its own right almost entirely due to the efforts of two clubs - Reading, who have provided one of the Nationwide League's more bizarre collections of songs, and Wycombe Wanderers, relatively new to the senior ranks but already showing considerable promise on the singing front.

That the area is not home to four of the most partisan sets of supporters in the country can be put down to one thing - location. The opening of the M40 has made the West Midlands easily accessible for residents of the Thames Valley, and with the bright lights and big names of London's footballing scene equally close to hand, it's easy to understand why the delights of Elm Park and the like have been unable to capture the imagination of the local populace. It seems that all of the country's big clubs have supporters associations in Oxford, Reading and the surrounding areas, and it is perhaps fair to say that you're equally likely to find a Berkshire voice leading the singing at Anfield or Highbury as you are on the South Bank or the London Road terrace. Swindon, of course, may not be quite as likely to haemorrhage support to London or beyond, but the County Ground seems to be an outpost of peace and tranquillity for some other less quantifiable reason.

Those supporters who are inclined to follow their local side have seen Oxford United weigh in with some fairly classy abuse of neighbours Swindon, but for their part, the Wiltshiremen have been unable to respond in kind and can only offer something which dates back to a long standing rivalry with Gillingham of all people.

There are no common themes in the area apart from *The Dambusters* tune which crops up at both the Manor Ground and Adams Park, and nothing which has spread across the country having first been heard in the M4 corridor - unless you count what was a relatively early version of *Winter Wonderland* from Elm Park or perhaps Oxford's somewhat tenuous claims to have been responsible for the "dead cat" version of *My Liverpool Home*, so all in all, the area is not really at the forefront of English terrace culture, but anywhere which has taken a lead from both Kylie Minogue and *Annie - The Musical* must be worthy of at least passing respect.

Oxford United

An odd contradiction from the Manor Ground in that present day supporters bemoan the lack of singing at the ground, whereas previous research dating back to the late 1970's reveals a vast array of songs and chants which totalled some two hundred and fifty different efforts! The vast majority of these - diligently recorded and transcribed over the course of fifteen games - were no more than the utterly run of the mill chants which crop up all over the place, but there were a few which need to be recorded here. The first of these sees the only other known occurrence of a strange shout which is also attributed to Peterborough United - and which is very simply *"Oooooooooooooh, Bastard, Bastard!"* (note the extra *"bastard"*!). When used at Oxford, this seemed exclusively to be directed at referees who incurred the displeasure of the home crowd, but again, no real indication of what rhythm the chant followed was given.

Next, gloomy news for Portsmouth supporters, in that their claim to have been the first to sing *"In Your Liverpool Slums"* has been rather shot up the arse!. Dating from a couple of years prior to Pompey's cup visit to Anfield - originally put forward as the first time the song had been heard - there is an instance of Oxford singing a very similar version of *My Liverpool Home*, with the same dustbin and dead cat references as the Fratton Park transcript, but directed at Swansea City of all people!

Other popular songs which were given an airing by the London Road terrace dwellers included an abbreviated version of the Evertonian anthem *When Skies Are Grey*, and an early appearance for the Dambusters theme (which subsequently formed staple fair at Wycombe and Old Trafford). The Oxford version, unlike these other two, was directed at the police by taking the form of *"We all hate pigs and pigs and pigs, pigs and pigs and pigs and pigs, pigs and pigs and pigs - we all fucking hate pigs!"*.

During the mid 1980's, there appears to have been a brief period when the Rotherham United "firework" song became the order of the day amidst those of a yellow and blue persuasion - possibly picked up from the South Yorkshire club during the spell in which both teams were in the same division. Unlike the Millers use of the song, though, which was purely and simply down to the admirable motivation of just being silly, the Oxford version was immediately followed by the chanting of Kevin Brock's name - a popular and long serving locally born midfielder who, of course, bore the same name as one of the country's leading manufacturers of pyrotechnic products! From a similar era there are mutterings of a version of The Beatles *Yellow Submarine*, but not even the slightest hint of what the words might have been was forthcoming, and not even the involvement of the Maxwell family with the club seems to have given rise to anything of note (unlike Derby County - another club to have attracted the attention of the late Sir Bob, but who celebrated his intervention in a more forthright style).

The villains of the piece at the Manor Ground when it comes to local rivalry are for the most part Swindon Town (although Reading are not always guaranteed a particularly warm welcome on their sorties into Oxfordshire), but there do not appear to be a great many songs dedicated to the forces of evil from Wiltshire. Apart from a few succinct chants, only one effort exists of any length and, considering the players who are mentioned, this dates from a good few years ago (around the late 1970's/early 80's). It is a strange combination of two songs, mostly drawing from the Newcastle and Sunderland contrivances of *Bless 'em All*, but which also contains elements of the *For Ever And Ever* chants from South Yorkshire (lyrically with regard to the latter, the tune following the former....).

> *Fuck 'em all, fuck 'em all,*
> *Kamara, McHale and Ford,*
> *And Rowland and Carter and Lewis and Bates,*
> *They're all Swindon bastards that we love to hate.*
> *And we're singing this song good and loud,*
> *Of the Oxford United we're proud,*
> *And we won't be mastered by no Swindon bastard,*
> *We're Oxford, we're the London Road.*

In order of appearance, the Swindon players blessed by an appearance in the above are Chris Kamara, Ray McHale, Andy Ford, Andy Rowland, Roy Carter, Russell Lewis and Chick Bates - and the inclusion of these seven makes this one of the longest roll-calls in any one song intended to abuse an opposing team. A few songs exist whereby a clubs' supporters will list their own teams' entire line up (*cf* Wolverhampton Wanderers) in order to assert their general loveliness, but such extravagant lengths are only really equalled at Swansea when it comes to the negative side of the equation - a fairly impressive point at which to leave the Manor Ground and its supporters.

Reading

And now, step if you will into the bizarre world of Elm Park's South Bank - a terrace on which such lunacy is perpetrated that the supporters must be acclaimed along with those at Orient as having probably the silliest selection of songs in the Nationwide League. As with other instances of such sublime idiocy, the majority of what follows was conjured up simply because the team used to be so inept that watching them was very much a chore, and one which could only be enlivened by a degree of foolishness which manifested itself in song. All of that which follows dates from the early 1990's when Reading were leading a largely pointless existence in the middle of the old Third Division - presumably their ensuing promotion and all manner of play-off jollity has meant that these songs are now more or less extinct, but their legacy lives on.

This first offering is just about as accurate a summation of the general theme as you could wish for, with *I Should Be So Lucky* by the inestimable Kylie Minogue benefiting massively from an amalgamation with the traditional football anthem which is *Molly Malone*....

> *In Brisbane's fair city,*
> *Where the girls are so pretty,*
> *I first set my eyes on sweet Kylie Minogue,*
> *She wheels her wheel barrow,*
> *Through streets broad and narrow,*
> *Singing....*
> *I should be so lucky,*
> *Lucky, lucky, lucky,*
> *I should be so lucky in love!*

....damn fine stuff indeed! On an equally silly tack, Reading supporters were one of the foremost purveyors of what was probably the most banal song in football history - endless repetitions of *"We know a song that'll get on your nerves, get on your nerves, get on your nerves, we know a songs that'll get on your nerves...."* which under normal circumstances would hardly merit a mention - apart from the fact that when this one finally came to a close, it would invariably be followed by....

> *This is the song that just never ends,*
> *It just goes on and on my friends,*
> *Some people started singing it not knowing what is was,*
> *And we will keep singing it forever just because,*
> *This is the song that just never ends....*

....at which point the whole thing was repeated, for as long as a game went on without some sort of incident taking place which broke the monotony. This second effort was shamelessly pinched from the supporters of Maidstone United, but it's difficult to know exactly when as it does not appear that the two teams actually played each other during the Stones' brief flirtation with the Football League. Originally, Kent's finest had picked up the song from the children's T V programme *Lambchops*.

25

Silly songs of the type which were Reading's forte lend themselves to being attached to particular players, and predictably there are some fine examples of this sort of thing - none finer than this....

> *To Morrow, to Morrow,*
> *Just give it to Morrow,*
> *He's only a pass away.*

....which was aimed at Steve Morrow during his short spell on loan from Arsenal, and which was based on the theme song from the nauseatingly twee film/musical *Annie*. Equally, striker Craig Maskell was to have a song assigned to him; to the tune of *Skip To My Lou*, and somewhat flexible depending on the quality of Maskell's contribution to the team this was....

> *Sell, Sell, Craig Maskell,*
> *Sell, Sell, Craig Maskell,*
> *Sell, Sell, Craig Maskell,*
> *He's a lazy bastard!*

....or, should things be going rather more according to plan, this would become *"Craig, Craig, Craig Maskell....Super Craigie Maskell!"* Of a rather more consistently positive nature were the songs for Trevor Senior - always a favourite at Elm Park. In his honour came one of the first versions of what has gone on to become a recurringly popular theme throughout the country....

> *Reading, are you listening,*
> *It's a goal that we're missing,*
> *So give it a punt, to Trevor up front,*
> *Scoring in a winter wonderland.*

A more quintessentially Readingesque song directed at the same player was....

> *Trevor, Trevor, he's our man,*
> *If he can't do it, no-one can!*
> *Wooooooooooooooooo!*

....which is largely inexplicable, unlike this next one which was created to reflect the sometimes less than reliable goalkeeping of St Albans born Gary Phillips. So dire were some of Phillips' occasional lapses that the only thing to which he could be compared were the legendarily inept custodians from north of the border (Rough. Leighton - players of that ilk), and thus the unequivocally English 'keeper became *"Scotland's number one - Scotland, Scotland's number one"* which, for a professional who seeks to make his living between the posts, is just about the most damning indictment of ability that can be imagined. Eager to search out new topics on which songs could be based, the South Bank then decided that the Reading kit merited some sort of idolisation - not

the famous blue and white hoops, though. It was the change kit whi
more interesting, and thus we find Dick van Dyke's soliloquy fr
Poppins appearing as

> *Chim-chiminee, chim-chiminee,*
> *Chim-chim cheroo,*
> *We've got a kit that's more yellow than blue!*

Similarly, The Beatles would no doubt have been proud to have heard the
inordinately repetitive effort which *"We all play in a yellow football strip, a
yellow football strip, a yellow football strip....."* - an obvious reprise of *Yellow
Submarine* (*cf* Hull City).

To close, a song of general jollity, engendered by a rather vague feeling of ill
will that exists at Elm Park towards the otherwise wholly inoffensive A F C
Bournemouth. The Cherries seem to have earned themselves inclusion in the
following for no less a sin than having inflicted a 2-0 defeat on Reading at
Dean Court during 1990/91 which featured one of the most tedious second
halves it is possible to imagine. Whatever - *Singing The Blues* gets some
predictably off-beat treatment by way of....

> *I've never felt more like feeling quite chuffed,*
> *As Reading win, and Bournemouth get stuffed,*
> *I'm happy, I'm really feeling quite chuffed.*

And there we leave Reading, their supporters feeling quite chuffed, and all the
more so for being acclaimed as one of the leading exponents in organised
football of that most laudable of things, The Utterly Stupid Song.

Swindon Town

Oh dear - an utterly dismal showing from The County Ground, and one which
should cause any amount of hilarity amongst Oxford United supporters. It
might reasonably have been expected that Swindon's chaotic last few seasons
(soaring up through the leagues, all manner of off-pitch wrangling, feats of
record breaking ineptitude in the Premier League, then a couple of relegation
seasons) would have provided a backdrop on which a wholly impressive vocal
tableaux could have been etched, but no - not in the slightest. Luckily, elevation
to the top flight did provide the club with sufficient television exposure for it to
have become clear that *Can't Help Falling In Love With You* has become a
regular theme on the Town End, but plagiarised Sunderland songs apart, there

is but meagre fare. Even the supposed enmity with Oxford United has failed to produce anything of note, and we have to look back to the 1980's for worthy contributions. With its roots in a bizarre rivalry which grew up with Gillingham throughout the decade (and which ended decisively in Swindon's favour with a win in the 1986/7 Division three play-off final), we find a splendidly abusive version of *Messing About On The River*....

> *Those bastards from Kent,*
> *They're all fucking bent,*
> *The blue and white wankers from Priestfield,*
> *Hillyard and Bruce*
> *Are no fucking use,*
> *They're blue and white wankers from Priestfield.*

Ron Hillyard and Steve Bruce (yes, that one!) are the players who feature in the above - both Gillingham stalwarts of the day. I vaguely recall that the song then extended to a verse, but recollections about the chorus but above are already sufficiently dim to preclude any speculation about how this went! The rivalry between the clubs was a strange affair, which I think started in the very late seventies when both clubs were vying for promotion to Division Two. The teams seemed to always meet very late on in the season throughout the following years, invariably with some sort of controversial victory for one ending the promotion ambitions of the other. Ultimately, after one such encounter, the mutual dislike erupted in a brawl in the tunnel between the players after a game at Swindon, and the simmering ill feeling between the clubs was only doused after the play-off game mentioned above saw Swindon move up and out of Gillingham's immediate sphere of endeavour. It would be interesting to see whether the old grudges would resurface should both teams find themselves in the same division again. And with that, enough of Swindon and their seemingly mute supporters!

Wycombe Wanderers

Another of the more recent recruits to the Football League by way of the so-called automatic promotion from the Vauxhall Conference, Wanderers have drawn on both recent and not so recent sources to augment their singing vocabulary. For many years, the club used to enter the pitch at Loakes Park (and latterly Adams Park) with *The Dambusters* theme blaring over the tannoy. Why this should have been deemed sufficiently relevant to have been considered as the club song is not entirely clear, but in non-league days, Wanderers always played a representative team from the R A F in the annual Battle of Britain Cup, so the link must lay in that direction. Anyway, near neighbours Slough Town had always been considered Wycombe's bitterest rivals (initially in the Isthmian league and latterly in the Conference - witness the ludicrously large attendances at the derby matches during Wanderers' promotion season of 1992/93), and as a result, although the opening bars of the tune were broadcast relatively unimpeded, the appropriate section would always be accompanied with a huge chorus of *"We all fucking hate Slough!"* which, four or five years down the road, still provides a local flavour to the pre-match proceedings of Wycombe's Nationwide League matches.

An equally well established part of the scene at Adams Park have been a group of supporters known as The Wycombe Rhubarbs. Having now followed the team for the best part of a decade, it would seem entirely reasonable to expect that initiation into the group would involve a similar rite as was required to join The Caveman Crew at Brighton, though obviously using a stick of rhubarb rather than celery. This assertion, however, is as unlikely as it is speculative, and we must make do with recording a terrace dance which the group have choreographed. The basic theme, along with the actions (energetic jumping up and down on the spot), were both shamelessly pinched from West Brom supporters after F A Cup encounters between the two sides a couple of seasons ago. Consequently, it does not take the mind of a particularly astute detective to deduce that Adams Park is now enlivened with regular bouts of *"Boing, boing, rhubarb, rhubarb!"* - an effortless transfer of the original *"Boing, boing, Baggies, Baggies"* effort from The West Midlands to darkest Buckinghamshire. Another enduring favourite with the Wycombe faithful is a verbatim performance of the original version of *Molly Malone* which - Reading and Watford's derivations notwithstanding - does not appear in this book attributed to anyone else. As the Wanderers section is a bit thin, then perhaps its listing here is as valid as it would be anywhere else though, of course, it should in no way be regarded as an exclusively Wycombe song....

> *In Dublin's fair city,*
> *Where the girls are so pretty,*
> *I first set my eyes on sweet Molly Malone,*
> *She wheeled her wheelbarrow,*
> *Through streets broad and narrow,*
> *Singing....*
> *clap, clap, clap clap clap, clap clap clap clap - WYCOMBE!*

Now on to players who have so impressed the Wanderers cogniscenti as to have been afforded their own songs. It would appear that only two such genii have ever worn the light and dark blue, the first of whom was Noel Ashford who brought gasps of admiration from the Loakes Park terraces in the late 1980's. So sublime were Ashford's talents that he was simply know to all and

29

sundry as God, with this heavenly monicker being intoned whilst spectators prostrated themselves before the divine being in a manner not dissimilar to the *Wayne's World* "we're not worthy" routine (though this actually pre-dated the film). It has even been suggested that when the teams were announced prior to matches, Ashford's name would be omitted from the roll call and replaced with *"at number ten - God!"*.

Some time later, after Ashford had left the club, a new messiah by the name of Dave Carroll bestrode the planet, and did perform footballing miracles of a most mighty nature. Having already had a God amongst their number, it was only natural that Carroll should be designated as Jesus - a role which he lived up to in spectacular nature by having a suitably messianic hair style and, so we are informed, by wearing sandals a lot! Here, the whole quasi-religious thing takes a bit of a nosedive as, far from there being soaring and inspirational hymns in Carrols' praise, a chant of *"Jesus, Jesus, Jesus"* is all that he has to show for being the embodiment of the reincarnated Christ on earth - which, you would have thought, deserved better.

Section Three
London

Arsenal

Barnet

Brentford

Charlton Athletic

Chelsea

Crystal Palace

Fulham

Leyton Orient

Millwall

Tottenham hotspur

Watford

West Ham United

London

Predictably, the concentration of clubs in the capital has given rise to a selection of songs which is more neighbour-orientated than anywhere else in the country, with the possible exception of the North East where a degree of geographical isolation has led to a similar preoccupation with abuse of local rivals.

With anything up to half a dozen clubs from London being in the same division at any one time, there is a proliferation of local derbies to be endured, and with the catchment areas from each club overlapping, it is almost certain that the supporters of one club will come into contact with those from at least a couple of others on a more or less daily basis. This rather claustrophobic circumstance has meant that London's songs have developed an air of exclusivity - one club will invariably pick up on the songs of another, and the need for influences from further afield to inject a bit of variety does not arise, as there are easily enough different tunes immediately at hand to provide a reasonable selection without having to import songs from South Wales, for instance.

This does not mean to say that London songs are only to be heard in the capital, as there are several which have been picked up on by supporters in the provinces. The likes of Chelsea, West Ham and Arsenal will always provide inspiration simply because they enjoy such a high media profile - witness the rise in popularity of songs based on The Red Flag since this became the Chelsea anthem (though obviously as The Blue Flag!) following their F A Cup run in 1994.

The smaller clubs in the capital provide interest in their own right as - seemingly as a reaction to the common themes of the Premier Division sides which have become so well known as to be almost boring - Brentford, Leyton Orient and to a lesser extent Barnet all have songs or themes which are entirely unique. There is obviously a degree of pride amongst the supporters of these clubs that they have decided to follow the small fry in spite of the fact that a multi-million pound super stadium is just down the road, and this seems to extend to a rejection of the bigger clubs' songs as well, which is rather at odds with the degree of common ground which the supporters of these clubs share.

With the existence of this double layer of songs (the well known themes of the leading clubs and the idiosyncratic foibles of the lesser lights) the capital can probably boast the widest variety of songs in any one region. However, sheer quantity should not be allowed to overshadow genuine quality, and for this reason, London cannot be considered as one of the most deserving cases when awards for singing are being bandied around - even when taking Watford's *Nellie The Elephant* song into consideration.

Arsenal

Unfortunately, however noble the achievements of this famous North London outfit may be, they have been saddled with the epithet *"Boring, Boring Arsenal"* ever since the chill hand of Don Howe and his coaching methods fell upon the club. With only the nature of *that* goal by Nayim and the messy dismissal of George Graham to stir the otherwise tranquil waters of London N5 in recent years, even the club's supporters have slipped into the sort of comatose state which simply does not engender any sort of decent football songs at all. However, there are some enduring favourites from the past, one of which is an updated version of a song first released on vinyl in 1971 to celebrate the club's double-winning triumph. Incidentally, the words to this were penned by a certain Jimmy Hill....

> *Good old Arsenal, we're proud to say the name,*
> *While we sing this song, we'll win the game,*
> *Good old Merson, we're proud to shout the name,*
> *While we sing this song, we'll win the game".*
> *(Tune: Rule Britannia - of all things)*

Can't imagine why Jimmy never embarked on a full-time career as a lyricist on the basis of this fine effort which, obviously, can be embellished by the addition of any Arsenal player's name in place of Merson. Anyway, onto something of more recent origins - the rallying cry which goes up at Arsenal tube station prior to matches at Highbury, and at away games when groups of travelling fans from North London encounter other like-minded parties:

> *Ooh to, ooh to be, ooh to be a - GOONER!*
> *Ooh to, ooh to be, ooh to be a - GOONER!*
> *(repeated incessantly until the "singers"*
> *are overtaken by boredom)*

A "Gooner" is basically any Arsenal supporter - the name which supporters of Highbury's XI have coined as their personal term of reference, and which is presumably a corruption of the club's official nickname. More specifically, it is also the name by which the club's more, err, confrontational supporters were known back in the good old days when footy fans used to punch the living daylights out of each other, when men were men and plastic seats were little more something you pulled out of the "posh" stands to chuck at other supporters. More often than not, back in seventies and early eighties, when the original Gooners did start lobbing seats about, the target would be fans of the other London clubs - the familiarity of all living in the same city breeding some particularly virulent contempt. Naturally, this rivalry was expressed in song, with West Ham's *I'm Forever Blowing Bubbles* being a favourite means with which to assert the merits of a particular club. The words to the bastardised version of *Bubbles* were more or less the same whether it was the Shed, the Shelf or the North Bank who were doing the singing - it's a simple matter of rearranging the order in which the clubs are mentioned to make the song particular to any one set of supporters; in Arsenal's case such a reinterpretation of the original score gives us....

> *I'm forever blowing bubbles,*
> *Pretty bubbles in the air,*
> *They fly so high, nearly reach the sky,*
> *Then like West Ham they fade and die.*
> *Tottenham always running,*
> *Chelsea running too,*
> *Arsenal are always running,*
> *'cos we're running after you.*

Of course, Arsenal's biggest rivalry has traditionally been with Spurs, but there is a surprising paucity of songs directly relevant to the enmity between the two clubs. There are plenty of chants along the *"You're the shit of North London"* sort of lines, but only one which seems to extend beyond a handful of words. This, to the tune of *She Wore A Yellow Ribbon*, surfaced after Spurs' manager David Pleat had been eased out of his job following a much publicised liaison with a young lady who worked nights at Kings Cross Station - and not as a member of the British Rail catering staff....

> *She wore, she wore, she wore a fishnet stocking,*
> *She wore a fishnet stocking and stilettos on her feet,*
> *And when I asked her why she wore that stocking,*
> *She said "It's for my client and his name is David Pleat".*
> *David Pleat, David Pleat, he's the famous Tottenham pervert*
> *And his name is David Pleat.*

Next, an example of something which defies any description other than "genuinely strange", and a song which avoids being relevant to the actual game of football by quite some distance. A speciality at away matches when seated in the upper tier of a stand, particularly Goodison Park or White Hart Lane, we have (to an inexplicable tune)...

> *Over and over and over again,*
> *"B'Jesus" said Paddy, "I sing it so well,*
> *I think I'll get up and I'll sing it again",*
> *So Paddy got up and he sang it again,*
> *Over and over and over again".*

This oddity is accompanied by the singers standing up, then sitting down again "en masse". It is, as one would expect, repeated for some time until the performers lose their momentum and then lapse into the considerably less taxing, but equally inane, *"Red Army, Red Army, Red Army, Red Army, Red Army, Red Army, Red Army, Red Army...."* On the subject of inanity, Highbury (and many other grounds come to that) has, over recent season, resounded to the ultimate in simplistic chants - the brief but no doubt heartfelt homage to The Gunners' goalscoring hero, Ian Wright. The tune is not dissimilar to the pertinent section of *Hot, Hot, Hot* by Arrow, and there are some slightly expanded versions at both Middlesbrough and West Brom. In a football context, though, this is very much the original....

> *Ian Wright, Wright, Wright*
> *Ian Wright, Wright, Wright!*

On a similar tack, the nation owes Arsenal supporters a debt of gratitude for having been the prime movers behind what has now probably the most overused chant in football history. Copenhagen, May 1994 - Alan Smith bangs in what proves to be the winner in the Cup Winners Cup final against Parma, and a pan-European audience is treated to thousands of Gooners belting out *"One nil, to the Arsenal, one nil, to the Arsenal, one nil, to the Arsenal"* for the rest of the evening, to the tune of *Go West* by the Pet Shop Boys. Unfortunately, so simple is it to adjust this chant to fit absolutely any footballing occasion (*"Six - four, to the Shrewsbury"*, *"Fuck off, you're just Bolton scum"*, *"We've won, at the Manor Ground"*, *"You're shit, and you know your are"* etc, etc, etc) that it swiftly became the most widely used tune in British football, and continues to annoy people to distraction to this day in any one of its forty three thousand different guises. In truth, however, it must be said that Arsenal have merely popularised this chant which actually first saw the light of day at The Hawthorns in the form of *"Go West, Bromwich Albion"* (so, no stroppy letters from the West Midlands, thank you).

Lastly in this section, it is my unfortunate duty to reveal the singularly most distasteful episode which was came to light during the research for this book. Quietly watching Fantasy Football League one Friday night, it became apparent that Frank Skinner was being suitably scathing about something which had appeared in an Arsenal F C matchday programme from a recent game. This item proved to be no less than an invitation to supporters to sign up to be an Official Arsenal Songleader! Apparently, by way of a proposed remedy by the club for the acknowledged lack of atmosphere at Highbury, supporters were requested to put themselves forward for this exalted position wherein, at predetermined times throughout the match, they would jump up and endeavour to start songs on cue. Obviously, such choreographed drivel is the complete and absolute antithesis of what "proper" footy songs should be, and we can only commend the vast majority of Arsenal supporters whose complete lack of enthusiasm for the objectionable scheme has ensured that it never seriously threatened to get off the ground.

Barnet

The thus-far brief and largely unspectacular Nationwide League career of North London's genuine footballing giants does not appear to have inspired a vast catalogue of impressive songs, even since the appointment of high profile managerial staff and a couple of passably successful seasons. In fact, it is necessary to look back to the Bees' non-league days to find anything of note. Back in the mid-eighties, when some distinctly mediocre seasons prefaced the steady rise to the big time which was to follow, the club's none-too-abundant successes in the netting department were reputedly greeted with....

> *Goal...! We have just scored a goal!*
> *We're fucking marvellous - woaaah-oh!*
> *Goal - we have just scored a goal,*

....all of which seems distinctly silly until you apply to the above lyrics the tune to Spandau Ballet's contemporary pop tune *Gold,* which instantly transforms a nondescript jumble of words and exclamation marks into a really rather fine effort.

From a similar era (Christmas '85 to be precise), good old Bing Crosby must have been spinning in his grave at an impressive number of revolutions per minute as Underhill resounded to a fine version of *White Christmas....*

> *We're dreaming of a nine-point Christmas,*
> *Just like the ones we used to know,*
> *Where goalposts glisten,*
> *And children listen,*
> *To hear the West Bank in full flow.*

Presumably, the West Bank was (and probably still is) the Underhill stand where the home side's more vocal supporters gathered in days of yore (running the length of the pitch opposite the main stand, as I recall). A particularly fine stand it was too, with one end roughly eight feet higher than the other due to the ground's notorious slope - though this architectural oddity appears never to have been immortalised in song.

Of a more recent vintage, an albeit half-hearted venture has been made into the world of the terrace dance with, to the tune of the ubiquitous *"Molby, what's the score, Molby, Molby what's the score?"* chants, the arrival of *"Barnet, do the twist, Barnet, Barnet, do the twist!"* on the scene. This is naturally accompanied with some appropriate hip-swivelling behaviour which, it would be fair to say, probably wouldn't be too close to the top if a list of the country's footy "dances" was compiled in descending order of merit. The seeds, though, have been sown, and you should keep an eye on Underhill in the future in case a more ambitious choreographer manages to exert an influence.

Barnet supporters, while perhaps then not the best at strutting their stuff, do however show a pleasingly aggressive side to their nature with their version of a chant which is popular at many other venues. Very often you will hear a struggling side - particularly if they are deemed by their supporters not to be trying too hard to rectify the situation - being encouraged with the chant *"Get into 'em"* followed by four claps, both elements being repeated in tandem a number of times. Bees' supporters, perhaps having seen more than their fair share of tepid performances from their team over the years, have slightly refined this by doing away with the clapping and inserting some additional lyrics, in as much as any less than wholehearted display by the team is now played out to a backdrop of....

> *Get into 'em,*
> *AND FUCK 'EM UP!*
> *Get into 'em,*
> *AND FUCK 'EM UP!*

....rather rude, I suppose, but with the *"And fuck 'em up!"* lines being shouted considerably more loudly than the others, it certainly has the ability to turn a few heads - particularly when performed during an otherwise uneventful game.

In a similarly simple vein, the club's nickname comes to the fore when bringing a sequence of clapping to a climax. As with other chants of this nature, this looks crap in print: *"clap - clap - clap-clap-clap-clap-clap BEES!"* being the offending rhythm - but it sounds thoroughly impressive when more than a handful of people get involved, and more so when the claps are replaced by a sharp kick on the back of a stand or whatever - oh, alright, I suppose you actually have to be there to appreciate this one, but just take my word for it, eh?

Brentford

Rightly dismissed as a cultural backwater in the first edition of *Dicks Out!*, Griffin Park has never been renowned as a vast amphitheatre resounding to all manner of fine songs - until now. Early '96 has seen the arrival of The Cheese Phenomenon which has rightly rocketed Bees' supporters to the very zenith of footballing stupidity. Rooted in the team's dismal away form which had produced litary win away from West London over the first four months of ~~9576~~ (in a First Round F A Cup replay at non-league Farnborough), the craze started at Bournemouth on the day of the Second Round match, during a pre-game drinking session (which always seems to be the case when it comes to these rather odd fads). An off the cuff comment about a song on the pub juke box being "a load of cheese" prompted a *"Cheese, cheese, cheese"* chant, to which the landlady responded by bringing out a vast tray of the said dairy derived comestible. Sufficient cheese was set before the Brentford supporters that they were able to eat their fill, then take the leftovers with them to the game, which the Bees duly won 1-0 to set the restorative qualities of the foodstuff in stone for the rest of the season. Already deprived of their former match day accessories (Chomp chocolate bars which were outlawed after they started to rain on to the pitch during goal celebrations and amidst chants of *"Chompionees, Chompionees, howay, howay, howay!"*), cheese soon became *de rigeur* on the terraces. Australian style hats also became vital fashion accessories, but instead of corks hanging from the rim, a number of small cheeses from supermarket pick'n'mix counters were attached. A supply of the foam "cheese wedge" hats, as sported by Green Bay Packers fans in the NFL was then sourced and these, too, became almost obligatory headgear for a time, and the craze continued unabated with the arrangement of a "Cheese Coach" to Carrow Road for the next cup tie. As far as songs went (ooh, back to the proper subject matter all of a sudden), the only enduring ditty seems to have been....

> *Hey Jude, don't make it bad,*
> *Just take a stilton, and make it cheddar*

...this somewhat stilted repertoire was, in part, explained by the stern vetting process which any likely cheese had to go through before being elevated to a song subject. Cottage cheese was out due to the Fulham connotations (local rivals/Craven Cottage and the like); French cheeses were ignored because of the nuclear testing row of the time, and blue cheese rarely appeared because of its tenuous link with Birmingham City. Norwich City supporters at the cup game then became unwittingly embroiled in the fun and games. With the Canaries campaign to oust chairman Robert Chase in full swing, it was but a short step from the *"Chase Out"* chants of the home supporters to the *"Cheese Out"* cry of the visiting multitudes. The Cheese Phenomenon was set to peak on F A Cup fourth round weekend, with a "Cheese Boat" being chartered to ferry Bees supporters from Kew Pier down the Thames to Charlton, but the game was postponed on its original date, and when Brentford lost the rearranged game shortly afterwards - the supporters having been unable to re-book their boat in time - cheese was declared distinctly passe and Griffin Park was allowed to slip once more into tranquil slumber - strange really, given that a defeat when cheese involvement was very much at a premium should have reinforced the magical qualities of the stuff.

Seemingly, the one enduring facet of the cheese era is that *Hey Ju___ ___.* Beatles and latterly Stockport County fame) has persisted to the present day, although the stilton/cheddar references as detailed above have now disappeared, and it is a faithful reproduction of the original lyrics which currently does the job of uplifting the red'n'whites, although obviously the climactic last line has been amended to *"Naaa, naaa, naaa, na, na, na, na; na, na, na, na - Brentford!"*

Being afflicted with the same nickname as Barnet, it might reasonably have been expected that Bees' supporters would have come up with some eulogy in praise of the noble insect - a reworking of Arthur Askey's *Busy Bee* song perhaps - but this has not been the case thus far, and it is from West Yorkshire that inspiration has been drawn for this aspect of the Griffin Park songbook - Leeds United's supporters having provided the basic framework for the *"We are Bees, we are Bees, we are Bees!"* chant which occasionally illuminates grey afternoons in West London and beyond.

Charlton Athletic

In spite of the lengthy exile from their spiritual home endured by Charlton supporters prior to their return to the Valley a couple of seasons ago, the Addicks' faithful have still managed to come up with some interesting contributions. One in particular, which really came to the fore during the enforced nomadic years, was by way of a lament for the sadly-missed Floyd Road stand at the Valley, which had been the equivalent of the Anfield Kop before the skullduggery which saw the club temporarily expelled from SE7.

Many miles have I travelled,
Many games have I seen,
Following Charlton,
My only team.
Many hours have I spent
In the covered end choir
Singing, Valley, Floyd Road.

Valley, Floyd Road,
The mist rolling in from the Thames.
My only desire is always to be there
At Valley, Floyd Road
(Tune: Mull of Kintyre - Paul McCartney & Wings)

This one is still going strong, particularly at away games, even now that Charlton have returned to their traditional home. Alternative contributions suggest *"On the travelling road"* as a possible option for the sixth line, but as this results in the rather forced rhyming of *"road"* with, err, *"road"*, it seems far and away the less worthy of the two.

On the subject of being on the travelling road with Charlton's vast army of supporters, the red and white hordes can claim a degree of notoriety for being the only terrace choir in footballing history to have made a chant out of 1960's hit *Riders In The Sky* - originally by The Ramrods, but made famous by a later release by The Shadows. Reliable sources have intimated that the shouty bit (!), *"Yippee-yi-ay; yippee-yi-oh!"* is regularly revived up and down the country, with no other lyrics being attached - unique and decidedly strange!

On a far more traditional tack, the erstwhile managerial partner of present incumbent Alan Curbishley was regaled with the following on the occasions that he left the sanctuary of the dugout to lead from the front on the pitch....

> Stevie Gritt, Stevie Gritt,
> Stevie, Stevie Gritt,
> He's got no hair
> And we don't care,
> Stevie, Stevie Gritt.

Boney M's *Hooray, Hooray, It's A Holi-Holiday* was obviously the inspiration behind this hymnal in praise of Mr Gritt's polished pate, as it was for similar songs across the nation when any such follically challenged individual was foolish enough to take to the field of play. However, Gritt has ensured that this fairly common song gets listed under the Charlton banner by the response given to his "anthem" before a game at Home Park, Plymouth, at the end of the 1990/91 season. Rather calling the bluff of his tormentors, Gritt took the field wearing a luxurious blonde wig which, we have subsequently found out, he supposedly wore for the first five minutes or so of the game before being rumbled by the linesman - only lengthy representations to the officials avoided a booking for ungentlemanly conduct!

Finally, we come to the Official Charlton Athletic Club Song - not many of which have made it into this spectacular publication. However, *The Red, Red Robin* deserves a mention not because it is played over the tannoy at home games to herald the arrival of the team, but in its role as a source for several other chants.....

> When the red, red robin,
> Goes bob, bob bobbing along, along,
> There'll be no more sobbing,
> When he starts robbing,

His own sweet song.
Wake up, wake up you sleepy head,
Get up, get up, get out of bed,
Cheer up, cheer up, the sun is red.
Live, love, laugh and be happy.
What if I'm blue, now I'm walking through
Fields of flowers.
Rain may glisten, but I still listen
For hours and hours.
I'm just a kid again, doing what I did again,
Singing a song.
When the red, red, robin comes bob, bob, bobbing along.

Although Charlton supporters have been known to intone this in its original format on the days when they are overtaken by a desire to extol the traditional virtues of their club, it has never really been adopted as a supporters song. Predictably, the common chant which has derived from this opus is far shorter, and is one of the game's truly universal efforts which can be heard at any ground in the country when one of teams are playing in red....

When the red, red robin,
Comes bob, bob, bobbing along,
Shoot the bastard, shoot the bastard,
Shoot, shoot shoot the bastard...!

Seems a bit harsh that the feathered harbinger of festive cheer should be dealt with in so callous a manner, but that's football!

Chelsea

Even when Stamford Bridge was still a sprawling shell of a stadium, with both ends arcing away from the pitch, Blues followers in the Shed and the West Stand still managed to kick up a fair racket when they put their minds to it - now, post improvements, the Bridge in full cry provides one of the game's most daunting arenas. Chelsea followers have always had (and cultivated, it must be said) a fairly, err, lively reputation, and many of their songs reflect this, harking back to the golden age of the seventies when being seen to wear the wrong colours in the Fulham Road meant an almost certain visit to the local infirmary. Recently, Millwall appear to have taken on the role of "public enemy number one" for Chelsea's supporters but, when the majority of the songs listed below were popular, it was Spurs who were the real villains of the piece, hence their inclusion in that which follows....

> Hey, Tottenham, d'you wanna fight?
> Fight the lads in Blue and White!
> Oh let's fight
> (clap, clap clap, clap - clap - clap - clap)
> Oh let's fight
> (more clapping)
> Well the West Ham ran, and the Arsenal too,
> And the Wolverhampton wankers down at Molineux,
> So let's fight....
> (Tune: Let's Dance by Chris Montez)

Two other London rivals make an appearance in the above, as do Wolves which helps to establish the song as a product of the 1970's - this being the last time that the Black Country team were challenging for major honours and that their supporters were perceived as potential rivals off the pitch. More of the same follows by way of...

> We went up to Wolves,
> We took their North Bank,
> We came down to Arsenal,
> They're not worth a wank,
> But take my advice,
> There's nothing so nice,
> As kicking the fuck out of Tottenham
> (Tune: Messing about on the River)

Obviously, the gist of this one is that no matter who else the forerunners to the Headhunters happened to get involved with, Tottenham were always the preferred targets! It would appear that this dislike of the Lillywhite's goes back to their 1967 F A Cup final victory over Chelsea, the memory of which overrides the proximity of Fulham, Q P R and Brentford when it came to conferring "most-despised" status on one of the capital's other clubs. On a less parochial playing field, the one club which is generally guaranteed to get Chelsea supporters spluttering into their beer with fury is Manchester United. Games between the two clubs a few years ago usually involved some sort of high spirited jinks between the opposing supporters, and the Blues celebrated the presumable successful outcome of such encounters with....

> We are the Shed, my friend,
> We took the Stretford End,
> We'll sing and dance, and do it all again.
> We live the life we chose,

We fight and never lose,
We are the Shed, oh yes we are the Shed.
(Tune: Those Were The Days by Mary Hopkins)

The illustrious *Wild Rover* tune then makes one of its rare appearances outside of its more usual confines of the North West of England, with the Stamford Bridge version doing away with the chorus and taking the tune of the verses only....

They came down to Chelsea in '75.
They took up the North Stand,
The Shed and the side,
But Chelsea were many, too many to ruck,
And the great Man United got battered to fuck.

We went to Old Trafford in '78,
The whole of Manchester was lying in wait,
But Chelsea went mental, 'cos we had our pride,
And the whole of Manchester United died,
Too der loo, too der loo,
And the whole of Manchester United died.

Still with their sights set firmly northwards, the next target for Chelsea's vitriol is good old Liverpool. The first song in this short subsection merits inclusion as it is an entirely unique version of the *Halls Of Montezuma* which adheres to a different formula when it makes an appears anywhere other than Stamford Bridge....

In the dark back streets of Liverpool,
Where the Mile End's never been,
Lies the mutilated body of a scouse git,
Where the North Stand kicked him in,
Fuck off to Man United,
Fuck off to Liverpool (they're shit)
We will fight, fight, fight for the Chelsea,
To win the Football League.

Not one hundred percent sure about line four of this one, as my admittedly unreliable geography suggests that the North Stand at Stamford Bridge was the old away end, however there used to be a rather odd stand on the North West corner of the ground, which is perhaps what is referred to here. Still with Liverpool, the Red's Roger Hunt obviously endeared himself to Chelsea supporters in some way, as he is afforded his very own song....

Standing on the Spion Kop end,
Throwing bricks at Roger Hunt,

Liverpool is one big brothel,
And he's the biggest cunt!
(Tune: Standing On The Bridge At Midnight)

Right, now a bit of a departure from the usual Chelsea song, as although the much vaunted violent tendencies of the supporters do get a mention in this next one, the virtues of a former player and of the club itself are given more prominence....

His name is Tommy Baldwin,
He's the leader of our team (what team?)
The finest fucking football team,
The World has ever seen.
We're the Fulham Road supporters,
And we're louder than the Kop (what Kop?)
And if you want to argue,
Then we'll kill the fucking lot
(Tune: Macnamara's Band)

Baldwin was a popular Blues striker who amassed the impressive tally of seventy four goals in just short of two hundred appearances over eight years with the club.

Maintaining the drift away from songs which are exclusively devoted to deeds of violence, we find Chelsea's supporters lamenting the occasions that they are required to leave the confines of the Bridge to follow their team away from home....

I would grow much weaker,
Weather would be bleaker,
If I spent a week away,
From Chel-el-sea.
Stamford Bridge,
You're the only ground for me.
That's where I go,
It's my home,
To see Chelsea

....this takes the tune of *Peek-a-boo* - not the Siouxsie and the Banshees release from 1988, but an earlier song of the same name by the New Vaudeville Band which claimed a top ten place in 1967.

Towards the end of this epic Chelsea section, we come to four songs which have all become synonymous with the club, one going back the best part of two and a half decades and the others of a more recent vintage. First, what is more or less *the* definitive club song, and one which must be known by everyone with even a passing interest in football....

> Blue is the colour,
> Football is the game,
> We're all together,
> And winning is our aim.
> So cheer us on in the wind and rain,
> For Chelsea, Chelsea is our name.

One of the very few official club songs ever to be enthusiastically embraced by supporters, this was recorded by the players of Chelsea F C in 1972. Obviously, the actual song as laid down on vinyl was considerably longer than this, but it's just the chorus which has gone on to take its place on the terraces. More recently, there can have been very few Chelsea games which have made it through the full ninety minutes without all of the following being heard at least once....

> Celery, celery,
> If she don't come,
> I'll tickle her bum,
> With a lump of celery.

....a chant which follows the *"We're the famous Darlington, and we're going to Wemb-er-ley"* sort of tune, and which for some months resulted in sticks of celery becoming a vital fashion accessory at matches (predictably, this was curtailed when the ever-accommodating Met Police decided that the harmless vegetable constituted a security risk, and it became the only such foodstuff to be banned from a senior football ground. Moving on, and when *Celery* is heard, this next chant is almost sure to follow....

> Carefree, wherever you may be,
> We are the famous C F C,
> And we don't give a fuck,
> Whoever you may be,
> 'Cos we are the famous C F C
> (Tune: Lord of the Dance)

The last of the trilogy - although perhaps not as popular now as three or four years ago - is still an important Chelsea theme. It's a fair bet that *"One man went to mow, went to mow a meadow"* will be performed in its entirety, up to eleven, with *"baseball bat"* taking the place of *"dog"* to add just a hint of Chelsea's violent past to an otherwise unthreatening and almost pleasant song. Briefly, the origins of the *Celery* chant at Stamford Bridge seem destined to remain shrouded in mystery, although the first stirrings of the chant on a wider stage were heard on the South Coast (see Brighton for more details).

Carefree has now become the most popular chant amongst Chelsea supporters, although it is by no means exclusive to the Blues, with many other clubs having there own versions - notably Manchester United. *One Man Went To Mow* reputedly first saw the light of day at an away game with Leeds, possibly as early as 1981, from which Chelsea supporters had ostensibly been banned. Naturally, the draconian ban didn't deter a large number of supporters from making their way North from London and, in the absence of the usual shirts and scarves (left at home to make entrance to Elland Road easier), the song was used as a rallying cry so that different groups of Blues fans were able to meet up in order that they could all enjoy a quiet pint or two together, or whatever other entirely legal pursuit they chose to undertake (with positively no slapping of heads on the agenda whatsoever!).

More recently, Chelsea's F A Cup exploits have meant that a new song has been vying for number one spot in the Stamford Bridge charts, and its popularity en route to two final appearances may well have installed it in pole position....

> *Flying high, up in the sky,*
> *We'll keep the Blue Flag flying high,*
> *From Stamford Bridge to Wembley,*
> *We'll keep the Blue Flag flying high....*

...a straightforward enough rehash of *The Red Flag,* but one which can gauge its popularity by the fact that another set of supporters have found it necessary to produce a slightly amended version - always the sign of a high-profile song (*cf* West Ham United). And finally (promise), a bit of a one-off, but one which may turn out to have had far-reaching consequences for one player in particular. During the 1995/6 run of Fantasy Football League, a fair few digs were made at Nottingham Forest's Jason Lee, not only because of some rather profligate finishing in front of goal, but because of his splendid "tied up dreadlocks" hair style which, as Messrs Skinner and Baddiel pointed out, was not dissimilar to a pineapple. With the programme on which this revelation was initially expounded going out on a Friday, Lee must have noted with dismay that Forest's game the following day was away at Chelsea - and his woes were compounded when he was subsequently required to come on as a substitute - having to run on to the pitch alone in the full glare of publicity. Stamford Bridge immediately rang to a chorus of *"Pineapple, on his head, he's got a pineapple on his head"* to the tune of the hymn *He's Got The Whole World In His Hands* (*cf* Wolverhampton Wanderers). Outwardly, this may have appeared a bit of innocent fun but, as then Forest manager Frank Clark was later to opine to the national press, the whole "pineapple" campaign had destroyed the unfortunate Lee's confidence and led to him being transfer listed at the end of the season, so even when Chelsea supporters were having a laugh, it seems that they retain the ability to hasten the end of someone's career!

Crystal Palace

For a stadium which was rightly crucified in the first edition of this book for having all the atmosphere of a particularly sedate vicarage tea party, no matter how many thousands of people were inside, Selhurst Park must now be regarded as one of the country's most improved venues as far as the amount of matchday noise on offer. The new stands have enclosed the once vast open spaces of the Holmesdale and Whitehorse Lane terraces, and Palace supporters now have a stage befitting their rather impressive repertoire. Apart from the less than inventive *"Eagles, Eagles, Eagles"* chant which is the standard song at Palace games, the club have adopted The Dave Clark Five's *Glad All Over* as their anthem. Burgeoning crowds during the 1990 F A Cup run saw the song rapidly gain popularity amidst a swarm of red and blue balloons, and it remains a current favourite, even though performances of the whole thing are rare....

You say that you love me,
All of the time,
You say that you need me,
You'll always be mine,

  And I'm feeling glad all over,
  Yes I'm glad all over
  Baby I'm glad all over,
  So glad you're mine

I'll make you happy,
You'll never be blue,
You'll have no sorrow,
I'll always be true

  repeat chorus

Other girls may try to take me away
But you know it's by your side I'll stay
Our love will last now,
'till the end of time
Because this love now,
Is only yours and mine

  repeat chorus

With a rare sortie into downright nastiness, ex-Palace favourite Ian Wright will always be assured of a warm welcome on returning to the club whose supporters felt that he was a bit too eager to jump ship when an Arsenal pay slip appeared over the horizon. Cheerily, *Poor Old Michael Finnegan* gets amended to....

> *Ian Wright is illegitimate*
> *He ain't go no birth certificate,*
> *He's got aids and can't get rid of it,*
> *He's an Arsenal bastard ....*

Crystal Palace are far from having a monopoly on this sort of song - it crops up at many other grounds in a variety of guises - but this provides an apt illustration of how a one time crowd favourite can swiftly becomes a hate figure when they move to a new (particularly local) club.

A number of Palace songs first saw the light of day in adversity. The infamous 0-9 hiding at Anfield in 1989 ended with *"We're going to score in a minute"* echoing round a fast-emptying stadium after the final whistle and, with the Palace contingent left on their own having been kept in by the police, the yawning expanse of the unpopulated Kop was viciously taunted with *"You're not singing any more"*. A possibly even more embarrassing hiding - going down 0-5 at Selhurst to Wimbledon of all people - prompted the bloke in charge of the P A to play Russ Abbott's *Oh What An Atmosphere* to a shell-shocked and silent crowd as they filed out of the ground. This was pounced on by Palace's song-starting supporters, and proceeded to get an airing at future matches when things were going rather better - notably during the second leg of the play-off win over Charlton at the end of 95/6.

South Norwood is evidently home to diligent followers of the latest music scene, as it took a very short time indeed for 2-Unlimited's *No Limits* to transmute into *"Bob Bob, Bob Bob Bob Bob, Bob Bob Bob Bob, Bob Bob Bobby Bowry"*, in praise of the ex-Q P R midfielder. Equally, the snappily titled *Poing*, apparently by Rotterdam Termination Source, soon permeated the Palace psyche and accompanies frenzied pogo-ing by way of *"Boing, Boing, Red'n' Blue Army, Boing, Boing, Red'n'Blue Army"*. This one, however, is not a Palace original and was yet again pinched from West Brom supporters who enlivened a crucial last-game-of-the-season affair at Fratton Park in 1994 with the similarly choreographed *"Boing, Boing, Baggies, Baggies!"*.

Going back a few years, the Victoria Ground Stoke in September 1978 reverberated to the outwardly rather oblique *"Rachid, Lend us a quid, Rachid, Rachid, lend us a quid"*, but light can soon be thrown on this one when Rachid Harkouk and Barry Silkman's contemporaneous arrest for allegedly forging bank notes is taken into account...! Oddly, diligent research has revealed that neither player actually appeared in the game in question, and that Harkouk had left the club some weeks earlier - but it was obviously considered so amusing as to warrant an airing regardless of the fact that the players concerned weren't in attendance.

48

To close, a couple of chants which are aimed *at* Palace by supporters of other clubs. Roy "Chubby" Brown, an alleged comedian, thrilled the country in 1996 with his version of the Smokie original *Living Next Door to Alice*, stamping his mark on the song by wittily shouting *"Alice, Alice, who the fuck is Alice?"* throughout. Unsurprisingly, this soon resurfaced as *"Palace, Palace, who the fuck are Palace"* at any number of grounds. Then, the notorious Eric Cantona incident caught the imagination of supporters up and down the country and the *Go West, "Ooh aah, Eric Cantona"* chant assailed Palace fans wherever they went - as did all manner of other pro-Cantona chants. Disappointingly for the Palace supporters, this treatment revealed that no matter how widely reviled Cantona was for playing for much-loathed Manchester United, there was widespread support for his action, and that kicking a Palace supporter was something with which many supporters could empathise - less popular than United - oh dear!

Fulham

Not only do Fulham have one of the most unfortunate nicknames in the league (although when "The Cottagers" was coined, the connotations about standing around in public toilets with feet in plastic bags probably weren't too widely known), but their demotion to Division Three in 1994 saw the team playing in professional football's basement for the first time in its illustrious history. However, a less inglorious past has left the club with a rich tradition of songs, the majority of which hark back to the early/mid seventies which culminated in the 1975 F A Cup Final appearance. Having ended Birmingham City's ambitions in the competition by defeating them in the semi, Hammersmith resounded to the likes of *"Bye bye Blues, Bog off Birmingham, We nearly won the Cup, We nearly won the Cup!"*, which was joined, after the Wembley defeat by West Ham, by...

> *All my life, I've been a-waiting*
> *Billy Bonds needs bloody castrating,*
> *Oh boy - we nearly won the Cup.*
> *But the world did see,*
> *That Fulham did grace Wembley*
> *(Tune: Oh Boy by Mud)*

During the game itself, and based on Status Quo's *Down, Down* tune, there was an almost incessant barrage of *"Down, Down, Chelsea are Down"* which was a relatively rare manifestation of West London rivalry and, naturally, celebrated the fact that Chelsea had just been relegated. The Stamford Bridge club came in for quite a bit of stick from their neighbours during the 70's, most notably by way of....

> As I was walking down the Fulham Road
> I met a Blue Filth boot boy,
> And he said to me "Are you off to see
> The team they call the Chelsea?"
> So I looked around and up and down
> And said "You must be joking,
> For if you could see the Fulham F C
> You'd know your team needs poking!"

Chelsea's extrovert Alan Hudson was singled out for personal abuse and had the gift of a song bestowed upon him by Fulham's supporters, though he would not, perhaps, have appreciated the lyrics....

> Here comes Alan Hudson,
> He's got something in his hair,
> Is it a royal blue ribbon?
> What's it doing their?
> Alan Hudson's a poof!
> (Tune: Something In The Air)

Next a departure from anti-Chelsea feelings, and something known as *The Rovers Song*, the tune to which seems rather vague (can't beat shoddy research, can you)....

> When you're born in Fulham, you'll never walk alone,
> Hike a hundred highways, to win away from home,
> Still, all in all I'm happy, the reason is you see,
> That I'll keep on following the great Fulham F C.

Another of the many songs which appear to be wholly unique to SW6, and another which dates back to the seventies is....

> I've just come back from Cardiff
> To see the Fulham play,
> They haven't won at home lately,
> They haven't won away.
> But I was very happy,
> Though my money was all gone,
> 'cos I swapped five photos of my wife
> For one of Leslie Strong
> And we were singing hymns and arias,
> Land Of My Fathers, right up your arse...!

There were many other shorter songs which made up the extensive Thamesbank repertoire of the mid 1970's, but the majority of these were simple chants based on individual players. The only other one of note is a fairly extensive version of *The Tennessee Wig Walk*, which surfaces at many other grounds in one format or another, but with only the A F C Bournemouth variant managing to exceed the length Fulham's rendition which therefore merits inclusion on that basis alone....

> *Bertie Mee said to Bill Shankly*
> *"Have you heard of the North Bank, Highbury?"*
> *Shanks said "No, go and have a po' (!),*
> *Sod off, you cockney bastard".*
> *But Bertie Mee said to Bill Shankly*
> *"Have you heard of the Thamesbank, Fulham F C?"*
> *And the Shank said "Yes,*
> *They're the loudest and the best,*
> *And they all support the Fulham."*

In fact, the Dean Court incarnation only appears to be longer than its counterpart in South West London because of the inclusion of several non-verbal "lah-ing" sections, so perhaps Craven Cottage should be recognised as the true home of this long-established and nationwide favourite after all - ample compensation for the retirement of Jimmy Hill indeed!

Leyton Orient

Well, here's a turn up - of all the clubs in London, it might reasonably have been expected that one of the leading lights may lay claim to having the most extensive repertoire of songs, but this mantle rests fairly and squarely with the residents of Brisbane Road in the light of their vast selection of (for the most part) shortish chants, spiced up with a couple of longer efforts. In the first instance, a couple of songs are performed in their original unadulterated forms, including improvised instrumental sequences, so expect to hear both the Leicester City anthem *When You're Smiling* and Erasure's *A Little Respect* next time you visit East London - it is not clear whether the former is complete with the same frenzied gesticulation as is found at Filbert Street, though.

As far as the proliferation of chants goes, much of the blame can be laid at the feet of a group of O's supporters who have christened themselves *The Donuts*. This rather peculiar name was adopted either because the shape of a donut reflects the outline of the initial letter of the club's name, or because it is not dissimilar to the basic structure of an equally palatable part of the female anatomy - conflicting reports support either hypothesis, so take you pick really. The rallying cry of The Donuts is *"Do you know what a donut is, doo dah, doo dah, do you know what a donut is, doo dah, doo dah day!"*, obviously to the *Camptown Races* tune, and this is always followed by a short burst of *"Silly, silly Donuts, silly, silly Donuts"*. Being residents of the Oliver Road terrace, The Donuts often assert both the geographic location of their patch, and their predilection for a few beers with *"We're the West Side, we're the West Side, we're the West Side alcoholics"* to which other factions on the terrace will respond with *"You're the West Side paraplegics"*. One such alternative faction is the Hood Squad who, apart from proclaiming their presence with the drawn out *"Hoooooooooooooood Squaaaaaaaaaaaaaad"* chant, also celebrate the questionable personal hygiene of a particular O's supporter (obviously quite a character on the terraces) with....

> *Yellow and green, yellow and green,*
> *Albert said "My teeth, my teeth,*
> *They've all gone yellow and green"*
> *Albert said "I've got genital warts,*
> *Genital warts"*

The loudest part of the above is the *"Yellow and green, yellow and green"* line, which naturally confuses the casual observer who might reasonably expect red and white to be the predominant feature in any O's colour-related songs. Not so much confused as just being bloody miserable, the police apparently took a dim view of a *"Yellows, yellows, yellows!"* chant which was aimed at a group of officers on duty at Brisbane Road wearing fluorescent bibs of an appropriate hue. Told to shut up, the supporters naturally continued with some other chants and, having been threatened with eviction from the ground should the innocent fun not cease immediately, they responded by humming the Christmas Carol *Silent Night* for the remainder of the match. This incident (in 1989) made the national papers, and possibly provided the inspiration for a Meadowbank Thistle performance of *The Lord's My Shepherd* in similar circumstances when under threat of imminent removal from Hamilton Academical's ground having performed some of the less politically correct of their many songs.

Back to the East End, and a swift resumé of some of the many brief chants which illuminate Brisbane Road. None of the following are believed to have any relevance to anything in particular, and are best dismissed as just "being silly": *"Who do you think you are kidding, Mr Kipling, with your bloody awful cakes"*, starts the ball rolling and is built around the theme tune to Dad's Army; *"Cheese and biscuits, cheese and biscuits, vinegar, vinegar"*, *"We like beans, we like sauce, we like sexual intercourse"*, *"We're all mad, we're insane, we eat Mars bars on the train"* and *"Lurpack, my baby loves lurpack"* all hint darkly at some sort of food related sexual deviation which is best left unexplored too deeply. Then, to everyone's surprise, football itself actually rears its ugly head, with the teams' rather extravagant kit of the early nineties being celebrated by way of....

> *Peter Eustace's red, white and black*
> *With a stupid yellow number on the back ARMY!*

West Ham are gently chided with a couple of standard efforts that seem to crop up just for the sake of appearances rather than as a reflection of any genuine antipathy between the neighbouring clubs but strangely, the real venom is reserved for Welsh clubs. The ubiquitous *Everywhere We Go* song, in its East End incarnation, is climaxed with *"...You're invited to Brisbane Road, to have a row with Cardiff City, oooooooh, we hate Cardiff and we hate Cardiff...."*, while *"We all follow the Orient"* from the *Land Of Hope And Glory* stable includes *"....over land and sea, AND NEWPORT!"* which is doubly strange given that County had ceased to be members of the professional ranks some time before this song became popular.

Unfortunately, Orient's on-field endeavours have showed little sign of matching the quality of the songs on the terraces, and this constant underachievement itself is now immortalized in *The Mid-table Mediocrity Song*....

> *We're not going up, and we're not going down,*
> *We won't win the league, and we won't win the Cup,*
> *We're not good, in fact we're bad,*
> *We are the Orient, WE'RE MAD!"*

....quite mad, obviously, and one last chant sums this up rather succinctly: Everyone will be familiar with the *"Woooaaaahh - you're shit"* thing that has been doing the rounds for some years to accompany goalkeepers taking place kicks but, from the area in which this chant may have its origins comes a unique variation. 'keepers taking such kicks in front of O's supporters no doubt think they know what's coming when the *"Wooooaaah"* bit builds up as they take their run up, but this stops abruptly when contact is made with the ball, and the stadium remains eerily silent until said ball returns to earth, when everyone shouts *"BOIIINNNNNGGGG!"* and bounces about in a suitably manic style - wonderful.

There is, unfortunately, just one thing wrong with the Orient claims to have one of the country's most extensive range of bizarre chants - on a visit to Brisbane Road towards the end of 1996/7 it has to be reported that I heard not one solitary song or chant during the course of an entire match which, having expected at least some of the above to make an appearance, was a bit disappointing to say the least!

Millwall

Not an awful lot to report from the New Den (or Senegal Fields or whatever this week's name for the new ground might be), but there is at least one song made popular by Lions' supporters which has spread right across the country since its inception in the late 1970's. Many other clubs may try to imitate, but there is only one group of supporters who are really able to do justice to....

> *We are Millwall, we are Millwall,*
> *We are Millwall, from The Den,*
> *We are Millwall, super Millwall*
> *We are Millwall, from The Den.*
> *No-one likes us, no-one likes us,*
> *No-one likes us, we don't care,*
> *We are Millwall, super Millwall,*
> *We are Millwall, from the Den.*
> *(Tune: Sailing by Rod Stewart)*

The reason that this has become so synonymous with the Lions is that, after the excesses of their notorious supporters over the years, they can genuinely claim to be one of the least popular clubs in the country and that, in actual fact, no-one does like them at all! Second in popularity only to *No-one Likes Us* is *Let 'em Come*, which is reputedly played over the tannoy before kick off. Some footage of a stupendous, beery rendition of this made it on to the TV (*Fantasy Football League*, again) early in 1996, and even Frank Skinner's mocking performances which followed could not detract from what is really a reather classy effort....

> *It's Saturday in Cold Blow Lane,*
> *We've all come down to cheer.*
> *We've had our jellied eels,*
> *And our glass of beer.*
> *Come rain or shine, all the time,*
> *Our families we'll bring.*
> *And as the Lions run out on the pitch,*
> *Everyone will sing loud and clear,*
> *Let 'em come, let 'em come,*
> *We'll only have to beat them again.*
> *We're the best team in London,*
> *No, the best team of all,*
> *Everybody knows us, we're called Millwall,*
> *Let 'em come, let 'em come, let 'em come,*
> *Let 'em all come down to The Den.*

Apart from these two though, singing fare at The Den is really rather frugal, in content if not in intensity. A scattering of the game's everyday chants enliven proceedings, but in the main there are just two other efforts which occur on a regular basis. The first of these is quite simply the name of the club repeated over and over to the rhythm of *Amazing Grace*, but there's something about the way in which it is done which gives the whole thing a very menacing air. Similarly, the name "Millwall" is again given a life of its own by way of a strange shout, more than a chant. This will start with just one person shouting *"Mmmmmmmmmmmmiiiiiiiiiiiiiiiii...."* on his (or I suppose her, in these enlightened times) own; gradually, more and more people join, maintaining the noise until enough momentum is reached for the whole thing to climax with *"......iiiiillllllwall, Millwall, Millwall!"* Again, this comes over in a particularly feeble manner using the printed word, but it sounds bloody impressive when a few hundred voices are giving it their all and the initial *"Mmmmmmiiiiii..."* bit has gone for a couple of minutes before the final crescendo.

Tottenham Hotspur

Oh dear - a really rather lamentable showing from White Hart Lane, and one which comes nowhere near rivalling the efforts of the capital's other top flight clubs. Quite why this should be the case is difficult to fathom - the fact that The Shelf was the first of London's traditional home terraces to fall victim to the bulldozers probably didn't help, but the new White Hart Lane still seems able to generate a reasonable atmosphere when the occasion demands. Perhaps it was simply the catalogue of embarrassing misfortunes that befell the club - mainly off the pitch - since the mid eighties which have knocked the stuffing out of Spurs' supporters and reduced them to silent acceptance of their rather unfortunate lot? Whatever the reason, at least the appearance of Arsenal can still be guaranteed to have the new East Stand and the Paxton Road in full voice, usually with something along the lines of the following....

> *Show me the way to go home,*
> *I'm tired and I want to go to bed,*
> *I had a little drink about an hour ago,*
> *And it's gone right to my head.*
> *Well, wherever I may roam,*
> *Through land or sea or foam (!),*
> *You will always here me singing this song -*
> *We hate Arsenal and we hate Arsenal,*

We hate Arsenal and we hate Arsenal,
We hate Arsenal and we hate Arsenal,
We are the Arsenal - haters!
(Tune: Show Me The Way To Go Home, lapsing into a traditional chant)

If the Spurs choristers cannot be bothered to prefix *"We hate Arsenal......"* with the seven line build up as above, it may be preceded by the more conservative *"Away in a manger, no crib for a bed, the little lord Jesus he jumped up and said...."*, which means that they can get on with the important sentiments of the chant without having to bother with the tiresome preamble.

Probably the best-known chant associated with Spurs is their version of the *Glory, Glory Hallelujah* hymn which has been adopted by so many other clubs since it surfaced at White Hart Lane in the early sixties. For the most part, the only lines actually sung nowadays are....

Glory, Glory, Tottenham Hotspur,
Glory, Glory, Tottenham Hotspur,
Glory, Glory, Tottenham Hotspur,
And the Spurs go marching on, on, on!

It is apparent that a much fuller version used to be performed back in the dim and distant past, with the *"Mine eyes have seen the glory of the coming of the Lord"* verse being the most popular addition to the above, but this seems to have fallen out of favour with the Tottenham supporters of recent years, apart form the fact that it provides the title for a Spurs fanzine. It has, though, gone on to wider use, notably at Nottingham Forest by way of a pro-Jason Lee song which came to light after the "pineapple" episode.

Only one other song of any real length seems to have found it's way into the Spurs repertoire, one which sees them join the select band - alongside Forest (again), Celtic, Linfield and Man United - who consider themselves to be of sufficiently noble lineage to merit a performance or two of....

Oh it's a grand old team to play for,
And it's a grand old team to see,
And if you know your history,
Well it's enough to make your heart go-ohhh...ohhh..ohhh!
We don't care what the red shite say,
What the hell do they know?
For we only know, that there's going to be a show,
And the famous Tottenham Hotspur will be there.

The "red shite" in question are obviously Arsenal, although the derogatory term is always used in this song - presumably the Spurs' fans can't quite bring themselves to utter the name of the residents of the Marble Halls.

A couple of chants as opposed to proper songs which seem to have faded from use with the demise of The Shelf were *"Hot dog, sausage roll, come on Spurs, score a goal"* and the rather odd *"What's the name of the game? - soccer, soccer, soccer!"*, although the former still occasionally crops up at other clubs, generally in the lower reaches of the Football League.

Unfortunately for the credibility of Spurs' supporters, the club seem to think it necessary to enlist the services of good old cockney knees up duo Chas & Dave to come up with a club song whenever Wembley hoves into view. This has resulted in the deplorable *Spurs Only Win When The Year Ends In One*, which never even came close to being adopted by the club's supporters, but also gave rise to the far more respectable *Ossie's Dream*, which has gone on to become an enduring terrace favourite, used by followers of many a club when they are on the Wembley trail (with suitable amendments, obviously), but which has remained synonymous with Tottenham in spite of its now much wider usage. The (slightly altered) words of the original chorus are those which have endured....

> *Spurs are on their way to Wembley,*
> *Tottenham's going to do it again,*
> *You can't stop 'em, the boys from Tottenham,*
> *The boys from White Hart Lane.*

Almost without exception, a rendition of the above prompts an immediate repeat performance by the supporters of the club which Spurs are playing - a far less savoury version which plays on Tottenham's Jewish connections (as do a number of other equally distasteful songs and chants) and which has become probably just as well known - however what with this book firmly ensconced on the moral high ground and the like, this version will not be making an appearance here!

Something of a far more acceptable nature to the patrons of White Hart Lane was the manner in which Arsenal managed to lose the 1995 Cup Winners' Cup final to Real Zaragoza - by way of a goal from ex-Spurs' player Nayim which sailed over a suitably nonplussed David Seaman from some fifty yards out in the dying seconds of extra time. Such a cherished moment naturally needed to be celebrated in song, and thus the North London contribution to the ever-expanding *Go West* stable was spawned, with just about the most popular song at White Hart Lane for the last couple of years subsequently being....*"Nayim, from the half-way line - Nayim, from the half-way line - Nayim, from the half-way line - Nayim, from the half-way line!"*

Watford

It would appear that (not unsurprisingly) Watford were done a great injustice in the first version of this noble publication wherein the depth of feeling that exists between them and Luton Town was grossly underestimated. Subsequent contributions from Vicarage Road have detailed a number of instances of spectacular violence at derby games between the two clubs, for the most part in the early 1980's, and mainly taking place at Kenilworth Road. Equally, the Watford songbook was crassly dismissed as being "crap", but needles to say this vacuous claim has also been refuted. There are, in truth, a number of rather fine Watford songs, most of them directed at Luton, and it is with the brooding malevolence of the Hertfordshire/Bedfordshire enmity that we must start.

Black Lace's jaunty hit from 1984, *Agadoo*, is probably one of the more unlikely songs to have been co-opted on to the terraces, but this derivative was supposedly popular on The Rookery (Watford's home terrace)....

> *Agadoo, do, do,*
> *We're the Watford wrecking crew,*
> *To the left, to the right,*
> *Luton are a load of shite!*

Of a similar ilk, though devoid of naughty swearies, we find the only recorded episode thus far of the Toy Doll's inestimable *Nellie The Elephant* having found its way into usage at a football ground, an event not to be sniffed at....

> *Ooooooooooh,*
> *Watford the Greatest scored a goal,*
> *And said Goodbye to the Luton,*
> *And off they went with a humperty hump,*
> *Hump, hump, hump!*

....again of 1984 vintage, this would have to be recorded as one of the better examples of a children's song having been adopted by a footballing audience - possibly only bettered by *Rupert The Bear* at Newcastle, and maybe Huddersfield's stab at the *Chigley* song. Of a far more mature nature comes this following effort from towards the start of the 1980's when both Watford and Luton were in the (old) Second Division. There does not appear to be any sort of tune, as such....

> *There's a hole in the ceiling (clap, clap!)*
> *And the Oak Road is leaking (clap, clap!)*
> *David Pleat's got no money (clap. clap!)*
> *And Eric Morecambe ain't funny (clap, clap!)*

What are we living for? (clap, clap!)
To see Luton in Division Four (clap, clap!)
What are we gonna do? (clap, clap!)
See Watford win Division Two (clap, clap!)

The Oak Road mentioned herein was the home terrace at Kenilworth Road and, as I'm sure everyone knows, Eric Morecambe was a director of the club. Similar Luton relegation celebrations came to the fore towards the end of season 91/2, when the Hatters went down on the final day courtesy of a defeat at already-relegated Notts County. To an indefinable tune there was....

Luton Town, Luton Town,
Is it true what people say,
You're going down - Oh Luton Town!

Back to the celebration of victorious sorties into battle against the old enemy, although not seemingly referring to a specific encounter, the old American Civil War tune *When Johnny Comes Marching Home* (*cf* West Ham United) was amended to....

The Luton went in one by one, hurrah, hurrah!
The Luton went in one by one, hurrah, hurrah!
The Luton went in one by one,
And one by one they all got done,
As The Horns go steaming in,
Bollocks to Luton Town!

This, of course, crops up at many other grounds up and down the country with the necessary alterations being made to change the relevance to the performing club and their chosen rivals. The "Horns" in this rendition are merely an abbreviated form of Watford's "Hornets" nickname. Now on to two songs - again popular at other venues - but which have been customised with a couple of alterations that are unique to Watford. The first, *Molly Malone*, is one of the most common songs across the British Isles with everyone from the late lamented Maidstone United to any number of Premier League clubs giving an airing to the same basically similar effort. Watford, however, work in a nice local reference to line five....

In London's fair city,
Where girls are so pretty,
I first set my eyes on sweet Molly Malone,
She wheels her wheelbarrow,
From Watford to Harrow,
Singing.....
(Clap, clap, clap, clap ,clap - clap, clap ,clap, clap)
WATFORD!

....it is obviously just a fortunate coincidence that Watford can make reference to Harrow (just five miles down the road) in order to personalise this song, and a similar circumstance means that they can also knock out a bit of a one-off from the tractor driving school of football songs....

> We can't read, and we can't write,
> But that don't really matter,
> 'cos we'll go up to Luton Town,
> And kick fuck out the Hatters!

....Luton's nickname fitting nicely into the last line. In conclusion, a couple of short chants that clearly illustrate how the same subject can be employed to entirely different ends by opposing sets of supporters. A decade or so ago, when Watford were a half-decent side, Elton John was in his first spell as chairman and the team was under the management of a certain Graham Taylor - not quite the personification of evil to football supporters nationwide then as he is now. With the Watford supporter's lot a reasonably happy one with the club progressing nicely under this administration, the fairly unchallenging chant *"Elton John's Taylor-made army"* was often heard to illuminate a quiet half hour or so on The Rookery. Supporters of visiting teams however, whatever their opinion of Elton and Graham's footballing relationship, could never quite manage to ignore the sexual proclivities of the spangled songster, and it was Manchester United's fans who decided that some voluble outing needed to be done, which resulted in a classic *Quartermaster's Stores* chant....

> He shot, his come, all over Taylor's bum,
> Elton John, Elton John!

This was a classic example of how any sort of behaviour by an individual - though outside of the immediate footballing sphere - considered to be anything other than the norm instantly became fair game when a subject for a song was needed. There are numerous other examples throughout this book of players and officials finding aspects of their erstwhile private lives being advertised loud and clear on the terraces, usually in an abusive or derogatory manner.

West Ham United

There is, of course, only one song with which we can start the West Ham section, the esteemed *I'm Forever Blowing Bubbles*. As inseparable from United as is *The Blaydon Races* from Newcastle (and equally likely to be picked up by supporters from other clubs), this is undoubtedly one of the most famous songs throughout football, though its connections with The Hammers are initially a little tenuous. Written in the 1920's by American songsmith James Brockman, the original song swiftly became popular with the general public on both sides of the Atlantic. It was first heard at Upton Park in about 1926 (and not, as is popularly thought to be the case, making its West Ham debut at the 1923 F A Cup Final), and was then, reputedly, adopted by a school adjacent to Upton Park as the "club song" for its junior football team. Having thus become established in the local area, it began to be played over the tannoy at The Hammers' ground before matches, and when an effort was made to replace it, after a few years, with *Maybe It's Because I'm A Londoner*, there was uproar and tumult amongst the West Ham faithful and it was swiftly restored to the turntables. Enjoying its zenith at the 1966 World Cup Final, when three West Ham players appeared for England, the song has since been irrevocably installed as the club anthem....

> *I'm forever blowing bubbles,*
> *Pretty bubbles in the air,*
> *They fly so high,*
> *Nearly reach the sky,*
> *Then like my dreams,*
> *They fade and die.*
> *Fortune's always hiding,*
> *I've looked everywhere,*
> *But I'm forever blowing bubbles,*
> *Pretty bubbles in the air,*
> *UNITED...UNITED!*

As with every song which becomes associated with a particular club, it is easy meat to the supporters of other teams who are looking to turn it around and abuse the original singers. This fate has befallen *Bubbles* even more readily than similar songs, and the general scheme of these bastardised arrangements is set out under Arsenal's entry, although any of the other London clubs are just as likely to give their particular arrangement an airing.

As mentioned, there was a move by the club to have *Maybe It's Because I'm A Londoner* adopted as the main club song and, although this scheme was put down by civil insurrection, the song still managed to find its way on to the pages of the Hammers' song book....

> *Maybe it's because I'm a Londoner,*
> *That I love London Town,*
> *Maybe it's because I'm a Londoner,*
> *That I think of her wherever I go.*
> *I get a funny feeling inside of me,*

Just walking up and down,
Maybe it's because I'm a Londoner,
That I love London Town.

....not being specifically a West Ham song, this is also used by several of the capital's other clubs on occasion - Chelsea more than most - but as a general rule, this should really be regarded as being more popular in the East End than anywhere else.

Another song steeped in East End tradition is *Me And My Girl*, taken from the stage production of the same name, though having being substantially rewritten for its transferral from the West End to West Ham....

Bow Bells are ringing, for the Claret and Blue,
Bow Bells are ringing, for the Claret and Blue,
When the Hammers are scoring,
And the South bank are roaring, And the money is pouring,
For the Claret and Blue.
No relegation for the Claret and Blue,
Just celebration for the Claret and Blue,
And one day we'll win a cup,
Or two or three or four or more!
For West Ham, and the Claret and Blue.

....Southampton are one of the few other clubs who have adopted this song.

On the subject of colours, a recent innovation at Upton Park has been the following splendid rewrite of Chelsea's *Blue Flag* song. Naturally wishing to pour scorn on song, club and colour, few Hammers' games during 1996/7 were complete without a few lusty choruses of....

Up your arse, right up your arse,
Stick your blue flag up your arse,
From Stamford Bridge to Upton Park,
Stick your blue flag up your arse!

The last of the really traditional Iron's songs shows a more general dislike for the other teams in the league, although with a tune that doesn't really bear straightforward comparison with any well known songs - other than perhaps having a passing resemblance to *The Halls Of Montezuma* - this one has tended to die out since the early 1980's....

Man United can stay at Old Trafford,
And Southampton can stay at The Dell,
And as for Tottenham Hotspur,
Well they can go to hell,

'cos we'll all drink to West Ham,
West Ham's the team for me,
Yes we'll all drink to West Ham,
West Ham United F C

Down an entirely different path, and one thing that was very much associated with West Ham during the 1970's and early 80's (apart from Trevor Brooking's bubble perm) was crowd trouble. London derbies were traditional and obvious flashpoints - although the Inter City Firm spread the gospel somewhat wider - and it was their excursions to Highbury that the West Ham gangs always enjoyed more than most. A sixth round F A Cup tie in 1975 was the high point for these invasions of North London - hundreds of Hammers' fans swarming onto the North Bank virtually unopposed, and it seemed only natural that this feat of bravado should be celebrated in song. As with Watford's choral festivities in memory of handing Luton Town supporters a similar hiding, *When Johnny Comes Marching Home* seemed an appropriate tune with which to work....

The West Ham went in three by three,
Hurrah, hurrah!
The West Ham went in three by three,
Hurrah, hurrah!
The West Ham went in three by three,
And took the North Bank, Highbury,
Da, da, da, da, da, da, d-da da da da, da, da!

Revelling in their reputation as one of the game's most feared hooligan crews, West Ham were not slow to acknowledge their violent image. Dick van Dyke's chimney-hopping ditty from *Mary Poppins* (a more inappropriate a source it is hard to imagine) became....

Chim chiminee, chim chiminee,
Chim chim cheroo,
We are the bastards in Claret and Blue.

....and even The Ramblers thoroughly inoffensive little song, *The Sparrow*, so often altered to a common theme at other clubs (*cf* Ipswich Town) ended up with a special Upton Park version....

He's only a poor little cockney,
His colour are Claret and Blue,
And one day this season,
For no fucking reason,
He's gonna kick shit out of you!

However, in more recent times, with the days of the butcher's coat and the silk scarf now long gone, and even the haute couture casual seemingly a thing of the past, West Ham supporters were forced to look to other directions via which they could make their mark on the game - so they came up with an irritating chant (a bloody irritating chant!). Luckily, even this has now begun to wane in popularity, but for a time in the late 1980's and early 1990's, not a single goal kick across the country could ever be completed without some amusing *(sic)* wag in the crowd going....

Wooooooooaaaaahhhhhhhh - YOU'RE SHIT! - aaaaaaaaarrgghhhhh!

....as the goalkeeper ran up to the ball and punted it upfield. The most diligent research has revealed it to be entirely probable that this nationwide craze was spawned by some spotty oik at Upton Park - and it's difficult to imagine anything much further removed from the rousing and rather noble chorus which is *I'm Forever Blowing Bubbles* - thank you, West Ham!

And it is with *Bubbles* that we shall end the West Ham section, as it has transpired that it is not only the supporters of other clubs who are wont to alter the original. Evidently short of something to do at some point around 1995, it became the vogue for Hammers' supporters to pervert their own anthem by singing the original words, but to the tune of *Chitty Chitty Bang Bang* (obviously some sort of unhealthy preoccupation with Dick van Dyke is starting to become apparent here!). Whilst you would have thought that the Upton Park faithful would have been the last people who'd want to sing anything other than the original, the remix became a popular way to celebrate when West Ham were winning and, having tried it out purely for research purposes, I am pleased to report that the new creation just about works (but only just!).

Section Four

East Anglia

Cambridge United

Ipswich Town

Northampton Town

Norwich City

Peterborough United

East Anglia

There are two distinctly different approaches from the clubs that make up this region - in the first instance we have Ipswich and Norwich, caught up in their local rivalry to the exclusion of almost anything else, then there are Cambridge United and Northampton who ignore the mundane matter of football and have instead chosen to tread the path of rank silliness.

Obviously, the approach taken by the two teams of less senior standing is the more impressive, and both have managed to set their stall out as leading proponents of the art of singing stupidity. At the Abbey, this comes through by way of the "moose" movement - a genuinely unique concept unless you can think of any other clubs which have sold foam antlers at one time or another! Sixfields, or more correctly the old County Ground, has managed to make its mark via two songs in particular - one about toilets (playing on that particular British preoccupation with lavatorial humour) and one about fondling young girls' bottoms (a different preoccupation entirely!).

Portman Road and Carrow Road are peculiar venues when it comes to song in that there are fairly extensive repertoires in evidence, but that they both have a rather dated air about them. *All Things Bright And Beautiful*, *On The Ball City*, *Onward Christian Soldiers* and the bizarre *Edward Ebenezer Jeremiah Brown* song - fine songs in their own right, but hardly at the cutting edge of the football song movement, and very much relics of yesteryear. It may be the case that this is the legacy of both clubs having enjoyed their last spells of prolonged success some years ago, with songs popular at the time being retained by today's supporters as a reminder of past glories, but whatever the reason, it seems that the recent resurgence in singing and chanting has either not yet reached East Anglia or has been deliberately ignored.

Cambridge United

To the casual observer, United seem to be one of those fortunate clubs where there is always something interesting going on. Whereas other clubs in the lower reaches of the league are either content or condemned to merely exist in the footballing equivalent of a persistent vegetative state, the U's forever appear to be up to one thing or another - whether it's a season (or three) of record breaking ineptitude, a cup run, some sort of of play-off involvement or a bucket of cold water applied to the testicles by way of some bizarre pre-match goings on. Supporters at the Abbey seem to reflect this spirited and vigorous approach to the game, and have originated an interesting variety of songs as a result.

Perhaps the first matter which should be addressed is the somewhat bizarre "moose" concept, which has been associated with the club since the late eighties and has manifested itself in song (albeit in a rather cursory manner) as well as receiving official sanction by the club through the production of "moose" souvenirs and the advent of a "moose" mascot. It may be a somewhat apocryphal story, but the origins of the movement are reported to lay in the actions of one particular supporter who, having returned from holiday by way of a long flight, made a United game his first port of call rather than going home for a bit of a wash and brush up, as more reasonable people might have been expected to do. The fetid air of a long-haul cabin had evidently not enhanced the said supporters personal freshness, and he was heard to comment that he "stank like a moose" - the accompanying impersonation of the relevant ungulate (a sort of mooing roar, whilst holding splayed hands aloft to approximate antlers) was all it took to set the ball rolling. Incidentally, diligent research by a contributor has revealed the game at which the above took place to have been away at Grimsby at the start of the 1989/90 season. As touched on briefly above, little by way of song has resulted from the moose movement. In fact, there seems to have been little else other than the substitution of the notorious *"You're shit, aaaargh!"* chant aimed at goalkeepers with the more oblique cry of *"Mooooooooo-OOSE!"* - growing in volume and ending with an anguished last syllable as with the original - but anything which gives rise to small children (and probably drunken adults for that matter) attending matches whilst wearing foam antlers can only be a good thing in our book (and, hey, it *is* our book so it is indeed a good thing!).

Away from the bestiary of the Northwest Territories, the 90/91 season (the away matches of which were designated as the *Moose Tour*, naturally as a result of the foolishness detailed above) saw United come with a late run on the rails to snatch the Third Division Championship from the grasping clutches of Southend United on the last day of the season. Such a triumph was inevitably

67

celebrated in verse, and henceforth numerous lives have been enriched by way of....

We beat the Aston Villa and we drew at Coventry,
We even drew at home against Manchester City,
And when we beat the Swansea, we won Division Three,
And we've never lost at Wem-ber-ley

Win, win, wherever we may be,
We are the famoose C U F C
And we'll see you all, wherever you may be,
And we'll see you all in the Premier League

Note the moose reference! The first half of this merry ditty (described by our contributor as being "deliberately stupid") is to the tune of *Macnamara's Band*, whilst the second should be instantly recognisable to all as *The Lord of the Dance*. The Villa, Coventry and Manchester City references have proved too vague to permit explanation, but the victory over Swansea was undoubtedly the 2-0 win at the Abbey which secured the title. The three other games must however have some significance, as they make an appearance in this song in place of any of the F A Cup victories which took United all the way to the sixth round during their championship winning season - strange indeed. Equally bizarre are the alternative lines used to finish of the first section, all of which were used at some time or another. The first variation, *"And we've never lost at Molineux"* seems fairly reasonable, but *"We've never lost in Ouagadougou"* and *"We've never lost on Button Moon"* are altogether less accessible. Whilst the latter is a straightforward reference to the magnificent children's. TV programme of the same name, quite why the capital of Burkina Faso (formerly Upper Volta) warrants a mention is unfathomable - deliberately stupid indeed!

In the pre-moose era, United supporters reputedly amused themselves with versions of *My Darling Clementine*, *Flower of Scotland* (which predictably saw the light of day as *Flower of Cambridge* - and by the way, *cf* Middlesbrough!) and the *Eton Boating Song* (*cf* Coventry City), but unfortunately the *Dicks Out* offices have not been furnished with the full words to these efforts (or even the partial words, come to that). There is, however, one anthem of the early 1980's which has been writ large for our delectation - a version of *Between the Wars*, by Billy Bragg, which was taken up by United's Inter City Trickle during their bleakest years at the start of the decade (Inter City Trickle being the name adopted by the increasingly small band of the club's travelling supporters, in deference to West Ham's Inter City Firm). Many a crushing defeat was played out to a chorus or two of....

I am a Cambridge man, I'm a United fan,
I'll support the Mighty U's, win, draw or lose.
I joined the I C T in times of victory,

And I'll support them ever more,
Win, lose or draw.
Oh show me a winning team,
Never to lose a game,
And buy me a drink,
And I'll give my consent,
To any Management,
That gets us back into Division Two

....a no doubt impressive song, and if only Billy Bragg had made more of an effort to get into the mainstream of eighties pop, we might even have some sort of idea as to how the tune went!

Lastly, and somehow appropriately, we come to one of the few documented cases of collective cringing embarrassment suffered by a group of singing supporters in the aftermath of a game (not counting people who think that the Arsenal Song Starters are a good idea). Back to United's momentous 1990/91 season, and picture if you will a packed and vibrant Abbey Stadium, enthralled as United stuffed the then Second Division Sheffield Wednesday in the 5th round of the F A Cup to secure a quarter final berth. *"We're going to Wembley, we're going to Wembley, your not, your not!"* sang the amber and black throng, not unreasonably it would seem, until you remember that Wednesday were then less than a fortnight away from completing a Rumbelows Cup semi-final win over Chelsea to secure an appearance in the shadow of the twin towers. United promptly lost to Arsenal in the sixth round, leaving the Wembley bound Owls supporters to reflect on the irony of the situation, and United supporters wishing that they'd kept their mouths shut.

Ipswich Town

As with many provincial sides, for whom the most important game of any season is always the big local derby (obviously against Norwich in this instance), the majority of Ipswich songs revolve around this rivalry. Before looking at some of these though, there are a couple of other efforts which have a rather wider target audience.

In the first instance, one which harks back to advent of Town's rather fine orange away kit of the early 1990's, the appearance of which coincided with the first broadcast of the "orange" Tango adverts on TV (fat bald bloke with rubbery hand - that sort of thing). It didn't take long for it to become necessary for any away win by an Ipswich side wearing the appropriate kit to be celebrated with a burst of....

> *You've been fucking tango'd*
> *You've been fucking tango'd*
> *La la la la - oooh*
> *La la la la - oooh!*

....to the all-pervading Conga tune. Some twenty five years or so earlier, Town's 1968 Second Division championship saw a Suffolk version of *Onward Christian Soldiers* make an appearance in the Blues' cause. With the tune being a straight reproduction of the renowned school assembly song, and a couple of references to notable Town players of the day, we have....

> *Onward Ipswich Town,*
> *Marching to the fore,*
> *With the flag of Ipswich,*
> *Going on before*
> *Crawford is our leader,*
> *Billy is our King,*
> *Listen to the North Stand,*
> *Listen to them sing.*

The first name check is for Ray Crawford, prodigal son of Portman Road who returned to the club to lead their promotion drive with a sixteen goal haul. *"Billy"* is the Mr Baxter of that ilk, who made over four hundred appearances for Ipswich in his role as central-defensive linchpin.

Dating from roughly the same period, and later committed to vinyl in the mid 1970's, we have one of the earliest examples of a traditional club song. This particular effort was specially commissioned by the club from a Mr G Hicks, and it fulfils one of the most important criteria for any such project in that it is for the most part incomprehensible drivel. It did, however, make it on to the terraces....

> *My name is Edward Ebenezer Jeremiah Brown,*
> *I'm a football supporter of Ipswich Town,*
> *Wherever they play you'll find me,*
> *I haven't missed a game since I was three,*
> *With my scarf and rattle and big rosette,*
> *Singing "Where was the goalie when the ball went in the net?"*
> *Follow the Town, up or down,*
> *My name is Edward Ebenezer Jeremiah Brown,*
> *But everyone calls me Ted!*

On a more controversial note (though unintentionally so), we find the renowned

Yorkshire anthem (*cf* Doncaster Rovers and others) having been refined for use in a blue and white context. Differing from other versions only by the substitution of one letter, and still to the *Cielito Lindo* tune, there was....

I, I R A, Ipswich Republican Army
Wherever we go,
We'll fear no foe
For we are the I R A

The potential for misinterpretation of the above is clear, and in hindsight it may not have been *the* most tactful of things to have sung this during an away game at Villa Park a few weeks after the 1975 Birmingham pub bombings. The Villa supporters were naturally enraged at what they construed as support for the Provisionals who had blown up their city centre, and violence on a grand scale ensued with many Ipswich fans getting arrested for singing what they properly regarded as a harmless football song.

Harking back to that 1968 triumph for a moment, the season in question saw the arrival of a short chant based around the *Macnamara's Band* theme, and including a mention of the manager of the time, Bill McGarry....

You've got your European, and you've got your F A Cup,
But we are Bill McGarry's boys, and we are going up.

....this is only really notably for the fact that its derivative leads us towards Town's litany of hatred directed at their local rivals, as the second version makes mention of the struggles of neighbouring Colchester United....

You've got your Bill McGarry, and you've got your Ipswich Town,
But Smith and Neil Franklin's boys are surely going down.

Neil Franklin was the then boss at Layer Road, and oversaw United's relegation to the Fourth Division. The *"Smith"* mentioned herein has unfortunately proved impossible to identity with any degree of certainty. Interestingly, attitudes towards Colchester have changed somewhat since the time of this song, as Portman Road was very definitely a haven of pro-United sentiment during the time that they were slugging it out with Barnet for promotion from the Conference towards the end of 1990/91. Several (none too interesting) anti-Barnet chants were the order of the day, mainly because Town's season had by then petered out to nothing, and something was needed to enliven the spectating experience a little.

Putting the varying degrees of loathing or otherwise which Colchester are afforded to one side, now on to the real matter in hand, and Town's revulsion towards everything of a canary yellow hue. Of an appropriately ornithological nature, we must first catalogue an Ipswich reworking of *The Sparrow* (which made the charts in October 1979 performed by the choir of Abbey Hey Junior School *aka* The Ramblers)...

> *He's only a poor little budgie,*
> *His shirt was all tattered and torn,*
> *He started to sing,*
> *So I filled the cunt in,*
> *And now he don't sing any more.*

The budgie reference is an obviously derogatory slant on Norwich's nickname, and this song has subsequently gone on to appear on a much wider stage, suiting the requirements of many supporters up and down the country, though more usually with lines three and four being *"He made me feel sick, so I hit him with a brick"* and with all manner of other names in place of *"budgie"* (*"Scouser", "Yiddo", Gashead"* and *"Scummer"* being just a few of many - the opposition of the day dictating which one is appropriate). However heartfelt the hatred of Norwich might be, it hasn't really prompted any entirely new songs, and another standard theme to be heard at East Anglian derby matches is the *Camptown Races* song (*cf* virtually everyone!)....

> *Who's the Shit of Anglia? Naarwich, Naarwich*
> *Who's the shit of Anglia? Naarwich is their name.*
> *Naarwich is their name, Naarwich is their name,*
> *Who's the shit of Anglia? Naarwich is their name.*

....*"Naarwich"* is used in preference to *"Norwich"*, as the inflexion of the first syllable is supposed to take the piss out of the Norfolk accent. This song is usually sung in conjunction with a second verse, which follows exactly the same pattern, but with the words *"Who's the Pride of Anglia? Ipswich, Ipswich!"* in place. Yet another popular song to get the Ipswich treatment is *John Brown's Body*, which is perhaps better known as *Glory Glory Hallelujah*. With a similar version often performed by other clubs, primarily directed at Tottenham, we have....

> *The famous Norwich City went to Rome to see the Pope,*
> *The famous Norwich City went to Rome to see the Pope,*
> *The famous Norwich City went to Rome to see the Pope,*
> *And this is what he said - FUCK OFF!*
> *Who's that team they call the Ipswich,*
> *Who's that team they all adore.*
> *They're the boys in blue and white,*
> *And they're fucking dynamite,*
> *And Micky Walker's mother is a whore.*

....the name in the last line is infinitely variable, depending on who the current manager at Carrow Road might be.

72

Finally, a few ditties with which players who have represented Ipswich have found themselves feted over the years. The first, a completely standard *Quartermaster's Stores* effort which was *"He's here, he's there, he's every fucking where, Johnny Wark"* wouldn't merit a mention at all were it not for the accompanying actions which set it apart from all the other versions. Simply, the first *"He's there"* sees the singers' left arm waved about (to the left), the second sees the converse right-arm action, and the *"he's every fucking where"* bit, somewhat predictably, results in both arms being waved about frantically - daft, but no doubt impressive. Secondly, school assemblies once again get in on the act as *Kumbaya* (the hymn which was recorded by The Sandpipers) was trotted out whenever Chris Kiwomya took to the field of play; *"Kiwomya, my lord, Kiwomya"* obviously being the amended lyrics. It would seem that this song neither followed Chris to Highbury after his transfer to Arsenal in 1995, nor similarly afflicted brother Andy during his tour of the Yorkshire clubs (or during a brief sojourn at Tannadice). In conclusion, there is yet again an air of South Yorkshire about this last one, as the Sheffield United/Brian Deane *Banana Boat Song* crops up as a devotional hymn in praise of Town defender Eddie Youds....

> Eddie, Eddie Youds,
> We want Eddie and we want him now;
> Not Glenn, not Frank, But Eddie Youds,
> The Ipswich defender and we want him now!

....not entirely sure about the sentiments expressed in this one, nor about the other players who get a mention. *"Frank"*, it's fair to say, is almost certainly Frank Yallop, another Town defender, but the only *"Glenn"* discovered in an Ipswich context seems to have been midfielder Glenn Pennyfather, who was at Portman Road only for the first few months of the Youds era.

Northampton Town

If ever confirmation was needed that the true songwriting talent of the British Isles is to be found in the lower reaches of the Nationwide League, no-one need look any further than to the Sixfields Stadium or, more correctly, Town's former home at the County Ground. Nowhere in the country is there a more wholly irrelevant piece of juvenilia, or a song which so completely ignores anything to do with football in its search for subject matter. Perhaps there was, at one time, some sort of relevance which the following had with something - however insignificant - to do with Northampton, but that is now long forgotten, and all we can do is reproduce the words and revel in the stupidity which is....

> *Dan, Dan the lavatory man,*
> *He's the leader of the shithouse gang.*
> *Spends his time cleaning sanitary towels,*
> *And listening to the rhythm of his rumbling bowels.*
> *Slip - slop, a sound is heard,*
> *The slip-slop-slip of a slimy turd,*
> *Down, down into the pan,*
> *Oochie coochie woochie,*
> *It's the shithouse gang!*

....no idea of the story behind this one - no idea of the history, no idea of the context - just no idea at all really! All we do know is that this dates from some time in the late sixties/early seventies, that it used to be performed almost exclusively during half-time at matches at the County Ground and that the tune is in all probability along the lines of Bonnie Lou's *Tennessee Wig Walk* (*cf* Scunthorpe United, Bournemouth and Fulham).

Still very much on the strange side of the fence, although this time at least with some sort of explanation, comes this - one of many variations of *Milord* by Frankie Vaughan....

> *We're from Northampton Town,*
> *So get you're knickers down,*
> *La la la la la, la la, la la la-laaa,*
> *We're coming on the grass,*
> *So we can touch your arse,*
> *La la la la la, la la , la la la-laaaa.*

This one appeared in the first version of *Dicks Out*, with the fourth and fifth lines listed as *"We're from the Hotel End, We'll drive you round the bend"*, but an anonymous contributor who claims to remember the match in question advises that the words produced above are correct, and in the context, they seem to make more sense. The songs dates back to 1968, and the visit of Brighton & Hove Albion to the County Ground. For some reason, Brighton took with them their own group of cheerleaders - all mini-skirts and taut buttocks - who proceeded to disport themselves nimbly in front of the Town supporter's terrace. The song - evidently a forerunner to the now common *"get your tits out for the lads"* type of thing - was supposed to encourage the cavorting lovelies to, well, get their knickers down, but unfortunately it appears not to have had the desired effect. Of a less perverse nature, and from some twenty years later, we find Northampton engaged in a First Round League Cup tie at Gillingham, in midweek, on the open away terrace, in what is euphemistically described as pissing rain. However, determined not to let the prevailing weather conditions diminish either their capacity for culinary criticism or their grasp of current chart music, *To Good To Be Forgotten* by Amazulu was swiftly rearranged to give a song by which the miserable night could be remembered....

> *We're just too wet to be forgotten,*
> *But what more can we do,*
> *The cheeseburgers here are rotten,*
> *We'd rather have dog stew.*

....and just in case being soaked to the skin, and having to subsist on reconstituted sheep offal wasn't enough for the travelling claret and white multitudes, Gillingham won the game 1-0 by way on an 87th minute winner - exactly what football is all about!

Back to the seventies again, and it transpires that Northampton supporters are a rare breed indeed, having produced a virtually unique version of *The Blaydon Races*, in that the content is entirely different in style to the St James' Park original and the vast majority of other derivatives....

> *Off we go on Saturdays to see Dave Bowen's aces,*
> *Frankie Large, John Fairbrother, skinheads in their braces,*
> *Eric Ross and Nobby Clarke and Felton pulling faces,*
> *Off we go on Saaaatuuuurdaaaaays,*
> *To see Dave Bowen's aces.*

As far as the identity of the Cobblers' heroes mentioned herein, Dave Bowen enjoyed two spells in charge at the County Ground before ultimately becoming a director of the club, (Graham) Felton was a reputedly pacey Town winger, and Messrs Large, Fairbrother, Ross and Clark were - it must be assumed - all contemporaries of his in the Town side of the day. It would seem reasonable to assume that there ought to be one or two additional lines to this Northamptonshire version of the famous Tyneside anthem (preceding the section given above), in order to make it better fit the structure of the original, but these were not forthcoming.

In closing, it should be noted that all the songs listed above pre-date Northampton's move from the County Ground to the aureate splendour of the Sixfields Stadium (no songs about toilets or young girls posteriors allowed under the new family-friendly ground rules!), so although Sixfields is certainly one of the better examples of the new breed of stadia, it still doesn't appear to have done much to enhance the atmosphere - chalk up another victory for the plastic seats!

Norwich City

The range City songs - for good or ill - seem to mirror the sort of thing that can be found at Portman Road, home of their dearly beloved neighbours Ipswich. This extends not only to the pre-eminence of songs directed at their rivals, but to the fact that Norwich are afflicted with a club song which dates back a good few years, and which is for the most part completely nonsensical. However, where as Ipswich's *Edward Ebenezer Jeremiah Brown* has its roots in the 1960's, the lineage of City's anthem goes back to before the turn of the century, and it must therefore be lauded as the Oldest Football Song in the World Still in Current Use (which, it has to be said, is a pretty impressive thing!). Without being able to pinpoint an exact date of its conception, *On The Ball City* was written at some time during the 1890's by a stout citizen going by the name of Albert T Smith. Originally intended as the club song (for want of a better phrase) for the Norwich Teachers F C, it was adopted by the newly formed City club on their inauguration (in 1902) which was presided over by two teachers, who may well have been something to do with the club for whom the song was initially written. Anyway, putting such historical imponderables to one side, we have, in all its glory, The Oldest Football Song In The World....

On the ball City, never mind the danger,
Steady on, now's your chance,
Hurrah! we've scored a goal.

In the days to call, which we have left behind,
Our boyhood's glorious game,
And our youthful vigour has declined,
With its mirth and its lonesome end,
You will think of the time, the happy time,
Its memories fond recall,
When in the bloom of our youthful prime,
We've kept upon the ball.

Kick off, throw it in, have a little scrimmage,
Keep it low, a splendid rush, bravo, win or die.
On the ball City, never mind the danger,
Steady on, now's your chance,
Hurrah! we've scored a goal.

Let all tonight then drink with me,
To the football game we love,
And wish it may successful be,

As other games of old.
And in one grand united toast,
Join player, game and song,
And fondly pledge your pride and toast,
Success to the City club.

To the surprise of no-one, visitors to Carrow Road are not treated to a full-length performance of this noble epic - it tends to be just the *"On the ball, City, never mind the danger"* section which still gets an airing on a pretty regular basis.

With regard to the Norwich - Ipswich enmity, there are further parallels between the two clubs in that City's repertoire does not include many genuinely original songs which have been assembled in order to abuse their Suffolk chums. The standard fare includes *Bread Of Heaven* by way of *"You're the shit of Anglia, Ipswich Town, Ipswich Town, you're the shit of Anglia"* (a straight role reversal of the Ipswich version of the same song) and a somewhat longer piece which is *"One man went to war, went to war with Ipswich; one man and his baseball bat, went to war with Ipswich...."* - as with the original (*One Man Went To Mow*), this goes on and on, until usually a dozen or so men are "going to war with Ipswich". Of a considerably more innovative nature comes this version of *Israelites* by Desmond Decker and the Aces which, given the identity of the two named players, must date back to the late 1970's....

> *Woke up in the morning,*
> *Eric Gates for Breakfast,*
> *Paul Mariner for tea,*
> *Oooooooohhh-woooh - Ipswich are shite!*

....and is really rather good. Along similar lines comes an adaptation of *All Things Bright And Beautiful,* with some subtle changes to the last two lines....

> *All things bright and beautiful,*
> *All creatures great and small,*
> *Norwich rule East Anglia,*
> *And Ipswich rule fuck all...!*

And that, with the exception of one or two utterly banal efforts which are so dire as to preclude themselves from publication, is just about it as far as the City song book goes - not a particularly spirited effort with the possible exception of the last two as detailed above. Even player-related songs at Carrow Road tend to be so predictable as to not warrant inclusion - except, that is, for one. The solitary player in the long history of Norfolk football to prompt any sort of reasonable chant in his honour was John Deehan, striker extraordinaire and one-time manager on the banks of the Wensum, who moved the City faithful to intone his name in time to the theme music from *The Pink Panther.*

Ridiculously simple, but strangely impressive nonetheless, it provides an appropriately uncomplicated denouement to City's section....."*Deehan, Deehan, Deehan Deehan Deehan, Deehan Deehaaaaaan, Deehan Deehan........*".

Peterborough United

Oh dear, not a particularly happy circumstance for any Posh supporters who wish to see how they have fared in the singing stakes when compared with their friends from Cambridge and Northampton, as Peterborough seem to have a selection of ditties which is meagre to say the least. Putting aside the seemingly obligatory East Anglian epic from the middle ages (we're saving that 'til later), the first two United efforts are somewhat apocryphal to say the least. There is, initially, a vague rumour doing the rounds that back in the 1970's those possessed of a lusty voice on the London Road terrace used to sing *The Last Waltz*, as taken to the top of the Hit Parade in 1967 by the very splendid Engelbert Humperdinck. Apparently a verbatim performance of the original lyrics, there was no suggestion made as to why the club might have adopted this song. Of an equally dubious heritage, there comes news of a strange shout, really, rather than a song or chant, which was again the preserve of those on the home terrace. With nothing available to give an indication of why this became popular, and only a hazily recalled notion of what it actually consisted of, the story behind *"Ooooooooooooooooooooooooooh BASTARD!"*, will have to remain untold for the moment (which is a shame). The only light which can be shed on this most uncomplicated of shouts is that it was the precurser for a very similar thing on the London Road terrace at Oxford United's Manor Ground - the fact that the only two recorded instances of the chant have both appeared on home ends with the same name can be no more than purely coincidental (or can it!).

On to a couple of songs, the usage of which is rather better recorded, and it seems that United were one of the many clubs whose supporters had a go at *Blue Moon*, during its heyday of the early 1990's. Nothing special about the lyrics to the Peterborough version though, just standard fare as per the popular arrangement (*cf* Manchester City). A season or two prior to the appearance of *Blue Moon*, United found themselves in the midst of a desperate run of results which threatened to plunge them into the relegation mire at the foot of the then Fourth Division (two wins in nineteen games which sent Posh plummeting nine places down the table and, seemingly, straight into a fight for survival with Colchester United who were languishing in 24th place). In order to reflect the plight of both clubs, *When The Saints Go Marching In* was taken as the the inspiration for....

The Football League (the Football League)
Is upside down (is upside down).
The Football League is upside down,
We're going up, with Colchester,
The Football League is upside down.

As with all such *When The Saints....* efforts, the second (bracketed) half of the first two lines is a repetition of the first, with each being sung by different factions on the terraces. Ultimately, Borough recovered their poise sufficiently to finish in a thoroughly healthy ninth place, but not before the spectre of a return to non-league football had been brought sharply into relief, and it is back to the club's non-league days that we go for their last song. It is not entirely clear whether or not this one actually made it on to the terraces (it would seem unlikely to be honest), but it relates to the F A Cup run of the 1956/57 season when Peterborough were still in the Midland League and a couple of seasons away from election to the professional ranks....

It's a non league team called Posh
That we are going to see,
At London Road we've watched them
Storm on to victory.
They beat their Midland League mates,
Divisions Two and Three,
A darn good F A Cup run,
We're sure you'll all agree.

It's Billy, Dennis, Andy,
The forwards who combine,
With Cockburn, Shaw and Rigby,
The strongest half-back line,
And then there's Barr and Douglas,
Who keep the wings supplied,
With Walls between the uprights,
The foes, they are defied.

Corby, Yeovil, Bradford,
Have fallen at their feet,
And now there's Lincoln City,
The latest to defeat.
They're on the road to Wembley,
Via Huddersfield's the way,
With guts and goals and glory,
Posh'll show you how to play.

This stirring chorus was to the tune of *The Yellow Rose Of Texas*, which had made the charts on three different occasions a year or so before United's cup run - a different performer having recorded it each time (Mitch Miller, Gary Miller and Ronnie Hilton if you really must know!). So, all in all a disappointing return from London Road, particularly when it is taken into account that the club has recently been touched by the Pudgy Hand of Barry Fry - which should surely have been enough to prompt some sort of lyrical activity on the terraces!

Section Five

The East Midlands

Chesterfield

Derby County

Leicester City

Mansfield Town

Nottingham Forest

Notts County

The East Midlands

A peculiar region this, in that the quality of the songs is entirely at odds with the general perception of the area in footballing terms. Mansfield Town and Chesterfield, I am sure, would be more than happy to agree that they are not usually considered as being amongst the country's most notoriously vocal supporters, but each has come up with a couple of cracking songs. At Chesterfield this takes the form of a superb hymn of praise directed at one-time goalkeeper Chris Marples, whilst Field Mill is illuminated by a fine song dating back to the miners' strike of the early 1980's, and by some not inconsiderable rudeness which touches on that most taboo of subjects, anal sex.

The peculiar relationship between Nottingham Forest and Notts County is also worthy of comment in that it is hard to imagine two other clubs who are situated so close to one another who share the same ambivalent attitude towards their neighbours. Admittedly, the two clubs have rarely crossed swords with league points at stake in recent years, but then neither have Burnley and Blackburn Rovers and in this case the hatred between the two sets of supporters has hardly been diminished at all. Forest, it has to be said, are far too consumed with their rivalry with Derby County to bother about County, bit it would be interesting to see what would happen should the two sides from opposite banks of the River Trent ever find themselves in the same division again.

Leicester City are in a strange situation, seemingly ignored by both Derby and Forest, they are almost more a part of the West Midlands scene, but then none of the sides in this area seem too bothered about the fate of The Foxes either. Luckily for City supporters, the Mark McGhee saga has enabled them to devote all their energies towards despising Wolves over the last couple of seasons, but should the man in question move on from Molineux (which is surely just a matter of time given his recent track record) then Leicester will again find themselves in their peculiar no-man's land, in which case they should take a leaf out of Shrewsbury Town's book and start having a go at a local non-league side; I'm sure a healthy rivalry could be generated with Shepshed Dynamo with a little effort!

Chesterfield

Not very much at all from the fleetingly famous Spireites - with even their virtually unprecedented jaunt to the F A Cup semi final seemingly unable to inspire their supporters to new heights of vocal dexterity. However, the limited information that has come to light reveals a couple of songs which are far more impressive than might reasonably have been expected from such an otherwise timid and undemonstrative set of supporters.

Back to the early 1990's first - a time when Doncaster Rovers' Belle Vue Ground afforded the most inhospitable environment for visiting supporters anywhere in the country. The remaining section of reasonably serviceable open terrace at the Rossington End of the ground had been enclosed on all four sides with stark, steel fences, making a cage into which away fans could be herded. It really was one of the worst enclosures of its kind, and became notorious throughout the lower divisions. In anticipation of a forthcoming afternoon to be spent in these charming surroundings, the weeks leading up to a visit to Belle Vue would find the Chesterfield supporters singing....

> *Daddy's taking us to the zoo tomorrow,*
> *Daddy's taking us to the zoo tomorrow,*
> *Daddy's taking us to the zoo tomorrow,*
> *To see Doncaster Rovers.*

....an obvious allusion to the cage, which really wouldn't have looked out of place at some run-down zoo, or one of those maximum security prisons for extreme nutters in the United States.

Having staged a suitably Steve McQueen like break-out from South Yorkshire - without, it would appear, resorting to any of the miners' strike tomfoolery in which supporters of Mansfield Town used to revel - it was back to the Recreation Ground to sing the praises of goalkeeper Chris Marples, who managed to combine his career between the sticks for the Spireites with a summer pursuit of being wicketkeeper for Derbyshire (really!). The Max Bygraves classic *You Need Hands* provided an eminently appropriate tune for the Marples anthem....

> *You need hands to keep goal for the Spireites,*
> *You need hands for catching cricket balls,*
> *You need hands to masturbate and juggle,*
> *You need hands if your name's Chris Marples,*
> *Chris, Chris, Chris Marples - Chris, Chris, Chris Marples!*

Obviously, the song lapsed into a straightforward chant for the last line, but I have to say that this in no way detracts from what is really a very fine composition indeed - very fine. Needless to say, Marples would react to this superlative accolade by turning to the Chesterfield supporters and waving frantically at them.

And that, rather disappointingly, is it. If ever there was a case of unrealised potential, then I think the Chesterfield supporters are it (?), as the genius which gave rise to the Chris Marples song should surely have been able to create some other masterpieces as well. But what did we get when the club were placed on centre stage recently - Old Trafford echoing to chorus after chorus of *"Blue Army!"* - tsk, tsk!

Derby County

One enduring image is left after any sort of contact with Derby supporters - that of people who harbour a pathological hatred of anything and everything to do with Nottingham Forest. The depth of the feeling that exists between the two clubs is on a par with most other such rivalries, though for some reason - perhaps as they are generally perceived as the least successful of the two clubs - County appear to despise Forest with more venom and intensity than the City Ground inhabitants reserve for the Rams. Apart from the antipathy being engendered by mere geographic reasons, the two clubs are apparently pushed further apart by the fact that they share so much history - championships under Brian Clough for the pair of them, the brooding presence of Peter Taylor in both camps and the regular exchange of players from one to the other. Whatever the reasons though, there can be little doubt that Derby really do not like Forest at all and, naturally, this comes through in their songs. The first, to the *Land Of Hope And Glory* tune, puts a new and entirely bigoted slant on a familiar theme....

> *We hate Nottingham Forest,*
> *We hate Forest too (they're shit!),*
> *We hate Nottingham Forest,*
> *And Forest we hate you...!*

....this often crops us elsewhere, but with the names of two or three different teams listed - this seems to be the only occasion on which one team is mentioned throughout.

Going back a few years to a time when Stan Collymore was still popular at Forest (before buggering off to Liverpool) he was, unsurprisingly, not an entirely well liked young man at the Baseball Ground. To this end, a version of *My Old*

Man's A Dustman was crafted in his honour, which drew heavily on the influence of other similar efforts from Swansea and West Brom....

> *Ooooooh - Collymore's a wanker,*
> *He wears a wankers hat,*
> *He plays for bastard Forest,*
> *'cos he's a fucking twat,*
> *He runs down the left wing,*
> *he runs down the right,*
> *He'll never play for England,*
> *'cos he's just fucking shite!*

No doubt Forest supporters would now not be too averse to singing something similar - it's difficult to imagine a case where a player has become so utterly despised by the supporters of one of his former clubs!

A couple of shorter songs also emphasise the esteem (or rather the lack of it) in which Forest are held, namely an appropriately amended version of the *Wings Of A Sparrow* song (cf Sheffield United), and *Always Look On The Bright Side Of Life*, the preferred Derby version of which is *"Always shit on the red side of the Trent"*. With Forest playing in red, a faithful servant of many a supporter over the years will also take a bow on occasion, this being the *"shoot, shoot, shoot the bastard"* version of the Charlton Athletic club song *The Red Red Robin*. An equally elderly song also makes brief mention of Forest, but is turning away from all-consuming hatred of all things arboreal towards more general themes....

> *We are the boys in white and blue,*
> *We've come to sing this song for you,*
> *We love to sing, we love to fight,*
> *We hate the boys in red and white,*
> *We sing a song in harmony,*
> *We sing a song of victory,*
> *The Villa fans will never mock,*
> *When they remember Bruce Rioch...Rioch!...Rioch!*

This is more of an extended chant than an actual song and, as such, it doesn't have a definable tune. Bruce Rioch was a very popular member of the great Derby side of the early to mid 1970's, though quite what he had done to Aston Villa I'm not too sure - though being Rioch, it probably involved scoring with a searing shot from sixty odd yards out, as was his forte.

Next a couple of chants of which Derby claim to be the instigators (not with all that much justification, it must be said). February 1983, and Bananarama are storming up the charts with the reissue of Steam's classic *Na Na, Hey Hey Kiss*

Him Goodbye - the Baseball Ground, should our sources be believed, was the first venue to benefit from the revamped version which was....

> *Na, na - na, na, na, na,*
> *Hey, hey - Derby County!*

....this was alternatively *"Hey, hey, Lincoln City"*, *"Hey, hey, Rochdale"*, or any one of the other eighty odd different versions which simultaneously sprang up at around the same point in history, but again it has to be said that someone, somewhere had to be the first, and in the absence of any other claims, it just may have been Derby who started this off. Far more controversially, County also claim to have started the *"I had a wheelbarrow, the wheel fell off"* movement which went on to become the full blown Notts County *Wheelbarrow Song* - but, once again, without any sort of back up story to explain the derivation, this is probably best put down as little more than an attempt to put one over a team from Nottingham.

Harking back to pet hates, if mention of Forest does not bring on apoplexy in Derby supporters, the name Robert Maxwell probably will. County were one of the unfortunate clubs which Maxwell saw fit to interfere with during the early 1990's, and however good intentioned (or otherwise) his period in charge of the purse strings might have been, his departure was hailed by all concerned with ill concealed glee - as was his mysterious death by drowning which was to follow. This, in particular, was cause for song or two in the Normanton Stand, with *What Shall We Do With A Drunken Sailor* providing the inspiration (as it always seems to be the case when celebrating a tale of woe is the order of the day - *cf* Bristol City)....

> *What shall we do with Robert Maxwell?*
> *What shall we do with Robert Maxwell?*
> *What shall we do with Robert Maxwell?*
> *Throw him in the ocean.*
> *Heave-ho and overboard,*
> *Heave-ho and overboard,*
> *Heave-ho and overboard,*
> *Now the bastard's drowning!*

....prior to his unfortunately damp demise Maxwell, when in charge at Derby, was not known for his regular attendance at games (although why somebody wouldn't want to watch an expensively assembled team of ex-Oxford United players get relegated from the First Division is quite beyond comprehension). This point was not lost on the County choir, and one of the very many *Quartermaster's Stores* chants was coined as a result - *"He's fat, he's round, he's never at the ground, Maxwell, Maxwell"* being the relevant effort. On the same subject, it seems that when any sort of ill-will exists towards a chairman or other figure of authority, a version of *My Darling Clementine*

86

won't be too far away (*cf* Brighton and Wigan). The Derby re-mix manages to be probably the most offensive of any such song....

> *Build a bonfire, build a bonfire,*
> *Stick Fat Maxwell on the top,*
> *Stab the fat cunt with a flicknife,*
> *And watch the bastard pop!*

And with both of County's most hated subjects having been roundly abused, time to wind up with a brief look at a less inflammatory song of devotion to the cause. A standard rehash of *Sailing*, this always seems particularly popular at the Baseball Ground, and will no doubt continue to be so at Pride Park....

> *We are Derby, We are Derby,*
> *We are Derby, Super Rams,*
> *We are Derby, Super Derby,*
> *We are Derby, Super Rams!*

Leicester City

An odd club, Leicester, from the singing point of view, as there invariably seems to be a good atmosphere at Filbert Street without there actually being much by way of any decent songs. For the most part, the everyday colour and name related chants suffice when it comes to whipping the Filbo crowd into a frenzy (*"Blue Army"* being a particular favourite!), but there are one or two notable items of more substance which deserve recording for posterity.

The first of these is the performance of a song of widespread popularity, but one which sets the standard by which all other versions should be judged, due to its inordinate length and its associated actions. *When You're Smiling* seems to have rather passed its sell by date as the undisputed City anthem in recent seasons, but it still manages to make sporadic and stirring appearances every now and then....

> *When you're smiling,*
> *When you're smiling,*
> *The whole world smiles with you*
> *And when you're laughing,*
> *When you're laughing,*
> *The sun comes shining through,*
> *But when you're sighing,*

You bring on the rain,
So stop your sighing,
And be happy again.
'cos when smiling, when smiling,
The whole world smiles with you,
Na - na - na - na - na!
The whole world smiles with you,
Na - na - na - na - na!
The whole world smiles with you!

The associated actions take the form of some coordinated waving which accompanies the last three repetitions of *"The whole world smiles with you"*. The left arm is thrust skyward on the first reprise, the right naturally follows with the second, and the climactic line is shouted as loudly as possible while waving both arms in the air - a largely pointless exercise, but one which helps to set the City version of this song high on a pedestal when compared to the efforts of other less committed proponents of the art.

Now, time for Messrs Skinner and Baddiel to squirm uneasily on their sofa as, if sources are to be believed, the whole "pineapple" episode which left Jason Lee a broken and shaven-headed man (see Chelsea's entry for details) was based on an idea which had been pinched from Filbert Street. The unfortunate Lee's tonsorial torment began at Stamford Bridge on January 20th 1996, a full year after a certain Jamie Lawrence had joined Leicester from Doncaster Rovers. Now, Lawrence had exactly the same hairstyle as Lee (it was certainly in place during his time at Belle Vue, but I'm not sure if it graced his handful of appearances for previous club Sunderland) and, an assertion has been made that *"pineapple on his head"* chants were conceived in Lawrence's honour almost as soon as he joined The Foxes (ie, in January 1995) - a full year in advance of when Fantasy Football League first pointed out the similarity between Lee's hair and a certain tropical fruit. So, it is entirely plausible that the Chelsea supporters who started the song in January '96 had first heard it at Filbert Street towards the end of 94/5 and, consequently, that the blame for Lee's fall from grace should lay fairly and squarely on the shoulders of the City supporters!

Of a more current nature, there can have been few Leicester games played out over recent times which will not have seen some concerted abuse of a certain Mr Mark McGhee. The circumstances under which McGhee left Filbert Street for the supposedly greener pastures of Molineux have been well documented elsewhere - suffice to say that the Filbo supporters did not send him on his way with cries of "best wishes" and "good luck, old boy" ringing in his ears. For the most part, McGhee is subjected to a run of the mill Daydream Believer ditty (with *"short four-eyed bastard"* or *"short Scottish bastard"* being the salient lines), but the real vehicle for the City abuse has been a far more succinct, and as it happens, far more pointed chant. Both the 95/6 play-off win which secured promotion to the Premiership and the 96/7 League Cup final were played out to a virtually non-stop barrage of *"Are you watching, Mark McGhee?"* to the ubiquitous *Bread Of Heaven* tune - an obvious reference to the success which City have enjoyed since McGhee jumped ship in December '95. Curiously, this same song also formed the backdrop to the 94/5 Reading v Bolton play-off final, with McGhee having left Reading in similar circumstances to those under which he departed from Leicester - he had bailed out of Elm Park in mid season to take up a more lucrative position - at Filbert Street! The same chant has yet more recently been confirmed as now being an utterly essential element to the end of any English league season when it was taken up in no small way by Barnsley supporters as they secured promotion to the top flight. In his role as Wolves boss, McGhee had managed to upset the Oakwell faithful by making some ill judged and condescending remarks about how his club were better suited for life in the big time than were Barnsley - needless to say this all blew up in his face as Wolves faltered during the run in, allowing Danny Wilson's side to secure an automatic promotion place. Wanderers supporters are already practising their interpretation of the song for the end of the 97/8 season, and after that - who knows? Hartlepool, Bury, Berwick Rangers - who will be next to take up what is currently football's most popular chant?

Mansfield Town

Two main themes seem to provide the mainstay of Field Mill's more substantial songs, drinking (with fairly straightforward connection being apparent given the importance of the Mansfield Brewery to the local economy) and anal sex (the predilection for which is not quite so easily explained). These subjects both have dedicated to them songs which are entirely unique to The Stags, while a third and altogether more predictable theme - a dislike of Chesterfield borne of local rivalry - seems to have been almost entirely passed over when the Mansfield compendium of vocal exhortations was being put together.

To drinking first, and one of the many "repetition" type chants (with no discernable tune attached in order that it might more properly be termed a song). The two halves of each line are shouted out by alternating sections of the crowd, with the whole thing then being repeated from start to finish as many times as the enthusiasm of the performers will allow. Football manages to escape mention entirely in this rather odd chant, the like of which does not appear anywhere else....

Oh when I die (oh when I die!),
Don't bury me alone (don't bury me alone!),
Just lay my bones in alcohol (just lay my bones in alcohol!),
And on my chest (and on my chest!),
Lay a barrel of the best (lay a barrel of the best!)
And tell my friend (and tell my friends!),
I've gone to rest (I've gone to rest!).

A wholly bizarre chant with which to embroider the rich tapestry that is life at Field Mill, I'm sure you will agree. The only half-way plausible derivation must lay in the direction of the brewery which was, in the not too distant past, one of the biggest employers in the town. It can only be assumed that the chant started as a drinking accompaniment used by some of the workers, who then introduced it to Field Mill on their excursions to watch the football.

If that bit of background seems somewhat dubious, I have no intention of even attempting to unravel the history behind this next effort. Another example of a chant with repeated elements, this mid 1980's composition simply defies explanation....

There's a lady in glitter (there's a lady in glitter!)
Who likes putting it up her shitter (who likes putting it up her shitter!),
Singing oh - oh - oh! (singing oh - oh - oh!)

Evolutionary mysteries notwithstanding, it's difficult to ever imagine a situation during the course of a game which would even begin to give this some sort of relevance. Clearly (and not entirely reprehensibly) it is simply a case of being rude for the sake of it, and it can only be imagined that the person who thought it up must have some sort of family tie with Hartlepool - home of the country's foremost purveyors of the Gratuitous Obscenity.

The majority of other songs from the North Terrace tend to be rather run of the mill (*yes!* - crap pun of the highest order). Even the proximate charms of Chesterfield (barely a dozen miles to the North West) don't seem to have prompted too much abuse aimed at patrons of the Recreation Ground, although derby matches would seem somehow incomplete without a few rounds of *"You can shove your fucking spire up your arse"* being directed at the followers of the team who take their nickname from the architectural oddity which is the famous twisted spire. Going back a few years, though, there was a song which was always aimed at Doncaster Rovers supporters (and probably those of other Yorkshire clubs) who had taunted Stags' supporters with chants of "Scabs" ever since the miners' strike in the early 1980's (see Donny's entry for a bit more background). Revelling in the fact that their Nottinghamshire based colleagues were back at work and earning money, while the South Yorkshire miners were still on the picket lines and relying on fighting funds and charitable handouts, the nursery rhyme *Old King Cole* was reinterpreted as....

Old King Coal was a merry old soul,
And a merry old soul was he,
He's took you bastards out on strike,
Now you've got nowt for tea.
In Arthur's court there's pie and peas,
And good roast beef to carve,
But you can stick to fucking soup,
We hope you bastards starve!

Quite a story to this one: "Old King Coal" was one of the names that the tabloid newspapers coined for miners' leader Arthur Scargill during the strike (as was King Arthur - hence the reference to "Arthur's Court"). There was a story put about at the time that while Scargill was spending his days touring the coalfields, preaching solidarity with the miners and indulging in a bit of PR work by handing out tins of soup and the like which had been collected for the strikers, at night he'd repair to his cosy little house and luxuriate in the splendour of vast meals while the members of his Union had to make do with whatever meagre fare they could scrape together. The song was definitely still doing the rounds as late as 1986, but I haven't personally heard it since, and it may well have now died out as memories of the strike fade with the passing years. Rovers supporters, meanwhile, still persist in calling Mansfield and Chesterfield supporters "scabs" well over a decade after the strike was broken.

Nottingham Forest

As is the case with their counterparts at Birmingham City, Forest supporters evidently took umbrage at the meagre nature of their section in the first edition of Dicks Out! and have taken great pleasure in setting the record straight in time for this update. First and foremost we have the song which has become as much an anthem at the City Ground as it has at Solitude, home of Cliftonville in Northern Ireland - *You've Lost That Loving Feeling* by the Righteous Brothers....

You never close your eyes any more when I kiss your lips,
There's no tenderness like before in your fingertips,
You're trying hard not to show it, baby,
But baby, baby I know it.

You've lost that loving feeling,
Wooaah that loving feeling,
You've lost that loving feeling,
And it's gone, gone, gone....

....not quite as extensive a reproduction of the original as is the case in Belfast, but it no doubt evokes an equally tear-jerking atmosphere nonetheless. This found its way on to the Trent End as part of the first wave of "non-football" football songs in the late 1980's/early 90's - but why this particular song was adopted has not been made clear.

A similarly abbreviated adaptation of a song made famous by other clubs sees *Over And Over* - an enduring favourite at Celtic Park where it makes a far more extensive appearance. Spurs and Manchester United have also taken the Celtic original on board, but Forest are the only club to have devised some alternative lyrics....

Through the seasons before us,
And down through history,
We will follow the Forest,
On to victory.

This could almost be said to bear more similarity to the structure of *Land Of Hope And Glory* than to *Over And Over*, but the rather awkward phraseology gives away its true origins.

Much has been made elsewhere of the ongoing saga of Jason Lee and his now infamous hairstyle, but what is perhaps not as well known as the Chelsea taunt and the subsequent downward spiral of Lee's career is that the Forest supporters came up with their own song to express a degree of solidarity with their beleaguered player during his crisis of confidence. *John Brown's Body* (or *Glory Glory Hallelujah* - whichever you prefer) was the chosen vehicle for....

My eyes have seen the glory of the coming of The Lord,
With number twelve upon his back, many goals has he scored,
His name is Jason Lee, he's got a pineapple on his head,
And the Reds go marching on, on, on!

Apart from the rather simplistic chant of *"Psycho, Psycho, Psycho"* which each and every appearance of Stuart Pearce prompted, Forest supporters seem to be far more willing to embrace the talents - or more correctly the lack of them - of the club's less successful players. Lee, of course, is a case in point, but the incomparable Brian Rice was also considered to be sufficiently poor to deserve immortalisation in song. The spectacularly inept Scottish winger was rarely lauded during his playing days at the City Ground but now, half a dozen years after he last transfixed the Forest faithful, dull moments are often illuminated with the Rice anthem, which takes the form of *Yellow Submarine*. Simply *"Number one is Brian Rice, number two is Brian Rice, number three is Brian Rice...."* is continued up to eleven, at which point *"We all live in a Brian Rice world, a Brian Rice world, a Brian Rice world"* brings things nicely to the boil. This, so it would seem, is particularly popular during the course of heavy defeats!

Apart from the aforementioned ditties, the Forest repertoire has been augmented over the years by a number of what might be considered the game's more basic chants. *The Red Flag* has its City Ground version, as does *You Are My Sunshine*, *The Sparrow* and even *Blue Moon* - all predictable enough in their content - but the far less common *Mull Of Kintyre* also makes one of its rare appearances. The format is very similar to the Charlton Athletic version, again with the proximity of a river to the ground in question being the main theme....

> *Oh, City Ground,*
> *The mist rolling in from the Trent,*
> *My desire is always to be there,*
> *Oh, City Ground.*

....a typical Forest song, this, in that it is very much an abridged version of the original - the Charlton adaptation extends to a complete verse in addition to the chorus.

Passing swiftly over a Forest claim to have been the first ever supporters to have chanted anything along the lines of *"Brian Clough's red and white army"* (intoned endlessly, over and over again for anything up to an hour) which seems spurious in the extreme, we come at last to the Nottinghamshire side of the Forest/Derby equation. As a reinforcement of the impression you may have garnered from the County section that it is they, not Forest, who feel more passionately about this rivalry, there have been only two songs submitted from the City Ground which are specifically directed at The Rams. Both are little more than regulation developments of commonplace ideas - the first being based on *There's A Tavern In The Town*, and harking back to the days of the Maxwell regime and Arthur Cox's tenancy of the Baseball Ground hot seat....

> *There's a circus in the town (in the town),*
> *Robert Maxwell is the clown (is the clown),*
> *And Arthur Cox has got the pox,*
> *And Derby County's going down (going down).*

Even this uninspiring fare seems vitriolic and full of malevolence when compared to the second anti-County production which follows - this is, however, a good illustration of a chant which has served many other sets of supporters well over the years (needless to say, with the name of their particular foe inserted in the appropriate places....).

> *We hate Derby and we hate Derby,*
> *We hate Derby and we hate Derby,*
> *We hate Derby and we hate Derby,*
> *We are the Derby - haters!*
> *Sheep, sheep, sheep shaggers!*
> *Sheep, sheep, sheep shaggers!*

The last two lines detailing the alleged proclivity amongst Rams supporters for a spot of ovine abuse often appear as a chant in their own right, but they sit nicely at the end of the first four line section, which is equally likely to be heard as a stand-alone effort. The whole thing is usually rounded off with an outburst of baaaa-ing for good measure.

So, on the whole, a far more commendable array of songs than was the case five years ago, but some extra thought really needs to be put into the abuse meted out to Derby if Forest are ever to claim a place in the higher echelons of football songwriting's roll of honour - could do better!

Notts County

Right, pay attention at the back now, as before the Magpies section can get properly under way, there is a brief lesson in the Physical Geography of the British Isles to be endured. Question - how many professional football teams are there in Nottingham? Well, there's Notts County and those other herberts, Forest, so that makes two doesn't it. Sounds eminently plausible, but if that's your answer, just pick up your pencil case and go and sit at the back of the class facing the wall in absolute, shamefaced disgrace 'cos you're wrong. County's pristine Meadow Lane ground may well be situated in the City of Nottingham, but the erroneously named City Ground on the south bank of the River Trent is, in fact, in the little known town of West Bridgford (it's all perfectly true - honest!). To celebrate this fact, and to remind everyone else that Forest inhabit what amounts to an ingnoble suburb of their great city, County fans have come up with a brief chant to the tune of Chicory Tip's *Son Of My Father*, it is, simply....

> *Ohhhh, Notts County,*
> *The only football team to come from Nottingham!*

Although this might seem to be a seemingly insignificant point to anyone not directly involved with either of the two clubs, an off-hand comment along the lines of "Oh, yeah, you're the *other* team in Nottingham aren't you" is likely to have County supporters foaming at the mouth. A similar reaction can be provoked in Tranmere Rovers supporters by labelling them as Scousers - and they too have come up with a song to correct this common misconception.

Municipal niceties notwithstanding, the real strength of an impressive County repertoire can be best illustrated by just one thing - *The Wheelbarrow Song*. A bizarre and exceedingly simple arrangement, this has really been associated with the club ever since a televised F A Cup tie at White Hart Lane in 1991 - County lost, but their supporters in the Park Lane end managed to keep the song going non-stop for the best part of an hour. As with West Brom's bout of "boinging" at Portsmouth a few years later, the song left the watching media utterly bemused, with no less a person than John Motson commenting on "the odd song that seems to have been going on for the entire second half". Anyway, to get things in perspective, background later, words now....

> *I had a wheelbarrow, the wheel fell off,*
> *I had a wheelbarrow, the wheel fell off,*
> *I had a wheelbarrow, the wheel fell off,*
> *I had a wheelbarrow, the wheel fell off....*

....and so on, interminably, to the tune of *On Top Of Old Smokey*. The roots of this exceedingly strange mantra can be traced back to Gay Meadow, home of Shrewsbury Town, on Tuesday April 17th 1990 (at about a quarter to nine in the evening - assuming the game kicked off at 7.30!). County (unsurprisingly) were the visitors, looking to get a point at the very least to keep them in the thick of the promotion race from the (old) Third Division. By half time, however, they were a goal down - a deficit which doubled with a second goal of the night by Dean Spink soon after the restart. In true footballing tradition, the County supporters evening then took another turn for the worse when it started to pour with rain, leaving those members of the travelling multitude who couldn't find shelter under the abbreviated roof of the Station End terrace in just about as miserable state as can be imagined - in Shrewsbury, on a Tuesday night, soaking wet, miles from home, watching your promotion dreams go up in smoke. The situation called for a song, and a nameless but now anonymously heroic figure in black and white took up *The Wheelbarrow Song* - it did, after all, look as if the wheels were about to irrevocably come off of County's promotion bandwagon. Almost immediately, though, as if moved by divine intervention, the Magpie's pulled a goal back through Tommy Johnson and then went on to secure a draw courtesy of Kevin Bartlett's equaliser. The drive towards the top of the table was thus sustained, promotion was eventually secured (via the play offs, admittedly), and the restorative and inspirational qualities of *The Wheelbarrow Song* were set in stone from that day onwards.

As if that is not enough, recent seasons have seen a spin-off from the original theme, with *Swing Low, Sweet Chariot* (the unofficial anthem of the England rugby union team) being amended to....

> *Swing low, sweet wheelbarrow,*
> *Coming for to carry me home,*
> *Swing low, sweet wheelbarrow,*
> *Coming for to carry me home.*
> *Abandoned wheelbarrows chasing after me,*
> *Coming for to carry me home,*
> *Abandoned wheelbarrows chasing after me,*
> *Coming for to carry me home.*

....which defies interpretation more stubbornly than did the original song itself. Since the heady days of wheelbarrow-inspired glory which swept County into the First Division, the Magpies fortunes have declined alarmingly, to such an extent that they are back in the basement for the start of the 97/8 campaign. Inevitably, individuals are singled out by supporters in order that the blame for such woes can be heaped upon their shoulders - justifiably or otherwise - and the load-bearer in this case was manager Colin Murphy. An obscure track by one-time Ska/2 Tone headliners The Beat - *Stand Down Margaret* - was chosen as the framework on which some anti-Murphy sentiment could be hung, and thus we have....

> *I see no joy, I see only sorrow,*
> *I see no sign of your bright new tomorrow,*
> *Stand down Murphy, stand down please,*
> *Stand down Murphy, stand down please!*

So, a compendium of vocal finery from Meadow Lane which provides an appropriate conclusion to the East Midlands section - an area which has seen its singing heritage develop out of all recognition from the paltry fare on offer in the first version of *Dicks Out!* (well, either that or it's been researched more thoroughly this time round) - *"You need hands to masturbate and juggle"* - sheer class!

Section Six

Humberside

Grimsby Town

Hull City

Lincoln City

Scunthorpe United

Humberside

One of the foremost songwriting regions in the country, this, with each of the four clubs providing a perfect example of the sort of creative talent which can be found in the lower reaches of the Nationwide League.

All the clubs have their own particular forte, with Hull City leading the way as being probably the finest exponents in the country of the art of taking a song from the charts and giving it some footballing relevance. Everything from *Karma Chameleon* to *Tiptoe Through The Tulips* has been given the Boothferry Park treatment over the years, although the recent traumas at the club have rather stifled the creative process as protest has become the order of the day.

At Grimsby, we have seen one of the most successful fanzine-inspired singing movements (on a par with the efforts of *AWOL* at Meadowbank Thistle and *Away From The Numbers* at East Fife) by way of the vast array of Christmas carols which were conceived by the staff at *Sing When We're Fishing*. These songs alone would have been better than what the majority of other clubs can offer, but when set along side the Hawaii Five-O dance which has also made an appearance in Grimsby colours, the club's supporters can really be said to have excelled themselves.

Rather lower-key fare from Lincoln City, but some laudable efforts nonetheless, and even Scunthorpe United's supporters have managed to come up with something of genuine quality by way of one of the few decent songs throughout the leagues dedicated to the shirts in which a team plays (a lament for the passing of their red and white kit during the early 1980's).

All in all, a really rather fine selection from Humberside, which would have been pushing hard for the title of Most Impressive Regional Selection of Songs if only there had been one or two decent ditties about local rivalries. Clearly, Hull City couldn't care less about Grimsby, Grimsby don't particularly like Hull but aren't all that bothered at the end of the day, Lincoln City seem to like everybody (apart from Barnet) and Scunthorpe; well, they seem quite pleased when anyone actually bothers to abuse them at all. So, with barely a cross word to be said by anyone, there is clearly something important missing from the songs on the East Coast - although the talent is evidently in place to come up with some real beauties should anyone ever be sufficiently bothered to do so.

Grimsby Town

Mariners' supporters have certainly done their club proud by way of the fine selection of idiocy which follows. Whilst the team may never quite have hit the heights when it comes to achievements on the pitch, there can be no doubt that the venerable Pontoon Stand at Blundell Park has, in its time, played host to some of the most commendably silly supporters the game has ever seen, mainly due, it must be said, to the promptings of the *Sing When We're Fishing* fanzine. Before considering the songs which abound on the East Coast, however, there is a far more pressing matter to address by way of Grimsby's entrant in the Great Terrace Dances Of Our Time competition - and one which in all probability would be pushing to claim the winner's spot. Picture if you will a dull, end of season encounter - the venue is immaterial - but Grimsby are the visiting side. As the match wanders towards its pointless end, a vaguely recognisable tune drifts across to your vantage point from the direction of the away terrace...."*d-da da da da da, d-da da da da daaah; d-da da da da daaa, d-da da da daaaa........*". "*Blimey*" you think, "*I know that, it's "Hawaiian Tattoo", as recorded by Belgian orchestral maestros The Waikikis, and later used for the theme music to top 1970's American cop drama Hawaii Five-O!*", and, as you begin to recall the adventures of Steve McGarrett and his faithful sidekick Danno, a line of black and white shirted Grimsby supporters hoves into view, snaking conga-like across the terracing, alternately "paddling" to one side, then the other in as fine as an approximation of the canoe-based title sequence to the programme as you're likely to see anywhere (with the possible exception of Carlisle). Unfortunately, the reason as to why Town supporters have taken to this particular behaviour has not been ascertained - although it's a fair bet that is has something to do with the nautical heritage of the town (what with all its fishing connections and all). However, the same cannot be true of the other exponents of the Hawaii Five-O tune, the supporters of Heart of Midlothian (who, incidentally, content themselves with the singing side only - no silly dancing at Tynecastle!).

If this has not slaked your thirst for terrace tomfoolery of a television related nature, do not despair, as a brief time spent in the company of Town supporters will, in addition to the Hawaiian lunacy described above, probably give you a chance to appreciate another famous theme tune....

> *Meet the gang 'cos the boys are here,*
> *The boys to entertain you,*
> *With music and laughter to help you on your way,*
> *To raising the rafters with a hey! hey! hey!*
> *With songs, and sketches, and jokes old and new,*
> *With us about, you won't feel blue,*

Soooo - meet the gang 'cos the boys are here,
The boys to entertain yooooooou!

....yes, hurrah, it's the theme tune to *It Ain't Half Hot Mum*, that quality televisual experience from two decades ago that unleashed Windsor Davies and Don Estelle on an unsuspecting British public. The relevance to Grimsby is, yet again, not easy to establish - being silly for the sake of it would appear to be as good a reason for the adoption of the song as any.

Now, it's high time that the real forte of Grimsby's support is addressed - Christmas carols. Dating from Christmas 1990 there is as fine a selection of festive tunes as you're likely to come across, with several traditional carols given the unique Grimsby treatment - all a far cry from what goes on elsewhere when a few choruses of *Jingle Bells* are all that the majority of other supporters can muster. Making an appearance on the East Coast, rather than at Brisbane Road as might have been expected, the first such gem is *We Three Kings*....

We're three fans of Grimsby Town,
Follow the team from ground to ground,
Emerson's, Appleby's, Peter Sheffield,
As long as they don't break down.

Ohhh-oh, Stevie Sherwood, Ian Knight,
Gilbert does and Cockerill might,
Cunnington, Lever, F A Cup fever,
A vision in black and white.

....a quality product indeed. The names in the first section are all coach companies, used by the Mariner's supporters on their sorties to away matches, while the second lists half a dozen players, all at the club when the song was conceived (David Gilbert, John Cockerill, Shaun Cunnington and Mark Lever being the four who are referred to by surname only).

Of a more match-specific nature, we then have *Away In A Manger* which, in this instance, tells the story of Town's 0-3 Littlewoods Cup (second round, 2nd leg) defeat away at Coventry during 1989/90 - a competition dear to Mariners' hearts, as they had knocked out Hull City in the first round....

Away in the West Midlands, where we love the police,
A Coventry player is flattened by Rees,
The folk in the away end look down where he lay,
And the referee's red card appears straight away.
The home crowd are baying, the ref he awakes,
By the Coventry player, no crying he makes,
We love you, our Tony, and though he's not dead,
We think you are heaven 'cos you stamped on his head.

....rather more of the original words retained in this one, which does not detract from its greatness in any way. Incidentally, although Grimsby may have taken extra delight in having defeated Hull City in the round prior to facing Coventry, the defeat would have been felt no more keenly than any other at Boothferry Park, as apparently, City supporters really couldn't care less about Grimsby, preferring instead to direct their ire at the considerably less proximate charms of Leeds United and Sheffield United - evidently emotions carried over from when all three teams were still in Yorkshire. Anyway - back to Grimsby - and the Cleethorpes remix of *God Rest Ye Merry Gentlemen*....

> *God rest ye Merry Mariners,*
> *Let nothing ye dismay,*
> *A cup defeat at Blackpool,*
> *Is just another day,*
> *We'll save ourselves up for the league,*
> *And never lose away,*
> *Oh, tidings to Al and the boys, Al and the boys,*
> *Oh, tidings to Al and the boys.*

....this makes reference to the 90/91 0-2 F A Cup reverse at Bloomfield Road, and to Alan Buckley, Grimsby manager of the day. A second version of the same song is rather more upbeat, and sings the praises of goalkeeper Steve Sherwood (he of *"oh, look it's Andy Gray, I think I'd better get out of the way and let him score the second goal in the 1984 F A Cup final"* fame)....

> *God rest ye Merry Grimsby-ites,*
> *Let nothing you dismay,*
> *For Town will top Division Three,*
> *With a win on Boxing Day,*
> *To save us all from Reading's shots,*
> *Big Stevie will be there,*
> *His saves bring us comfort and joy, comfort and joy,*
> *His saves bring us comfort and joy.*

...as it transpired, Mr Sherwood must have had a bit of a Wembley flashback, as Grimsby lost 0-2 on their festive trip to Elm Park, and stayed in second place, only to next top the league at the end of March - after beating Reading 3-0 in the return match at Blundell Park (spooky!).

And there's more - with the peculiarly one sided Grimsby - Hull hostility once more rearing its head in this manifestation of *The Holly And The Ivy*....

> *Oh the Hull-ites get a hiding, every New Year's afternoon,*
> *And all the teams in Division Two can say goodbye soon.*
> *For the tigers are quite hopeless, even their fans are sure,*
> *That Division Three is where they're off, or maybe even Four.*

To complete the array of nativity related strangeness, there are also versions of *Deck The Halls, Silent Night* and *Little Donkey*, but even the most noble of song catalogues must contain a few duds, and these three are far less impressive than the other detailed above, although *"Silent Knight, Holy Knight"*, dedicated to injury-prone defender Ian Knight was almost sufficiently splendid to merit inclusion in full (but not quite). To bring the Grimsby section to a close however, it is necessary to move away from the Christmas scene, and consider the thoroughly uncomplicated chant with which Grimsby fans have now been associated for some little time. An adaptation of the ubiquitous *Jauntanamera* by The Sandpipers, which appears in many other guises throughout the country, the staple industry of Grimsby is set upon a pedestal by way of....

Sing when we're fishing, we only sing when we're fishing,
Sing when we're fishing, we only sing when we're fishing

....which, amongst other things, gave rise to the aforementioned fanzine title and also prompted the craze for inflatable fish (known as *Harry the Haddock*) which were a regular sight at Grimsby matches throughout the early 1990's. By way of a footnote, it should be recorded that Grimsby are one of two teams who get a mention in what is a genuinely unique song, in that it extols the virtues of two Nationwide League teams at once. However, this exceedingly strange circumstance is more fully explained under Lincoln City, the other team involved, as Grimsby have compiled a worthy selection of songs, whereas City's efforts are altogether more meagre, and need padding out!

Hull City

As with Grimsby, the supporters of Hull City have seemingly set themselves the objective of producing as many unique and original songs as possible but, instead of drawing on Christmas carols for their inspiration, it seems very much as if chart songs of various eras are taken as the raw material from which to work. With the addition of several more run of the mill chants, this adds up to City having one of the league's more impressive array of songs which provides a stark contradiction to a statement in a 1949 edition of *Tiger Mag* (an early forerunner to today's fanzines) that *"supporters at Hull were not known for their vocal encouragement"*. Contemporary with the *Tiger Mag* comment - though perhaps unknown to its writers - there was a really rather fine song already in existence, to the tune of *Sioux City Sue*, and which persisted on the terraces up to the mid 1970's....

I took my wife to a football match to see Hull City play,
We waited for a trolley bus for nearly half a day,
And when we got to Boothferry Park, the crowds were rolling in,
The bus conductor said to me "Do you think that they will win?"
Shoot City shoot! Shoot City shoot!
The grass is green, the ball is brown,
And we got in for half a crown,
Shoot City shoot, Shoot City shoot!
There ain't no guy as sly as our goalie Billy Bly

....quality material from the decade of powdered egg and whale meat pie, and notable as being one of the half dozen or so oldest songs in the country. The evidently fox-like Billy Bly was to remain in possession of the City goalkeeper's jersey for some fourteen years up to 1959. The following decade saw Cliff Britton's City promoted to Division Two, largely due to the goalscoring feats of Ken Wagstaff who went onto be lauded by one of the more traditional versions of *Cielto Lindo* (*cf* Wolves, Doncaster Rovers *et al*)....

Aye, aye, aye, aye, McKechnie is better than Yashin,
Waggy is better than Eusebio,
And Carlisle are in for a thrashing.

....from around the time of the 1965/66 Third Division championship, and with a couple of well known World Cup figures thrown in for good measure (Russian goalkeeper Lev Yashin, and Portugal's Black Pearl, Eusebio). Ian McKechnie - here compared favourably with Yashin - signed for the Tigers from Southend United, although why Carlisle warrant a mention is unknown.

Continuing along the chronological path through City's songs, we come next to the early 1970's, and the first recorded outbreak of a food related song (an art more recently refined by both Orient and Doncaster Rovers). Though not strictly a Tigers' original, the following still originated in Hull, as it was first heard at Craven Park, home of Hull Kingston Rovers rugby league club....

Mrs Hull's sausage rolls are the best,
Mrs Hull's sausage rolls are the greatest,
'cos they're made from the milk from her tits,
Mrs Hull's sausage rolls fall to bits

....this is to the universally popular *Here We Go!* tune. Evidently being more than a little proud of locally produced foodstuffs, there follows a refrain which is based on *Bread Of Heaven* which extols the virtues off four such items....

Bread of Skelton, Bread of Skelton,
Feed me 'til I want no more, want no moooore,
Feed me 'til I want no more.

Chips from Carvers, chips from Carvers,
Feed me 'til I want no more, want no moooore,
Feed me 'til I want no more.

Pies from Fletchers, pies from Fletchers,
Feed me 'til I want no moore, want no moooore,
Feed me 'til I want no more.

Curries from Shezan, curries from Shezan,
Make you shit for ever more, ever moooore,
Make you shit for ever more,
Na, n-na, na na na - oooh, he's from Hull and he's from Hull.....

....the last line (which is repeated for as many times as the enthusiasm of the performers permits) sees a sudden departure from the format of the rest of the song, and would seem to bear more than a passing resemblance to Sheffield United's *"He's a blade"* silliness - possibly the *Prince Charming* version. It can only be assumed that *Shezan* is an Indian restaurant, much loved (or possibly loathed) by City supporters.

Next, a bit of East Coast exclusivity (and military history, for good measure), as the bizarre *Millhouse Fusiliers* song makes its way south from Victoria Park, Hartlepool, and turns up at Boothferry Park in circumstances initially as inexplicable as those which surround its appearance in Cleveland. The band of sexually earnest soldiers named in the title has peculiarly changed from *"Millhouse"* to *"Sledmere"*, and on this basis alone, it is possible that the song was originally used by locally-raised conscript regiments as a way of asserting regional identity. Extremely diligent research has revealed that there was, indeed, a First World War Volunteer Transport Regiment made up of workers from the estate of Sledmere House (some twenty five miles north of Hull), but they were officially known as the Walls Wagoners, and *"Sledmere Fusiliers"* was, in all probability just a local term for this band of patriotic young men. Whatever, historical inaccuracies notwithstanding, the song as it appears at Boothferry Park is....

Eyes right, foreskins tight, arses to the front,
We are the boys who make the noise, we're only after cunt,
We are the heroes of the night, we'd rather fuck than fight,
We're the heroes of the Sledmere Fusiliers, (Fusiliers, Fusiliers!)
We're the heroes of the Sledmere Fusiliers

If, as seems to be the case, this is an original dating back to the time of the Great War, this would be one of the oldest songs ever used in a footballing context (of a similar era to the Hartlepool effort, and also to *Good Old Sussex By The Sea* - cf Brighton and, of course, Hartlepool).

Considerably more up to date, now, and time to consider the plethora of chart/terrace crossovers which became all the rage on Humberside during the 1980's. Foremost amongst this selection has to be the City version of *Caravan Of Love*, by Hull band The Housemartins, which topped the charts in December 1986; a little tweaking of the original gives us....

> *Every woman, every man, join the transit van from Hull*
> *Tigers...! Tigers...!*
> *Every living City fan, join the transit van from Hull,*
> *Tigers...! Tigers...!*
> *I'm your brother, I'm your brother don't you know,*
> *She's my sister, she's my sister don't you know.*

From three years earlier, we find that *Karma Chameleon* by Culture Club (fronted by the inestimable Boy George) had also been seized upon by the City songsmiths, who came up with the following (which also crops up at other clubs, with the requisite alterations obviously being made to give it parochial relevance)....

> *Karma, karma, karma, karma, karma, come on you Hull,*
> *Come on you Hull, come on you Hu-u-u-ull.*

Other popular themes which were considered worthy of alteration included Bob and Marcia's *Young Gifted And Black*, which naturally became *"Young, Amber and Black"*, K C and the Sunshine Band's *Give It Up*, which was reprised as *"City's going up, City's going up!"* and *Yellow Submarine* by The Beatles which was more comprehensively changed to....

> *We all follow a black and amber team,*
> *A black and amber team,*
> *Who sometimes play in green*
> *We all follow a black and amber team*
> *A black and amber team,*
> *Which sometimes play in green.*

....evidently, City's change kit was green! One particular occasion on which Hull's proclivity for pop-song bastardisation had particularly dire consequences was the visit of Millwall in September 1983. Macolm Maclaren's *Double Dutch*, already popular through the chanting of the *"B-bum bah bah, b-bum bah bah; b-bum bah bah, b-bum bah bah"* section (which also appeared at Turf Moor, Burnley) was refined with the provocative addition of *"The Millwall die, the Millwall die"*. Evidently hearing this, coupled with the fact that their team was being handed a 5-0 hiding, was sufficient to prompt a vigorous reaction from the visiting supporters, who rioted spectacularly.

On the subject of violence, City's Kempton Terrace was the part of the ground where the club's more recalcitrant supporters had assembled during those halcyon days of the 1970's, when few games were completed without a good natured scuffle or two. In order to affirm their possession of this particular corner of England, the following invitation was tendered to any travelling supporters who might have fancied livening up proceedings in the traditional manner....

> Tiptoe, through the Kempton,
> With your boots on,
> Get your head kicked in,
> So tiptoe through the Kempton with me

This type of derivative from *Tiptoe Through The Tulips* also appears elsewhere (*cf* Manchester United).

Onto another regular subject for song, although it would seem that only one of City's players of the more modern era has been considered sufficiently noteworthy to have had an aria commissioned in their honour, and having first recovered from the shock that this player is not Duane Darby, it is a pleasure to record that the splendid Frank Bunn was so enobled during his service in the black and amber. Unfortunately, it was not Mr Bunn's sterling displays on the pitch which elevated him to greatness - rather an unfortunate physical quirk which saw him compared to - among others - Bruce Forsyth. Manfred Mann's *Mighty Quinn*, in one of its many different guises, must therefore be set out as....

> Come on without, come on within,
> You ain't seen nothing like Frankie's chin!

One last contribution from Humberside, and a heartfelt one for that, in that it dates back to the late seventies/early eighties when no matter what Hull City achieved on the pitch (not too much, to be entirely honest) they were destined to be overshadowed by the egg-chasing frolics of the twin rugby league superpowers that were Hull and Hull Kingston Rovers. Exhibiting an attitude which was to resurface in Wigan with the growing pre-eminence of Central Park's rugby team a few years later, we find a jolly old Cockney singalong number (*My Old Man Said Follow The Van*) somewhat pointedly reinterpreted as....

> My old man, said "Be a rugby fan",
> I said "Fuck off, bollocks, you're a cunt!"

....succinct and definitely not open to much misinterpretation, but lacking the depth of similar offerings based on the same song, which can be found under Hartlepool United's entry.

Lincoln City

Not an awful lot of terribly exciting things to report from Sincil Bank but, as alluded to in Grimsby's section, the club are party to what is a genuinely unique song - the like of which appears nowhere else (ooh - tautology of the finest kind!). The roots of this strange offering lay in the town of Market Rasen, marooned as it is amidst the featureless void of the Lincolnshire Wolds and, but for three miles (in Lincoln's favour) equidistant between Sincil Bank and Grimby's Blundell Park in Cleethorpes. It is apparent that there are (or at least were) a group of football supporters in the town who could never categorically decide which way they should journey along the A46 come match day, south west to the lofty spires of Lincoln, or north east to the oilskin clad fisherfolk of Grimsby. Evidently, it was a decision which was far too weighty a matter ever to be decided firmly one way or the other, so they followed which ever one of the two clubs seemed to be enjoying the better fortunes at any one time. Lincoln's demotion from the Football League in 1986/87 seemed to settle the matter once and for all, and Grimsby looked like the only place to be, but the following season, with the Imps soaring back into the big time on the back of crowds which were 86% up on their relegation season, the old uncertainty reared its ugly head once more, and prevarication was once more the order of the day. The upshot of all this indecision is that there is a song heard in the pubs of Market Rasen which pledges allegiance to the cause of the two separate clubs: the tune chosen to accompany this ground breaking composition is none other than *Mull Of Kintyre* by Paul McCartney (*cf* Charlton Athletic)....

> *Lincoln, oh Lincoln, my love how I wish,*
> *To be there at the dockside collecting the fish,*
> *In beautiful Grimsby, The Imp smiling down,*
> *Cunningham, Batch, Ford, Bell, City, my Town.*

....mentions there for both clubs, and players from each (Tony Ford and Nigel Batch from Grimsby, Tony Cunningham and Derek Bell from City). The players help to put a date to this song - very much early to mid eighties. The Imp mentioned above, incidentally, is a gargoyle type stone carving in the roof of the Angel Choir of Lincoln Cathedral, from which the club took their nickname!

Looking back a decade or so from when this bizarre schizophrenia was the vogue, we find City awaiting the arrival of Derby County for the second leg of a League Cup, 4th round match. On the visit to the Baseball Ground, the team had achieved a very creditable draw against what was then one of the country's foremost teams, but off the park, the City supporters had taken a right hiding off the County boot boys. Keen to present a more united front should Derby fancy more of the same at the return match, City's livelier supporters organised themselves into a gang, which swiftly became known as The Clan and the terrace on which this posse of likely lads stood - The Railway End - was unofficially renamed the Clanford End in their honour. The next evolutionary step was, unsurprisingly, for The Clan to conjure up a song, and so it was that Lee Marvin's *Wanderin' Star* (from *Paint Your Wagon*) was amended to....

> *I was born under the Clanford End,*
> *I was born under the Clanford End,*
> *Knives are made for stabbing,*
> *Guns are made to shoot,*
> *If you come down the Clanford End,*
> *We'll all stick in the boot.*
> *I was born under the Clanford End,*
> *The Clanford, Clanford End.*

Unfortunately, it is not known how the return bout with Derby worked out, but since then, the Railway/Clanford End has been demolished and replaced with the Stacey West Stand, which is named in honour of two City supporters who tragically died in the horrific fire at Valley Parade, Bradford in 1985.

Other City songs tend to centre around the thrills and spills of promotion and relegation, which the club seem to embrace in equal amounts with some gusto. Whilst on the way down to the Fourth Division in 1985/6, the following became popular, as the club's supporters had come to regard Division Four as their spiritual home, largely due to an unbroken fourteen year stint in the basement (up to 1976) which preceded a decade of archetypal yo-yo style instability....

> *Division Three, kiss my arse,*
> *Division Four we're home at last,*
> *With a nick nack paddywhack,*
> *Give a dog a bone,*
> *Lincoln City's coming home*

....whether a prepubescent Skinner, Baddiel or Broudie chanced across this ditty and it planted the seed that was to go onto become *that* "coming home" song or not is open to conjecture - probably not! What is clear is that both Bournemouth and Everton also have songs based on the same tune - though neither are of such a self depreciating manner.

Having revelled in relegation back down to the familiar and comfortable surroundings of Division Four, City supporters must have been slightly less impressed when the same fate befell their team at the end of the following season and they found themselves out of the Football League and contemplating life in the Vauxhall Conference. Fortunately, this sojourn in the game's nether regions was to last just one season, but it took a nail-biting finish after a ten month scrap with Barry Fry's Barnet before The Imps were able to secure promotion. A degree of hostility inevitably developed between the two clubs during the campaign, with much of the Lincoln ire directed at Fry, whose brash assertions that his club would come out on top were not popular in the Wolds. Fully aware that Fry was, in essence, just a front for the real motivating force behind the club - the larger-than-life chairman Stan Flashman - it didn't take too long for the following Wiganesque chant to develop, another in the long line of *Knees Up Mother Brown* derivations....

> *Who's up Flashman's arse,*
> *Who's up Flashman's arse,*
> *Barry, Barry, Barry Fry!*
> *Barry, Barry, Barry Fry!*

Towards the end of the season, Fry was seen on television, assuring all and sundry that Barnet were definitely going up, and that he was so sure of this outcome that he'd willingly *"put his house on it"*. Such a rash statement lead to City's last couple of games being played out before many a joyous chorus of *"Got no house, got no house, got no house...."* to the omnipresent *Here We Go* rhythm. The final victory of the season also saw *She'll Be Coming Round The Mountain* adapted for extensive and boisterous use as a farewell to the Bees boss, who was left behind in the Conference with the cheery refrain *"Singing bye bye Barry, Barry Fry, bye bye Barry Barry Fry...."* ringing in his ears.

Scunthorpe United

Somewhat out in the sticks in a footballing context (never having really got embroiled in the Humberside scene, a bit too far away from Lincoln to harbour any deep seated hatred for all things Impish, and very much on the periphery of goings on in South Yorkshire), Scunny supporters could be excused for taking a thoroughly introverted view of things, and not bothering to come up with any lyrical goings on at all. Fortunately for the student of the football song though, a couple of matters have prompted some semblance of creativity in the cradle of the British iron industry.

Perhaps as a result of being in such an ambivalent location, it was evidently deemed necessary on the terraces of the Old Show Ground (pre-Glandford Park days) to assert a bit of civic pride and dignity, and what better than the aforementioned industry for which the town is so well known for subject matter. As a reflection of this, the team are nicknamed The Iron (and have a rather silly girder thing on the most recent incarnation of their badge as a result), so it was Peter Sellers' interpretation of the old music hall song *Any Old Iron* that was taken on board by way of....

> Any old Iron, any old Iron,
> Any any any old Iron,
> You look sweet, walking down the street,
> Bottle in your hand and boots on your feet,
> Dressed in style, always with a smile,
> We'll sing "Up The Iron",
> Oh we don't give a damn,
> About Donny Rovers fans,
> Old Iron, old Iron.

Strangely, for a traditional London song and given that West Ham are known as The Irons, this has never cropped up at Upton Park, and it should therefore be considered as unique to Scunthorpe.

Afforded a brief mention in the above are Doncaster Rovers, who provide the second source of inspiration for Scunny creativity. As touched upon in the Rovers section, the rivalry between the two clubs is a strange beast, in that it only really comes to the fore when Rotherham United (the real *bêtes noirs* for any Belle Vue acolyte) are engaged in a footballing sphere other than that which Donny may find themselves. In simple terms, if both Millers and Rovers are in the same division, no-one really cares about Scunthorpe, but if the Millmoor outfit are enjoying one of their occasional excursions to a higher division, Rovers supporters grudgingly concede that they'll have to make do with Scunthorpe as local rivals. For their part, adherents to the Scunthorpe cause seem grateful for anyone else to simply acknowledge their existence, and thus it is the occasional foe from Belle Vue who find themselves abused by the Glandford Park hordes, both in the song detailed above, and in the South Humberside version of *The Red Flag* (which is exactly the same as the Doncaster version, but with the names of the two teams reversed).

Next, to pressing matters of sartorial elegance - shirts, and the colours thereof. The 1980's were certainly a decade of change for Scunny, as not only did 1988 see the last game at The Old Show Ground and a move to the salubrious surroundings of Glandford Park, but the start of the decade had seen the team return to their old, traditional colours of claret and sky blue, doing away with the red and white outfit that had sufficed for the previous twenty five years or so (and briefly preceded by a sortie into white, amber and blue!). At the time of the changeover, most Scunny fans of an age where singing at games was the done thing had never known anything other than the old red and white, and the following arose as a lament for the 1960's/70's kit....

When I was just a little boy,
Scunny were red and white, oh what a joy,
Now we are claret, now we are blue,
Why, we ain't got a clue.
Tell me mam, me mam,
They've dressed us up like West Ham,
We look like blue paint and spam,
We look like West Ham

...a song of the utmost quality, and to the tune of *Que Sera Sera* (which, interestingly, charted in 1966, at the hands of Geno Washington and the Ram Jam Band!).

During the red and white era of the late 1970's, Scunthorpe's cause was served (albeit in fairly limited fashion) by a certain Ron Wigg, who made such an impression on the home supporters on the Doncaster Road End terrace that they thought he deserved his own version of Bonnie Lou's *Tennessee Wig Walk* (*cf* Northampton Town, Fulham and Bournemouth); thus he was regaled with.... ·

I'm a bow legged chicken,
I'm a knock kneed hen,
I ain't had a drink since I don't know when,
I walk with a wiggle and a giggle and a squawk,
Doing the Donny Road Wigg Walk

Harking back to the assertion of identity, for the purpose of which the vast majority of clubs have a couple of chants incorporating little other than just their name, Scunthorpe have managed to come up with something more substantial than a mere shout or two of *"United, United!"*. They have chosen to show off their grasp of the English language by spelling out their name, to the rhythm of a popular chant which also turns up in the North East (*cf* Newcastle United and Sunderland) and which is very loosely hung onto the metre of the climactic lines from *Flash, Bang, Wallop What A Picture....!*

With an S and a C and a U, N, T;
An H and an O and an R, P E,
U, N, I, and a T, E, D - Scunthorpe United, F C!

And with that triumph for the education policy of Scunthorpe District Council, it is almost time to draw a veil over the choral efforts of United's supporters, apart from one last offering which saw all the good work of previous years in establishing an identity for the club which endures a peculiar sort of isolation, undone over the course of a few minutes. Springfield Park, Wigan, August 14th 1993 and, as a result of some peculiar goings on in the transfer market during the closed season, United take to the green sward for the season's opener with no less than seven players making their first team debuts (Russell Bradley, Paul Mudd, Steve Thornber, Matt Carmichael, Mark Smith, Chris Hope and Neil Trebble). Cue a certain degree of bemusement amongst the travelling Scunny contingent, and then one of the very few occasions on which that immortal question, to the *Bread Of Heaven* tune, has been directed towards a team by its own supporters - it was, of course....

> *Who the fucking hell are you?*
> *Who the fucking hell are you?*
> *Who the fuck, who the fuck?*
> *Who the fucking hell are you?*

....hardly a Scunthorpe original, but an appropriate inclusion in their section given the bizarre nature of the circumstances in which it was used!

Section Seven

Yorkshire

Barnsley

Bradford City

Doncaster Rovers

Huddersfield Town

Leeds United

Rotherham United

Scarborough

Sheffield United

Sheffield Wednesday

York City

Yorkshire

A peculiar state of affairs in Yorkshire for the diligent student of the football song to consider as the proximity of so many clubs might reasonably be expected to have produced all manner of songs directed at local rivals - as is the case in London. However, apart from the deep-seated hatred between the two Sheffield clubs, there seems to be a peculiar sort of tolerance that exists between the other teams who - as a general rule - all seem to put up with one another to a greater or lesser extent, with none of the desperate loathing which exists in other comparable areas being in evidence. Obviously, the likes of Leeds and Bradford don't particularly like each other, but the team from Valley Parade wouldn't number particularly highly on a list of despised clubs collated in the Revie Stand - the likes of Manchester United and Chelsea are far more probable to feature. Similarly, Barnsley and Huddersfield mightn't welcome each other with open arms on the occasion of derby matches, but there isn't the degree of dislike that you get with other pairs of clubs a similar distance apart.

Why this should be the case is somewhat open to conjecture, but perhaps it's simply because there are too many clubs in the area for specific rivalries to grow and fester - the vitriol of a Yorkshire football supporter has to be spread pretty thinly if everyone within a reasonable distance is to get their fair share!

The songs that do exist in this rather strange environment provide rich pickings for any interested parties, with a couple of county-wide themes being fairly evident. The *Yorkshire Republican Army* song (to the tune of *Cielito Lindo*) is more or less obligatory material for any self respecting supporter who fights under the banner of the White Rose, and *Marching Altogether* - once the preserve of Leeds United - has slowly but surely spread throughout the other clubs within the county. There are also some singularly superb efforts - the incomparable *Annie's Song* at Bramall Lane, the sheer idiotic splendour of Barnsley's *Eric Winstanley* efforts, and the deranged ramblings from Belle Vue where the Doncaster Rovers supporters can claim the Nationwide League's finest song about cakes amongst their repertoire!

When also taking into account the Scarborough claims to have been possibly the first supporters in the country to have come up with alternative versions of *Three Lions* and *Daydream Believer*, it becomes apparent that Yorkshire must be considered one of the real centres of singing excellence in the game - and all without a single mention of Ilkley Moor!

Barnsley

Whatever it was that inspired Danny Wilson's side to promotion during the 96/7 season, it's a fairly safe bet that it wasn't the impassioned vocal support of the Oakwell faithful which seems somewhat lacking in both quality and quantity (apart from an utterly bizarre song based on a track by The Fall - more of which later). Innovation is certainly not a byword on the Pontefract Road End, and for the most part Reds' supporters content themselves with what might be regarded as a typical Yorkshire repertoire, with *Marching Altogether* (*cf* Leeds United), *Yorkshire's Republican Army* (*cf* Doncaster Rovers) and *For Ever and Ever* (*cf* Sheffield United and Doncaster Rovers) all being aired, obviously, with the requisite amendments having been made to give them some relevance to Barnsley (*ie* the substitution of *"Reds, Reds, Reds"* for *"Leeds, Leeds, Leeds"* in the former). One song did become synonymous with the club during its progress to the Premier League, but even this has strong connections to at least one other club with Brighton claiming to be the original exponents of the *Blue Moon* derivative which was.... *"Brazil - it's just like watching Brazil; it's just like watching Brazil; it's just like watching Brazil"*. Followers of both clubs offer the same explanation as to the appearance of this song in that, particularly towards the end of the season, their teams were doing so well as to be beyond compare with some of the rubbish they had seen previously and, to all intents and purposes, they might well have been "watching Brazil" (obviously, Brighton's late season rally can only be considered impressive when compared to the pathetic fare that the team had served up over the first six months of the season!).

To find a genuine Barnsley original, it is necessary to backtrack to the late 1980's when David Currie, Steve Cooper and Steve Lowndes held the Barnsley public in thrall with all manner of scintillating performances. Currie, in particular, endeared himself to Reds' supporters with his goalscoring exploits, and it was the old music hall favourite *Side by Side* which provided the inspiration for....

> *Oh we ain't got a barrel of money,*
> *But we've got Cooper and Currie,*
> *With Lowndes on the wing,*
> *Doing his thing,*
> *Side by Side*

The local press ensured the popularity (albeit short-lived) of this song by printing the lyrics, and it was a firm favourite prior to Currie leaving Oakwell for Nottingham Forest in January 1990.

Apart from this effort, there appears to have been only one other substantiated Oakwell contribution of note - a wonderfully succinct chant from the mid

1980's which dispenses with all superfluous content in an effort to clarify its message - *"Fuck you lot, we're alright, we support the Red and Whites - BARNSLEY clap,clap,clap BARNSLEY!"* - not much chance of misconstruing the sentiment behind this one!

Next, a sortie into the realms of the positively paranormal, and brief mention has already been made of what may prove to be one of the oddest songs ever to have graced the nation's football grounds. In simple terms it was a hymn in praise of Barnsley's coach under the Allan Clarke regime of the mid to late eighties, one Eric Winstanley. Quite why Eric was considered worthy of his own song has not been revealed, neither was our contributor entirely sure of the lyrics and - as with Bristol Rovers' *Paint it Black* effort - the song seems to have been the preserve of none but a select few, but nonetheless, it would appear wholly incontrovertible that *Hey! Luciani*, a single released by The Fall in 1986, was used as the basis for....

> *Hey! Eric Winstanley,*
> *The future's hip today,*
> *Hey! Eric Winstanley,*
> *The future's hip to stay,*
> *Hey! Hey! Eric Winstanley,*
> *And all the cows are black,*
> *Hey! Hey! Eric Winstanley*
> *Bop, bop, bopop, bop,bop!*
> *Bop, bop, bopop, bop bop!*
> *Hey! Hey! Eric Winstanley.*

....err, right, and to coin a phrase, I think you probably had to *be* there to stand even the remotest chance of getting a handle on what this was all about. Don't forget that alongside the sheer stupidity of this song, it would have all been performed in the broadest of Yorkshire accents, just to give it a bit of extra flavour! From what I can remember of late nights listening to John Peel playing endless Fall tracks on Radio One, the words are basically taken from the original (apart, obviously, from the Eric Winstanley bits!), although the order seems to have been altered - a fact which may be accounted for by our sources' failing memory. Whatever, there really doesn't seem to be any rational explanation behind this one at all, and it really must be roundly applauded as the most surreal song to have been submitted during the course of research for this updated publication. Incidentally, it would now seem almost obligatory for Burnley supporters to apply something along the lines of the above to defender Mark Winstanley...! Such a Lancastrian effort would, by the way, be a suitably bizarre reflection of the fact that the video for another Fall song, *Kicker Conspiracy,* was filmed at Turf Moor - so arses in gear, Clarets supporters, and let's have more Mark E Smith inspired lunacy on the terraces!

Bradford City

A pleasant surprise from Valley Parade now, as City supporters have managed to conjure up a few interesting songs without ever having had much of a reputation for being one of the country's foremost purveyors of the art. Firstly, it should be noted that followers of the Bantams are not immune from Yorkshire's county-wide predisposition to a few basic songs. Leeds United's *"When I was just a little boy"* crops up in a claret and amber guise with the requisite alterations being made to (somewhat perversely) convey a heartfelt hatred of the song's originators; similarly, the *Yorkshire Republican Army* anthem has been known to make a few appearances in the City cause.

Of a far more noteworthy nature, we find what must be one of the country's older songs, as it makes mention of City's one-time local rivals Bradford Park Avenue, who were last playing in the Football League over a quarter of a century ago. The tune may well be *We're A Couple Of Swells*, in which case it is taken from the exceedingly jolly musical *Easter Parade*, starring Fred Astaire and Judy Garland, but being the world's leading authority on football songs has rather precluded my development of an equally astounding knowledge of such films and it may, therefore, be called something completely different and come from a entirely different source. Anyway, the lyrics proceed thusly....

> *Oh, we'd go up the Avenue,*
> *But we're not all that hard up,*
> *We would go to the Avenue,*
> *But they've got no beer to sup,*
> *So we'll stay with the City,*
> *'cos we know they're going up,*
> *Yes we'll stay with the City,*
> *We'll stay with the City,*
> *Yes we'll stay with the City*
> *'til they're up - right up!*

Of a rather more contemporary derivation comes this next offering, a sort of devotional song designed to revel in the camaraderie of simply being together and supporting the same team (eeeuch!); inspired by *Crazy, Crazy Nights* as served up by the rather silly rock band, Kiss, we have....

> *Your are my people,*
> *This is my crowd,*
> *This is our team,*
> *And we watch 'em proud,*
> *These are crazy, crazy, crazy, crazy nights*
> *These are crazy, crazy, crazy, crazy nights.*

Luckily, this is about the only occasion where one of these ridiculous "cock-rock" anthems has made it onto the terraces of our beloved game. I for one would not be happy if encounters towards the foot of the Nationwide League were played out to a backdrop of bastardised versions of other drivel by Bon Jovi, The Tygers of Pan Tang, Aerosmith or other spandex-clad nincompoops.

Putting self-opinionated musical critiques to one side for the moment, we now come to what must be regarded as one of the great events in British football history. Since the release of the original song in the 1960's, scores of supporters at many different clubs must have been sorely tempted at one time or another to eulogise any member of their team named "Ron" by putting together some sort of song based on *Da Doo Ron Ron* by New York's Phil Spector-inspired Crystals. In every case, though, these same supporters stepped back from the brink, no doubt deciding that the resulting work would have been at best silly and at worst, a complete embarrassment. Come the mid 1980's, however, Bradford City supporters showed no such inclination to dither, and the relevant half of that fine footballing double act, the Futcher brothers, was accordingly humiliated by the appearance of....

> *I met him on a Saturday, my heart stood still,*
> *Da do, ron, ron, ron, da do ron, ron,*
> *Somebody told me that he was evil,*
> *Da do ron, ron, ron, da do ron, ron.*
> *Yeah - he's got no hair,*
> *But - we don't care*
> *'cos, when he sticks it in,*
> *We love Ron, Ron, Ron, we love Ron, Ron*

....and you thought the Kiss song was sad!

On a considerably less offbeat path, City number themselves amongst that fairly broad selection of clubs who perform a version of *Just One of Those Songs* (*cf* Manchester United). This time, the old favourite follows what is more or less the standard format at everywhere other than Old Trafford, or when it takes the form of the Hartlepool "nasty" song....

> *We're Bradford City, the Pride of the North,*
> *We hate Newcastle, and Leeds of course,*
> *We drink all our whiskey and bottles of brown,*
> *The Bradford boys are in town.*
> *Na, na, na, na na na na na, na na na na na......*

Finally, the 1996/97 season showed that City supporters draw inspiration from either Underhill, home of Barnet Football Club, or Der Parkstadion, Gelsenkirchen, home of Germany's Schalke 04. This can be deduced by the appearance of the same clapping rhythm which precedes shouts of *"Bees!"* at Barnet or *"Seig!"* in the Ruhr Valley - the latter also being imitated by supporters of the German national team (boo!) during Euro '96. Unfortunately, the quality of the effects microphone at Sky TV's coverage of City's game against Q P R on the last day of the season was not sufficiently sensitive to reveal exactly what was shouted after the seven-clap preamble, but hopefully it was something obscene!

Doncaster Rovers

Suitably feted in the original incarnation of *Dicks Out!* for having one of the league's more irrelevant selections of songs, the grim times endured by the club over the intervening years have fortunately not seen the Belle Vue songbook diminish, as might have been expected. As was the case five or so years ago, the majority of entertainment for supporters at Rovers' games is unlikely to come from the efforts of the team on the pitch and it has therefore been necessary for Yorkshire's finest to look to dance as a possible source of amusement. Whilst never really rivalling either Grimsby's Hawaiian gyrations for artistic merit, or Cardiff City's *Do the Ayatollah* goings-on for sheer idiocy, the Pop Side at Belle Vue is regularly host to what is certainly one of the country's most enthusiastic efforts. Quite simply, all that is required in order to join in is to be able to bounce up and down vigorously, pushing and shoving anyone in the vicinity, whilst shouting out part of the chorus of that famous number *Centrefold (My Baby is a Centrefold)* by the J Geils Band. Even if you have no idea of how the song goes, you will need to witness just one performance before becoming word-perfect, as the actual lyrics are entirely ignored in favour of the....

> *Na, na - na na na na - na na na na, n-na na, na, na - na,*
> *Na, na - na na na na - na na na na, n-na na, na, na - na.*

....shouty bit (yet another one which makes little or no sense on paper, but which is wholly impressive if you ever see it in the flesh!). Still steering clear from what can genuinely be considered a song, there is a real old fashioned chant which has remained popular with Rovers supporters over the years; without a tune, but simply shouted out as loudly as possible, we have....

> *Zigger Zagger, Zigger Zagger DONCASTER!*
> *Zigger Zagger, Zigger Zagger DONCASTER!*
> *D (d), O (o), N (n), C (c), A (a), S (s), T (t), E (e), R (r).*
> *The Rovers (clap, clap, clap), The Rovers!*

The third line sees each letter shouted, then repeated, by different sections of the crowd, usually with so little space between each one that the whole thing merges into one long shriek which is ultimately punctuated by the *Rovers!* shouts at the end - again, tricky to convey using the printed word, but a real belter if a few people join in!

Now onto something a little more conventional in that it actually has a definable tune. Rovers supporters are always good for a few renditions of a song which has been adopted almost without exclusion by all the teams based in Yorkshire - mirroring the fact that on the other side of the Pennines, virtually every club in Lancashire has a version of *The Wild Rover*. Clubs under the banner of the White Rose have taken a fancy to something to the tune of *Cielito Lindo* (*cf* Wolves), the words to which are common to all the sides who perform it....

> *Y - Y R A,*
> *We're Yorkshire's Republican Army (we're Barmy!)*
> *Wherever we go,*
> *We'll fear no foe,*
> *'cos we are the Y R A.*

....this is usually followed by a burst of *"Yorkshire, Yorkshire, Yorkshire!"* for good measure. Being very aware of their county's identity, even ten years after the event, Rovers supporters occasionally hark back to the Miners Strike for an excuse to have a go at opposing fans. Miners from Nottinghamshire and Derbyshire were the first to break the strike after the long stoppage, leaving their former Yorkshire colleagues to fight on alone, and for this reason, Mansfield Town and Chesterfield supporters are always referred to as "scabs" by anyone with a Rovers allegiance. On a similar tack, there is still the occasional outburst of *"One Arthur Scargill, there's only one Arthur Scargill"* (to the standard *Juantanamera* tune) at Rovers matches, in praise of the leader of the miners' Union at the time of the strike.

More recently (towards the end of 96/7 as a matter of fact), Rovers found themselves embroiled in the scramble to avoid relegation from the Third Division to the G M Vauxhall Conference - only being assured of safety on the penultimate Saturday of the season. This precarious position, though, didn't stop the club's supporters from baiting the players at similarly struggling teams that were encountered during April, and both Darlington and (prophetically) Hereford stumbled to defeat accompanied by the strains of....

> *Thirty pounds a week,*
> *Thirty pounds a week,*
> *G M Conference calling you!*
> *Thirty pounds a week*

....to *The Camptown Races* tune, and obviously based on the assumption that relegation to the part time ranks would see players turning out for suitably meagre remuneration.

From songs which have their roots in something quantifiable, we move swiftly to an episode which leans rather more towards the utterly daft end of the scale. As mentioned previously, Rovers' supporters had a tendency to ignore on-pitch goings on when looking for a bit of amusement, and a few suitably irrelevant chants were heard during the course of a 0-2 Autoglass Trophy defeat at Burnley in November 1991. The Clarets supporters in attendance were alternately serenaded with the likes of *"Where were you when Elvis died?"*, *"There's only one Nanette Newman"*, and *"Bake you a souffle, we're going to bake you a souffle"* - all of which were largely inconsequential. However, one such effort, the now legendary *"Would you like a piece of cake?"* chant, was to have far reaching consequences. Evidently the person who came up with the chant had taken some cake to the game, and proceeded to wave the aforementioned bunlike comestible towards the Burnley supporters whilst singing the song - a gesture which the ever observant members of the constabulary on duty initially construed as threatening behaviour. Several police officers were despatched to the away terrace to put an end to this apparently provocative chanting, and began to note the names of the perpetrators, as they are want to do. Unfortunately, it transpired that the first few supporters thus impeached shared the same surname, and when another member of the family arrived to investigate, the police were regaled with the chant *"All called Hepworth, you know we're all called Hepworth"*. Amazingly, rather than resorting to an immediate barrage of CS gas and truncheon-related mayhem, the police actually saw the funny side of things and all parties ended up dissolving into hysterics. A few weeks later, Rovers returned to Turf Moor for a league fixture and, in recognition of the unnatural good humour of the police, an impressive array of cakes was transported to the game in order that they might be offered to the coppers on duty - hence, one of the finest songs in the long history of football was born, when said upholders of the law were regaled with....

> *And so this is Burnley,*
> *And what have we done,*
> *We've lost here already,*
> *Would you like a cream bun?*

....obviously to the tune of Lennon's *And So This Is Christmas*. Of a similar vintage there is another song which does not help to further any claim by Rovers supporters to be wholly sane, in that a number of away games during the early 1990's were enlivened by full-length performances of William Blake's epic hymn *Jerusalem*. Each rendition was made relevant to a particular match by amending the *"England's green and pleasant land"* bit to include the name of town or ground at which the game was taking place - with Maidstone being the first venue so ennobled during a 2-2 draw in October 1991 (*cf* Linfield).

121

As far as individual players are concerned, and typically for a lower division club, the turnover of staff at Belle Vue is usually so rapid as to preclude any one man being around long enough to have verses of praise penned in his honour. However, Darren Moore (Rovers' central defensive colossus afforded national stardom when being shown on T V getting sent off for twatting Brighton's Ian Baird during the last ever game at the Goldstone Ground) proved sufficiently popular during his two year spell at the club that he has two songs to his credit. The first, which sees his name given the *Wonderwall* treatment (*cf* Manchester City), is hardly noteworthy, but the second is rather more interesting in that the old *Robin Hood* theme was amended to....

> *Darren Moore, Darren Moore,*
> *He's our number four,*
> *Darren Moore, Darren Moore,*
> *He's our number four.*
> *He eats raw meat, he won't be beat,*
> *Darren Moore, Darren Moore, Darren Moore*

Bizarrely, it should be noted that Darren joined Rovers from Torquay United who, as recorded in their section, were the first club to use the *Robin Hood* theme by way of their 1960's Robin Stubbs original - strange indeed.

And still it goes on, with Rovers' adoption (again circa April 1997) of a more widely used song following an incident where one of the numerous I R A "security alerts" of the time lead to Doncaster station being closed after a bomb scare. All the matches which took place between the time of the event and the end of the season were to see at least one rendition of the following, which takes the tune of the traditional hymn *Sing Hosanna*....

> *Keep St George in my heart, keep me English,*
> *Keep St George in my heart, I pray,*
> *Keep St George in my heart, keep me English,*
> *No surrender to the I R A.*
> *No surrender, no surrender, no surrender to the I R A!*

Lastly (and not before time) it is time to address the subject of local rivalry. For Rovers supporters, this has always seemed to be a matter which is infinitely flexible, as when I were a lad (during the 1970's), and Barnsley were both shite and in the Fourth Division, it was the Oakwell team who bore the brunt of the abuse from the Pop Side. Since the Reds' elevation to Division Three and beyond however, it has been alternately the Uniteds of Scunthorpe and Rotherham who have brought down the wrath of Rovers' followers in equal proportions, depending on which of the two happened to reside in the same division as Donny at any given time. Recently, it has been Scunthorpe who have taken most of the flack - usually endorsed by way of the Belle Vue mix of *Scotland the Brave*....

Downtown the lights are flashing,
We're going Scunny bashing,
Da da da da da da da, da, da da da!

....which is followed, occasionally, by an extended exploration of the tune, with several more lines getting the *da, da, da-da* treatment)

....and through constant (albeit thoroughly unoriginal) renditions of *"Five nil, we beat the scum five nil"* in celebration of a thumping Rovers win at Glandford Park in April 1995. "Scunny", as United are known to most followers of lower division football, also find their way into the Rovers' version of what is another universally popular composition, but which seems to include the first section only in its Yorkshire variants. This initial section takes the tune of *Oh Sole Mio* (from the Cornetto adverts), with the second part being a straightforward theft of *The Red Flag....*

Forever and ever, we'll follow our team
The Donny Rovers, they are supreme,
We'll never be mastered,
By no, by no Scunny bastard,
We'll keep the red flag flying high.

Flying high up in the sky,
We'll keep the red flag flying high,
And when the Rovers win the league,
We'll keep the red flag flying high.

However, putting Scunthorpe on the back burner, the ongoing tribulations and ultimate relegation of Rotherham were digested with increasing glee at Belle Vue as the 96/7 season progressed, and it looks as if some new songs may well be in order to celebrate the renewal of this particular rivalry,. which seems set to take centre stage on the South Yorkshire scene after Sheffield United blew their chances to renew acquaintances with their chums from Hillsborough.

Huddersfield Town

Even a move to the impressive McAlpine Stadium has been unable to stir Terriers' supporters out of the catatonic state which left them damned with faint praise on the first occasion that their singing repertoire came under scrutiny. With no new and entirely substantiated submissions since received, it is still a case of there being just two songs of note to record, but both manage to maintain the generally high standard set by other Yorkshire clubs. The first does so by including the most dated reference encountered thus far to noble deeds of yesteryear - there can be few other clubs who have either the inclination or the heritage to go back to the 1920's to find something worth singing about....

> *Those were the days, my friend,*
> *We'd thought they'd never end,*
> *We won the League three times in a row,*
> *We won the F A Cup, and now we're going up,*
> *We are the Town, oh yes we are the Town,*
> *Na na na na na-na, na na na na, na-na...etc*

The good old days indeed, as Mary Hopkins' ubiquitous *Those Were The Days* makes another of its many appearances, this time in order to heap praise upon the fabled Huddersfield team managed by Herbert Chapman which won three successive League championships, finished as runners-up for the two seasons after the third triumph, and managed three F A Cup final appearances (winning once) during the same decade.

Since the aforementioned departure from Town's traditional stomping ground for the banana-trussed splendour of the McAlpine, the second Huddersfield song has also taken on a somewhat redundant air, as it eulogises the terrace at the Leeds Road end of the old ground, which became known as The Cowshed to those who stood upon its steps. Thus far, nothing similar has been introduced to idolise the architectural splendour of the Kilner Bank or Riverside stands, and it is a particularly fine version of *Waltzing Matilda* which reflects on those halcyon days when Huddersfield supporters welcomed visiting fans to their ground with a cheery smile, a warming cup of Bovril proffered in friendship, a dish of pie and peas - and a swift punch in the mouth....

> *Waltz in the Cowshed, Waltz in the Cowshed,*
> *Who'll come and waltz in the Cowshed with me?*
> *'cos we'll kick you, and brick you,*
> *And chop your fucking bollocks off,*
> *If you come and walk in the Cowshed with me!*

Excellent - a traditional warm Northern welcome if ever there was one! Quite how this famous Australian anthem came to find itself bastardised in the heart of industrial England is wholly mysterious, but that does not preclude the song from being one of the finest numbers dedicated to good old fashioned thuggery that has been recorded in the course of this book. Other than these two slightly archaic efforts, there seems little else of interest to catalogue apart, that is, from a rumour that a number of theme tunes from children's television programmes were wont to make an appearance, mostly at away games, during the early part of the 96/7 season. It may well be that this is no more than another example of the archetypal "me and a few mates down the pub" scenario, but word has reached us that the (new) *Blue Peter* theme has been vocalised in the Huddersfield cause, along with the resurrection of one of the finest ditties as performed by the late and very sadly lamented Pastor Milne's Black and Tan Army of Meadowbank Thistle fame - namely, the Half Man, Half Biscuit version of the title song from the magnificent *Chigley*....

> *Time flies by when you're the driver of a train,*
> *Speeding out of Trumpton with a cargo of cocaine,*
> *Under bridges, over bridges to our destination,*
> *Don't spill your fucking beer, Eugene, it causes condensation.*

....the lyrics as given above differ from the actual Chigley original (no!), the version as laid down on vinyl by the Liverpudlian pop surrealists and, by definition, from the Meadowbank Thistle version (what with the last two being the same, and all), although it retains at least a few words from either incarnation. Quite why this particular effort has been reanimated in the pubs of West Yorkshire is - as with *Waltzing Matilda* - sadly unknown, but with songs of this quality, there simply does not have to be a reason, as their mere existence is justification in itself.

Leeds United

In spite of the efforts of the recent managerial incumbents to suffocate the atmosphere at Elland Road through the sheer stultifying dullness of the team's play, Leeds remains one of the few truly intimidating venues that can still be found, and the old Kop, although now all-seater and renamed the Revie Stand, retains its ability to generate an atmosphere of unadulterated hatred - particularly when the visitors are from Old Trafford.

The first entry, though, merits inclusion on a rarity basis, rather than for being a particularly virulent effort, as it is one of the very few songs which share the tune to the Liverpool anthem *Poor Scouser Tommy*, and originally taken from the song *Red River Valley*. Presumably dating back to the early 1970's, we have....

> *In the Black Country town, Wolverhampton,*
> *Where most of the fighting was done,*
> *It was there that a young Leeds supporters,*
> *Was stabbed by a Wolverhampton fan.*

> *As he lay on the terraces dying,*
> *With the blood gushing out of his head (gush, gush!)*
> *As he lay on the terraces dying,*
> *He turned to his comrades and said....*
> *Are you there, are you there, are you there...?*

The rather odd last line starts somewhat quietly, and increases in volume with each repetition until it reaches a rousing crescendo after a dozen reprises or so. There is an alternative, later, version of 1979 vintage which differs from the above only in that the last line was replaced with a chant of *"Adamson OUT!, Adamson OUT!"*, which reflected the supporters' disenchantment with the then manager Jimmy Adamson.

Conceived at a similar point in history to the above, we find another relative rarity in the shape of an official club song which has been taken on board by the supporters, in much the same way that *Blue Is The Colour* did at Chelsea (and unlike, ooh, virtually every other club song you care to mention). Released on April 15th 1972, with "Leeds United Football Team and Supporters" listed as the artistes, was the evocatively named *Leeds, Leeds Leeds!* which has gone onto greater things under its popular title of *Marching On Together*. It is the second half of the chorus which has really been adopted by the United supporters, although the whole chorus makes sporadic appearances, and it has been known for the whole thing to be run through from beginning to end, though this is a rarity nowadays....

> *Here we go, all the way with Leeds United*
> *We're going to give the boys a hand,*
> *So stand up and sing for Leeds United,*
> *They are the greatest in the land*
>
> *Every day, we're all going to say,*
> *We love you, Leeds, Leeds, Leeds!*
> *Everywhere, we're going to be there,*
> *We love you, Leeds, Leeds, Leeds!*
> **Marching on together,**
> **We're going to see you win,**
> **La la la, la la-la,**
> **We are so proud, we shout it out loud,**
> **We love you Leeds, Leeds, Leeds!**
>
> *We've been through it all together,*
> *And we've had our ups and downs,*
> *We're going to stay with you forever,*
> *At least until the world stops going round.*
>
> (*repeat chorus*)

As stated, it is the second half of the chorus (the bit in **bold**) which has gone onto become popular on the terraces, although in these less than enlightened times the words *"we love you"* tend to be dropped, as it's hardly the sort of thing you want to be singing if you're trying to intimidate a load of rival fans! The song, originally written by that famous duo of Mason and Reed (!), has proved to be a favourite not only at its intended venue, as with subtle variations (*cf* Barnsley) it has appeared at Oakwell, Valley Parade and Belle Vue, and has become probably *the* definitive Yorkshire song.

By far the most gleeful time for United supporters in recent years must have been the championship winning season of 1991/92, not only because of simply winning the league, but because despised rivals Manchester United were overtaken at the last and dumped into second place. This was a time of much rejoicing, and more involved songs were ditched in favour of shorter efforts which could be belted out at full volume, purely by way of celebration. Typical of this ilk was....

> *Ee aye, ee aye, ee aye oh,*
> *Up the Football League we go,*
> *Now we've won the title,*
> *This is what we'll sing:*
> *We are the champions, we are the champions,*
> *Sergeant Wilko's King - oi!*

....to the tune of *Knees Up Mother Brown*; this was a development of a song which had proved very popular during the promotion season a couple of years beforehand, when the third line had been *"When we win promotion"*. *Blue Moon* then found itself as part of the Elland Road repertoire, with Man. United (universally known as "the scum" to all Leeds fans) being regaled with *"Hey, scum, look what we've gone and done, we've won Division One, we are the Champions"*. Similarly, *Tie Me Kangaroo Down, Sport*, in another bizarre Australia/West Yorkshire crossover, became *"Who's the champions, now, scum, who's the Champions now? Who's the champions, now, scum, who's the champions now?"*. Both of these two songs were repeated over and over again, as many times as was humanly possible. On the subject of repetitive songs of a championship winning vintage, it would seem churlish not to mention that Leeds' supporters were the first to anoint the eardrums of the world with the eclectic masterpiece which was *"Ooh, aah, Cantona, I said ooh ah Cantona"*. Naturally, in praise of the French maestro, this chant was based on the chorus from *Oops Upside Your Head* by The Gap Band, a tune which completed a neat circle with Cantona's later defection to Old Trafford, as it had first begun to grate on the national consciousness in the form of *"Ooh, ah, Paul McGrath"* during the central defenders' eight seasons with United in the early 1980's (and having nothing at all to do with Aston Villa, just in case anyone decides to perpetuate that particular myth!). In turn, this chant was an (albeit slight) misinterpretation of the original, which had again been directed at McGrath, but by supporters of the Republic of Ireland national team. Yet more confusingly, this had found its way onto the international scene via Celtic supporters who, whilst supporting the Republic, were wont to ejaculate the (then original) Gap Band based chant of *"Ooh, ah, up the Ra!"* (basically *"up the I R A"*). This version was picked up on by The Wolfetones in their song *Celtic Symphony*, from where - erroneously - many people thought it first came! And there, in a nutshell, is the potted history of one of the game's simplest chants, but one with the most circuitous heritage!

Anyway, (and about time too!), back to the matter in hand, and a rather fine effort directed at that great favourite in the United side of the late 1970's/early 80's, Tony Currie, who was ultimately to leave the club for Q P R, citing his wife's homesickness for the capital as being the reason for his impending departure. Not unreasonably, Leeds supporters had encouraged their hero to stay by chanting *"Tony, shoot your wife, Tony, Tony, shoot your wife"* which, disappointingly (for the fans at least), he didn't.

Ever onward, and time to consider the rivalry which exists between Leeds and Chelsea, almost exclusively because of their encounter in the 1970 F A Cup final. In the first instance, we find another trendsetting song to the tune *Que Sera Sera* - one which has gone onto wider usage....

> *When I was just a little boy,*
> *I asked my mother "What should I be?*
> *Should I be Chelsea, should I be Leeds?"*
> *Here's what she said to me:*
> *"Wash you mouth out, son,*
> *And go get your father's gun,*
> *And shoot all the Chelsea scum,*
> *Leeds are Number One"*

In case you're still in some doubt as to exactly how Chelsea are perceived at Elland Road, there is also the following cheery number (the tune to which hangs loosely onto the structure of *Macnamara's Band*, and which has a direct counterpart at Middlesbrough), which neatly sums up the relevant attitude....

> *If you're feeling tired and weary,*
> *And you're wearing cockney clothes,*
> *And you want you're fucking head kicked in,*
> *Just come down Elland Road.*
> *And as you pass the Gelderd End,*
> *You'll hear a mighty roar*
> *Fuck off you Chelsea Bastards,*
> *We are the Revie Boys.*

Somewhat unusually, we then find evidence of an outbreak of rare good humour at Elland Road towards the end of the 1996/97 season, as the somewhat less than flamboyant George Graham looked back on his managerial achievements with pride, noting that United has finished the campaign with one of the lowest ever "goals for" totals in the long history of top flight football, and that exciting striker Tony Yeboah had been virtually forced out of the club after what had euphemistically been described as a "clash of personalities" with his dour boss. Memories of an equally austere time flooded back, as Vera Lynn's wartime classic *We'll Meet Again*, was amended to....

> *We'll score again, don't know where, don't know when,*
> *But I know we score again some sunny day.*
> *We'll score again, don't know where, don't know when,*
> *But I know we'll score a goal some sunny day!*

In closing, it seems appropriate to set out the words to the chant with which Leeds supporters have become most readily associated in recent seasons. With a neat return to the simplistic style with which we opened by way of the *Leeds, Leeds, Leeds!* song, there can be very few matches during recent years in which United have taken part which have passed without at least one or two performances of the forthright assertion of identity which is....

> *We are Leeds, we are Leeds, we are Leeds,*
> *We are Leeds, we are Leeds, we are Leeds....*

....repeated for as long as the endurance of the performers will allow, this follows the all-pervading *"Here we go"* rhythm and, with the fervent thousands in full cry, provides one of the games' most intimidating chants (*cf* Brentford),

Rotherham United

Making a sterling recovery having been entirely ignored in the original *Dicks Out!*, United's supporters have recorded a splendid, if slightly sparse selection of songs second time around. Their first effort is instantly commendable in that it is based on a song by the inestimable Cliff Richard, with *Batchelor Boy* finding itself amended to....

> *When I was young, my father said,*
> *Son, I have something to say,*
> *And what he told me I'll never forget,*
> *Until my dying day.*

He said "Son, you are a Rotherham fan,
And that's the way to stay,
Happy to be a Rotherham fan,
Until your dying day".

He said "Son, you are a Rotherham fan,
That's the way to stay,
Happy to be a Rotherham fan,
Until your dying day".

...pity a few more of the virginal volleyer's ditties haven't received similar treatment really. Anyway, this is reputedly a bit of an "old time" favourite, but one which saw an impressive revival in April 1996 when United were at Wembley for the Auto Windscreens Shield final against Shrewsbury. In its first flush of youth, this song formed part of the repertoire which secured Rotherham the BBC Television *Sportsnight Kop Choir* crown at some time in the early 1970's - an accolade of the highest order.

Lacking the pop pedigree of Cliff's contribution, but more than making up for it by way of rampant silliness, comes this veteran of a 1983 League Cup tie at Anfield which must have taken place on or about the 5th of November....

A banger, a banger - boom, boom, boom!
A rocket, a rocket - zoom, zoom, zoom!
A sparkler, a sparkler - ssssss, ssssss, ssssss!

....a chant of genuine quality (*cf* Oxford United) which was further enhanced by the participants waving their hands about to accompany the climactic *"sssssss"* noises, evidently to approximate the sort of waving that everyone does as soon as they get hold of a sparkler - top stuff!

From much the same era (so we are lead to believe) comes another chant, rather than a song, the rhythm of which seems rather familiar, unlike its origin and purpose which are far less clear....

Rotherham, you've got me wondering, Rotherham,
You've got me wondering, Rotherham,
You've got me wondering.
One banana, two banana, three banana four!
One banana, two banana, three banana, four!

....more than a hint of the old *Blue Moon* approach to the first three lines of this one it would appear, and another Manchester City parallel through the Banana Splits reverence in the last two, so unless Rotherham are to sensationally swipe the mantle as instigators of one of the country's most enduring terrace themes (from Crewe Alexandra), it's a fair bet that the above first saw the light of day somewhat later than our contributor would have us believe (Alex having previously nailed down the footballing debut of *Blue Moon* to have taken place in February 1989).

So, a hint of controversy on which to end the Rotherham section - one which otherwise typifies the virtue of quality over quantity, whilst at the same time encouraging dangerous and juvenile pranks with fireworks - excellent!

Scarborough

A small but not insignificant section for one of the Football Leagues' newer recruits, with the supporters at the McCain Stadium claiming to be the instigators of what is probably the singularly most popular singing theme the game has ever seen, and also of being more or less in equal first place when it came to taking up the second most common anthem. In the first instance, Borough fans assert that they were the epoch-shaping revolutionaries who first applied anything other than the original words to the now hugely popular Skinner & Baddiel anthem *Three Lions*. If true, this would appear to have been purely a quirk of fate, rather than as a result of any extraordinary creativity on the part of the North Yorkshire hordes, as it is believed that Scarborough took part in one of the very first pre-season friendlies of the 96/7 season (barely a fortnight or so after the tragic denouement of Euro 96) and for this reason alone they were the first supporters to sing *"We're going up, we're going up, Borough's going up!"* - which exhibited some extraordinary optimism as well as showing that they had a good ear for a popular tune!

Similarly, Borough assert that their version of *Daydream Believer* was second only to the Sunderland original on the Darwinian evolutionary ladder of football songs. It must by definition follow that Scarborough supporters were the first to spot the latent potential for abuse that Simply Red and White's recorded version contained, and furthermore that York City manager Alan Little was the first person to be afforded the honour of being named in an alternative rendition of the song. If this is genuinely the case then....

> *Cheer up Alan Little, Oh what can it mean,*
> *To be a short ugly bastard with a shit football team*

....is a song which needs to have its lyrics set in stone, having been the first of oh so many others along similar lines, and after all, *someone* had to be the first to have sung this version, and in the absence of any contrary claims, why shouldn't it be the Borough supporters who take the accolade?

Less controversially, it appears that apart from these two (allegedly) ground-breaking efforts, all is relatively quiet on the North Eastern front. On purely geographic grounds, York City come in for a bit of stick via any of the bog standard chants you think may be appropriate (hence the Alan Little episode), and even fanzine-inspired campaigns to whip the Borough faithful into a maelstrom of vocal frenzy have failed to produce much of a reaction. However, if our sources are to be believed, no-one will be able to even come close to deserving the level of quasi-religious deference which Borough merit in their (as yet unsubstantiated) role as Originators of the Two Most Popular Songs in the History of Football, which for an otherwise nondescript Third Division club is probably more than enough to be going on with.

Sheffield United

In simple terms, what follows is in my opinion the finest football song ever to have graced the British game. It's difficult to quantify what gives it such an air of greatness; it may be the contrast between the lyrics of the original - a lilting ballad by homespun American songsmith John Denver - and the Blades version with its uncompromisingly Northern imagery, or perhaps the manner in which each was sung. To the accompaniment of an acoustic guitar, Denver - all soft woollen pullovers and little round glasses - would drivel out his version, full of sweetness and harmony, while the flattened vowels of a thousand beery Yorkshiremen in full voice batter the tune into submission, leaving only a string of deadpan sentences to be shouted out in succession, and climaxed with a guttural roar. Whatever it is, the Bramall Lane version of *Annie's Song* is a superb, truly stirring anthem which, even grudging Wednesday fans must admit, sits proudly at the forefront of the noble game's songwriting heritage (and not a hint of pro-United bias anywhere in this book's publication team - honest!). Anyway, enough pathetic preamble, and onto the song itself....

> *You light up my senses,*
> *Like a gallon of Magnet,*
> *Like a packet of Woodbines,*
> *Like a good pinch of snuff,*
> *Like a night out in Sheffield,*
> *Like a greasy chip butty,*
> *Oh Sheffield United,*
> *Come thrill me again.*
> *La la la la la - laaaaa la.*
> *La la la la laa la la - OOOOAAARGHFFF!*

By way of clarification, Magnet, as mentioned in line two is a local beer brewed by John Smith's at Tadcaster, and line six has given the song its universally recognised colloquial name of *The Chip Butty Song*.

It might be reasonable to assume that in the shadow of such magnificence as detailed above, the rest of the United repertoire would be a small, rather dank affair of little or no interest, but it is a pleasure to report that there are several more rather fine efforts to record. The first few come under the category of songs dedicated to particular individuals (a rather unwieldy name for a category, and one that I shall strive to improve on as this book progresses). Always impressive (without ever quite qualifying as "prolific") goalscorer, Brian Deane, was a firm favourite at the Lane during his six years or so in the red and white stripes, and he was rewarded for his commitment to the cause by way of a rewrite of Harry Belafonte's *Banana Boat Song* (recently revived through the *Trio* chocolate bar adverts, and to be found in a slightly different format at Portman Road, home of Ipswich Town)....

> *Deano, De-e-eano,*
> *We want a goal and we want one now!*
> *Not one, not two, not three not four,*
> *We want a goal and we want one now!*

Deane's most profitable season came in 1988/89 when he formed a lethal partnership with Tony Agana (the pair garnered forty six league goals between them, as the team secured promotion from Division Three). Naturally appreciative of the efforts of their striking duo, the Bramall Lane choral society revived an old favourite in their honour....

> *Brian Dean and Tony Agana*
> *Wibbley, Wobbley, Woo!*
> *Put 'em together and what do you get?*
> *Wibbley, Wobbley, Woo!*

This had formerly made an appearance a decade or so earlier, when the team was under the joint managerial stewardship of Harry Haslam and Danny Bergara (later of Stockport County fame). With a subtle difference, apart from the obvious name changes, the original was....

> *Harry Haslam, Danny Bergara,*
> *Iggledy, Boggledy, Boo!*
> *Put them together and what have you got?*
> *Iggledy, Boggledy, Boo!*

....a classic example of the way in which songs evolve over time here, with the transition over ten years from *Iggledy, Boggledy, Boo* to *Wibbly, Wobbly, Woo* - a development so complex as to utterly defy explanation (ha!).

Another former Blade afforded the glory of having a song dedicated in his name was the noble Barry Butlin - though the degree of pride he would have felt on hearing said song was wholly dependent on the quality of performance he was turning in, as the words altered to reflect what was seen on the pitch. An outstanding contribution to a match would have been acknowledged by the following, to the tune of *Chitty Chitty Bang Bang*....

> *Aye, oh, Barry, Barry Butlin,*
> *Barry Barry Butlin, we love you*

....but any form of substandard display saw this swiftly altered to *"....Barry, Barry Butlin, you are shite!"*. Only one United player of more recent times looks to have been deemed sufficiently capable to deserve some sort of song - the free-scoring Norwegian, Jan-Aage Fjortoft, who wandered down the A1 from Middlesbrough in the early part of the 96/7 season. The song in its own right barely merits a mention - being merely the player's christian name(s) repeatedly shouted out to the *"Red Army, Red Army"* rhythm (*"Jan-Aage, Jan-Aage!"* to be precise), but it is virtually unique in that it is one of the very few player-related songs that has accompanying actions: Fjortoft always celebrates goals by wheeling away from the penalty area, arms outstretched and pretending to be an aeroplane, and those that see fit to intone his name in the manner set out above are obliged to do so whilst, err, holding their arms outstretched and pretending to be an aeroplane!

Away from the adoration of those that ply their trade in the red and white stripes, Blades supporters were not averse to a bit of good old fashioned stupidity, witness this following effort which illuminated the otherwise drab proceedings during a goalless draw with West Brom towards the end of the 1987/88 season....

> *There are green alligators, and long legged geese,*
> *Some humpty-backed camels and some chimpanzees,*
> *Some cats and rats and elephants,*
> *But as sure as you've been born,*
> *You'll never see no unicorn*

....an old Bachelors song being performed with the original lyrics intact, for no good reason whatsoever (unless the chimpanzee reference was an early foretaste of what Peter Reid was later to experience - *cf* Newcastle United). On a similar tack, a Group Cup match at Blundell Park, Grimsby, must have been equally as enthralling as the travelling United supporters spent most of the game jumping around on the terrace singing *"He's a Blade and he's a Blade and he's a Blade and he's a Blade......."* to the tune of *The Can Can* - at the same time pointing at each other in the sort of self-aggrandising manner that only footy supporters can manage. Evidently tiring of this particular number, something else soon appeared along similar lines, but this time to the tune of *Prince Charming* by Adam and the Ants....

> *He's a Blade, OOOOH! he's a Blade, OOOOH!*
> *Sheffield Wednesday are nothing to be scared of!*

Only one of the handful of popular Yorkshire-based songs seems to have gained a foothold at Bramall Lane, that being a version of *For Ever And Ever* (*cf* Doncaster Rovers), which this time round tells the tale of the *"supreme"* Sheffield United never being mastered *"by no Wednesday bastard"*, but there is a popular song of much wider national usage which has become synonymous with United. Infinitely adaptable to suit the requirements of any set of supporters who are committed to the concerted loathing of a local rival, we find this variant of *My Bonny Lays Over The Ocean*....

> *If I had the wings of a sparrow,*
> *If I had the arse of a crow,*
> *I'd fly over Hillsborough tomorrow,*
> *And shit on the bastards below,*
> *Shit on, shit on, and shit on the bastards below, below,*
> *Shit on, shit on, and shit on the bastards below!*

It's all too easy to see how this can be altered to make it relevant to any other cross-town rivalry, but for some reason, it has become increasingly peculiar to the divided loyalties of the Steel City, although with Wednesday apparently unwilling to reciprocate with the *"fly over Bramall Lane"* retort, it would seem to be an exclusive to the red and white half of the equation.

Sheffield Wednesday

There is, of course, only one song with which we can start the Wednesday section - the interminable tune popularised by the club's notorious band, and since adopted by virtually every other group of supporters across Great Britain. Unfortunately, being almost exclusively an instrumental effort, it is impossible to set out how it goes in writing (and I'm bloody sure I can't be bothered to learn how to transcribe sheet music just for this thing!), but suffice to say that anyone who has been at or near a game of football anywhere in the Northern Hemisphere at any time since mid 1996 will have heard the "tune", which in this particular context sees fifteen seconds or so of "lah-ing" followed by a shout of *"The Wednesday"*, followed by more "lah-ing", another similar shout, then more of the same, continuously, without a break, ever more repetitively, for about an hour at a time. However, by way of compensation for the dismal inability to produce any sort of cogent written approximation of the tune, we have a bit of background information. Most people with much more than a cursory interest in the game will have heard of, if not seen, the Wednesday supporter universally known as Tango. A rather rotund (!), bald figure, he is wont to attend Owls' matches during the depths of winter devoid of warming *vêtements*, and occasionally painted orange (as per the character in the television adverts from whence he gets his name!). This semi-mythical figure was reputedly visiting The Netherlands during the late summer of 1996, and went to a game involving F C Utrecht. This particular club, once renowned for having some of the most violent supporters in the Dutch league, now boast a band (as do many other clubs in Holland) who played the above mentioned tune throughout the course of the ninety minutes. Recognising this as a tune that had first been heard sparingly during the course of Euro 96 (at the Dutch games), Tango returned home, explained roughly how it went to his mates in the nascent Wednesday Band, and thereby inflicted the arrangement upon the unsuspecting British footballing public for ever more. Strangely, no-one at the offices of the burgeoning Sheffield Wednesday Band plc could furnish us with the name of the tune, other than to say that it has colloquially become known as *The Hillsborough March*. As with all the other songs and chants which appear in this book listed as having universal appeal, a simple test is all that is needed to check the viability of *The Hillsborough March* for inclusion in this category - if you know the tune, just think of any team, and fit the name to the song; it should be possible to get at least a recognisable portion to scan. For instance, take someone whose name should be implausibly difficult to work into any other songs, Hamilton Academicals for instance; barely a moments thought is required to paste a shout of *"Accies!"* in position and, hey presto, a thoroughly plausible chant. Anyway, putting such pointless exercises to one side, it should be remembered that Wednesday do actually have one or two other songs, in spite of the fact that they've all virtually disappeared following the advent of *T H M*. The first couple of these worthy of consideration are relevant to the intense rivalry with Sheffield United, and are both based on *Singing The Blues*. Option one was so popular at Hillsborough that striker Terry Curran was moved to make a recording of it (in 1980)....

> *I never felt more like singing the blues,*
> *The Wednesday win, United lose,*
> *Oh Wednesday, you've got me singing the blues.*

....and so on, in a continuingly uninspiring vein. The second and rather more interesting version perhaps puts the cross-city animosity into its true perspective as, although it might be viewed from afar as one of the less intense such rivalries, this ditty leaves little doubt as to what the real feeling between the two sets of supporters is....

> *Oh I've never felt more like kicking a red,*
> *In the head, until he's dead,*
> *Oh Wednesday, you've got me kicking a red.*

We then find the Yorkshire preoccupation with basing chants on the work of rather unlikely artists (*cf* Rotherham United and Cliff Richard) coming to the fore once again. Leo Sayer would probably have been hard pushed to have imagined *Raining In My Heart* finding its way onto the terraces when it was released in 1978, but it did....

> *Sky is blue, clouds are white,*
> *That's 'cos God's a Wednesdayite,*
> *Na na na na, na na na na na.*

Equally, Jeff Beck may not have anticipated *Hi Ho Silver Lining* becoming one of the main themes of Sheffield's footballing heritage, but it has been taken up by the supporters of both of the city's clubs, usually when rival factions find themselves gathered on opposite sides of a room during some sort of social function when etiquette dictates that the ascendancy of one team or the other must be determined by some other means than the more traditional fist fight. Alternating choruses of *"And it's hi ho, Sheffield Wednesday, everywhere we go"* and *"And it's hi ho Sheff United...."* will be shouted by the relevant supporters, with whoever can muster the loudest rendition claiming to be vastly superior in every way to their less strident foes.

Being lucky enough to play their home games at one of the country's foremost stadiums is evidently a source of pride to the Wednesday faithful as, in a rather more forthright manner than is the case with the "garden shed" song from the West Midlands, they are quick to ponder aloud on the merits of whatever other grounds they find themselves at on their travels (including Wembley Stadium). *Bread Of Heaven* provides the tune for the chant of....

> *What a fucking - what a fucking,*
> *What a fucking shitty ground!*
> *What a fucking shitty ground!*

....the sentiments of which are not open to too much misinterpretation. Civic pride once more emerges in what is one of the most popular songs at many other clubs - *When The Saints Go Marching In* being the tune for an effort which has been put forward as a Wednesday original....

> *Oh Sheffield - oh Sheffield!*
> *Is wonderful - is wonderful!*
> *Oh Sheffield is wonderful,*
> *It's got tits, fanny and the Wednesday,*
> *Oh Sheffield is wonderful.*

It's easy to see how this has become such a common chant, as any town or city can be substituted for "Sheffield" (and any nickname or suffix for "Wednesday") to make it instantly relevant to another team. Easier still is the way in which the chant can be turned around by supporters of the opposing team, in attendance when it is sung....

> *Oh Sheffield - oh Sheffield!*
> *Is full of shit - is full of shit!*
> *Oh Sheffield is full of shit,*
> *It's full of shit, shit and more shit,*
> *Oh Sheffield is full of shit!*

Either version is equally popular, as a rendition of the first version always requires an immediate rejoinder by way of the second. More subtle variations on the theme also crop up, usually referring to a particular player - see West Brom's Kevin Bartlett number for an example.

For a short time during the mid 1980's, a hint of the mystic North East was brought to South Yorkshire when a slightly altered arrangement of the Hartlepool United nasty song became flavour of the month....

> *My brother's in borstal,*
> *My sister's got pox,*
> *My mother's a whore down on Liverpool docks,*
> *My uncle's a flasher,*
> *My aunty's a slag,*
> *And the Yorkshire Ripper's my dad,*
> *La la la la la la la la, la la la la la!*

Sharing the *Just One Of Those Songs* tune with the original, the pertinent amendments see the maternal parent now plying her trade on the banks of the Mersey rather than near Hartlepool docks, uncle's perversion has been more specifically referred to, aunty's madness is defined as nymphomania and dad has become a figure from more recent local history. The basic gist of this decidedly odd song, however, remains the same.

Lastly, a recurring South Yorkshire favourite was given the Wednesday treatment, as a peculiar version of Frankie Vaughan's *Milord* appeared at Hillsborough during the latter part of the 1970's....

> *We've travelled far and wide,*
> *We've been to Merseyside,*
> *But there is only one place I wanna be,*
> *And that is Hillsborough,*
> *Where it is magnifique,*
> *And all the Blades lay down on their faces.*

An eminently sensible song - until the last two lines in which the plot seems to have been lost in a particularly irretrievable manner. Doncaster Rovers (them, again!) provided a rather more cogent interpretation of the same song at around the same time, with the first three lines being the same, but the last three changing to *"....That's on the Belle Vue end, Where you can stamp your feet, And all the Barnsley fans lay dead underneath!"*. The Wednesday version is actually closer to the original, but makes considerably less sense as a result. And therein may lie the reason why The Hillsborough March has become so singularly popular since its inception - Wednesday do have a number of other songs, but those that are more or less exclusive to Hillsborough all seem to be a little awkward, for the want of a better word - lacking the simple effectiveness of what is now undeniably the most prevalent arrangement in the blue and white half of the Steel City - if not the World!

York City

A somewhat perplexing collection of tunes from Bootham Crescent, in that City supporters have, over the years, come up with some novel arrangements of the game's more obscure chants without ever composing anything of real substance. Manfred Mann's *Mighty Quinn* - often used elsewhere in connection with players bearing the appropriate surname - is a case in point, as City are almost certainly the only club to have sung this along the following lines....

> *Come on without, come on within,*
> *You've not seen nothing like a City win!*

The nearest anyone else has come to this arrangement is the Millwall version - *"Come on with us, come on with them, you ain't seen nothing like the Millwall team"* - which may be more than just coincidence as the terraces of the old Den are the only other venue in the league apart from York to have played host to the following rehash of Jim Reeves' *Distant Drums* - *"I hear the sound of distant bums, And do they smell? - like fucking hell!"*

A similarly exclusive arrangement exists with Sheffield United - the only other proponents of anything based on *Prince Charming* by Adam and the Ants. Whilst the Blades' version owed more to sheer silliness than anything else, City supporters used the tune to laud their favourite son - striker Keith Walwyn....

> *Keith Walwyn - oooh!*
> *Keith Walwyn - oooh!*
> *Defenders are nothing to be scared of!*

The goalscoring feats of the prodigal Jamaican (honest - check in Rothmans') were also celebrated by way of a short extract from the *Red Baron* song (with uncharacteristic honesty, I have to say I have absolutely no idea whatsoever who originally sang this!).

> *Ten, twenty, thirty, forty, fifty or more,*
> *Big Keith Walwyn keeps running up the score.*

....which is crying out for another couple of lines or so to finish it off in spectacular style, but which seems to go no further than this.

The are only two City songs which extend beyond more than a couple of lines - a standard reprise of Molly Malone (*cf* Wycombe Wanderers), and the North Riding version of *Halls Of Montezuma*, which merits inclusion for no other reason than that the York section would be pretty threadbare without it....

> *From the banks of the River Ouse,*
> *To the shores of Sicily,*
> *We'll fight, fight, fight for the City,*
> *'til we win the Football League,*
> *To hell with Donny Rovers,*
> *To hell with Scarborough,*
> *We'll fight, fight, fight for the City,*
> *'til we win the Football League.*

Scarborough have been included in this example purely because the Seadogs don't appear to like City very much - the original submission which pre-dated the advent of league football at the McCain Stadium listed Hull City in their place - more down to being a convenient rhyme than anything else, I think.

And that, with the dismal realisation that no-one on the Bootham Crescent terraces ever managed to come up with anything along the lines of *Nigel Pepper's Lonely Hearts Club Band* to mark the midfielder's sojourn in City colours, is that (something with which Bradford City supporters can now work, perhaps...?).

Section Eight

The North East

Darlington

Hartlepool United

Middlesbrough

Sunderland

Newcastle United

The North East

When the first edition of Dicks Out! made an appearance some five years ago, the introductory page to this section carried a note that an increase in success for the clubs of the region would probably lead to a much needed upturn in the quality of songs on offer - the subsequent return to the big time on the banks of the Tyne, Tees and Wear has now seen this happen in no uncertain terms. Even though Middlesbrough and Sunderland have been unable to sustain their challenges in the Premier League, the crowds have flocked back to the traditional heartland of the game in their thousands, and the atmosphere at the grounds has improved beyond all recognition from the rather lacklustre fare which sufficed towards the end of the 1980's. Needless to say, the majority of songs in the region (including the material from Feethams and Victoria Park) are dedicated purely and simply to the abuse of local rivals. Newcastle and Sunderland seem to expend a good 95% of their singing efforts in slagging each other off, Middlesbrough stand rather aloof on the sidelines, letting fly at both of these two in more or less equal amounts, and whilst Darlington do manage to direct a little ill-feeling towards Hartlepool, this is swamped by the all-consuming torrent of obscene invective which floods back in the opposite direction. There is no other area of the country which can come close to matching the North East for the degree of scorn which each club pours on its local rivals, and coupled with the renewed fervour which has swept the region in recent years it can perhaps now rightly be said to have regained its reputation as having the most passionate support in Britain.

The material is for the most part a mixture of both old and new, with the time honoured strains of *The Blaydon Races* and *We Shall Overcome* being heard alongside much newer material such as *Daydream Believer* and modern reworkings of more traditional efforts - an appropriate illustration of how the renaissance of the clubs has given new impetus to what have been always perceived as the traditional virtues of the supporters in the region.

It only remains for an as yet unknown billionaire benefactor to finance the rise of Hartlepool United to Premiership status so that a wider audience may fully appreciate the quality of the songs from Victoria Park for the North East to have its singing supremacy endorsed for time immemorial, but until this happens, you'll just have to make do with the descriptions over the following pages - which are probably quite enough to be going on with.

Darlington

Given the oh so hackneyed reputation that the North East has for being a seething cauldron of footballing passion, it seems entirely reasonable to begin the section with a look at a group of supporters who barely seem able to raise much more than a stilted whisper in praise of their club. Feethams, thoroughly nice ground though it may be, is utterly overshadowed by Hartlepool when considering the relative singing merits of the two neighbouring clubs, and hopefully this stinging criticism may prompt some sort of remedial action to be taken in order that the balance might be redressed.

There are however one or two stirrings on the Cricket Ground terrace, the first of which involves the revival of another of those notorious club songs. The roots of this one, unusually for its ilk, are difficult to ascertain, but as it dates from the 1960's and takes the tune of *John Brown's Body/Glory Glory Hallelujah* it may well have been inspired by the Tottenham original of the day. The words, largely forgotten by the Feethams patrons for a couple of decades or so, were uncovered by Darlo fanzine *Mission Impossible* in the early nineties, and measures were then put in hand to rekindle some sort of enthusiasm for the song, though a recent visit to the North East would seem to indicate that this initiative failed to get off the ground....

> *Come on the Quaker men, the boys in black and white,*
> *We cheer them every morning, every afternoon and night,*
> *Feethams is our home ground, where we score goals galore,*
> *And now we shout for more, more more!*
> *We'll sing Darlington for ever,*
> *We'll sing Darlington for ever,*
> *We'll sing Darlington for ever,*
> *As the Quakers go marching on, on, on!*

....if anyone has even the vaguest idea as to why this didn't really take off after its relaunch, perhaps you'd be good enough to let us know!

Of a slightly more contemporary feel, Ten Pole Tudor's 1981 mega hit (!) *Wunderbar* made some sort of impression in County Durham, in that verbatim performances of long sections of the song were very much the order of the day. Unfortunately, even had such performances been of sufficient length to include the whole song, the lyrics are barely worth recording as the single word *"Wunderbar"* virtually constituted the whole of the complex vocal arrangement.

Apart from these two thoroughly ignoble efforts, there are just two other Darlington songs of which news has been received. The first is a rather meek reciprocation of the ill-feeling which pours in torrents towards Feethams from Hartlepool, and takes the tune of *The Wild Rover*....

> *In the back streets of Darlo I used to frequent,*
> *I found Billy Horner, his arse up for rent,*
> *I kicked him until on the roadside he lay,*
> *I'll hate Poolie bastards 'til my dying day.*

> *And it's Darlington, Darlington F C,*
> *We're by far the greatest team,*
> *The world has ever seen.*

....this does, reputedly, extend to a second verse, but the words to this were not included by our contributor. With regard to timing, this must have first appeared between either 1976 and 1983, or 1984 and 1986, which were the dates of Horner's two spells in charge at Victoria Park.

To conclude, an example of what is no more than a rather silly shout when it appears at other grounds but which carried somewhat deeper significance during airings by the Darlington posse during the mid 1970's....

> *Ogley, Ogley, Ogley - oi, oi, oi!*
> *Ogley - oi! Ogley - oi!*
> *Ogley, Ogley, Ogley - oi, oi, oi!*

....not just making a row for the sake of it in this instance, but a "song" dedicated to one-time Darlo goalkeeper, Alan Ogley, and quite possibly the only occasion on which this peculiar chant has ever actually meant anything!

Hartlepool United

It's always a treat to come across a group of supporters who seem to take genuine pleasure in their singing, and this would appear to apply to the followers of Hartlepool United who, eschewing the more normal selection of songs which can be found more or less anywhere, have set their stall out purely and simply to become the most foul-mouthed terrace choir in the country. There would not seem to be any particular reason behind the flood of four letter expletives which has inundated Victoria Park, and therein lies their magic - gratuitous swearing just for the sake of it. Take, for instance, this almost poetic creation, lovingly crafted using some of the Anglo Saxon language's choicest profanities in order to abuse Darlington....

If you wear a black and white shirt,
And you're a Darlo fan,
Then you're a fucking wanker,
Or so says my old man,
You're just a Darlo bastard,
And you don't know how to fight,
Your team are fucking useless,
And your fans are fucking shite!

....utterly peerless in a Larkinesque sort of way and, according to our contributor, this is a fairly recent (1993'ish) composition, so it cannot even claim to be merely a relic from the bad old days of the seventies and eighties when the air at every other ground was turned blue on a Saturday afternoon - this is the Hartlepool contribution to the new, friendly face of family football! The tune, by the way, is along the lines of *My Old Man's A Dustman.*

More high quality obscenity in this next contribution, too, which is the Cleveland incarnation of the regimental rallying cry of the Sledmere Fusiliers (*cf* Hull City). Not quite such a wealth of background information available for this version as there is for the one from Humberside, but suffice to say that Mill House is an area of Hartlepool which has given its name to the road on which the main stand at Victoria Park is built (and consequently to the stand itself) and, it is reasonable to assume, to a volunteer militia unit raised in the area to fight in the Great War. Accordingly, this (as is the case with the Hull City version) has to be considered one of the oldest songs still in circulation in a football environment....

Eyes right, foreskins tight, bollocks to the front,
We are the boys who make no noise, we're only after cunt,
We are the heroes of the night, and we'd rather fuck than fight,
We're the heroes of the Mill House Fusiliers (Fusiliers, Fusiliers!)
We're the heroes of the Mill House Fusiliers.

....more good, clean and wholesome family fun. And there's more of the same in this next song which follows the *Macnamara's Band* tune, although this one tones down the swearing a little, in favour of extolling a wider, more rounded sort of depravity. As with most of the other 'Pool songs, no idea was given as to any sort of reason behind the co-option of this one in to the Town End repertoire....

We've got a nasty reputation for soliciting little boys,
For raping old age pensioners and nicking kiddies toys,
We're the perverts of the nation,
We're the worst you've ever seen,
We're a pack of foul mouthed bastards,
And they call us Hartlepool!

145

....oh how the hearts of the dignitaries of club and town must swell with pride as they hear this one belted out at grounds across the country!

On a slightly different tack, it is apparent that the actual players rarely move the Hartlepool faithful to song - not even the striking partnership of Paul Baker and Joe Allon, whose goals were virtually the only thing that stood between 'Pools and footballing oblivion throughout the late 1980's and early 90's (although, to be strictly fair *"Joe, Joe, Joe Allon"* did make a few appearances). About the only semi-worthwhile effort along these lines was aimed in the direction of another striker, John Borthwick, whose lamentable tally of just seventeen goals in one hundred and thirty six appearances for United made him the butt of many a joke on the Victoria Park terraces. Imagine the delight of the 'Pools followers when Borthwick was not only sold, but sold to much despised Darlington, and imagine how this delight was compounded when barely two months in to his new career Borthwick lined up against Hartlepool in a derby game at Feethams, turned in a dismal performance, and was substituted. This, of course, deserved a song and it was *Thank U Very Much* (by The Scaffold) which became....

> *Thank you very much for buying Borthwick,*
> *Thank you very much, thank you very, very, very much,*
> *Thank you very much for buying Borthwick,*
> *Thank you very, very, very much.*

....this has also cropped up in wholly different circumstances elsewhere (*cf* Wolverhampton Wanderers, and in the Cadbury's Roses adverts!).

With apologies for that brief departure from the more regular sort of Hartlepool song, normal service shall now be hastily resumed. First, to what is simply known as The Nasty Song, which has subsequently been exported to such disparate venues as Exeter City and Sheffield Wednesday. To the tune of *Just One Of Those Songs* we have....

> *My brother's in borstal,*
> *My sister's got pox,*
> *My mother's a whore down on Hartlepool docks,*
> *My uncle's a pervert,*
> *My aunty's gone made,*
> *And Jack the Ripper's my dad,*
> *La, la, la, la la la la la, la la la la la....*

And finally, a blinding return to form after that brief obscenity-free interlude, with a song that (again) enjoys nationwide usage in innumerable different guises but which, given the nature of their other contributions, would seem to be the quintessential Hartlepool song. Our Cleveland correspondent simply said that 'Pools *"also sing the Don't Dilly Dally song, with all the references* to Darlo", but it is a fair bet that by assembling the partial lyrics which have dribbled in from other sources (cf Shrewsbury and Newcastle) we'll end up with a reasonable approximation of what goes on, and such machinations leave us with something along the lines of....

> *My old man said "Be a Darlo fan",*
> *I said "fuck off, bollocks, you're a cunt"*
> *We took the Feethams in half a minute,*
> *We took the Feethams with the Darlo in it,*
> *With hatchets and hammers,*
> *Stanley knives and spanners,*
> *We taught the Darlo bastards how to run,*
> *So if you are a Darlo fan and wear your black and white,*
> *Then we'll sing "fuck off you cunt".*

Quite simply, with this last effort in place, there is no doubt whatsoever that Hartlepool are the runaway winners of the (entirely fatuous) Award for Mindless Overuse of Foul and Abusive Language, but I would suggest that the inclusion of all their rather rude songs also provides an indispensable service to you, our readers. Should you wish to submit a letter of complaint about the use of obscene language throughout this book, don't bother to tediously trawl through all three hundred or so pages, itemizing each and every example; simply refer us to the preceding dozen or so paragraphs to illustrate your point, because no matter how hard you look, you won't find anything more offensive than this anthology of Hartlepool vulgarity.

Middlesbrough

Turbulent times indeed for Boro as this book is prepared for the printers - cup final defeats and controversial relegations being very much the order of the day - but in spite of these setbacks, the club has proved to be one of the most forward-thinking in the country over recent years, and songs at the new Riverside Stadium have begun to reflect this brave new world.

Firstly, though, one for which the departure from Ayresome Park seems to have sounded the death knell, in that it makes mention of the old home terrace - The Holgate End - the counterpart of which at The Riverside is the thus-far tediously named North Stand. The sentiments expressed in the song would suggest that 'Boro are right in the thick of a triangular North Eastern rivalry (with Newcastle and Sunderland) but, in reality, these other two are far too busy with their own mutual loathing to really spare the Teesiders much thought. Although games which pitch Boro' against the Mags or the Mackems are hardly likely to lack atmosphere, there is very much a feeling that these other two clubs don't really despise Middlesbrough as they certainly do each other. Nonetheless, Boro' fans have used *Macnamara's Band* to illustrate their feelings for Newcastle....

> *When you're feeling lonely, and when you're feeling sad,*
> *Just go down to the Holgate, and you won't feel so bad,*
> *'Cos when you're in the Holgate, you'll hear a mighty roar,*
> *Fuck off you Geordie bastards, and don't come back no more!*

Sunderland are given measurably less obscene treatment via this next effort, which takes the tune of *Hey Girl Don't Bother Me*, originally by The Tams....

> *Sunderland, don't bother me,*
> *Sunderland, don't bother me,*
> *Go away, come back another day,*
> *Just don't bother me*

Back to Newcastle United, and a version of the curious juxtaposition of *Glory, Glory Hallelujah* and *Ally's Tartan Army* (Andy Cameron's song for the Scotland World Cup bid in 1978), the likes of which also appears at Portman Road (*cf* Ipswich Town)

> *All the Geordies went to Rome, just to see the Pope,*
> *All the Geordies went to Rome, just to see the Pope,*
> *All the Geordies went to Rome, just to see the Pope,*
> *And this is what he said:*
> *Who's that team they call the 'Boro,*
> *Who's that team they all adore,*
> *And they play in red and white,*
> *And they're fucking dynamite,*
> *And we'll support the 'Boro ever more.*

Whether or not the Pope finishes off line four with *"Fuck Off"*, as in most other versions of this, has not been made clear!

Away from abusing their disinterested neighbours, Middlesbrough were one of the earliest clubs to import a non-football song onto the terraces. In place at Ayresome Park before the end of the 1980's, and now very much a favourite (it was particularly voluble during the 1997 League Cup Final replay at Hillsborough), we find *We Shall Overcome*, the anthem of the American Civil Rights movement which was recorded by Joan Baez in the early 1960's. Given the current plight of the club, the words are more relevant now than at any stage during the song's popularity on Teeside....

148

We shall overcome, we shall overcome,
Deep in my heart,
I do believe,
That we shall overcome some day.

....this is the chorus, for want of a better word, which is the bit that can always be heard clearly during matches - even a 'Boro fan accosted in the street on F A Cup Final day (oh dear) was unable to say with any conviction if any more of the song actually gets sung or not. Of a similar nature, although with a couple of slight alterations from the original in place, there is then the Teesside remix of *Flower Of Scotland* - another which had found its way into the Ayresome repertoire for no obvious reason....

Oh team of England,
When will we see,
Your like again?
We've fought and died for,
And we'll do the same again

Let's turn against them,
Who? - the Geordie armies,
And send them homewards,
To think again.

The terrace is bare now,
They've ran away once again,
We will defend thee,
And be that team again.

On a far more straightforward tack, the influx of assorted foreign genii to the Riverside during 1996 and '97 was always going to result in a few new songs. By far the most popular of the imports was the Brazilian Juninho and, by way of introducing a bit of a samba flavour to Teeside, the little maestro found himself lauded with this version of *Hot, Hot, Hot,* originally by The Arrows and re-released by Pat & Mick in 1994....

Howay, howay, howay, howay,
Juninho-ho-ho, Juninho-ho-ho.

....the repetition of the players name in the second line is to a rhythm which is very similar indeed to the way in which *"Ian Wright - Wright - Wright!"* is chanted at Highbury, which perhaps indicates that the 1984 Arrows original was the inspiration behind this enduring North London theme as well as the Boro' version a dozen years later. Another central tenet of Boro's new order was Gianluca Festa, brought into shore up a leaking defence midway through 96/7. His surname was, predictably, a godsend to the Riverside artistes and his first game in a Boro' shirt (against Sheffield Wednesday) was punctuated by the theme tune to *The Addams Family* (complete with finger clicking), and Johnny Mathis' *Winter Wonderland* being swiftly rearranged to....

> *There's only one Uncle Festa,*
> *One Uncle Festa,*
> *Walking along, singing a song,*
> *Walking in a Festa wonderland.*

....rumour has it that the unfortunate player entirely misunderstood the application of the *Addams Family* effort, and thought that the Boro' fans were taking the piss out of him because he was ugly...!

Apart from the seemingly unacknowledged Emerson and Mickel Beck, the last of Boro's costly new foreign recruits was Fabrizio Ravanelli, who was afforded an exceedingly silly chant - again to the *Addams Family* theme - which reflected his now famous goalscoring celebration of pulling his shirt over his head and running around in circles. The sober hand of common sense, however, apparently put an end to this chant after a couple of months or so - it was evidently deemed just too daft to become properly established (and rightly so)....

> *His name is Ravanelli,*
> *He's always on the telly,*
> *Showing us his belly,*
> *His name's Fabrizio*

....how the Silver Fox must have longed for the more mature and sensible atmosphere of the Stadio Delle Alpi back in Turin, where he was no doubt feted by some sweeping operatic number from the more classically inclined Juve supporters. It is imagined that he would have been similarly unimpressed by another Boro' effort, lyrically along the same lines but which jogged along to the *Macarena* tune - perhaps this had a more appropriate Latin feel, but just as much of an anathema to the Italian star as the *Addams Family* version!

Newcastle United

Far and away the most successful of the three resurgent teams in the area (in that they're the only one of the trio not to get relegated yet!), United's renaissance under the benevolent deity which is Sir John Hall has seen the atmosphere at St James' Park improve beyond recognition from the dark days of the 1980's, but it is in this period of despair and near-relegation to the (old) Third Division that we must begin. Regardless of what degree of success the team might have been enjoying, there was always one song which was (and still is) utterly synonymous with the Toon Army. One of the genuine classics of its ilk, mention Newcastle and one of the first things anyone will think of is *The Blaydon Races*, a traditional song from the area dating back to the last century, and sung at United matches for as long as anyone can remember. Revel in the full, unexpurgated glory which is....

We went to Blaydon Races, 'twas on the ninth of June,
Eighteen hundred and sixty two, on a summer's afternoon,
We took the bus from Bamburghs, and she was heavy laden,
Away we went along Collingwood Street, that's on the road to Blaydon.

(chorus)

Oh, me lads, you should've seen us gannin',
Passing the folks along the road just as they were standin'.
All the lads and lasses there, all with smiling faces,
Gannin' along the Scotswood Road to see the Blaydon Races.

We flew past Armstrong's factory and up to the Robin Adair,
Just gannin' down to the railway bridge, the bus wheel flew off there,
The lasses lost their crinolines and veils that hide their faces,
I got two black eyes and a broken nose in gannin' to Blaydon Races.

repeat chorus

When we got the wheel put on, away we went again,
But them that had their noses broke, they came back over home,
Some went to the dispensary, and some to Doctor Gibbs,
And some to the infirmary to mend their broken ribs

repeat chorus

Now when we got to paradise, there was many a bonny game begun,
There was four and twenty on the bus, man, how they danced and sung,
They called on me to sing a song, I sang them "Paddy Fagan",
I danced a jig and swung me twig (!) that day I went to Blaydon

repeat chorus

We flew across the Chine bridge right into Blaydon town,
The bell man he was calling there, they called him Jacky Brown,
I saw him talking to some chaps, and them he was persuading,
To go and see George Ridley's show in the Mechanics Hall at Blaydon

repeat chorus

The rain it poured all the day, and made the ground quite muddy,
Coffy Johnny had a white hat on - they yelled "Who stole the cuddy?",
There was spice stalls and monkey shows and old wives selling ciders,
And a chap with a ha'penny roundabout shouting "Now me lads for
riders".

repeat chorus

Predictably if unfortunately, it is only the chorus and occasionally the first verse which usually get sung - a complete rendition would probably take longer than the available ninety minutes! Taking into account, however, some of that which follows on the next couple of pages, Newcastle supporters might like to consider making the last verse a regular addition, what with its mention of *"monkey shows"*! The version above gives the entirely traditional words (although with the more obscure Geordie dialect phrases having been "translated"), and these are the exclusive preserve of the Newcastle supporters - where the song makes an appearance elsewhere, it is always quite extensively altered (*cf* East Fife). Without being too much of a pedant, the song is basically the tale of bus load of revellers on a day out to the unofficial horse races and fair which took place at Blaydon, south east of Newcastle. The Scotswood Road has now rather less romantically been designated the A695, although it retains its original name when entering the city near the Central Station (a mile or so south of St James'). I would not like to hazard a guess as to exactly what "swinging ones twig" might entail!

As already touched on briefly, Sunderland are not exactly *the* most popular team on Tyneside, and the revulsion with which the two sets of supporters regard each other is as virulent as any other such rivalry you care to mention - if not more so. Naturally, there are a number of songs directed at Mackems (the name given to Sunderland supporters who are born and bred on Wearside), not all of them entirely complimentary, to whit....

I love to go a-wandering,
Along the cliffs of Dover,
And if I see a Sunderland fan,
I'll kick the bastard over, and over, and over.

...which are probably not quite the same sentiments as were expressed in the original version - *The Happy Wanderer* by the Obernkirchen Children's Choir!

My Bonny Lays Over The Ocean is also used as a vehicle to illustrate attitudes to the red and whites, with *"Roker"* being inserted into the same structure as exists for the version listed under Sheffield United, though presumably this will change to "Wearmouth" as from late 1997, to reflect Sunderland's move to a new home (currently with the working name of the Wearmouth Colliery Stadium). A variation of *My Old Man Said Follow The Van* also crops up - substantially different from other renditions....

> *My old man said "Fuck Sunderland,*
> *And fuck Man United on the way"*
> *Off went the van with the boot boys in it,*
> *I ran behind and said "Wait a minute"*
> *We dillied, we dallied,*
> *We fucked them in the alley,*
> *We lost our way and don't know where to go,*
> *If you can't find the van with the boot boys in it,*
> *Then we're on our fucking way home!*

If there is one aspect of Sunderland-hating which has proved a real boon for the Toon Army in recent years, it's the appointment of Peter Reid to the managerial position at Roker (or at Wearmouth - whatever). In the first instance, *Cheer Up Peter Reid* provided an almost ready-made means by which the ex-Evertonian could be metaphorically beaten about the head. Notwithstanding the Scarborough claims to have been the first to thus pervert the original, the most popular derivative from Simply Red & White's effort must be....

> *Cheer up Peter Reid,*
> *Oh what can it mean,*
> *To a sad Mackem bastard,*
> *With a shite football team.*

Almost as popular on the Gallowgate End has become a slightly newer innovation which is a rehash of The Beatles *Yellow Submarine*. Reid is unfortunately famous for his - how shall we say - somewhat simian appearance, and this has been gleefully embraced by the Newcastle supporters - an exercise made more appropriate not to say harmonious given the Geordie pronunciation of "head", which becomes "heid" in the local dialect and therefore rhymes almost exactly with Reid. An anatomical observation of which the most studious anthropologist would be proud thus gives us....

> *In a town called Sunderland,*
> *Lives a ma-a-an with monkey's heid,*
> *And his name is Peter Reid,*
> *And his na-a-ame is Peter Reid*
>
> *Oh, Peter Reid's got a fucking monkey's heid,*
> *A fucking monkey's heid,*
> *A fucking monkey's heid,*
> *Peter Reid's got a fucking monkey's heid*
> *A fucking monkey's heid....etc*

....the advent of this has also tended to see line three of *Cheer Up Peter Reid* become *"a monkey-faced bastard"*, rather than the initially popular lyric as given above. Moving tactfully on from such Reid-baiting activities, it's time to look at a few player-related chants. The most substantial of these is undoubtedly the rewrite of *Lola*, initially by The Kinks, but now a hymnal extolling the virtues of David Ginola....

> *Now, we are the world's most passionate fans,*
> *And we look real cool 'cos the Geordies rule,*
> *With Ginola, la, la, la, Ginola, he'll score us a goal-a.*
>
> *She walked up to me and she asked me to dance,*
> *I said "Fuck off Mackem, I'm from France,*
> *Me name is Ginola, la, la, la Ginola, la, la, la Ginola.*

....a sterling effort, and one which would certainly top this particular category (if anyone was sufficiently cretinous to carry out any sort of survey) were it not for the far more impressive song which has been devised for the purpose of deifying Belgian defender Philippe Albert. Cast your minds back to 1971, when Jackie Lee saw fit to record the *Rupert The Bear* song, and you will be able to make some sense of the following (*cf* Larne)....

> *Philippe, Philippe Albert,*
> *Everyone knows his name!*

Onto songs of a more traditional style, and the almost obligatory *Macnamara's Band* variant which, in this case, dates back to 1968/69....

> *They call us Newcastle United,*
> *The best team in the land,*
> *And here's to Joe Harvey,*
> *With the Fairs Cup in his hand,*
> *We're better than Glasgow Rangers,*
> *We're better than Celtic too,*
> *And if you don't support us,*
> *You must be a Sunderland jew.*
> *Joe, Joe, Joe Harvey, Joe, Joe, Joe Harvey!*

One can only imagine that Joe Harvey (featuring in the chanted additional last line) must have played a prominent role in United's 6-2 aggregate win over Ujpest Dozsa!

Then a small taste of mystic Humberside can be found up on the Tyne, by way of a suitably amended performance of the Scunthorpe United "spelling" song....

154

With an N and an E and wubble-U, C,
An A and an S and a T, L, E,
A U, N, I and a T, E, D,
Newcastle United - F C!

With yet further alterations, this then becomes a Sunderland favourite (see next section for details).

To finish, a rather succinct chant which typifies the way in which Newcastle have rocketed from struggling underachievers to being one of the biggest clubs in the land almost overnight. It wasn't so very long ago that crowds of under ten thousand were rattling around St James' Park, and included in this throng were obviously a number of die hards who watched even in the very bleakest of times. Now, with everything about the club being tuned for success and a 30,000 capacity ground packed to the rafters for every game, there's just a hint of bitterness towards the new wave of supporters from the old brigade, and every now and then a plaintive cry goes up from the Gallowgate, directed at the newcomers in the refurbished Leazes End. The inestimable *Bread Of Heaven* is once again the tune for....

Where were you when we were shite?
Where were you when we were shite?
Where were you, where were you,
Where were you when we were shite?

Sunderland

Not much doubt as to which has been the most well know Sunderland song over the last couple of years as *Cheer Up Peter Reid* has swept the country from Berwick to Bournemouth with virtually everyone coming up with their own version. The first time that the song appeared in a footballing context was towards the end of the 1995/6 season, with Sunderland poised to clinch promotion from Division One. Recorded by a group of Sunderland supporters under the name of Simply Red & White, it reached 41 in the national charts, shifted 10,000 copies during its first week in the shops, and outsold Oasis in record shops on Wearside. The tune is taken from an original song called *Daydream Believer* - and don't think it entirely escaped the attention of Newcastle fans that it was first performed by The Monkees (strangely appropriate, perhaps?). Anyway, cheap jibes aside, the words to the version as laid down on vinyl are....

Oh I could fly without wings, on the back of Reidy's kings,
At three o'clock I'm happy as can be,
'cos the good times they are here,
And the Premiership is near,
So watch out world as all of Roker sings....

Cheer up Peter Reid,
Oh what can it mean,
To be a Sunderland supporter,
To be top of the league.

We once thought of you, as a scouser dressed in blue,
Now you're red and white through and through,
We had all dreamt of the day, when a saviour would come our way,
And now we know our dreams are coming true

The initial concept for the song came out of the terrace version of the chorus, which was started because, well, because Peter Reid just looks so bloody miserable most of the time. Now, of course, it has gone onto be one of the most widely used tunes in the history of the game and, along with *Three Lions*, very much helped to make 1996 the year that football supporters really rediscovered their voices.

Before *Cheer Up...*, Sunderland were probably best known for one of the first wave of songs that graduated to football having initially had nothing to do with the game whatsoever. Elvis Presley's *Can't Help Falling In Love* was the real theme song of the Fulwell End from the late 1980's, and it persists to the present day. As with all such instances of songs being imported from the real world, the words remain as per the original....

Take my hand, take my whole life too,
For I can't help falling in love with you.

Like a river flows,
Surely to the sea,
Darling so it goes,
Some things are meant to be.

Wise men say, only fools rush in,
But I can't help falling in love with you.
SUNDERLAND! SUNDERLAND!

Throughout the history of the game, any number of songs have come into existence for the purpose of recording some particularly triumphant moment for posterity - Manchester United and their European triumphs, Peterborough United and the F A Cup run that dates from their non-league days, and Doncaster

Rovers sticking five past Scunthorpe. All of these, however, pale into insignificance when set alongside the monumental effort from Roker Park which tells the story of how Sunderland went up via the play-offs at the end of the 1989/90 season, beating Newcastle in the semi final, then losing to Swindon at Wembley but still ultimately going up after the Wiltshire team's demotion for having made irregular payments to players. Incidentally, Sunderland's promotion wasn't confirmed until June 13th, which must be the latest date on which any club has finally secured elevation from one division to another. The song loses some of its dignity by having somewhat boringly pinched the *Blaydon Races* tune (the bit from the verses, anyway), but that apart, it is really rather splendid....

We went to Wembley Stadium on the twenty eight of May,
Heading for the play-offs, Swindon Town to play,
We didn't win a trophy and we didn't win a cup,
But what really riles the Geordies is we lost and still went up

It started twelve days earlier at St James' Park,
We were soaking, we were freezing, but wasn't it a laugh,
The Geordies made some noise that night, they really made a din,
But you should have heard the Leazes End when Marco's goal went in.

They came on from the Milburn Stand, the Gallowgate the same,
Dancing round like arseholes as they tried to stop the game,
The got stopped on the halfway line by all the boys in blue,
We had just one complaint that night, they should've let them through!

The Mackems finished under us, the play-offs are all wrong,
We were six points ahead of them, the Geordies moaned along,
The tears they flowed into their "broon", oh how the Geordies cried,
But I'll never forget that magic night Newcastle fucking died.

This basically tells the story of the second leg of the play-off semi final, after the first game had finished goalless at Roker. Eric Gates and Marco Gabbiadini gave Sunderland a 2-0 lead at St James' Park which prompted a spectacular pitch invasion by the Newcastle supporters. Pouring on from all corners of the ground, they were determined to either get the game abandoned, get to visiting Mackems in the Leazes End or ideally both, but they were stopped by a line of policemen who hastily took up position across the middle of the pitch. The game was eventually allowed to continue, the scoreline remained unchanged to the final whistle, and Sunderland went onto Wembley and eventually their controversial promotion. Newcastle were not best pleased.

With the brooding dislike of all things Geordie still to the fore, there is next an interesting example of how a song can be updated to keep it current over the passing seasons. The first example of this Sunderland song, to the tune of

Bless 'em All, must have first served the Fulwell regulars in the early 1970's, as the players named were all disporting themselves in the black and white of Newcastle at that time....

> *Fuck 'em all, fuck 'em all,*
> *John Tudor, MacDonald, McFaul,*
> *We'll never be mastered,*
> *By those black and white bastards,*
> *'cos Sunderland's the best of 'em all.*

By the time that the start of the 1996/7 season came around, this song of a twenty year vintage had been updated to....

> *Fuck 'em all, fuck 'em all,*
> *Ferdinand, Shearer and all.....*

....and presumably there were a number of similar efforts during the intervening years which included Newcastle players of the 1980's.

As if it were not enough for Roker park to have seen the first stirrings of *Daydream Believer*, a case can be made for another of the games now immensely popular themes having made its debut on the Fulwell End. The lyric-less *Triumphal March* from Aida which is now "lah'd" at grounds up and down the country, usually to the accompaniment of swirling scarves, was definitely a Sunderland pastime towards the end of the 1990/91 season which is certainly the earliest reported sighting of this particular phenomenon.

In order that the Sunderland section might finish on what I am sure their supporters would consider a thoroughly worthy sentiment, it is now time to recall that the Mackems are partial to an occasional performance of Newcastle's lexicographic effort. For the most part exactly the same as the Tyneside version, your attention should be drawn to the small but oh so lovingly crafted alteration to the closing phrase which gives the whole thing some added piquancy....

> *With an N and an E and a wubble-U, C,*
> *An A and an S and a T, L, E,*
> *A U, N, I and a T, E, D,*
> *Newcastle United - FUCK OFF!*

Section Nine

The North West

Blackburn Rovers

Bolton Wanderers

Burnley

Everton

Liverpool

Manchester City

Manchester United

Oldham Athletic

Preston North End

Stockport County

Wigan Athletic

The North West

The most notable factor about the songs from Greater Manchester and Merseyside has been that there are so many tunes which are shared by two or more clubs in the area. Even the otherwise irreconcilable supporters of Liverpool and Everton, and Manchester United and Manchester City, have a good deal of common ground when it comes to the songs that they sing, and a similar degree of melodic interbreeding is also apparent further down the Football League.

The singularly most popular song in the region must be *The Wild Rover*, which makes an appearance at a good half a dozen different clubs. This, it seems reasonable to say, is probably as a result of the song first having been imported to these shores by the vast number of Irish immigrants who descended on Manchester during the last century and, as they spread more widely across the region, so the song went with them until it was established throughout the length and breadth of Lancashire and beyond. It is fair to say that no other song has become quite so synonymous with one area as has this particular ballad, although there are other tunes which are more widespread when the country is looked at as a whole (*Three Lions*, for instance!).

Apart from the efforts of Manchester City, and one or two of the excursions into television-related tomfoolery at Wigan, the songs from the North West all seem to be rather serious, without the regular descents in to abject silliness which feature elsewhere. It must therefore be assumed that the game is viewed as a matter of the utmost gravity in the region - not something that can be taken too lightly or ever reduced to the status of a mere joke, with even the renowned Scouse wit from Anfield only being evident in a couple of silly chants based on players' names. This is illustrated no more clearly than by the desperate, almost psychotic hatred of Blackburn Rovers by the supporters of Burnley, which is one of a very few English rivalries which comes close to the loathing which exists between Glasgow's Old Firm - although Rovers' supporters have enjoyed the luxury of looking down on their neighbours from loftier divisions for long enough for the feelings at Ewood to have paled a little over recent years. Unfortunately, the two teams seem destined never to meet in league football again, which is a shame, as I for one would like a chance to experience the atmosphere at a Burnley v Blackburn game at first hand - I imagine it would probably be a touch lively!

160

Blackburn Rovers

As good a starting point as any for this tour of the North West, as Rovers are - or certainly were - one of the foremost exponents of that most popular of local themes, *The Wild Rover*. It can only be imagined that this essentially Irish tune was brought over from the Emerald Isle by the many Irish immigrants who flocked to Manchester in the 19th century, and that from there, it spread throughout the region as the Irish community became more widely dissipated in their search for employment. Whatever the reason, the song is now firmly woven into the fabric of the area's footballing heritage, and the Ewood Park version is a fine example....

> *There's an alehouse in Burnley I used to frequent,*
> *I met Chrissy Waddle, his money all spent,*
> *He asked me to play and I answered him 'Nay',*
> *'cos I'll hate Burnley bastards 'til my dying day.*
>
> > *And it's no, nay, never - no, nay, never no more,*
> > *Will we play Burnley bastards, no never, no more.*
>
> *Now I've followed the Rovers for many a year,*
> *And I've spent all my money on football and beer,*
> *But I've one aim in life, before I am gone,*
> *That's to follow the Rovers in Division One.*
>
> > *And it's no, nay, never - no, nay, never no more,*
> > *Will we play Burnley bastards, no never, no more.*
>
> *Now ten years later, our team reign supreme,*
> *The league and the cup have been won by our team,*
> *And as for Chris Waddle, he's now on our side,*
> *Because he sweeps the rubbish on our Riverside,*
>
> > *And it's no, nay, never - no, nay, never no more,*
> > *Will we play Burnley bastards, no never, no more.*

The numerous mentions of Burnley and their current manager reflect the intense rivalry which exists between the two clubs (in this example it's newly installed boss Chris Waddle who can be found sweeping the Riverside, which was the huge partially terraced stand to the right of the away end at the pre-Jack Walker Ewood Park). Although the rivalry has barely had a chance to manifest itself on the pitch in recent years, with Rovers buying their place in football's elite while Burnley grub about in the lower divisions, the feeling between the two sets of supporters seems to run as deep as ever. The nadir for

The Clarets was the years between 1985 and 1992, when they found themselves in the Fourth Division - a state of affairs so pleasing for the Rovers supporters that it simply had to be celebrated in song. *There's A Tavern In The Town*, so beloved of Nottingham Forest supporters, was deemed to be the ideal starting point, and thus we have....

> *There's a circus in the town, in the town!*
> *Brian Miller is the clown, is the clown!*
> *And Burnley bastards are in Division Four,*
> *Where we won't see them any more, any more!*

Miller was one of four managers who oversaw Burnley during their time in the basement - Tommy Cavanagh, Jimmy Mullen or Frank Casper could equally have found themselves designated as clown prince in this song.

Away from matters of local pride, the embodiment of the new Walker-backed Rovers of the 1990's was undoubtedly Alan Shearer, whose goals went a long way towards seeing the team crowned Premiership champions in 1994/5. Each and every one of his thirty four strikes throughout this season would prompt the following from the Blackburn supporters - an already popular song, but one which became particularly associated with the ex-Southampton striker during his time in the blue and white halves....

> *There's only one Alan Shearer,*
> *There's only one Alan Shearer,*
> *Walking along, singing a song,*
> *Walking in a Shearer wonderland.*

This is a typically modern rendition of a song which first saw the light of day in a footballing context at far less salubrious surroundings - the likes of Underhill and Elm Park (*cf* Barnet and Reading). It has since gone on to eulogise the talents of all manner of other players, and is now standard fare for the less inventive supporters at many clubs.

The other chant synonymous with at least the early years of the Walker reign at Ewood was inspired by Harry Enfield's 1988 *Loadsamoney* record. Initially, this was more commonly used by the notoriously wealthy supporters at White Hart Lane, who would wave the "wads" at any stereotypically impoverished Northerners that they encountered. The infusion of cash on the banks of the River Darwen, however, meant that Rovers supporters could chant *"Loads and loadsa money"* at the supporters of anyone at all - impoverished Northerners and wealthy southerners alike - all of whom were paupers when compared to the vast fortunes that Blackburn now had at their disposal.

Recalling the less opulent days of the early 1980's, there is a song which records the events of the last day of the 1981/2 - a day which Rovers started as favourites to clinch promotion to the (then) First Division. Results, however, went against them - notably a win by Swansea City over Preston North End that sent the Swans up and ensured that Rovers wouldn't see the promised land for the best part of another decade. *John Brown's Body/Glory Glory Hallelujah* was the tune to a peculiar lament for the way in which things turned out....

> *On that famous Saturday, the second day of May,*
> *We met a bunch of Swansea fans, on the motorway,*
> *We said we'd win promotion and we said we'd win the cup,*
> *But on that famous Saturday, Preston fucked it up!*
> *Na na na n-na na na na,*
> *Na na na n-na na na.*

And that is rather disappointingly that. For a team at the forefront of the game for some five years or so - and one with an illustrious history to boot, a more impressive collection might reasonably have been expected, and perhaps Sir Jack should make his next priority the purchase of some rather more innovative fans from one of the many Nationwide League clubs who can justifiably claim to put their loftier counterparts in the Kidder Street stand to shame when it comes to singing.

Bolton Wanderers

A not inconsiderable revelation from the North West in that it appears that the repertoire of Bolton songs might actually extend to something beyond the collection of imbecilic Munich chants which is generally perceived as being the extent of the Wanderers' song book. For the most part, though, Bolton supporters *do* spend their entire lives abusing Manchester United by way of any number of songs based around the 1958 air disaster. Ably lead by the club's fanzines, Whites' supporters embraced the whole Munich episode with glee, virtually to the exclusion of any songs which may have actually been about their own club - until one of the more culpable fanzines *(Here We Go Again)* printed the words to a song known as *Look Who's Coming Up The Hill, Boys*. Initially having appeared in print at some point during the early nineties, the lyrics first made it onto the terraces at an away game with Wigan Athletic during 92/3, some twenty five years or so after it had first become popular (and subsequently faded from use). The tune, unfortunately, rather defies description, and doesn't really tie in with any more well known ditties, nonetheless, the words are as follows....

Look who's coming up the hill, boys
The Wanderers are coming up the hill, boys
They all laugh at us,
They all mock us
The say our days are numbered.
Born to be a Wanderer,
Victorious are we,
So you'd better hurry up,
'coz we're going to win the cup,
We're the pride of Division Three! Two! One!
Victorious and Glorious
We took the Stretford End
Between the four of us,
Glory be to God that there ain't no more of us,
'coz the Lever End took the lot.

....rather an impressive effort, it must be said, and one which shares the same rather hazy history as does this next (considerably shorter) contribution. To a tune as inexplicable as that of *Look Who's Coming Up The Hill*, we have....

The world is a football, that goes round and round,
For ever and ever, where football is found!

This rather odd affair is made up of two lines of a much longer song (details of which have not been forthcoming) which originally used to be played over the tannoy at Sealand Road - the home of Chester City before the club moved to the Deva Stadium. How and why the song made the short journey up the A56 has remained a complete mystery.

Of a far more straightforward derivation came the chant *"Can we play you every week?"* (to the *Bread Of Heaven* tune) which was sung by the Bolton supporters during the course of their 4-1 win at Middlesbrough in mid-February 1996. The win represented only Wanderers' fourth three point haul of the season (and the first away from home), and the inference is obviously that Bolton would have had a far more successful season had they been able to play Boro more often!

A chant almost entirely exclusive to the North West of England - and one which became particularly associated with Bolton during the latter part of the 1980's is the splendidly silly effort....

Here we go again,
Bobbing up and down like this,
Ooooooooooh.....
Here we go again,
Bobbing up and down like this.....

Another of the many "repetition" songs, this, but one which is used to best effect on terracing and has therefore suffered more than most with the arrival of the seats. The initial *"Here we go again"* line closely resembles the tune of *"we shall not be moved"*, but thereafter it descends into its own peculiar rhythm. Needless to say the *"bobbing up and down like this"* bit has associated actions which can be either frenzied leaping about, or the more lyrically accurate "bob" with hands by the sides and no more than a gentle bend at the knees. In addition to the few efforts detailed above, there is one chant which can always be guaranteed an airing at every Bolton match - the *Juantanamera* derivation which is *"Hate Man. United, We only hate Man United, Hate Man Uniiiited, We only hate Man United"* - as apt and succinct an illustration of the overriding emotion which consumes all Wanderers supporters as can be imagined, and one of the intangible parts of Burnden Park which will certainly be woven into the fabric of the new Reebok Stadium when Bolton take up residence in 1997.

Burnley

Another famous old club with a rich heritage of which a not insubstantial part is an almost insanely virulent hatred of Blackburn Rovers. It would seem that this is no more than a product of the two clubs being situated so closely together - a local rivalry of the most straightforward fashion - but what sets the mutual loathing apart from other similar instances is that it has remained so intense while the two teams have spent so much time in different divisions. It's hard to recall exactly when Burnley and Rovers last crossed swords in pursuit of league points (1982/83 in Division Two, at a guess), but at Turf Moor at least, there has remained only one real enemy over the intervening fifteen years. The main song which is used to put over the feelings reserved for Rovers is, predictably enough, the Burnley interpretation of *The Wild Rover*. Broadly similar to the Rovers version, it gives probably the best illustration yet of how one song can be altered to suit the common needs of two otherwise utterly irreconcilable sets of supporters....

> *There once was an alehouse I used to frequent,*
> *I saw Kenny Dalglish, his money was spent,*
> *He asked me a question, I answered him "Nay",*
> *I said "Rubbish like yours we can beat any day"*
>
> *And it's no, nay, never - no nay never no more,*
> *Will we play Bastard Rovers, no never, no more.*

Ewood Park is now empty, it's getting knocked down,
Bastard Rovers play their games on a piece of waste ground,
With Dalglish on the touchline - say, something's not right,
There's far more players than supporters in sight.

And it's no, nay, never - no nay never no more,
Will we play Bastard Rovers, no never, no more.

Now five years have passed and Burnley reign supreme,
The league and the cup will be won by our team,
Bastard Rovers are bankrupt and they've long since died,
And down Ken Dalglish sweeps Burnley's Long Side.

And it's no, nay, never - no nay never no more,
Will we play Bastard Rovers, no never, no more.

The fate of the respective managers in the two versions provides the most direct link, with the Rovers boss finding him self clearing up on the Long Side terrace at Turf Moor, while his Burnley counterpart is destined for a similar job but this time on the old Riverside Stand at Ewood. Rovers' home would seem to be in the most urgent need of a bit of spit and polish, if the words to this next song are to be taken literally....

One man went to shit, went to shit on Ewood,
One man and his dog - Spot! - went to shit on Ewood,
Two men and their dog, went to shit on Ewood,
Two men and their dog - Spot! - went to shit on Ewood....

....and, it is imagined, so it goes on until a complete complement of eleven men (not forgetting Spot the dog) are "shitting on Ewood". This is, of course, based on *One Man Went To Mow*, of which Chelsea are probably the leading exponents.

Appearing for once outside its more usual context in which it celebrates some sort of unfortunate event which has befallen either local rivals or an unpopular figure (*cf* Bristol City and Derby County), *What Shall We Do With A Drunken Sailor* was wont to echo up and down the Long Side - predominantly in the late 1970's after it had been heard on an episode of Blue Peter in which the presenters were demonstrating hornpipe dancing, if our contributor is to be believed!

We hate Blackburn Bastard Rovers,
We hate Blackburn Bastard Rovers,
We hate Blackburn Bastard Rovers,
We hate Bastard Rovers.
Aye-oh we are Burnley,

Aye-oh we are Burnley,
Aye-oh we are Burnley,
We hate Bastard Rovers.

This is another song which makes much of the fact that the supporters of either of the two teams involved in this long standing Lancastrian rivalry refer to the other club and its followers simply as "bastards". If it were needed, this next song provides even more evidence of this....

Walking down the Brunshaw Road,
Are Clarets by the score,
Marching off to Ewood Park,
Marching off to war.
The Bastards they were everywhere,
In Bastard blue and white,
But they ran like fuck when we tried to ruck,
Too fucking scared to fight.
Run, run, Bastards, run,
Show you're full of fear,
Run, run, Bastards run,
The Burnley boys are here!

This is a real rarity in English football, in that it takes the tune of *We're No Awa' To Bide Awa'*, which in its original form is the basis for one of Glasgow Rangers most famous songs *"As I was walking down Copland Road"*. The only other ground at which this makes an appearance is Rugby Park, Kilmarnock, so how it ever came to feature on the Long Side is a bit of a mystery. The only possible link may be that there has long been a Linfield supporters club branch in the North West known as the Lancashire True Blues, and the connections between Linfield and Rangers are well known (both clubs being staunchly protestant and loyalist). It's feasible, then, that Rangers songs could quite plausibly have made an appearance in Lancashire, although the Lancs True Blues always used to be based in Blackburn which makes any subsequent Burnley involvement seem rather unlikely! The Brunshaw Road, incidently, runs alongside the Bob Lord Stand at Turf Moor.

Turning away from the less than friendly relationship that exists between Burnley and Blackburn, its time for a brief look at a couple of songs which have been used to acclaim some favourite players in the claret and blue. As already mentioned, Kurt Nogan's stint at Turf Moor saw what had already become his own personal theme tune - the *No Limits* adaptation of his surname - adopted on the Long Side (the song following him North from the Goldstone Ground). A more edifying chant came out of the loan spell which goalkeeper Andrew Marriot spent at Turf Moor during the early 1990's. Taking his place in the Burnley line up just after the Rugby Union World Cup, it was not too surprising when *"Swing low, sweet Marriot, coming for to carry me home"* became the vogue. A decade or so earlier, another goalkeeper, Roger Hansbury was afforded an entirely unique song which had much to do with the fact that he returned to the English game with Burnley after spending some time playing in Hong Kong. Earnest students of this book will by now have noted that I am more than a little impressed with songs that have their roots in children's television programmes, and Hansbury - superbly - found himself regaled with a particularly noble effort: *"Hong Kong Hansbury, number one super guy; Hong Kong Hansbury, quicker than the human eye"* - oh that the Burnley fans had remembered more than just these two lines from the theme to the fine cartoon *Hong Kong Phooey*!

Finally, a bit of a dance, although not one which Burnley can claim as their own. Apparently, it was not only the supporters of Hull City who careered dangerously up and down the terraces of the late 1980's while singing bits out of Malcolm Maclaren's entirely silly *Double Dutch* song - Burnley's fans also enjoyed a bit of boisterousness to the *"B-bum bah bah, b-bum bah bah, b-bum bah bah, b-bum bah bah"* bit, but apparently they managed to do so without upsetting any Millwall supporters!

Everton

A rather dated collection of songs from Goodison, but one which contains five unique arrangements - probably more than appear at any other single club. Quite why this should be the case is not certain, but it's a fair bet that the historic rivalry with Liverpool - the subject of most of the songs - has been the catalyst behind most of the Evertonian creativity. Witness this first particularly stirring effort, which in part bears some resemblance to *The Halls of Montezuma*, but which is predominantly exclusive to those who used to stand on the Gwladys Street terraces....

> *We hate Bill Shankley, we hate St John,*
> *But most of all we hate Big Ron,*
> *And we'll hang the Kopites one by one,*
> *On the banks of the royal blue Mersey.*
> *To hell with Liverpool and Rangers too,*
> *We'll throw them all in the Mersey,*
> *And we'll fight, fight, fight with all our might,*
> *For the lads in the royal blue jerseys.*

Interesting to note the Rangers reference in the fifth line, which is a legacy from the days when there was a religious as well as footballing divide on Merseyside. Everton were the predominantly Catholic club, and Liverpool Protestant - hence the dislike of Rangers who have always been the epitomy of anti-Catholic sentiment in footballing circles. "Big Ron" can only have been Liverpool legend Ron Yeats, and "St John" is obviously Ian of that ilk.

From a similar era - the 1960's - comes this next effort, which is a brief celebration of the win over Sheffield Wednesday that secured the F A Cup in the same year as England's World Cup triumph. The tune, rather contrary to the Catholic connections of the club, is very similar to that of *The Sash My Father Wore*, which is one of the leading loyalist songs at Ibrox....

> *It was on a Saturday afternoon,*
> *In the merry month of May,*
> *That we all went to Wembley,*
> *To see the Toffees play,*
> *There was Alex Young and Gabriel,*
> *And we played in royal blue,*
> *We gave the Wednesday two goals start,*
> *And still beat them three-two.*

Some twenty years or so later, we find a song which must have been conceived towards the end of the 1980's, as it refers to Liverpool's league and cup double of 1986 and to a game which must have taken place early in Kenny Dalglish's reign at Anfield (from 1985 onwards). Evidently, one of Dalglish's first managerial encounters with Everton ended in defeat, and Reds' supporters were calling for his head - but all was forgiven when the double was landed....

> *There was a famous derby game,*
> *Some four years ago,*
> *When all the Kop were chanting,*
> *"Kenny, Kenny, you must go"*
> *But now you've done the double,*
> *And Kenny is your pride,*
> *You two-faced Liverpool bastards,*
> *You're the shit of Merseyside!*

The tune to this one would seem to be something along the lines of *Macnamara's Band*, but a case can also be made for *Glory, Glory Hallelujah* to fit the bill - so take your pick really!

Back to the sixties again for this next one - a somewhat lengthier effort which is once again centred around attitudes towards the red half of the city. The now standard Evertonian confusion once more prevails about which tune the song actually takes, with *(If You Ever Go) Across The Sea To Ireland* being the first suggestion, but with the whole thing having more than a passing similarity to the structure of the Liverpool song, *Red River Valley* (colloquially known as *Poor Scouser Tommy* and which, on reflection, might well be exactly the same as *Across The Sea To Ireland* anyway!)

> *Now there's a team across the park at Anfield,*
> *Whose players have no ideas at all (ideas at all),*
> *Now they'd be better off playing snakes and ladders,*
> *It's a shame to let them use a brand new ball (a brand new ball)*
>
> *If you ever go across the park to Anfield,*
> *If it's only to see the Toffees play (the Toffees play),*
> *Be sure to take your macintosh and wellies,*
> *Unless your liable to float away (to float away)*
>
> *Now those Kopites will piss on you in the morning,*
> *Those Kopites will piss on you any time of day (time of day),*
> *For those Kopites don't go to see good football,*
> *They only go to swear and drink bad beer (and drink bad beer).*

The last two sections both make reference to that delightful Anfield tradition of simply not bothering to move from your spot on the Kop if you wanted to go to the toilet - it was simply a case of *Dicks Out!* and off you go!

Now, away from Goodison's array of unique songs to one which has seen service at the majority of other grounds throughout the country over the years. Simple substitution of another club's name is all that is required to make *You Are My Sunshine* appropriate to a different venue, but the song was particularly popular at Everton during the halcyon days of the mid 1980's - hence its inclusion in this section....

> *You are my Everton,*
> *My only Everton,*
> *You make me happy,*
> *When skies are grey,*
> *You'll never know just*
> *How much I love you,*
> *Until you've taken my Everton away.*

....for good measure, the whole thing was then usually "lah'd" all the way through, although such behaviour was occasionally cut short at other grounds after just two lines - the whole thing then being brought to a climax with a loud *"ooooaaarghhhhff!"* shout, similar to those which round off *Annie's Song* at Bramall Lane and *Just One Of Those Songs* at Old Trafford.

Mention of Manchester United brings us to the Gwladys Street's appreciation of United's erstwhile captain, Bryan Robson. Games between the two clubs -

particularly those at Goodison - always produced an electric atmosphere, and rarely would such an encounter pass without at least a couple of renditions of....

> *This old man, he told me,*
> *Bryan Robson's got VD,*
> *With a nick nack paddy whack,*
> *Give a dog a bone,*
> *Man United fuck off home!*

For such a well known and easily adaptable tune, it is perhaps surprising that *Nick Nack Paddy Whack* has only really seen the light of day at relatively few clubs - Bournemouth and Lincoln City being the other venues at which it has been heard (with the Dean Court version also aimed at Man United!)

To finish off, the last of the quintet of Everton songs which have no real parallel anywhere else - a somewhat qualified assertion in the case of the previous four, but a cast iron certainty when it comes to this last one. A contemporary of the Sheffield Wednesday F A Cup Final song from 1966, this is a truly bizarre homily to centre forward Fred Pickering who endeared himself to the Everton faithful by averaging better than a goal every other game during his three year stint at Goodison. With inspiration somewhat harder to come by on the blue side of Stanley Park (whereas top pop tunes of the day were finding themselves adopted on the Kop at Anfield), Fred had to make do with the theme tune to *The Beverley Hillbillies* as the tune for his particular song....

> *Now come listen to a story about a man called Fred,*
> *He could score goals with his feet and his head,*
> *Then one day when playing against the 'pool,*
> *He slipped past Yeats and scored one so cool,*
> *- Goal, that is, worth two points!*
> *When that goal went in all the Kop was in despair,*
> *And all the Evertonians threw their hats in the air,*
> *Even John Moores shouted out with glee,*
> *Freddy Pick - you're the man for me,*
> *Fred - hail is the king of E F C!*

It's difficult to imagine anything of this nature actually being sung on the terraces, but it's no less strange than a good many of the other offerings in this book, so perhaps Mr Pickering did actually hear this one as he cavorted about on the Goodison turf. Anyway, safe in the knowledge that nothing which the present day Everton supporters come up with will ever be able to rival the Freddy Pickering song for sheer unsingability, or the *Royal Blue Mersey* one for passion, it's time to trek the few hundred yards or so across Stanley Park to sample the fare at Anfield....

Liverpool

Being members of the fairly select group of clubs, all of whom have a particularly well known song associated with them, Liverpool's entry can only really start in one way - with the lyrics to *You'll Never Walk Alone*. First adopted on the Kop after the release of the Gerry and the Pacemakers original in 1963, the song has gone on to become utterly synonymous with the club - particularly in the wake of the Hillsborough disaster, when it was re-recorded and released as a fund raiser for the victims of the tragedy. The words as sung on the terraces are a verbatim performance of the song which reached number one in the charts on two separate occasions, twenty two years apart....

> *As you walk through the storm,*
> *Hold your head up high,*
> *And don't be afraid of the dark,*
> *At the end of the storm,*
> *Is a golden sky,*
> *And the sweet silver song of the lark,*
> *Walk on through the wind,*
> *Walk on through the rain,*
> *Though your dreams be tossed and blown,*
> *Walk on, walk on,*
> *With hope in your hearts,*
> *And you'll never walk alone,*
> *You'll never walk alone.*

Performances of the whole thing as detailed above have become increasingly rare with the passage of time, but this has been counteracted by a tendency for the last four lines to be repeated several times, occasionally punctuated with a pair of claps between each pair of syllables (to give a *"You'll ne-(clap, clap)-ver walk-(clap, clap) a-lone"* sort of effect) which, as with many other songs that weren't initially conceived for the printed page, sounds an awful lot better than it looks!

However, in spite of the popularity and international fame of *You'll Never Walk Alone*, Liverpool are by no means a one song club. Another far longer effort is equally likely to be heard wherever the Reds are playing and, in my humble opinion, this second song is at least the equal to its more famous counterpart. Unfortunately, the complete words do not appear to be all that widely known, and performances tend to stumble along in a bit of a subdued fashion until they get to the fifth section, the lyrics to which must have reached a far wider audience, as this is the bit that can always be heard loud and clear. The song, generally known as *Poor Scouser Tommy* takes the tune of *Red River Valley* which, as mused upon in the Everton section, may or may not be exactly the same as *(If You Ever Go) Across The Sea To Ireland* - this second option seeming more and more plausible with every passing day given that the song is of traditional Liverpudlian extraction, with all the Irish links that particular sort of heritage entails. If anyone is sufficiently interested to establish exactly what the tune is, it was recorded by Billy Maher, and can be found (amongst other places) on a compilation called *You'll Never Walk Alone* (catalogue number GAFFER 4). Anyway, enough idle banter and on with the matter in hand....

Let me tell you the story of a poor boy,
Who was sent far away from his home,
To fight for his King and his country,
And also for the old folks back home.

They put him in a higher division,
Sent him off to a far foreign land,
Where the flies swarm around in their thousands,
And there's nothing to see but the sand.

The battle it started next morning,
Under the Arabian sun,
So remember that poor scouser, Tommy,
Who was shot by an old Nazi gun.

As he lay on the battlefield dying (dying, dying),
With the blood gushing out of his head,
As he lay on the battlefield dying (dying, dying),
These are the last words he said:

Oh I am a Liverpudlian,
From the Spion Kop,
I like to sing, I like to shout,
I go there quite a lot,
I support a team that play in red,
A team that you all know,
A team that we call Liverpool,
To glory we will go.

We've won the league, we've won the cup,
We've been to Europe too,
We played the Toffees for a laugh,
And left them feeling blue
One, two - one, two, three,
One, two, three, four - FIVE-NIL!

Now, this really is a quality song, and I'm surprised that Leeds United are the only other club to have crafted their own (substantially shorter) version. For what it's worth, the song must be of considerably more recent vintage than might seem to be the case, as the term "Nazi" was only coined in or around 1930 (historical and/or etymological pedants please direct all queries on this point to the publishers of the Oxford English Dictionary - thank you!)

Next, a far more succinct song than either of the two preceding epics, and one which shares *Show Me The Way To Go Home* as its inspiration with a more expansive Tottenham version....

Show them the way to go home,
They're tired and they want to go to bed,
'cos they're only half a football team,
Compared to the boys in Red....

....and there it ends, awkwardly in mid air and desperate for a couple of additional lines to finish it off - but none were forthcoming.

At this juncture, it might be prudent to embark on one of my occasional historical interludes - this time about the derivation of the term "kop" (*cf* Birmingham City, of all people). Obviously, this is the name given to the famous terrace at Anfield on which Liverpool's most passionate and vocal supporters used to stand, but what is not generally such common knowledge is that it was Arsenal's original Manor Ground (in Plumstead, south of the river) where the first genuine kop was built. In essence, this was basically a bank of terracing - thrown up to cover a huge sewage outfall pipe - which used to accommodate crowds made up of a disproportionately high number of military men (attached to the Royal Arsenal munitions works from which the club took its name). This terrace was erected during 1904 - four years after the Boer War at which a particularly messy encounter was fought on a hill called Spion Kop in Natal. With many veterans of the South African campaign now regulars at the Manor Ground, the new terrace swiftly became nicknamed the Spion Kop - no doubt due to its resemblance to the hill of the same name. The Liverpool connection was not to come about until two years later when, after the opening of a redeveloped Anfield which included the forerunner to the famous terrace, a local sportswriter suggested that the new open bank should be officially called the Spion Kop as a memorial to the many Liverpudlian soldiers who had died during the battle six years previously - and thus a famous name was added to football's vocabulary.

And now (with grateful acknowledgements to Simon Inglis!) back to more relevant themes. Over the years, the Liverpool crowds have seen more than their fair share of quality players disporting themselves in red shirts, but - in contrast to the vast majority of other clubs - none of these players have been celebrated with any songs of real note. It's only in comparatively recent times that individuals have been singled out for a bit of vocal deification, with Stig

Inge Bjornebye, Steve Macmanaman, Jason McAteer and Phil Babb all having their names immortalized in song. First to the Norwegian defender, who has been afforded that most esteemed of accolades in that an old glam rock classic was dusted off in his honour. Gary Glitter's *I'm The Leader Of The Gang (I Am)* became (in part) *"Bjornebye in our gang, our gang, our gang, Bjornebye in our gang - oh yeah!"* which is probably a more worthy effort than was the introduction of Jason McAteer's name into Los Del Rios' now omnipresent *Macarena* tune....*"He runs down the wing and his name is McAteer, he runs down the wing and his name is McAteer, he runs down the wing and his name is McAteer -woooooah, McAteer!"* One of the original Liverpool Spice Boys is no doubt less impressed with a similar sort of thing now popular at Old Trafford (*cf* Manchester United). Next, the splendidly named Macmanaman, who must have thought that a surname like his would keep him relatively safe from such silliness, he unfortunately, though, reckoned without the *Mah Na Mah Na* song by Pietro Umiliani. A simple but effective amalgamation of song and name resulted in *"Macmanaman, mah na, mah na mah, Macmanaman mah na mah na...."*, and so on in similarly silly style! Now, though, to the Kop's crowning glory, and even if any of those famous names of yesteryear had ever been celebrated in song, it's a fair bet that nothing would have surpassed the "song" now designated to Phil Babb. Everyone must surely know the theme to Match of the Day - and it was a revelation of near biblical proportions when it was realised that Babb's surname fitted nicely into the rhythm of the tune - altogether now: *"Babb, Babb, Babb, Babb, B-Babb, Babb Babb Babb, Babb Babb B-Babb, Babb Babb; Babb, Babb, Babb, Babb B-Babb, Babb Babb Babb, Babb Babb B-Babb Babb Babb......"* and so on, right the way through another twenty single *"Babb's"* and six more *"B-Babb's"* to the rising cadence of the nine final repetitions over the climactic bar or two - store this one away for future reference, and Saturday evenings need never be the same again!

Manchester City

Seemingly always at the forefront of whatever the latest singing fad may happen to be, although not always managing to be the actual instigators, City's supporters have rightly gained a reputation for being the prime movers behind some of the most enduring aspects of terrace life over the last decade or so. A case in point is the *Blue Moon* phenomenon, which became inextricably linked with the club over the early part of the 1990's - although it should never be forgotten that the song had made its footballing debut at the instigation of Crewe Alexandra supporters a full six months before City muscled onto the scene.

The Rogers and Hart number, originally written back in the 1930's, subsequently charted at the hands of such luminaries as Elvis Presley, The Marcels and Showaddywaddy, but it was Bob Dylan's arrangement which was seized upon by the Gresty Road throng and was then adopted in Moss Side. Its first senior appearance in the Sky Blue colours, so to speak, was at Anfield in August 1989 - City's first game back in the top flight after promotion the previous season. It was, however, to take another eight months or so before it became an established part of the Maine Road scene - prompted by the publication of the lyrics in the fanzine Electric Blue - and those lyrics were....

> *Blue moon, you saw me standing alone,*
> *Without a dream in my heart,*
> *Without a love of my own.*

> *Blue moon, you knew just what I was there for,*
> *You heard me saying a prayer for,*
> *Someone I really could care for.*

> *Then suddenly they'll appear before me,*
> *The only one my arms could ever hold,*
> *I heard someone whisper "Please adore me",*
> *And when I looked, my moon had turned to gold.*

> *Blue moon, now I'm no longer alone,*
> *Without a dream in my heart,*
> *Without a love of my own.*

As well as swiftly becoming almost obligatory fare for the supporters of any other team who had played in anything even approaching some sort of vaguely blueish colour at any time during their history, the song bounced back and forward across the short distance between Maine Road and Old Trafford, reflecting any salient points in the Mancunian rivalry. The red faction gleefully celebrated the retrieval of a draw having been 1-3 down in the 1990/91 derby with *"Blue moon, you started singing too soon, you thought you'd beat us 3-1, now Howard Kendall has gone"*, which made mention not only of the match in question, but also of the fact that Howard Kendall had controversially dropped the managerial reins at Maine Road as soon as the opportunity to scuttle back to Everton was presented to him. City responded with a pointed reminder of the thrashing handed out to United a season earlier - *"Blue moon, you started singing our tune, You won't be singing for long, 'cos we still beat you five - one!"* The song continued to reverberate around the city for a couple of years or so, a new version cropping up every time something of significance came to light but, having really taken a grip in the aftermath of the five goal hiding handed to United in September 1989, the song·rather faded from the scene when the Reds wiped the slate clean with a similar victory in November 1994.

At more or less the same time that *Blue Moon* was sweeping all before it in the race to become the undisputed City anthem, the nationwide craze for "inflatables" was gathering pace with City's chosen "weapon" being large yellow bananas. Naturally, the arrival on the Kippax and at grounds up and down the country of hordes of otherwise perfectly normal Northerners wielding three foot long Fyffes needed some sort of song (as these things do) and what could be more appropriate than the theme from that icon of school holiday television from the 1970's *The Banana Splits*. Reintroduced into the public consciousness by The Dickies in 1979, City's version was no more than a word for word reproduction of the original....

> *One banana, two banana, three banana four,*
> *Five banana, six banana, seven banana more,*
> *Tra la la, la la la la,*
> *Tra la la, la la la la!*
> *Four banana, three banana, two banana, one,*
> *All bananas playing in the bright warm sun,*
> *Flipping like a pancake, popping like a cork,*
> *Fleagle, Drooper, Bingo and Snork,*
> *Tra la la, la la la la,*
> *Tra la la, la la la la.*

For anyone in their thirties reading this who might now be appalled by the *Tellytubbies* and other rubbish that masquerades as kids telly in these enlightened times, just reflect a while on what you used to watch twenty odd years ago - a lion who was clearly on drugs, a grossly overweight dog of some kind who wore a fireman's helmet, a mute elephant with vast sunglasses, and some sort of gibbon thing that grinned as if it had synthesised a particularly potent mescalin substitute - all of whom drove round in beach buggies (mind you, I quite liked the *Arabian Knights* cartoons - *"size of a mouse!"*). More to the point, had you ever considered that the song heralding the appearance on your TV of this bunch of pharmaceutically invigorated characters would find its way onto the terraces of our national game some years later - no? - thought not!

To matters of a more mundane nature, and it is more than a little surprising that there is a bit of a paucity of City songs dedicated to the vilification of United. One of the best of these few, however, is this abbreviated extract from *The Wild Rover*....

> *Old Trafford they say is a wonderful place,*
> *But I know it's really a fucking disgrace,*
> *And as for United, I know they should be,*
> *Shovelling shit on the Isle of Capri.*

It is to be assumed that this is either followed or preceded (or possibly both) by the standard format of chorus which in this instance would be *"And it's Manchester City, Manchester City F C, we're by far the greatest team, the world has ever seen"*. The enduring thread which is common through the majority of other anti-United songs is the oft-quoted assertion that only a relatively small proportion of Reds' supporters actually come from Manchester. Carefully avoiding any sort of sociological dissertation on this subject, it should be noted that a favourite from Meadow Lane is used to make the point, by way of *"Ohhhhh, Man City - the only football team to come from Manchester!"* which though unequivocally true, is a point about which United supporters care very little (oh, and by the way, *cf* Notts County!). A very surprising point to bear in mind when considering the City/United situation is that the Munich songs so beloved of Bolton and Leeds fans (and very much less so at post-Hillsborough Liverpool) are almost entirely absent from the Maine Road battery of abuse aimed at the Reds. Why this should be the case is not certain, but contemporary newspaper reports and subsequent books about reaction to the air crash in Manchester made an awful lot of the fact that the entire city was in mourning, and not just United supporters. Perhaps this feeling has endured over the forty odd years since, but whatever the reason, City supporters have to be seriously provoked before the Munich songs are allowed to resurface.

Now, something else which sets City supporters apart from the rest of the herd is that they are far more likely to burst into song in order to acclaim a manager than they are a player. Just two player related songs were received (a thoroughly dull affair about Niall Quinn, and a strange effort about Georgiou Kinkladze as detailed a bit later) but three managers, all from different eras, have been lucky (!) enough to have lyrics lovingly crafted in their honour. In chronological order, Joe Mercer was the first, by way of the following which records his achievements having overseen City's restoration to Division One in 1966....

> In 1962, we fell into Division Two,
> The Stretford End cried out aloud,
> "It's the end of the Sky Blues!"
> Joe Mercer came, we played the game,
> We went to Rotherham, we won one - nil,
> And we were back into Division One.
> Since then, we've won the league,
> We've won the cup,
> And played in Europe too (and won!)
> And when we win the league this year,
> We'll sing this song for you.

A confusing number this, as not only were City actually relegated at the end of the 1962/3 season, but the tune is about as inexplicable as a tune can get. Nothing by way of any recognisable song fits in any shape, manner or form, and it can only be assumed that it was based around some contemporary effort, long since forgotten. Of a far more accessible nature is the 1980's entry in City's Managerial Song Contest which sees the inestimable John Bond serenaded to an arrangement of *There's No-one Quite Like Grandma* by the St Winifred's School Choir! Best described as a silly song, there would appear to be more just a hint of facetiousness about it....

> *John Bond we love you,*
> *Oh John Bond, we do!*
> *Though you may be far away,*
> *We will follow you.*
> *And on Monday when we're champions,*
> *We'll look back and say,*
> *There's no one quite like John Bond,*
> *He's helped us on our way!*

As far as the contender from the 1990's goes - well, it can only be one thing can't it? The passion that the Brothers Gallagher have for City has been well chronicled elsewhere, and the rise of Oasis to international superstardom has seen their songs become the most sought after material on which new terrace anthems can be based. First on the bandwagon, no doubt as a result of Liam and Noel's penchant for the Blues, City supporters took *Wonderwall* to their hearts within days of its release - with their interpretation being a word for word reproduction of the first half of the original - all bar one small but significant alteration....

> *Today is gonna be the day, that they're gonna throw it back to you,*
> *By now, you should've somehow, realised what you've got to do,*
> *I don't believe that anybody feels the way I do about you now.*
>
> *Back beat, the word is on the street that the fire in your heart is out,*
> *I'm sure you've heard it all before, but you never really had a doubt,*
> *I don't believe that anybody feels the way I do about you now.*
>
> *And all the roads we have to walk are winding,*
> *And all the lights that lead us there are blinding,*
> *There are many things that I would like to say to you,*
> *But I don't know how,*
>
> *Because maybe, you're gonna be the one that saves me,*
> *And after all, you're my Alan Ball!*

(all of which is probably © Creation Records Ltd but, hey, give us a break eh?)

Less complete renditions can omit either the first two sections, or the first three, which leaves just the last two lines (which contain the amendment!). Where the song has appeared elsewhere, it is very much just this closing phrase which does the job - with *"the one that saves me"* being anyone and everyone from *"my Darren Moore"* at Donny Rovers to *"my Ashley Ward"* at Derby, via virtually every other professional footballer whose name fits.

Back at City, there has been a suggestion that lines seven and eight might be changed to *"And all the runs that Kinky makes are winding; And all the goals that City score are blinding"*, but I am of the opinion that this never really got off the ground, and that the virtually unadulterated version is the only one that will be tolerated.

With this in mind, and remembering how *Blue Moon* was also twisted to deviant ends some years ago, it is not at all surprising to learn that United supporters have also decided that *Wonderwall* needs singing. The Red version though, as flexible in length as it is elsewhere, finishes off with a pointed reference to City's lack of silverware over the last twenty one years by way of *"And after all - you've won fuck all!"*

To finish - two songs (well, one song and a chant) which couldn't be much further removed from the lengthy intonation of *Wonderwall*. The first, as briefly mentioned earlier, is a rare City "player" song which features the darling of Moss Side, Mr Kinkladze. The tune, though a little dismembered in this arrangement, would seem to be *A Scottish Soldier*....

> *There was a man, a man from Dynamo,*
> *Kinkladze was his name, and football was his game,*
> *Oh Frannie Lee said, just sign him up and,*
> *Bring him back to Maine Road*
> *Kinky, Kinky, wooaah-oh!*
> *Kinkladze was his name!*

...."Dynamo" being Georgiou's former club, Dynamo Tbilisi. And finally, one of the finest "off the cuff" chants that has been sent in - from a City game against West Ham in or around 1987. Half time, and a West Ham supporter wanders down a gangway in the seats above the Chicken Run at Upton Park, in plain view of the City supporters on the South Bank. The supporter in question has obviously just returned from the tea bar, as he is clutching a hot dog - a journey with which he is evidently not unfamiliar as, to coin a phrase, he was a fat bastard. Seconds later, and the unfortunate gentleman is squeezing his ample frame between the seats to an accompaniment of *"There's gonna be a diet! There's gonna be a diet!"* which, you may remember, more usually took the form of *"There's gonna be a riot!"* - I reckon the "fat bloke" version is by far the better of the two, though!

Manchester United

As befits a clubs which enjoys a reputation for numerically huge and occasionally voluable support, the full spectrum of songs and chants can be found at Old Trafford - enduring anthems, recurring favourites, adaptations of existing ideas, innovative efforts, decidedly silly numbers and things which have clearly been pinched from other people.

Very much belonging to the first category is the song which has been recognised as the United theme since back in the 1970's. Based on *Just One Of Those Songs* - a common enough tune - this is one of the very few versions which extends to a second verse....

> *We are just one of those teams that you see now and then,*
> *We sometimes score six but we seldom score ten,*
> *We'll beat 'em at home and we'll beat 'em away,*
> *We'll kill any bastard that get's in our way,*
>
> *We are the pride of all Europe, the cock of the North,*
> *We hate the Scousers, the Cockneys of course (and Leeds!),*
> *We are United, without any doubt, we are the Manchester boys,*
> *La, la, la, la la la la la, la, la, la, la, la - WHOOOOOARFFFFF!*

For quite some time during the 1980's the first half of this one was more or less a closed book to the majority of United supporters and complete performances were few and far between, but it became more widely known (and used) as the 90's progressed, at around which time the anguished roar also began to be tacked on to the end with some regularity.

Being situated in the North West, United are naturally obliged to number *The Wild Rover* amongst their songs, but the verses as listed below are now heard only very occasionally. The "chorus" takes the standard format as for more or less any version outside of Blackburn or Burnley, and it is a simple matter for the name of any number of other teams to be inserted to make this part into a short song in its own right.

> *From the dark snows of Munich back in '58,*
> *I remember those players who once were so great,*
> *Their memory it still lingers on in my mind,*
> *So I'll follow United 'til the end of my time.*
>
> *Chorus*
>
> *And it's Man. United, Man United F C,*
> *We're by far the greatest team,*
> *The world has ever seen.*

We went down to Wembley one sweet night in May,
The crowd were all happy and singing away,
And when it was over and when it was done,
We'd beaten Benfica by four goals to one,

> *Chorus*

The first came from Bobby, he outjumped the rest,
The second it came from wee Georgie Best,
The crowd were all cheering, they roared "United!",
And the third goal it followed from young Brian Kidd

> *Chorus*

The crowd were all calling and shouting for more,
So Bobby obliged by making it four,
That night I'll remember when I do recall,
Manchester United - the greatest of all.

> *Chorus*

We've fought all our battles in Manchester's name,
So listen you bastards, you'll all die in vain,
Some others will rise and some others will fall,
But Man United stay the greatest of all.

> *Chorus*

It's glory and honour, the great man he said,
There's nothing on earth like being a Red,
I'll follow them far and I'll follow them near,
And I'll follow United on whisky and beer.

> *Chorus*

A few historical points to note in this epic saga which are, in order: line one's references to the Munich air crash in 1958; the third, fourth and fifth verses all relating the story of the European Cup Final ten years later, with "Bobby" being Bobby Charlton and, in the sixth verse, "the great man" is Matt Busby. As you can imagine, this does not often appear during matches in its full unexpurgated glory, with complete renditions being more the stuff of beery evenings down the pub.

Of an even older vintage, the pre-Munich days of the 1950's saw a recording made by an unfortunately nameless artiste of a song called *The Man United Calypso*. Having faded into obscurity for the best part of forty years, this suddenly made a comeback onto the terraces during United's resurgence in the early 1990's. The tune was commissioned especially for the recording, and as such, doesn't bare much similarity to anything which might be rather better known....

> *If they're playing in your town,*
> *Be sure to go to that football ground,*
> *For if you go there you will see,*
> *The football taught by Matt Busby,*
> *Manchester, Manchester, Manchester United,*
> *The team they call the Busby Babes,*
> *The team they should have knighted!*

....this, of course, is all very silly (more so if you do happen to know the tune), but it really took a hold in the run in to the 1992/93 championship winning season.

A couple of seasons earlier, United secured the Cup Winners Cup with a win over Barcelona in Rotterdam. With the Red Army cavorting around Europe, throughout the preceding rounds, two songs in particular came to symbolise the run to the final. In the first instance, this was the time that *Always Look On The Bright Side Of Life* came to the fore and, although everyone should now know that this was an Exeter City original, it was United supporters who really brought it to the attention of a wider audience. Another song synonymous with the cross channel forays was *Sit Down* by indie band James. Rendered exactly as per the "proper" lyrics, this was picked up on simply because it was a jaunty "good time" song, performances of which would virtually guarantee to have everyone on their feet! The rain-sodden night of the final itself saw another long standing song of more general popularity *(Lord Of The Dance)* given a new lease of life by way of....

> *Drink, drink, wherever you may be,*
> *We are the drunk and disorderly,*
> *And we don't give a shit and we don't give a fuck,*
> *'cos we're coming home with the Cup Winners Cup!*

The following season saw this version performed either with line four rewritten in the past tense, or with the two expletives swapping positions and being followed by *"'cos we're coming home with the championship"*. The last legacy of the Cup Winners Cup win was the revival of a twenty three year old song which had initially recounted tales of European glory from 1968. Taking the tune of Liverpool's *Red River Valley*, and updated to feature the teams encountered en route to Rotterdam, there was....

> *If you ever walk down Warwick Road in Salford,*
> *Buy a ticket for the cantilever stand,*
> *So you can go and watch the famous Man United,*

183

> *Hammer every other bastard in the land.*
> *We've beaten all the Polish and the Frenchmen,*
> *We've beaten Barcelona, pride of Spain,*
> *We were there in Rotterdam to see United,*
> *Become the champions of Europe once again.*

The Poles of Legia Warsaw and France's Montpellier find themselves mentioned by nationality in this one, along with Barcelona of course, but not even the vaguest reference is made to Hungary's Pecsi Munkas or Wrexham who were beaten in the first and second rounds respectively.

Mention of Liverpool brings us to a further category of United songs - those directed at teams of whom the Old Trafford crowd are none too enamoured. It is the Anfield club who bear the brunt of this verbal assault with, in the first instance, a second verse to the Oxford United/Portsmouth composition *In Your Liverpool Slums*. Following the first section which is the same as these other incarnations we find....

> *In your Liverpool slums,*
> *In your Liverpool slums,*
> *You speak with an accent exceedingly shit,*
> *Your ma's on the game and your dad's in the nick,*
> *In your Liverpool slums.*

A far more inventive second swipe is then taken at Liverpool by way of a splendid reworking of Chuck Berry's *My Ding A Ling*....

> *When I was just a little bitty boy,*
> *My grandmother gave me a wonderful toy,*
> *Hundreds of Scousers tied up with string,*
> *She told me to kick their fucking heads in!*
> *Kick their heads in, kick their heads in,*
> *She told me to kick their fucking heads in!*

From a far more recent perspective, the showdown at Anfield towards the end of the 1996/7 season saw the United supporters come up with a (rather rude) derivative of the Jason McAteer/*Macarena* song. The unfortunate Steve Macmanaman also has his name somewhat taken in vain....

> *Fuck Macmanaman and fuck McAteer,*
> *Fuck Macmanaman and fuck McAteer,*
> *Fuck Macmanaman and fuck McAteer,*
> *They're bo-o-oth fucking queer!*

The matter of abusing City in song has not been given quite as much thought as one might have imagined would be the case, with there only being a couple of such pieces that extend beyond a couple of lines. The first is a now somewhat dated effort that celebrates the famous afternoon when a win by Luton Town at Maine Road relegated City in place of of the Hatters and prompted David Pleat's now legendary dance across the pitch. *The Laughing Policeman* provides the tune for....

> *City versus Luton was heading for a draw,*
> *Final Saturday of the season,*
> *It'd just turned half past four,*
> *David Pleat sent on his sub,*
> *To see what he could do -*
> *He knocked it in,*
> *And sent the Blues,*
> *Into Division Two*
> *Aaaah-ha-ha-ha-ha-ha-ha-ha......*

The one song which can always be guaranteed an airing on derby day is the very popular ditty based on *The Camptown Races* which - relevant number increasing with every passing season - points out just how many years it is since City last had their hands on some silverware. To date this has reached the dizzy heights of....

> *City is our name, City is our name,*
> *Twenty one years and won fuck all,*
> *City is our name!*

Harking back to the days when derby matches used to be marred by crowd violence, there are a couple of songs relating to fisticuffs on the old Kippax terrace at Maine Road, which has subsequently been replaced by a shiny new three tier grandstand. The first such song takes the tune of *Tiptoe Through The Tulips*....

> *Tiptoe through the Kippax,*
> *With a flick-knife,*
> *And a sawn-off shotgun,*
> *Tiptoe, through the Kippax with me.*

....obviously suggesting suitable weapons with which acts of the most severe violence could be perpetrated upon the City supporters. Of a similar nature there is a somewhat longer effort which, immensely irritatingly, I simply have not been able to remember the name of the tune (pity, really, as the whole thing had been quite well researched up to now!). Anyway, whatever it may be called, the tune is the same as is used for the likes of *"....Walsall boys, we are here, shag your women and drink your beer"*, and *"Can you hear the Rochdale sing, no-oh, no-oh, can you hear the Rochdale sing, I can't hear a fucking thing"*, all of which must make it one of the best known tunes in the game, and even more embarrassing than it already was that I can't think of the tune! Still, inadequate background information notwithstanding, United's song goes....

If I die on the Kippax street, wo-oah, wo-oah,
If I die on the Kippax street, wo-oah, wo-oah,
If I die on the Kippax street,
There'll be ten blue bastards at my feet,
Wo-oah, wo-o-oah, wo-o-oh!

A second verse will sometimes follow with *"use your hands and use your feet"* replacing the *"If I die on the Kippax street"* parts, which shows an admirable return to low-tech scrapping after the advocation of flick-knives and sawn-off shotguns in the previous song - the old ways are the best, eh!

As far as Leeds United are concerned - with whom United have probably their most visceral and malicious rivalry - there is only really a single chant. Taking a leaf out of the Wycombe Wanderers song book, The Dambusters Theme has given sterling service over recent years in the guise of *"We all fucking hate Leeds - we all hate Leeds and Leeds and Leeds, Leeds and Leeds and Leeds and Leeds, Leeds and Leeds and Leeds, we all fucking hate Leeds!"* which claws back through intensity and sheer venom what it loses through being so utterly simplistic.

While any of United's main rivals (not to mention Bolton) occasionally stoop to the use of Munich songs to taunt Reds' supporters, it should not be forgotten that United fans themselves are equally prone to plumb the depths by way of a retort. Hillsborough, Heysel and the deaths of Bill Shankley, Don Revie and Joe Mercer have all been considered fair game over the years as far as songs go, but strangely, in spite of all the incitement from Bolton, there have never been any songs in response about the 1946 Burnden Park disaster when thirty three supporters were killed and four hundred injured due to overcrowding on the Railway Terrace during an F A Cup game against Stoke City. Fortunately, performances of this type of song - from both United and their opponents - have become far less frequent as the 1990's have progressed, and they may soon disappear forever in all but the most bigoted corners of football grounds in the North of England.

On to far less distasteful matters, and songs which over the years have been used to convey the esteem (or lack of it) in which certain players at Old Trafford have been held. One of the first players to have prompted hymns of praise from the Stretford End was Denis Law, who found his name worked into a re-write of *Lily The Pink* by The Scaffold....

We'll drink a drink a drink,
To Denis the King the King the King,
'cos he's the leader of our football team,

He's the greatest centre forward,
That the world has ever seen.

Whilst Denis Law remains the original King of Old Trafford, it is a measure of the affection in which Eric Cantona was held when, the best part of thirty years after the first version had appeared, he became the only other player ever to have had his name included in this song (obviously *"Eric the King"* was substituted for the original lyrics). The 90's remix had an added element in that it became all the rage to extend the first word of the song for as long as possible before launching into the rest of it. Apart from the "coronation" song, and being lauded by the same Wolfetones/Gap Band chant that had sufficed at Elland Road, Cantona's name also appeared in one other guise. No doubt in order to make him feel at home, and at the instigation of the *Red Issue* fanzine, his name and its obligatory "ooh ahh" suffix were repeated over and over to the tune of the French national anthem *La Marseilleaise*. Another 60's favourite to have a 90's equivalent was to another French song *Alouette*. Originally it was *"Nobby, Nobby - Nobby, Nobby Stiles"* who featured, with Jordi Cruyff taking over more recently, but the really notable version of this was from the late 1980's when the incomparable Ralph Milne was so celebrated. Milne - a pedestrian winger recruited from Bristol City after a spell at Charlton and a surprisingly successful time at Dundee United - became a real cult figure with United supporters of the day, largely because he was so useless. The song, in turn, became even more popular than the player, and the strains of *"Ralphy, Ralphy, Ralphy Ralphy Milne - Ralphy Milne! Ralpy Milne! ooooooooooooh, Ralphy, Ralphy...."* can still be heard on occasion, getting on for seven years after Milne last held the First Division in thrall. Equally, more recent times have seen a *Quartermaster's Stores* derivative, celebrating the relationship between one of United's players and a certain television presenter - *"He's here, he's there, he's shagging Danni Behr, Ryan Giggs, Ryan Giggs!"* being a noble successor to the Brian McClair original, and also one of the longest songs ever dedicated to a United player has appeared. Roy Keane is the man in question, and he now careers around kicking people to the accompaniment of....

Roy Keane he is magic,
He wears a magic hat,
And when he saw United,
He said "I fancy that".
He could have signed for Arsenal,
Or Blackburn - but they're shite,
He signed for Man United,
'cos they're fucking dynamite!

Now - and not before time - just two more songs with which to round off this extended trawl through United's singing heritage, both of which have become enduring favourites. By far the more established of the two is a simple song to the same *Marching Through Georgia* tune which lends itself to one of the foremost songs at Rangers' Ibrox Park. A genuine United anthem of many years standing is....

> *Hello! Hello! we are the Busby boys,*
> *Hello! Hello! we are the Busby boys,*
> *And if you are a City fan,*
> *Surrender or you'll die,*
> *We all follow United!*

And finally, to the singularly most popular song of recent years, which has already undergone some tinkering in order to keep it current. United's championship triumph in 1996 was climaxed with a 3-0 win at Middlesbrough's Riverside Stadium, and the traditional Black American song *Down By The Riverside* immediately became....

> *We're going to win that Football League again,*
> *Down by the Riverside, down by the Riverside,*
> *We're going to win that Football League again,*
> *Down by the Riverside, down by the Riversiiiiide!*

Having featured at virtually every game throughout the following season up until early Spring, it then became apparent that an upcoming game at Anfield was going to be crucial to the outcome of the title race, and a swift alteration saw the song suitably amended to....

> *We're going to win that Football League again,*
> *This time on Merseyside, this time on Merseyside,*
> *We're going to win that Football League again,*
> *This time on Merseyside, this time on Merseysiiiiide!*

And that - safe in the knowledge that United are away at Barnsley on the last day of 97/8, so we'll be hearing *"....this time on Dearne-side, this time on Dearne-side"* before too much longer - is that.

Oldham Athletic

We now embark on an Oldham section considerably expanded from the meagre selection which constituted the Boundary Park bill of fare in the first *Dicks Out!*, but which has only been enlivened by any one contribution of real note (more of which later). Latics' supporters seem content to subsist on a diet of common Lancastrian themes for the most part, but there is one song which although not unique the club is of sufficient rarity to warrant inclusion. This is a version of Doncaster Rovers' *Zigger Zagger* chant which, so legend would have it, was also a Stoke City favourite at some time in the past, even though - which characteristic lethargy - no Potters' fans could be arsed to write in with any details. Anyway, the Chadderton Road End has most definitely provided a forum for....

> *Zigger Zagger, Zigger Zagger ATHLETIC!*
> *Zigger Zagger, Zigger Zagger ATHLETIC!*
> *One, two, three, four,*
> *Listen to the Chaddy roar!*
> *clap, clap - clap, clap, clap - clap, clap, clap, clap,*
> *OLDHAM!*

Having sought inspiration from East of the Pennines for this one, some attitudes and ideas most definitely rooted in the red rose county account for the bulk of Oldham's repertoire. Citing Blackburn as their main rivals, the Burnley tendency to refer to the Ewood Park club exclusively as *"Bastards"* once again rears its head: *"If you hate Bastard Rovers clap your hands" (She'll Be Coming Round The Mountain)*, the chorus to the Burnley version of *The Wild Rover* and *"We hate Bastards and we hate Bastards, We are the Bastard - haters!"* are all instances where Blackburn's alternative name makes an appearance.

From the same era that saw the resurrection of *Alouette* at Old Trafford (in its Ralph Milne incarnation), the Latics' Frankie Bunn was similarly lauded at Boundary Park - mainly as a result of his six goal contribution to a Littlewoods Cup slaughter of Scarborough (see Hull City for another Bunn anthem), but Oldham's premier song of a player-related nature is unusually reserved for a defender. Alan Lawson was the man in question, whose five year stint as a hero of the Chaddy End saw him earn a reputation as an uncomplicated and sometimes brutal tackler. Andy Stewart's *A Scottish Soldier* (later to resurface at Maine Road) was the means by which Lawson's particular talents were celebrated....

> *There was a half back, a Scottish half back,*
> *And Lawson was his name, and clogging was his game,*
> *He came to Oldham, when Celtic sold him,*
> *And Alan Lawson was his name.*
>
> *For on the green fields, down at Boundary,*
> *There's a'melee there, with bodies everywhere,*
> *For on those green fields, down at Boundary,*
> *Alan Lawson reigns supreme.*

And Barry Stobart, and Jimmy Fryat,
He sent them far away, to the infirmary,
He clogged victorious, he clogged so glorious,
And Alan Lawson was his name.

Fryatt was presumably a victim of a Lawson assault during his spell as a Stockport County player, although such was the ex-Celts' reputation that he may well have "clogged" the luckless Jimmy during the time that both were team mates at Boundary Park. The significance (or otherwise) of Barry Stobart has not proved so easy to ascertain - suffice to say that he must have been another notable scalp claimed by Lawson.

In conclusion, time for another rash assertion based on the now reasonably well established assumption that even the most widely used of chants must have initially started at one particular club. It is to Oldham's everlasting glory, therefore, that they are hereby recorded as the instigators of a chant which has gone on to be the bane of any supporter who appears to be rather more heavily built than might normally be considered reasonable. As no other set of supporters have made a similar claim, it is to be assumed that the now commonplace version of *Knees Up Mother Brown* used to berate fat bastards nationwide was first directed at a plump visiting supporter on the Rochdale Road End. Thank you, Oldham, for the classic which is....

Who's ate all our pies?
Who's ate all our pies?
You fat bastard! You fat bastard!
You've ate all the pies!

Preston North End

With the departure of Stoke City from the Victoria Ground at the end of the 1996/97 season, Deepdale has recently taken over the mantle of the Nationwide League's oldest ground but, perversely, recent years have seen the development of an atmosphere at the stadium which is far removed from the respectful hush you may think appropriate at such a venerable old venue. 1993 saw the appointment of John Beck to the manager's job at Deepdale, and the archetypal sleeping giant was given an equally proverbial kick up the backside which, in spite of Beck's departure in November '94, would ultimately lead to promotion from the Third Division after a couple of seasons spent languishing in the basement. The inherent excitement of the "shit or bust" approach to the game which Beck brought to Preston, combined with the improving fortunes of the team, saw attendances soar and, naturally, more people meant more noise. The impression given by our correspondent from the Town End is one of an almost relentless barrage of noise from the PNE supporters, underscored by a backdrop of drumming and occasionally illuminated by the efforts of a Mr Dave Hovis (made up name?) and his trumpet but, unfortunately, it appears that this cacophony contains little of note for the student of the football song. With the advent of serious vocal encouragement at Deepdale not seeming to have much of a history, it is perhaps inevitable that what songs there are are of a somewhat obvious nature and, with there being few things in football less obvious than outpourings of hatred towards local rivals, Blackpool are regularly serenaded with....

Who's that jumping off the pier?
Who's that drowning in the sea?
Oh it's Megson and his boys
Making all the fucking noise,
'cos they cannot beat the famous P N E
(Tune - Ally's Tartan Army)

....Blackpool manager of the time Gary Megson earning himself a mention in this one. To the nascent Preston choral society, the imprisonment of Blackpool chairman Owen Oyston in the summer of 1996 must have seemed like manna from heaven and, with Oyston firmly detained at Her Majesty's pleasure and Euro '96 still fresh in the memory, the opening weeks of the 96/7 season were predictably played out to one of the many derivatives from the burgeoning *Three Lions* stable....

He's sewing bags, he's sewing bags,
He's sewing - Oyston's sewing bags.

....though given the nature of the offence for which Oyston was convicted (sexual naughtiness of a most grievous nature with young female "models" in hotel rooms), this seems a good deal more restrained than many other songs which could have been invented in his honour with a just a bit more thought. The traditional prisoner's task of sewing mail-bags provides the subject matter in this (rather muted) instance.

Another consequence of the relatively recent arrival of Preston's supporters on the singing scene is the eagerness with which any current fads are embraced - both the utterly ubiquitous *Triumphal March* from Aida and the equally inane *"Barmy Army"* type chants are currently popular, with the former actually being played over the tannoy at the start of matches, and it can only be assumed that cries of *"....the North End"* regularly climax performances of that other mid-nineties favourite, *The Hillsborough March*.

Now, the preceding paragraphs may have given the impression that although Preston supporters are loud and enthusiastic singers, there isn't actually much substance to their repertoire, well, reconsider if this is your opinion, as the following gem has been submitted from someone who claims to have heard it *"just before Gordon Lee was sacked"*, which dates it to the middle of the 1983/4 season....

> We've just lost eight on the bounce,
> We've just lost eight on the bounce,
> Bye bye, Gordon, bye bye,
> Don't cry, Gordon, don't cry,
> Now we're bottom of the Third,
> Just fuck off you baldy turd!

....patently, one of the all too rare occasions on which a song by undoubted musical greats Brotherhood of Man gave rise to a terrace anthem, with *Save All Your Kisses For Me* being the inspiration for this noble effort. Feverish thumbing through the relevant copy of Rothmans has revealed that Lee's departure was, in fact, preceded by an eight-game losing streak (a club record to this day, it seems) but that North End never quite hit rock bottom as a result (they were in 22nd place after the eighth defeat, and later recovered to finish 16th). What cannot be denied, however, is that Gordon Lee was bald.

Stockport County

An embarrassing silence was all that emanated from Edgeley Park when responses were collated for the first incarnation of *Dicks Out!* but things have improved apace in the intervening years between then and now. Until promotion from the old Fourth Division, County had always been regarded as one of the perennial strugglers of the game, along with the likes of Crewe and Rochdale, but The Hatters (not to mention the transient Cobras!) have barely looked back since they said goodbye to the basement with a 5-0 hiding of Scunthorpe United on the last day of the 1990/91 campaign. The very next season saw them on the brink of a second successive promotion (defeat in the play-off final by Peterborough put paid to that, though). but things were now definitely on the up - on the terraces as well as on the pitch.

In order to earn their Wembley berth against Peterborough, County had to overcome Stoke City in the play-off semi and, having won the first leg 1-0 at home, they scored within a minute of the start of the return tie at The Victoria

Ground. By this point in history, City's preoccupation with *Delilah* was common knowledge, and a new version suddenly became appropriate....

> *Bye, bye, bye, Delilah,*
> *Bye, bye, bye, Delilah,*
> *And so, before, you sing that song any more,*
> *Remember Stoke City, you're not going up any more,*
> *Remember, Stoke City, you're not going up any more!*

This was sung repeatedly throughout the game (ultimately a 1-1 draw) and was accompanied by some cheery waving (during the first two lines) in the direction of the increasingly animated City supporters on the Boothen End.

Away from the thrills and spills of play-off football, Ralph McTell must have thought that his wistful folk song *Streets of London* had suffered the ultimate indignity when it was covered by Tunbridge Wells punk band The Anti-Nowhere League in the late 1970's. Little did he think that a dozen or so years further down the line, his pleasant ditty was going to resurface at a rather dingy football ground in the North of England, but that's exactly what happened, and County's supporters have inexplicably now taken to butchering the unfortunate Ralph's pride and joy....

> *So how can you tell me, you're lo-one-ly,*
> *And say for you that the sun don't shine,*
> *Let me take you by the hand,*
> *And lead you through the streets of Stockport,*
> *I'll show you something,*
> *That'll make you change your mind.*

A verbatim performance of the original, other than the insertion of *"Stockport"* in place of *"London"* of course, this is right up there with the very best of the other "sung for no apparent reason whatsoever" efforts which have come to the forefront of popular terrace culture in recent years and, of course, to reveal the reason behind its adoption at Edgeley Park would deprive it of this status, so I'm not going to.

They certainly don't believe in just churning out the usual songs in Stockport - witness this next effort which defies much explanation either about its derivation, or the tune (which just might have something to do with *Standing on the Bridge at Midnight*)....

> *At the turn of the century, in the clear blue skies over Edgeley,*
> *There's a roaring and a thundering like you've never heard,*
> *On the pitch, the boys in blue,*
> *They beat the Palace and West Ham too (thank you...!)*
> *And their fans cried, and their fans died,*

And we buried them together on the Popular Side.
We used our hands, and we used our feet,
And they ran like fuck down Castle Street.

....any ideas anyone? A little further back towards the mainstream, County's popular former manager, Danny Bergara, was regularly serenaded with the old Irish favourite *Danny Boy* - presumably a word for word performance of the original - although the now positively ancient Sheffield United *Iggledy, Boggledy, Boo!* chant in praise of the Uruguayan youth international does not appear to have followed him across the Pennines.

As mentioned previously, promotion from the old fourth division appears to have been the catalyst for the upsurge in County creativity, and it certainly coincided with the advent of the *"We're Too Sexy...."* movement which sprang up at the start of 1991/92. A blistering start to the season, which kicked off with a 5-0 thrashing of Swansea, had the County faithful anticipating immediate elevation to a higher division and, with Right Said Fred riding high in the charts at the time, *"We're too sexy for the Third"* soon became a popular theme on the terraces, though strangely the "proper" tune was never used and the chant followed the more traditional *Bread of Heaven* rhythm. County proceeded to blaze a trail to Wembley for the play-off final, by which time the club shop had picked up on the *"Too Sexy"* idea - all manner of merchandise was produced accordingly, and many a County fan watched the defeat by Peterborough whilst carrying a *"We're too sexy for Wembley"* flag/scarf/thermos flask/ painted walnut in team colours or whatever.

Anyway, away from such trivia, and the chant which we were advised has become the supporter's real anthem over recent seasons, if anthem is not too strong a word for the chorus to *Hey Jude* with the word *"County"* inserted - *"Naaa, naaa, naaa, na, na, na ,na; na, na, na, na County!"* - hmmmm, more of a *refrainette* than an anthem, but probably quite impressive nonetheless.

Wigan Athletic

A brave footballing outpost in the cherry and white epicentre of rugby league country, Springfield Park may not at first glance seem to offer any worthwhile morsels for the connoisseur of football songs, but the Latics faithful - in a manner which is typical of supporters of clubs from the lower reaches of the league - have come up with a fair selection of chants, the majority of which have little to do with the game itself. It is fair to say that Rugby League is not popular on the Springfield terraces, mainly because the town's club - particularly during the reign of chairman Alec Lindsay - seemed to get everything that was going by way of fiscal assistance from the town council, while the footy club were more or less left to their own devices. Substantial subsidies for the ongoing development of Central Park always seemed to gravitate towards the already overflowing coffers of the rugby club and this perceived injustice gave rise not only to the ever popular chant of *"....Hate Wigan rugby, we only hate Wigan rugby, hate Wigan rugby, we only hate Wigan rugby"* (to the *Juantanamera* tune), but also to the rather more specifically targeted...

> *Who's up Lindsay's arse, who's up Lindsay's arse?*
> *We all, we all, we all know, half the council's had a go!*

....to the tune of *Knees up Mother Brown*. Similarly, any number of the rugby club's players are roundly abused for any slight misfortune which may befall them (particularly in their personal lives), but apart from the (no doubt categorically untrue) suggestion that Joe Lydon was once prone to, errr, getting his knob out in public and waving it at ladies which is *"He's here, he's there, he's flashing everywhere, Joe Lydon, Joe Lydon"*, the publication of the vast majority of these is far too likely to end in a messy libel suit to permit their inclusion here (boo...!)

Still manfully avoiding a certain eleven-a-side game by way of subject matter, there was a time, not so very long ago, when no Wigan game was complete without the performance of a catalogue of chants based on characters from T V soaps. This saw the inception of *"Mrs Mangel's Blue and White Army"*, along with abuse for Rita Faircolough's one time lover on *Coronation Street*, Alan Bradley, and an assertion that *Emmerdale's* Annie Sugden had some sort of pharmaceutical based addiction. *EastEnders*, unfortunately, did not posses the requisite "street credibility" to allow for the appearance of any of its characters in song.

And then suddenly, without any prior warning, there are some songs about footy. Being in Lancashire, it is inevitable that Wigan should have a version of *The Wild Rover*, and while we were not furnished with the complete words, it is surely just a matter of inserting references to the Springfield Pop Side and John Deehan in the relevant places to give a pretty shrewd idea of how it pans out. Far more impressively, there is then the Springfield version of *My Darling Clementine*, which is a surprisingly rare visitor to the rarified atmosphere of Britain's football stadia but which is used here to convey the less than amicable relationship which Wigan supporters have with the followers of other clubs in their vicinity.

> *Build a bonfire, build a bonfire, stick Bolton on the top.*
> *Put Blackpool in the middle, and burn the fucking lot!*

On the subject of local rivalry, prior to the Graham Jones inspired revival in 1996/7, the Latics invariably seemed to come off second best in the majority of games which could be considered derbies but, in early January 1993, much despised neighbours Preston North End were beaten 2-1 in the Autoglass Trophy and - what with it being the festive season and all - it seemed appropriate to taunt the visiting supporters with....

> *So here it is, Merry Christmas,*
> *Everybody's having fun,*
> *Bollocks to you Preston cunts,*
> *We've beaten you two-o-o-one*

....obviously to the tune of Slade's well known yuletide anthem, and spectacularly rude for good measure. Similarly, when the paths of Wigan and Blackpool cross, the following very pertinent question is asked (and answered, come to that) by supporters of a blue and white persuasion....

> *Who's the shit of Lancashire - Blackpool, Blackpool,*
> *Who's the shit of Lancashire, Blackpool A F C!*
> *Blackpool A F C, Blackpool A F C,*
> *Who's the shit of Lancashire - Blackpool A F C!*

....a rather fine adaptation of *The Camptown Races* and one which would seem to be ripe for adaptation to fit more or less any other side in the league, which indeed it is (with the possible exception of *"Who's the shit of Northamptonshire - Northampton Town, Northampton Town"* which would frankly be a bit of a mouthful).

A latent talent for ornithological impersonation of which the late lamented Percy Edwards would have been justly proud brings Wigan's section to a close. A visit to Gresty Road in 1989 seemed fairly run of the mill, until it was spotted that the Alexandra custodian went by the name of Dean Greygoose. Now safely ensconced between the posts at Northwich Victoria, Greygoose probably still shudders at the memory of the day that his place kicks were accompanied by....

> *Woooooaaaaahhhhhhhh - gobble, gobble, gobble, gobble, gobble!*

....obviously an extension of the *"Woah - you're shit"* chant, but climaxed with as fine an approximation of the sound of a goose as has probably ever been heard at a senior football stadium anywhere, in the whole world, ever!

Section Ten

The Potteries and Marches

Crewe Alexandra

Hereford United

Port Vale

Shrewsbury Town

Stoke City

Tranmere Rovers

The Potteries & Marches

Luxuriating in semi-retirement at a vast mansion in the Welsh Valleys, hips creaking and stiff from so much prolonged swivelling, it is a fair bet that Tom Jones has probably never considered himself to be one of the major inspirational characters behind the football songs of this sceptered isle but, of course, he has obviously reckoned without the rather strange behaviour of the supporters of Stoke City and Port Vale. First *Delilah*, then *What's New Pussycat?* found themselves imported into the footballing arena, and instead of performances being accompanied by various pairs of ladies panties being thrown on stage, the former at least would have seen the air thick with oatcakes as another bizarre Stoke ritual gained momentum. There is no particular reason behind the adoption of either of these two songs, but of course, had there been any sort of rational explanation, the craze would have lost much of its intrinsic appeal and probably died out after a fortnight or so. As it is, *Delilah* is entering something like its fifth year as the Stoke anthem as we go to press, and although *What's New Pussycat?* has been somewhat superseded by the equally irrelevant *The Wonder Of You* on the Bycars End at Vale Park, the legacy of Tom Jones has been indelibly stamped on our game, and looks sets to remain in place for some years to come.

The other teams which fall under the auspices of this rather hazily defined area have all made sterling efforts to keep up with events in The Potteries. Crewe can number the genesis of *Blue Moon*, one of Britain's finest terrace dances and a vastly impressive interpretation of a Monty Python song amongst their many triumphs; Shrewsbury must deserve some sort of accolade for reserving most of their ire for a local non-league club, Tranmere remain stoically aloof from the rather bland fare which is on offer across the Mersey and even poor old Hereford have managed to come up with some really rather noble efforts during their twenty five years or so in the professional ranks. So, all in all, one of the more productive regions of the country when it comes to songs which, when viewed in the context of the paucity of genuine success enjoyed by any of the clubs over the years, serves as a fine endorsement of the oft-made assertion in this book that it is the supporters of the "smaller" clubs who usually come up with the best material - you can bet that no-one in the Premier League will come up with anything to better Crewe's version of *The Bruces' Philosophers Song* in the foreseeable future.

Crewe Alexandra

Prior to the Dario Gradi-led renaissance which saw the club ascend to the lofty heights of the First Division in 1997, Alex were generally perceived as one of the game's hopeless cases for the majority of the other one hundred and five years of their existence as a professional club. Seven applications for re-election to the league (one unsuccessful) and an unbroken stint of two decades spent in the Fourth Division up to 1989 saw the Gresty Road club flirting with oblivion on numerous occasions, but they survived and have at last gone onto greater things. During the bleak years of the 1970's and 80's, it seemed that even the supporters were losing heart with attendances always amongst the lowest in the league but hope sprang eternal - and what an absolutely superb song was used to express what little ambition there was. The Monty Python team have unwittingly provided the source for a couple of football songs - the *Dennis Moor* theme based on an original Robin Hood film score has prompted one or two efforts, and of course there was *Bright Side Of Life* which dominated the scene during the early 1990's - but only one club's supporters have ever had the temerity to rearrange the not-quite-so-well-known *Bruce's Philosopher's Song*. I would imagine that not too many of you out there will have ever heard the original of this (a bizarre ditty about how most of the great thinkers in world history were complete alcoholics) which is a very great shame, as appreciation of what follows does rather depend on knowing the tune, but no matter. You'll just have to take my word for the fact that this is truly one of the great songs, and hope that one day you may chance across one of the rare televised repeats of the Python's performance....

> *Weeeeeeee're Alex boys, at making noise,*
> *When drunk we're more than able,*
> *We've just one dream, to see our team,*
> *Go soaring up the table,*
> *Left out of sight are Chester shite,*
> *Like Houghton, Croft and Abel,*
> *But to follow Crewe in Division Two*
> *Is quite un-be-liev-able.*
> *For nearly twenty years we've been stuck in Division Four,*
> *Our chances of promotion are exceeding-aly poor, but....*

....at which point the whole thing is repeated. A couple of pronunciational alterations have to be made for the words to actually fit the structure of the song, with "unbelievable" in line eight being split into four very distinct sections (the last of which must rhyme with "table") and with "exceedingly" in the penultimate line having a rather extended last syllable. With regard to the time at which this stupendous effort was conceived, it must have been sort of mid 1980's - what with the reference to having spent "nearly twenty years" in

Division Four, and also because of the fact that the Chester City players named were all on the scene at that sort of time. This is, incidentally, the only time that any sort of rivalry at all is mentioned by anyone in connection with Crewe - usually one of those clubs who more or less everyone has a bit of a soft spot for - but evidently Chester were not entirely popular at Gresty Road, with Peter Houghton, Brian Croft and Graham Abel all being disliked with sufficient enthusiasm for them to warrant a namecheck.

Of a less obscure but equally as impressive a nature comes Crewe's real claim to fame on the singing circuit, in that they would appear to have been the first supporters to use *Blue Moon*, some sixth months before it hit the big time at Maine Road when Manchester City's supporters introduced it to a far wider audience. All manner of verified reports in both local and national newspapers of the day confirm that the words to the soon-to-be-City-classic were first intoned on the away terrace at Edgeley Park on February 10th 1989, but as is often the case in these circumstances, there is nothing to suggest exactly why the song was given its debut on this occasion. The only possible reason that comes to mind is that through some bizarre circumstance, Alex were required to play the match wearing their change kit (of a definite blue tendency), but this seems sufficiently unlikely as to make it a virtual non-starter. In any case, the lyrics are rather thoughtlessly set out in full under the Manchester City entry as, although Crewe should be warmly applauded as the instigators, it would be foolish to pretend that the song was ever popularised by anyone other than City. Eight years on, it was noticeable that *Blue Moon* is still very much part of the Crewe supporter's vocal armoury, as it was heard in abundance at the 96/7 play-off final against Brentford.

More plaudits are now to be waved in the general direction of Cheshire as it can be revealed that Crewe are the performers of one of the finest dance accompaniments to any song you're likely to come across. More of that shortly though, as the song itself must also be considered vastly impressive in its own right. To the tune of *The Chatanooga Choo-Choo*, and presumably something to do with Crewe's well documented railway heritage, we have....

> *We're riding along on the Alexandra Special,*
> *Woooo-woo, woooo-woo!*
> *Just riding along, singing our song,*
> *The Alexandra, The Alexandra!*

....and as if that were not enough, now to the "dance" element, which consists of punctuating each "woooo-woo" sound by thrusting an arm skywards, then mimicking the action of pulling the whistle cord on one of those old steam trains that Casey Jones was always messing about with. The combination of sound and action must make for a singularly impressive sight! A couple of other items of interest to consider from Gresty Road, the first of which is a peculiar custom known as *The Gresty Clap*. Odd in the extreme, this seems to refer to a habit which the locals have of clapping, very politely, any aspect of the game of football which impresses them (such deeds are equally well received if performed by the visitors or by any Alex players). The closest approximation as to what The Gresty Clap entails is perhaps the sort of luke warm applause you get at Wimbledon whenever an eleven year old Albanian prodigy has completed a straight-sets victory over the latest British hopeful - almost grudgingly given, but with an air of definite appreciation nonetheless.

Delving way back into the mist of time for the last contribution from Crewe, and it is reported that thirty odd years ago (pre-1965) a song known as *Now Is The Hour* was a favourite with those who took an unnaturally close interest in Alexandra's fortunes. Somewhat uselessly, I can reveal that this song (being of Maori origin) was sung by Dame Kiri te Kanawa at the closing ceremony of the 1990 Commonwealth Games in Auckland, New Zealand, so if you remembered to video said ceremony, you can now play it back and evoke the atmosphere of Gresty Road in the 1950's - if you didn't, you won't have the faintest idea of how the song goes, but rest assured that you won't be alone if this unfortunate circumstance has befallen you.

Hereford United

Right, that's it, enough prevaricating over United's future as a league club - they're in as far as the *Dicks Out* offices are concerned, regardless of whatever bizarre decision the Football League Management Committee come up with about whether or not Brighton's continued fiscal naughtiness is going to get them thrown out of the professional ranks or not! It has to be said that purely on singing terms Hereford certainly deserve to retain their league status, as their repertoire is at least the equal of many supposedly superior clubs and a damn sight better than some! To begin with, the record must be set straight with regard to an error made in the first edition of this book when the United club song was attributed to a certain Dave Lee - the man in question was in fact the inestimable Danny Lee, who can now rightly be acclaimed as the moving force behind....

> *Hereford United, we all love you,*
> *We'll always support you,*
> *And will follow you through,*
> *Our supporters are the best,*
> *And they do their thing,*

> *When the lads take to the pitch,*
> *This is what they sing....*

....with "what they sing" actually being the whole thing again in its entirety. It must be said that I was initially somewhat dubious as to whether or not this was actually sung on the terraces but it was given a lusty rendition by Hereford supporters on that infernal *Sky Soccer AM* programme (again) and must therefore be fully acknowledged as part of the great singing vista at Edgar Street. Initially recorded at some point during the 1971/2 season just prior to United's elevation to league status, the song was subsequently re-recorded in a contemporary disco style during 1979 - it will be a surprise to no-one that it failed to chart on either occasion!

Having cleared up that little misunderstanding, it is now time to take an extend stroll through the rest of the Hereford repertoire, starting with a few efforts from the five years or so before their election to the league in 1972. Firstly, an early version of the *My Old Man's A Dustman* theme which has subsequently been revised and updated by many other sets of supporters....

> *We don't carry meat hooks,*
> *We don't carry lead,*
> *We only carry hatchets,*
> *To bury in your head,*
> *So if you feel like fighting,*
> *We'll see you all outside,*
> *As we are the boys,*
> *Of the Merton Meadow End.*

On a similarly threatening theme, a performance of Don McLean's *American Pie* is the next offering, with the original lyrics intact and utterly without parallel throughout the rest of Britain....

> *So it's bye, bye, Miss American pie,*
> *Drove my Chevy to the levee,*
> *But the levee was dry,*
> *Them good old boys,*
> *Drinking whiskey and rye,*
> *Singing this'll be the day*
> *THAT YOU DIE!*

The climactic last line was shouted out in a voluble and suitably menacing manner, with index fingers thrust in the general direction of the opposing supporters at whom the threat was directed - frightening indeed!

A last relic from the Southern League days was the adoption of Torquay Uniteds *Best Behaved Supporters In The Land* song - reputedly pinched off the Plainmoor faithful following an F A Cup tie between the two sides in 1968. The more northerly of the two United's were later to add both the *'But we're a right load of bastards when we lose"* verse, and another which was along the lines of *"But we are the team that never lose"* which rather negated the impact of the former!

The 1970's (Danny Lee's club song apart!) saw a bit of a cessation in the creative processes which had seen these songs develop, but there was one other product of the decade which must be recorded for posterity - a rather exclusive version of *My Liverpool Home* (which can now be said not to have been a Portsmouth original with some degree of certainty!). Reflecting the lack of neighbourly affection with which United regard teams from Wales, there was....

> *In your Cardiff slums,*
> *In your Cardiff slums,*
> *You look in the dustbin for something to eat,*
> *You find a dead dog and you think it's a treat,*
> *Dead dog and mustard is something to eat,*
> *In your Cardiff slums.*

So, not only had the more popular deceased feline been replaced with a dog in a similar state of health, but an additional line (the fifth) has been inserted to suggest that some of Colman's traditional condiment would make a suitable accompaniment for a meal of putrid pooch - a serving suggestion which is both thoughtful and entirely unique to the Hereford version.

Of a slightly more recent vintage comes the most extensive performance submitted of *Knees Up Mother Brown*. Several other clubs cite part of the song amongst their repertoires, but none can match what follows....

> *Knees up Mother Brown,*
> *Knees up Mother Brown,*
> *Under the table you must go,*
> *ee aye ee aye ee aye oh*
> *And if I catch you bending,*
> *There'll be a nasty shock,*
> *For down will come my trousers,*
> *And in will go my cock!*
> *Oh my, what a dirty dick,*
> *What a dirty dick*
> *What a dirty dick,*
> *Oh my what a dirty dick,*
> *What a dirty singer too!*

Fine use of the gratuitous obscenity in this one, and yet another example of something which is found nowhere else in this particular format other than at

203

Edgar Street. Anti-Welsh sentiment seemed to come to the fore in the 1980's with the advent of both *"Score in a sheep pen, you only score in a sheep pen"* to the Juantanamera tune, and a rather more edifying chant to The Gap Band's Oops Upside Your Head which was *"You've got a sheep wrapped round your cock - you've got a sheep wrapped round your cock!"* Both of these obviously refer to the alleged predilection in the principality for developing friendships with sheep that extended to more than just a simply platonic relationship.

From 1990, there was a nice adaptation of a very popular piece which appeared when United faced Wrexham in the Welsh Cup Final (which they won 2-1). With manager Ian Bowyer (not to mention son Gary) at the forefront of the bid for glory we find....

> *We're on the march with Bowyer's army,*
> *We're going to the Arms Park,*
> *And we'll really shake 'em up,*
> *When we win the Welsh Cup,*
> *'cos United are an English football team!*

....naturally to the tune of *Ally's Tartan Army*, and with Cardiff Arms Park being the fortress on which Bowyer's army were marching.

Continuing the array of unique Hereford songs (which must by now be starting to rival that of Everton) we find one to the tune of *Beat On The Brat* by the Ramones. Though the tune has inspired other chants (*"Hit him in the head, Hit him in the head, Hit him in the head with a baseball bat - oh yeah!"* being just one) it is the subject matter which raises this particular incarnation above the ordinary....

> *Kick him in the belly,*
> *Kick him in the belly,*
> *Kick him in the belly,*
> *With a Sun Valley welly - oh yeah!*

....this somewhat odd creation refers to the Sun Valley poultry processing company, one of Hereford's largest employers who have gone onto actually sponsor the team over recent years. A "Sun Valley welly" was one of a pair of a particular type of rubber boots which workers at the company were required to wear whilst in the factory as part of some hygiene regulation or other. The song, incidentally, preceded the adornment of United shirts with the Sun Valley logo by some ten years or so. Prior to this, a similar sort of thing had already made an appearance at Molineux where - in the true tradition of other 1970's thug anthems - it was performed as *"Stab 'em up the arse, stab 'em up the arse, stab 'em up the arse with a Banks's glass - oh yeah!"*. Banks' were a Midlands brewery, whose hop-related concoctions had probably fuelled much of the bravado which lead the Wolves fans to go around stabbing people up the arse with glasses in the first place!

The final and most pertinent point yet to be addressed is whether United's songs will grace Division Three or the G M Conference in the immediate future - all I can say is that if league positions are decided on singing merits, the club should most certainly be in the Premiership!

Port Vale

Marvellous - at last we reach the section which details the songs belonging to a group of supporters who have apparently set out to be as ridiculous as possible, and who have achieved their aim with consummate ease. Even five years or so ago, it was clear that Vale Park's Bycars End was home to some pretty odd songs, but diligent application since has ensured that Vale are now very close to the top of the tree when it comes to rank silliness, if not perched proudly on top.

Take, for instance, that most widely known terrace phenomenon from The Potteries - the Tom Jones school of football songmanship. Alright, it may well have been the case that Stoke City supporters started the ball rolling when *Delilah* was taken up as their theme tune, but did Vale really have to pick on *What's New Pussycat?* to be their contribution to the movement....

> *Pussycat, pussycat, I love you,*
> *Yesss I dooooooo,*
> *You and your pussycat nose -*
> *You and your pussycat eyes -*
> *You and your pussycat lips -*
> *Ohhhhhhh-What's new pussycat?*
> *Woaaahoaaahoaahoh!*
> *What's new pussycat?*
> *Woaaahoaaahoaahoh-ohh!*

....couldn't have made do with something sensible like *It's Not Unusual* or *The Young Mexican Puppeteer* could they? Oh no, it had to be the one song which was guaranteed to sound as stupid as possible didn't it - but, in fairness, what a superb effort this really is - and one which has done much to enhance the reputation of Vale's supporters since it made its first appearance during the course of a League Cup tie at Anfield in October 1991.

Of course, you wouldn't really have expected anything other than this sort of behaviour from the supporters who had previously concocted one of the most extensive reworkings of *Yellow Submarine* to have made an appearance thus far (not counting the interminable *"Number One is Willie Boyd..."* sort of thing, which is clearly cheating). The Vale version seems to have been doing the rounds for quite some little time - an enduring quality born of sheer class if you ask me....

> *In the town where I was born,*
> *There's a team we go to see,*
> *First we have ten pints of ale,*
> *Then we go to see the Vale,*
> *TO SEE THE VALE!*
>
> *Ooooooooooooooooooooooh,*
> *We all piss in a red and white pot,*
> *A red and white pot, a red and white pot,*
> *We all piss in a red and white pot,*
> *A red and white pot!*

Naturally, the *"red and white pot"* into which the Vale supporters metaphorically piss with ill concealed glee is a reference to the colours of local rivals Stoke City. A far more recent arrival on the scene has been *The Wonder Of You* - probably best known by way of Elvis's recording of 1970 (re-released in 1977), but which had made an earlier appearance at the hands of both Ronnie Hilton and Ray Peterson. The song seems to have found its way to Vale Park as a bit of a reaction to the Tom Jones situation which, as mentioned, was really a Stoke City thing - perhaps the supporters were looking for something which had its own identity, distinct from a fad which had started on the Boothen End at the Victoria Ground. Anyway, whatever the reason, Elvis' posthumously re-released song was very much a part of the Bycars experience during the course of 1996/7....

> *When no-one else can understand me,*
> *When everything I do is wrong,*
> *You give me hope and consolation,*
> *You give me strength to carry on,*
> *And you're always there to lend a hand,*
> *With everything I do,*
> *That's the wonder - the wonder of you.*

The last of Vale's more substantial songs is one which rears its head during the festive season, being based on *The Twelve Days Of Christmas*. This was first heard during the latter part of the 1980's and therefore pre-dates the *"Twelve Cantona's, eleven Cantona's.......and an Eric Cantona"* thing from Old Trafford which is perhaps the most current version of the song. Vale's rendition celebrates that most important of Christmas's many glorious facets - drink....

On the twelfth day of Christmas,
My true love sent to me,
Twelve pints of Bass,
Eleven pints of Bass,
Ten pints of Bass,
Nine pints of Bass,
Eight pints of Bass,
Seven pints of Bass,
Six pints of Bass,
Five Pedigrees,
Four pints of Bass,
Three pints of Bass,
Two pints of Bass,
And a pint of Bass in a straight glass - oooh aaah!

Bass is obviously a noble pint brewed by, err, Bass, whereas Pedigree is a particularly fine ale produced by Marston, Thompson & Evershed - both quality tipples from local Staffordshire breweries. By way of clarification and to answer a question posed in the previous book, it has subsequently been disclosed that when this song was popular it was indeed sung in its entirety, from *"On the first day of Christmas, my true love sent to me"* right through to the last part as detailed above, by way of the ten intermediate stages - this, as can be imagined, took some time. The accepted form seems to have been that more and more people would join in with each successive stage until the entire contingent (or whatever the collective noun for Vale supporters might be) were contributing lustily by the time the climactic coup de grace was reached.

And with that, it's time to move onto some of the less extensive songs and chants which have featured at Vale Park and other equally exotic locations over recent years - perhaps the most succinct of which is....

Boom, boom, boom - let me hear you say Vale - VALE!

....a noble chant in the style of *Boom Boom Boom* by the Out There Brothers, and one which was big during the early part of 1997. The same Valiants' supporters who partake of this particular chant may well have also been prime movers behind a clandestine movement of the 1980's whose stated aim was to try and get into as many grounds as possible (where Vale were playing) for the price of a child's admission ticket. Needless to say, those that attempted this gross fraud were all of an age at which they should have been paying full price, but to give themselves a more plausible air of childishness chants such as *"Port Vale, Port Vale, rah, rah, rah!"* and *"P-O-R-T - V-A-L-E - we like Port Vale, woo woooh!"* were very much the order of the day.

Shrewsbury Town

Not generally perceived as being home to some of the Football League's most fervent supporters, Gay Meadow has surprisingly thrown up a couple of interesting songs - a markedly different version of a popular classic in the first instance, and a strange preoccupation with a local non-league team in the second.

To the Shrewsbury version of *My Old Man Said Follow The Van*, then, with a few peculiarities to look out for....

> *My old man said "Follow the Town,*
> *And don't dilly dally on the way",*
> *We'll take the Station End and all that's in it,*
> *All get your boots on, we'll be there in a minute,*
> *With bottles and spanners, hatchets and spanners,*
> *We don't care what the fucking coppers say,*
> *'coz we are the boys from the Gay, Gay Meadow,*
> *And the kings of football songs,*
> *THE SHREWSBURY clap - clap - clap THE SHREWSBURY!*

Line three throws up the first inconsistency with the naming of the Station End as the objective for the Town supporters' sortie. In almost every other instance of this song (*cf* Hartlepool and Tranmere) it is the ground of a club's local rivals which is in the sights of the singers, but the Station End is the away supporters terrace at Gay Meadow - a far less ambitious target! Line four, again, is entirely unique to Shropshire's premier footballing superpower as are six, seven and eight, although the last of this trio is something of a moot point given the nature of what follows.

Telford United - a thoroughly inoffensive Conference team who do nothing of note other than putting together a biannual run to the third round (or thereabouts) of the F A Cup. Nothing to get worked up about at all, it would seem, but - on purely geographical grounds it must be assumed - Shrewsbury don't like 'em! The two teams seem to meet on an infrequent basis in the Shropshire Senior Cup (which, due to the lack of other teams in the county, has been relegated to little more than a pre-season kickabout), and these less than titanic struggles have evidently been enough to sew the seeds of a rivalry of sorts. From the Shrewsbury perspective this takes, for the most part, the form of abusing the Telford supporters for being of the young "casual" variety - exceptionally brave and mouthy as long as there's more than four hundred of them in a group, but no more than spotty and irritating if their number should drop below this level. To this end, *Hersham Boys* by Sham 69 has been amended to *"Telford boys, Telford boys - nappy rash and Tonka toys!"* with the obvious inference that the Telford supporters are of sufficiently tender years to still play with toy trucks. *Ally's Tartan Army* has also provided a vehicle by which the Bucks Head club can be baited, in this instance the popular tune becomes....

> *Who's that team they call the Telford?*
> *Who's that team they all adore?*
> *And they play in black and white,*
> *And they are a load of shite,*
> *And they won't be very happy going home!*

....a thoroughly standard interpretation in all but the last line, which can only be a comment on the doleful journey away from Gay Meadow after being ignominiously defeated, but which is rather odd to say the least.

Of a more straightforward nature, *Winter Wonderland* made an appearance as part of the Shrewsbury/Telford rivalry, but in a substantially different format from that which has now become the norm....

> *There's only one team in Shropshire,*
> *There's only one team in Shropshire,*
> *Telford are shite, Telford can't fight,*
> *You'll never take the Shrewsbury Riverside!*

Presumably this assertion of the invulnerability of Shrewsbury's home terrace became *"There's only one team in Salop"* during the years that Shropshire's name was temporarily consigned to the constitutional dustbin. A similar theme was expounded by the brief chant *"Chelsea tried, Chelsea died, no-one takes the Riverside, la la la la, la la la la, la la"* which was popular after the Blues visited Gay Meadow for an F A Cup game in the latter part of the 1970's. Whether this was a statement of fact, or a case of bravado after the fact is not clear, but it would be surprising indeed if Chelsea's notorious supporters had mounted an assault on the Riverside and been beaten back by the home supporters.

To close, a very strange song from the *Blue Moon* stable which makes brief reference to an incident involving Town striker Micky Brown (at Gay Meadow during the late 1980's and early 1990's) and someone of a somewhat higher profile....

> *Oh, Micky Brown - he plays for Shrewsbury Town,*
> *His favourite group are The Doolies,*
> *And Brian Clough grabbed his goolies!*

Only briefly alluded to in a local newspaper report, it would be intriguing to learn more about this incident - additional information very welcome!

Stoke City

Gleeful news for Port Vale supporters now, as the dismal and utterly pathetic array of songs from the Victoria Ground (and, no doubt, from the Britannia Stadium, or Sideway, whatever it eventually becomes known as) means that the contest for the right to be regarded as the superior singing force in the Potteries is the archetypal one horse race which Vale win by a country mile.

City supporters may well have become infamous for one song not only because it was quite newsworthy in its own right, but because it is more or less their *only* song - a lamentable state of affairs from a club who have always managed to command decent attendances and who should really have done considerably better.

The one effort which has become synonymous with the Boothen End and its inhabitants is, of course, Tom Jones' *Delilah*. Very much on the scene since the early 1990's, the adoption of the song has a simple story behind it, in that it was heard on the jukebox of a pub prior to an unspecified away game. The Potters' supporters thus enlightened, and suitably uninhibited after sampling the wares of the hostelry in question, proceeded to give the song several loud and lengthy reprises at the match and it just caught on for no real reason whatsoever. As is often the case, it is a measure of how firmly the song has become entrenched in the Stoke psyche that other clubs have subsequently begun to alter the words to belittle City (see Stockport County!) - a fate which has previously befallen West Ham's *Bubbles* and Manchester City's *Blue Moon* to name but two other examples. The words to the City anthem are simply those of the original, with the chorus being the most frequently performed part....

> *My, My, My Delilah,*
> *Why, why, why Delilah*
> *So, before, they come to break down the door,*
> *Forgive me Delilah I just couldn't take any more,*
> *Forgive me Delilah I just couldn't take any more!*

For the sake of padding out the otherwise thin City section a little, it might as well be recorded that a measure of devotion to sometime manager Lou Macari was put forward by the Stoke supporters through the use of *"Lou, Lou, Skip to my Lou; Lou, Lou skip to my Lou, Lou, Lou skip to my Lou, skip to my Lou Macari"*, to the obvious tune and which was wont to be amended to *"Lou, Lou, who the fuck's Lou....."* by City's opponents on occasion.

Now desperately struggling to fill even a solitary page with the machinations of some of the country's quietest supporters, it's time to report that - in the absence of much singing - the City fans decided to jump onto the "throwing things about" bandwagon which has also seen Weetabix arcing through the air at Bristol Rovers games and Chomp bars attaining cult status at Griffin Park, Brentford. Oatcakes were the tools of the trade at the Victoria Ground - a delicacy peculiar to the Potteries, not dissimilar to Chorley cakes or Eccles cakes, but devoid of pastry and (not entirely surprisingly) consisting mainly of oats. In a ritual dating back to Alan Ball's tenure of the City managership (sort of late 1980's), the team would be welcomed onto the pitch prior to games with a hail of oatcakes but given the highly aerodynamic nature of the round, flat comestible, it wasn't long before they started to be thrown prodigious distances at any point during games. This was all fine and dandy until the South Yorkshire Police took a very dim view of such cake-bunging activities at Bramall Lane in 1989, and started throwing the throwers out of the ground citing the usual "oh, look, football supporters having a bit of harmless fun, let's steam in and arrest the bastards" justification for their over-reaction. And with that, oatcake hurling began to fade into obscurity, and Stoke supporters returned to the comatose state from whence they had come - until *Delilah* rudely awakened them.

Tranmere Rovers

A short but rather impressive selection from The Wirral, with a couple of rather fine songs which are very much at odds with assertions from Rovers supporters that the atmosphere at Prenton Park is - and has been for some time - "completely shit" (to quote a contributor!).

Rovers' supporters seem to be a rather hard done by bunch - with several of their songs having an axe to grind with someone or other. The first of this is aimed at the world in general, whose misconception of anyone with a Tranmere allegiance being a "scouser" is the singularly most irritating factor in the lives of those who frequent The Cowshed. In order to set the record straight, this rather fine ditty has been set to the tune of a verse from *The Wild Rover*....

> *Don't be mistaken and don't be mislead,*
> *We're not fucking scousers, we're from Birkenhead,*
> *You can shove your cathedrals and shove your pier head,*
> *We all follow Tranmere and that's in Birkenhead.*

The "cathedrals" are Liverpool's twin religious edifices (one Roman Catholic and one Anglican) which feature in the opening titles of Brookside, and the "pier head" is from where the "ferry across the Mersey" operates - Liverpudlian icons all three, and therefore not popular at all with Rovers followers.

Next, another illustration of how football supporters can easily go from adoring someone to perceiving them as the embodiment of all evil and something to be despised with a passion. Such a contentious individual in the minds of the Prenton Park faithful is one time Rovers' chairman Peter Johnson. All round hero and thoroughly super chap during his time in the Prenton boardroom, the millionaire businessman is now viewed as absolute scum since he took his cash across the Mersey to Everton, not exactly leaving Rovers in the shit, but effectively curtailing what was becoming a spectacular rise from Fourth Division also-rans in the late 1970's to a position where they looked as if they were on the brink of Premiership football. Johnson had made his fortune by selling Christmas hampers, and it was a typical *She'll Be Coming Round The Mountain* adaptation which now sees his memory sullied by chants of *"You can stick your fucking hampers up your arse, you can stick your fucking hampers up your arse...."*. A little more inventiveness has left a more thoughtful legacy which sees occasional outbursts of *"You're a long haired fucker from Liverpool; and we don't believe a word you say; You're a long haired fucker from Liverpool; fuck off and just get on your way"* which is obviously based on the fabulous *Long Haired Lover From Liverpool* by the enigmatic genius who was Little Jimmy Osmond, and reflects the fact that Johnson used to have (and may indeed still have) shoulder length hair. (Although it has to be said that I think there's some confusion with that Moores bloke at Liverpool here!)

With conscious efforts having been made to divorce themselves from the Merseyside football scene, Rovers traditional rivals have always been Chester City - with the Deva Stadium being barely a dozen miles down the M53. This will not, though, be remembered as one of the most bitter rivalries in football history, and on the singing front, Chester merit only a cursory mention in the Tranmere version of *My Old Man.....*

> *My old man said "Follow the 'sheds,*
> *And don't dilly dally on the way",*
> *We took the Wrexham in half a minute,*
> *We took the Chester and the bastards in it,*
> *With bottles and hammers, chisels and spanners,*
> *We're the boys who never run away....*

....and as well as being *"the boys who never run away"*, they are also the boys who have never come up with the last two lines to this song - which leaves it stranded in mid flow in a rather silly manner. The *"'sheds"*, by the way, were the more boisterous members of the Cowshed assembly.

And that leaves us with the two most disappointing aspects of the Rovers songbook to be addressed. The first of these is that there has been no discernable influence on the terraces of Prenton Park by the work of some of the club's more high profile supporters - the acknowledged surrealists of the late 1980's pop scene, Half Man Half Biscuit. While some of the Biscuits numbers have found there way into the repertoires of other clubs (Huddersfield and the sadly missed Meadowbank Thistle for instance), the supporters of the club followed by the band have remained staunchly aloof from such potential classics as *Fucking Hell, It's John Aldridge, The Bastard Son of Dougie Anderson* or even the obvious *All I Want For Christmas Is a Tranmere Rovers Away Kit*. The fact that such inspirational fare has fallen on deaf ears, though, pales into insignificance when it is realised that an alleged Rovers classic - the "prostitute" song alluded in the first edition of *Dicks Out!* - has still defied our best investigative processes and remains shrouded in mystery. The song reputedly is a lengthy and largely obscene narrative which tells the story of a Rovers supporter's night of passion with a prostitute who is covered from head to foot in tattoo's, including one *"just above her fanny of Al Jolson singing Mammy"*. Sadly, this can still only be filed alongside Southampton's *Old Brown Cow* in the Extremely Rude but Probably Very Good If Only We Could Find The Complete Words box - which is a shame.

Section Eleven

The West Midlands

Aston Villa

Birmingham City

Coventry City

West Bromwich Albion

Wolverhampton Wanderers

The West Midlands

Some very variable material has been submitted from the clubs in this region, with page after page of quality material having flooded in from Molineux, a smaller but no less impressive selection arriving from The Hawthorns, standard fare from St Andrews and an embarrassing lack of anything even remotely decent from Villa Park. Coventry City remain quite content with their two-song repertoire (which is at least vaguely commendable if only for its Jimmy Hill connections), and The Bescott Stadium is still shrouded in mystery, with nothing at all being sent in by those who would prostrate themselves in adoration at the feet of The Saddlers.

Of course, Wolves are still utterly pre-eminent in the region - if not in the country as a whole - as a result of their collection of quality songs, most of which are of inordinate length, and which cover the widest range of topics imaginable from curries and beer to the sexual preferences of cartoon characters. West Brom, however, have improved their range vastly since the first edition of Dicks Out! and, as well as having instigated the obscenely popular *Go West* chants, have also managed to conjure up some more substantial efforts as well.

For a region which covers such a relatively small area there seem to be very few songs which crop up at more than one club, but this may be as a result of a conscious decision by the various sets of supporters to try and keep their identities as separate from one another as possible, but what can be seen from the contributions from the West Midlands is the way in which football songs have evolved over the years. Take, for instance, the Wolves numbers from the 1960's - virtually all of them are songs extolling the virtues of players in the Old Gold, and of general support for the team. More recently, the fashion has been to abuse rivals, as can be seen in the West Brom songs about Steve Bull and those that cover Birmingham City's relationship with Villa. This, of course, has been a national trend and not one specific to this area, but the older efforts from Molineux provide some of the best examples of the older, more positive style of song in the country.

Aston Villa

In spite of having a vastly impressive stage on which to perform by way of the huge Holte End at Villa Park, Villa supporters have managed to drivel out a collection of "songs" which, to be completely honest, is little short of pathetic for a club of their stature (and which would probably still deserve an epithet along the lines of "piss poor" if they were a struggling semi-professional outfit languishing at the foot of the Midland Combination with only the likes of Blackheath Electrodrives with which to stand comparison). Quite why this is the case is difficult to imagine, as the club possess all the criteria which usually guarantee a more than respectable repertoire - a long and distinguished history, regular large crowds, a fervent local rivalry (with Birmingham City) and even a European triumph or two thrown in for good measure. Whatever the reason, the degree of invention shown at Villa Park when it comes to singing is utterly feeble. There are only a very few chants which ever seem to rouse the claret and blue army from their slumber, and none of these are particularly edifying. The first (and probably the most popular) is merely the *volte face* version of neighbouring Birmingham City's favourite chant - *"Shit on the City"* following the same structure as is laid out in the Blues' section for their *"Shit on the Villa"* effort, but obviously with the pertinent word substituted throughout.

The second contribution which Villa have made to the boiling cauldron of terrace emotions (more of a simmering saucepan in their case) seems to make an appearance at more or less any game, regardless of who they happen to be playing. Everyone from Crewe to Newcastle United have been treated to a few lusty choruses of *"Who the fuck are Man United"* to the tune of *Glory, Glory Hallelujah* courtesy of Villa supporters over recent seasons. This particular chant is a bit of a relic from the 1992/93 season when Villa and United were the two main protagonists in the Championship race, but for some bizarre reason it seems to have persisted long after the destiny of said race was decided in United's favour.

On the subject of relics, there is one chant of which we were advised which seems to have been prevalent during the two year reign of Willie Bell as manager at St Andrews, and must therefore date back to sometime between 1975 and 1977. Some readers may remember the old Pepsi television adverts with their *"Lip smacking, thirst quenching......"* song (a similar effort was recently used on Sky T V to promote their coverage of Rugby League, if you're interested) and, to the same sort of rhythm, Bell and City were rather rudely abused by way of *"Willie, Willie Bell and his cock-sucking, dog-fucking, blue and white homosexual BASTARDS!"* which must rank as one of the most gratuitously obscene chants to have come to light in the research for this book (almost sufficiently obscene to be mistaken for a Hartlepool chant, in fact!).

Apart from the lackadaisical efforts listed overleaf, there really is not much else to speak of. Some laughable attempts were made to affirm that Villa supporters were the first to have sung anything along the lines of *"Ooh, aah, Paul McGrath"*, and therefore instigated the whole Cantona thing, but this sort of nonsense is barely worthy of a mention at all. More recently there has been talk of some sort of Dwight Yorke song based on the famous *New York, New York* (a favourite of Frank Sinatra) and this does seem to have some credence, but needless to say, no-one could supply the lyrics.

Villa's derisory collection of songs does, however, mean that there is sufficient space allocated to them to permit a detailed explanation of how the club's supporters have earned themselves the nickname of "Seals" - by which they are known throughout the West Midlands, primarily by supporters of West Brom. The oldest stand at Villa Park is the Trinity Road, which over recent seasons has increasingly become the habitat of shrieking schoolkids and family groups as the livelier (!) elements of the crowd have gravitated to the newer parts of the ground. With inventiveness not a Villa forte at the best of times, it is unreasonable to expect anything too reactionary on the singing front from the Trinity's thermos flask and travel rug brigade and, in a suitably inane manner, the chant of *"Villa, Villa, Villa!"* is just about all that emanates from beneath the gabled roof. Surprisingly, efforts are made to enliven this tawdry effort - feet are stamped and hands clapped to punctuate the words - and it does not required a quantum leap in imagination (merely the addition of some beach balls balanced on noses, and the substitution of *"Villa"* with a suitable barking noise) for the perfect performing seal scenario to be in place - hence the name. Really, the use by the Baggies of their derogatory Seals name for Villa fans seems wholly justified on the basis of the feeble showing on the songwriting front from what is perversely one of the country's foremost venues - and bearing in mind that they got slated in the first edition of this noble publication and no-one (not even Nigel Kennedy !) wrote in to redress the balance, it seems to be a situation which is set to persist for the foreseeable future.

Birmingham City

Perhaps one of the more unjustly-treated clubs in the first edition of this book with regard to the poor selection of Blues' songs included, City's supporters have since gone some way towards putting the record straight, having sent in one or two interesting submissions. With the club having enjoyed a qualified renaissance under the Sullivan/Brady/Fry administration, and with a much admired old boy now at the helm in the shape of Trevor Francis (well, it actually *is* Trevor Francis come to that, not just someone the same shape as him!), things appear to have livened up somewhat at St Andrews, and the club's latent support have once again climbed aboard the bandwagon, bringing some much improved matchday atmosphere with them.

First and foremost, the one song which can be guaranteed an airing at virtually every City game is *Keep Right On To The End Of The Road*, a traditional, rambling effort in true West Midlands style and one which can sound singularly impressive when a few thousand voices are giving it their all....

> *All through life it's a long, long road,*
> *There'll be joys and sorrows too,*
> *As we journey on, we will sing this song,*
> *For the boys in royal blue:*
> *We're often partisan, la, la la,*
> *We will journey on, la, la la,*
> *Keep right on to the end of the road,*
> *Keep right on to the end.*
> *Though the way be long,*
> *Let your hearts be strong,*
> *Keep right on round the bend.*
> *Though you're tired and weary,*
> *Still journey on,*
> *'til you come to your happy abode,*
> *With all your love, we'll be dreaming of,*
> *We'll be there - where?*
> *At the end of the road*
> *Birmingham, Birmingham...!*

The traditional nature of this song make for some rather strange words, but it still provides a pretty impressive racket when belted out by a big crowd - one of its more impressive airings in recent years being at the 1995 Auto Windscreens Shield final against Carlisle United at Wembley.

With regard to the origins of the song, it appears that its introduction by City player Alex Govan en route to the 1956 Cup Final against Man City (as set out in the last edition) is rather less than the whole story. Govan has reputedly perpetuated this myth on a club video, but we are now reliably informed that the song predates this occasion and was doing the rounds for some time beforehand. This is revealed by the fact that the local Brum paper, the Sports Argus, issued a special Cup Final edition which went on sale a week or so before the game and carried the banner headline "Keep right on to the End of the Road", so Govan was merely popularising a song which already had links with the club.

Having already made mention of the 1995 Auto Windscreens Shield final, it is now wholly appropriate to look at what is the second most popular song in the City supporter's repertoire. Simple, straightforward and to the point, it is the inestimable....

> *Shit on the Villa, shit on the Villa tonight,*
> *We're gonna shit on the Villa,*
> *Shit on the Villa tonight*
> *(repeat these three lines twice, then finish off with...)*
> *Why should we shit on the Villa?*
> *Because they're full of shiiiiiite!*
> *(Tune: Roll out the Barrel)*

This has been doing the rounds for ages, but sprang to prominence after the Carlisle game when winning-goalscorer Paul Tait whipped off his City shirt to reveal a *"Birmingham City - Shit on the Villa"* tee shirt. No-one took too much notice at the time, but the good old Sun newspaper *(sic)*, ever keen to get make something out of nothing, printed a piece the following day which condemned the shirt, and by association, the song as *"deliberately provocative"* and *"a mindless obscenity"*. A few days later, the Birmingham Evening Mail grasped pathetically at The Sun's coat-tails after the song had made an appearance during a league game at Brentford, noting that the City supporters *"committed themselves to obscenely insulting Villa"*. The furore resulted in Tait being fined a fortnight's wages - the song, needless to say, became even more popular on the terraces.

Before the *"Shit on the Villa"* furore, City supporters were perhaps most fondly remembered for the rather nasty tendencies of their lunatic fringe, the Zulu Warriors. Throughout the eighties, the St Andrews experience could never be considered complete until you'd been chased across the waste ground outside the stadium by a load of hooligans chanting *"Zulu, Zulu, Zulu!"* - few people at the time probably stopped to think why the kicking they were being handed was preceded by this rather than the more usual *"You're going to get your fucking heads kicked in"*, but all can now be revealed. The old terrace on the Coventry Road side of the ground was one of many such stands to be nicknamed the Spion Kop (see Liverpool for the full story behind this) and, it became apparent to a group of Blues fans in the early 1970's that there was some sort of African connection involved in the derivation of this name. However, not fully grasping the real historical background, it was decided that this must have something to do with the Zulu wars of the late nineteenth century, and thus a rugby song known as *Zulu Warriors* became the vogue. Extending to little more than a chant of *"Get on down you Zulu Warriors; Get on down, you Zulu boys"*, it was elaborated upon after the timely release of the Michael Caine film *Zulu*, which contained scenes of the native "impi's" jumping up and down on the spot with arms held stiffly by their sides in some sort of pre-battle ritual. Not only the dance, but the accompanying warcry (no words - just a bit of co-ordinated shouting really) which became know as *The Banana*, immediately transferred to the Coventry Road Kop and, when City's fighting crew were looking for a name for themselves, Zulu Warriors was the obvious choice.

In a less confrontational style, City's recent sojourn in the lower reaches of the league obviously took them to some of the country's rather less impressive stadia and, safe in the knowledge that St Andrews was well on the way to becoming a decent ground, residents of the more shambolic venues were regaled with....

> *My garden shed, is bigger than this,*
> *My garden shed is bigger than this,*
> *It's got a door and a window,*
> *My garden shed is bigger than this.*
> *(Tune; When The Saints Go Marching In)*

To wind up, a bit of social history for you. Birmingham is notorious for the somewhat less than rhapsodic accent with which locals are afflicted, but even residents of the second city consider their dulcet inflexions to be sweeter than the Black Country drawl of Wolverhampton. In particular, the Wolverhampton usage of "y'am" has been picked up on (this is actually a corruption of "you are", which has become "you am" and is then abbreviated to "Y'am"), and this has resulted in residents of the town - and particularly supporters of the Black'n'Gold outfit - being known as "Yam Yams" to everyone who lives a couple of junctions down the M6. This, then, is the explanation behind the thus far mysterious chant from the Blues supporters at City v Wolves matches of *"Yam Yams, give us a song"* and is one of a very few examples which exist of local dialect making an appearance in a chant.

Coventry City

The perennial struggle against relegation from the top flight which City have developed into an art form over recent seasons seems not to offer a particularly rich environment in which songs can develop. While it could be argued that the desperate end of season scramble to preserve Premiership status should generate exactly the sort of frenzy from which classics grow, evidence would suggest that their are too many fingernails being chewed throughout Highfield Road for Sky Blues' supporters to set aside some time for the light relief offered by a good shout. This is a shame, as on the odd occasion that the spectre of relegation is lifted from the shoulders of the Highfield hordes, they have shown themselves capable of some laudably enthusiastic singing - albeit largely by way of just one song.

For such an example of unencumbered frivolity, there is no need to look any further than the 1987 F A Cup Final against Spurs, when the twin towers resounded to *The Sky Blue Song* throughout the entire afternoon. Before we set out the words to this, however, it is necessary to relate the history of the song which is the second in this book to have been composed by that poet laureate of terrace anthems, Jimmy Hill. The Chinned One's long-standing involvement with City is well documented, and whilst manager in the 1960's a conscious decision was made to come up with a club song. Enlisting the help of John Camkin - a City board member and football commentator for Anglia T V - Hill embarked on the creative process, imbued with inspirational qualities which come from the bottle of gin which was allegedly emptied during the writing session. Temporarily flagging from their task, the pair decided to listen to the radio in search of ideas, only for *The Eton Boating Song* to drift across the airwaves. Grasping the moment, the words were hastily scribbled down and the song was soon committed to vinyl, with someone by the name of Ted Heath doing the singing (not sure whether this was the bloke who went on to become prime-minister or not!). The words to the song were then printed in the matchday programme for a game against Barnsley which, fortunately, was subject to a break in proceedings when thick fog descended over the pitch. Shoving the public address microphone and a copy of the words in front of club chairman Derrick Robins (not averse to public performances after a flirtation with amateur opera), Hill marched out onto the pitch and lead the crowd through the first performance of the song, with Robins belting out the lyrics on the tannoy. Were anything of this nature to take place nowadays, the perpetrators would no doubt be booed off the pitch, but this being the swinging sixties, the crowd took the song to heart and it has been City's anthem ever since - time for the words, then....

> *Let's all sing together,*
> *Play up Sky Blues,*
> *While we sing together,*
> *We will never lose,*
> *Tottenham or Chelsea,*
> *United or anyone,*
> *They can't defeat us,*
> *We'll fight 'til the game is won.*

In fact, it is believed that the three teams mentioned in the original were *"Proud Spurs or Bolton, Wolverhampton or anyone"*, but as (at least) one of them has since declined from the pinnacle of footballing endeavour, they have been usurped by some slightly more contemporary names to give the thing a suitably nineties feel.

Evidently being of the opinion that nothing could ever surpass this fine effort, City's fans have been loathe to introduce many new songs over subsequent years. Obviously, the usual chants have been tailored to their own needs, but it was not until the 1991/92 season that something new(ish) made an appearance. This season was right in the middle of the craze for adopting pop songs in their entirety and singing the whole thing through without any alterations (see Sunderland, Cliftonville and the like for other examples) and the West Stand choir were soon giving virtuoso performances of The Beatles' *Twist And Shout*. The reason behind the adoption of this song, unfortunately, has eluded the best efforts of our stringent and otherwise flawless investigative processes. So, a paltry two songs seems to be the sum total from seventy-five odd years of senior football in Coventry, a poor return and one deserving of severe castigation - were it not for the fact that their club song has been written by one of the game's leading pundits when horribly pissed!

West Bromwich Albion

Supporters of the Albion have had a pretty raw time of late, stagnating in what is now the First Division and even plumbing the depths of the Second for a couple of years since their demotion from the top flight some ten years ago. Luckily, the lack of success on the pitch has driven the fans to seek alternative entertainment and, in between regular fancy dress jaunts around the country, they have come up with a rather fine variety of songs - two of which have gone on to wider fame.

Firstly, Albion are the true claimants of the crown for having been the instigators of all the Pet Shop Boys *Go West* chants (originally a Village People song, by the way) which, as already noted, were really brought to the nation's attention by Arsenal supporters at the 1994 Cup Winners' Cup final in Denmark. For some time before the Gooners turned this into one of the stock songs for supporters across Europe, the Baggies following had been intoning *"Go West, Bromwich Albion, Go West, Bromwich Albion, Go West, Bromwich Albion, Go West, Bromwich Albion"* - laying the foundations for what must now be one of the games most all-pervading chants.

The second effort - and one for which West Brom's supporters have received rather more critical acclaim is the exemplary *"Boing, Boing, Baggies, Baggies!*

....*Boing Boing, Baggies, Baggies!"*. Initially coined from a Dutch techno track (see Crystal Palace - one of the clubs who have since embraced the chant) this took centre stage at Fratton Park during the last game of the 1993/94 season; equal on points with Birmingham City at the start of play, a 1-0 win for the Baggies was good enough to send City down on goal difference. Huge celebrations were therefore in order, and the chant was accompanied by some rather fine jumping up and down and skyward thrusting of arms which, along with the apparently nonsensical words, suitably perplexed the members of the media in attendance. The phenomenon now known as "boinging" became sufficiently well established as to warrant investigation by a team from Birmingham University, though quite what they were looking to discover is a bit of a mystery. Anyway, with the local and national papers also showing an interest in the bizarre goings-on, it is fair to say the "boinging" has probably become the most well known of the few terrace dances which currently exist, although it perhaps lacks some of the fulsome splendidness of the Grimsby and Crewe efforts, and doesn't quite match Cardiff City's *Ayatollah* for sheer stupidity.

Now time for a bit of neighbourly taunting, and a short song which appeared during the 91/2 season shortly after the arrival of Bobby Gould in the Hawthorns hot-seat. Wolves are, of course, Albion's genuine local rivals, but this didn't stop the Birmingham Road Kop giving an airing to....

> *If you like kick and rush,*
> *Played by dumb gorillas,*
> *Don't waste your time at the Albion,*
> *Fuck off down the Villa*
> *(Tune: One Man Went To Mow)*

Having mentioned Wolves, one thing that can usually be guaranteed to stir up the Baggies is mention of Steve Bull - Wanderers prolific striker who arrived at The Hawthorns on a free transfer from Tipton Town in August 1985, scored three goals in five appearances and was then sold to Wolves for the pathetically meagre sum of £35,000 three months later. The rest, as they say, is history, with Bull going on to international recognition and to put together one of the finest goalscoring records in the history of the game - West Brom appear to have shot themselves spectacularly up the arse when they allowed him to leave! Anyway, suffice to say that Mr Bull is not *the* most popular player on show whenever Wolves visit the Throstle's nest, so much so that he has had the chant of *"Bully is a tatter, Bully is a tatter"* conceived in his honour. Rather odd though this may sound to anyone not versed in the colloquial peculiarities of the Black Country, its purpose becomes clearer when it is realised that a "tatter" is a local term of abuse for a grubby old gyppo in the Harold Steptoe mould. The term has also found its way into the extended version of the chant, which takes the tune of *My Old Man's A Dustman*....

Woooooooaaaaah - Stevie Bulls' a tatter,
He wears a tatter's hat,
He lives in Wolverhampton,
And he's a fucking twat,
He runs down the left wing,
He runs down the right,
He couldn't score a goal,
If he tried all fucking night.

....which is not only factually incorrect (Bull may indeed be a twat, but he certainly scores plenty of goals), but is pinched from Swansea City where a far longer version is used to belittle the entire Cardiff line-up.

As far as fêting their own players goes, Albion supporters came up with a few ditties to illustrate the affection in which they held some (now departed) favourites. Don Goodman's four and a half years in the blue'n'white stripes was punctuated by stirring performances of....

Hark now here the West Brom sing,
The king is born today,
His name is Donald Goodman
And he's better than Stevie Bull - SHIT!
(Tune: Mary's Boy Child by Boney M)

....before he moved on to Sunderland and beyond. More recently, Andy Hunt has precipitated the introduction to The Hawthorns of a bit of samba flavour, as the striker who completed his fifth season with the club at the end of 96/7 has found himself the recipient of one of the Ian Wright/Juninho stylee chants based on Arrow's *Hot, Hot, Hot* - following the increasingly popular format, this is obviously....

Howay, howay, howay, howay,
Andy Hunt, Hunt, Hunt!
Andy Hunt, Hunt, Hunt!

....which seems to lend itself to being used to rather less complimentary ends by supporters of Albion's opponents!

Back to the 1980's, and Kevin Bartlett's brief tenure of an Albion shirt (sandwiched between spells at Cardiff City and Notts County) saw him regaled with a *When the Saints Go Marching In* derivative which was....

Oh Kevin B; Oh Kevin B,
From Cardiff C; From Cardiff C
Oh Kevin B from Cardiff C,
He's got a head like a malteser,
Oh Kevin B from Cardiff C !

Evidently being a celebration of the boy Bartlett's smoothly shaven head, the copyright for this passed to Meadow Lane along with his registration papers and soon became a favourite with the Magpie's supporters. To the same tune, the equally popular John Thomas, or *"Johnny T from Wednesbury"* to quote the relevant lines, was proclaimed to all and sundry as being *"Johnny T from Wednesbury - He's got a stall on the market, Oh Johnny T...."*. Presumably, not only did Mr Thomas originate from Wednesbury but, err, he had a stall on a market - strange what trivia is deemed to deserve inclusion in songs!

Now, time for Baggies fans to feel a little less smug than they may have done with the assertions in the opening paragraphs of this section that they were the originators of two very fine chants - a third that they have always claimed as their own is, in fact, the property of someone else! The 1969 Harry J All Stars number *The Liquidator* became a firm favourite at the Hawthorns after it was played over the tannoy before games. Unfortunately, it is impossible to describe this in writing, other than to say that everyone hums or lah's the tune, adding a sequence of four claps and a shout of *"West Brom"* in appropriate places. So attached has this become with the Albion that the country's number one Baggie Frank Skinner has been known to perform it on stage during his one-man gigs - erroneously, as it has transpired, in the belief that it is a West Brom original. Apparently, this is without doubt a Chelsea number - to the extent that a version of *The Chelsea Liquidator* has been committed to vinyl, with the relevant shouts and claps in place - far more impressive than West Brom having to improvise to the original unembelished recording! Anyway, if you fancy hearing what this mysterious tune sounds like, either go to the Hawthorns, venture to Stamford Bridge and ask the bloke who does the P A to play it (he's got a copy!) or pay a visit to your local purveyor of fine gramophone recordings and buy one for yourself (the Chelsea recording in question - by Billy Blue Beat - being on *Blue is the Colour* - catalogue number MONDE 19CD). Failing this, part of the tune was sampled in *Fascinating Rhythm* by Bass-o-matic.

Far less controversially, a song which is most definitely exclusive to West Brom in a football context (well, since the demise of Meadowbank Thistle, anyway) is the 23rd Psalm (Crimond arrangement!) known to all and sundry as *The Lord's My Shepherd*. History would suggest that this, along with a few other hymns, found their way into Albion hearts when a hymn book was found in a pub during a pre-match drinking spree, with the 23rd proving to be the most popular. It has since served the Baggies cause in instances of both anguish and joy, taking the form of a requiem during a game at Twerton Park which saw the team relegated to the old Third Division, and then as an uplifting, joyful anthem during a Wembley play off win over Port Vale.

Mention of Port Vale brings us to a version of Harry Belafonte's *Banana Boat Song*. More usually employed in a style along the lines of its Sheffield United incarnation, it was rewritten during the course of Albion's '96/7 visit to Vale Park a week or so after the home side had richly entertained a nationwide T V audience by spectacularly throwing away a four goal lead against Queens Park Rangers. The inhabitants of Burslem were reputedly not amused when they were regaled with....

Daaay-oh, Daay-aay-ay-oh,
Four - one up and you drew four - four
Not one, not two, not three but four!
Four - one up and you drew four - four!

Of a less specific nature, two other Midlands favourites also form part of the Baggies bag of tricks, with both *Shit On The Villa* and the "garden shed" version of *When The Saints Go Marching In* (*cf* Birmingham City) earning regular run-outs and, in addition to the other material catalogued, this all adds up to what is really a most impressive collection of songs from another set of supporters who give the impression of always being determined to enjoy themselves regardless of what is happening on the pitch.

Wolverhampton Wanderers

Right, get yourself comfortable, open a couple of tinnies and settle down - this is going to take a while. Wolves have quite simply got the biggest collection of songs this side of Hadrian's Wall. They may not be necessarily the best, but only Glasgow's two Old Firm clubs can exceed the sheer quantity of chants to which Molineux plays host. Apparently, it is a source of great pride to Wolves fans that they lay claim to having football's finest selection of songs and, although the luxury of an extensive back catalogue means that there are very few new ones doing the rounds in the Black Country (no need to bother making any up, really), it seems reasonable that they should retain their position - as conferred upon them in the first edition of *Dicks Out!* - as easily "the singing champions of the West Midlands" and, very probably, the leading exponents of the art countrywide.

The Wolves fans' talent seems to be one for taking an idea which first shook the rafters at a different club, then altering it (usually by the addition of forty odd verses) and making an already decent song yet more impressive. Their first contribution is a classic example of this sort of thing - everybody at some time or another has had a go at the *"Everywhere we go"* chant, but no-one has ever come close to rivalling this....

Everywhere we go - everywhere we go!
People want to know - people want to know!
Where the hell are you from? - where the hell are you from?
We're from Wolverhampton - we're from Wolverhampton!
Lovely Wolverhampton - lovely Wolverhampton!
Colourful Wolverhampton - colourful Wolverhampton!
Buy a corner shop now - buy a corner shop now!
Selling cheaper lager - selling cheaper lager!
Tennants' Pilsner - Tennants' Pilsner!
Seventy two pee a can - seventy two pee a can!
Tennants' Extra - Tennants' Extra
Eighty four pee a can - eighty four pee a can!
Banks' Mild - Banks' Mild!
Sixty eight pee a can - sixty eight pee a can

Everywhere we go - everywhere we go!
People want to know - people want to know!
Where the hell are you from? - where the hell are you from?
We're from Wolverhampton - we're from Wolverhampton!
Lovely Wolverhampton - lovely Wolverhampton!
Colourful Wolverhampton - colourful Wolverhampton!
Buy a take away now - buy a take away now!
Selling cheaper curry - selling cheaper curry!
Chicken Madras - chicken madras!
Two pounds twenty - two pounds twenty!
Chicken Vindaloo - chicken vindaloo!
Two pounds eighty - two pounds eighty!
Try a popadom now - try a popadom now!
Forty two pee a piece - forty two pee a piece!

Everywhere we go - everywhere we go!
People want to know - people want to know!
Where the hell are you from? - where the hell are you from?
We're from Wolverhampton - we're from Wolverhampton!
Lovely Wolverhampton - lovely Wolverhampton!
Colourful Wolverhampton - colourful Wolverhampton!
Buy a football club now - buy a football club now!
Call it Wolverhampton - call it Wolverhampton!
Sack the Bhatti's - sack the Bhatti's!
Get promotion - get promotion!
In the second season - in the second season!
WANDERERS (clap, clap, clap!), WANDERERS (clap, clap clap!)

.... and that's all there is to it! The most diligent research has revealed that a complete rendition of this would take just over two full minutes which - not counting things such as singing *"Billy Bonds' Claret and Blue Army"* over and over again - makes it just about the longest proper song on offer at any football ground in Great Britain. Obviously, the general gist of its performance is that a handful of people shout out the first "half" of each line, with the massed ranks of the Wolves faithful joining in to belt out the repetitions. Not content with this phenomenal effort, Molineux's North Bank have also come up with another epic (ooh, now that's a story in itself as, when organised singing first started at the ground back in April 1965, it was said North Bank which housed the majority of the singers; in the late eighties, post-Taylor safety restrictions forced the closure of this terrace and the voluble elements of the home support decamped to the equally decrepit South Bank at the opposite end of the ground. In due course this too was threatened with closure and Wolves faced the prospect of playing at a ground with just one serviceable stand. Then came the timely intervention of millionaire businessman Sir Jack Hayward, the first tangible benefit of which was the raising of the new Stan Cullis Stand on the site of the old North Bank. This traditional home ground was then swiftly reclaimed, thus completing the almost unique circumstance of a club's home terrace moving from one end of a ground to the other and then back again!) - err, right, back on track after that brief geographical interlude, and the aforementioned second epic from Wolves supporters (to the tune of *The Camptown Races*):

We all know a famous bear; Yogi, Yogi,
We all know a famous bear; Yogi, Yogi, bear,
Yogi, Yogi bear, Yogi, Yogi bear,
We all know a famous bear, Yogi, Yogi bear.

Yogi's got a little friend; Booboo, Booboo,
Yogi's got a little friend; Booboo, Booboo bear,
Booboo, Booboo bear, Booboo, Booboo bear,
Yogi's got a little friend, Booboo, Booboo bear.

Booboo takes it in the arse; backshot, backshot,
Booboo takes it in the arse; backshot, backshot bear,
Backshot, backshot bear, backshot, backshot bear,
Booboo takes it in the arse, backshot, backshot bear.

Yogi's got a girlfriend; Suzi, Suzi,
Yogi's got a girlfriend: Suzi, Suzi bear,
Suzi, Suzi bear, Suzi, Suzi bear,
Yogi's got a girlfriend, Suzi, Suzi bear.

Suzi takes it in the mouth; blowjob, blowjob,
Suzi takes it in the mouth; blowjob, blowjob bear
Blowjob, blowjob bear, blowjob, blowjob bear,
Suzi takes it in the mouth, blowjob, blowjob bear.

Yogi's got an enemy; Ranger, Ranger,
Yogi's got an enemy; Ranger, Ranger Smith,
Ranger, Ranger Smith, Ranger, Ranger Smith,
Yogi's got an enemy, Ranger, Ranger Smith.

Yogi is a Wolves fan; South Bank, South Bank,
Yogi is a Wolves fan; South Bank, South Bank bear,
South Bank, South Bank bear, South Bank, South Bank bear,
Yogi is a Wolves fan, South Bank, South Bank bear,

Yogi went to Scarborough; vandal, vandal!
Yogi went to Scarborough; vandal, vandal bear!
Vandal, vandal bear, vandal, vandal bear,
Yogi went to Scarborough, vandal, vandal bear.

There does actually appear to be some sort of tenuous connection between Yogi Bear and being a Wolves supporters - lots of veiled references in their fanzines and the like - but the by now standard shoddy research has been unable to ascertain the real facts behind this strange preoccupation with the Hannah Barbera creation. The last verse of this song is somewhat easier to explain, as it makes reference to Wolves' visit to Scarborough for the home side's first game as a Football League club - thousands of fans travelled up from the Black Country and rioted spectacularly, wrecking the roof of one of the Seamer Road Stadium's stands (pre-McCain Oven Chip days this, being at the start of season 1986/87). Also, notice the reference in the seventh verse to the South Bank - this song being conceived when this was the "home" terrace, as detailed on the preceding page.

On a far less obtuse note comes the following - a cheery refrain which indicates where the real rivalry lies when it comes to Wolves and their fellow Football League sides....

Oh I do like to be beside the seaside,
Oh I do like to be beside the sea,
Oh I do like to walk along the prom, prom, prom,
Where the brass band plays
Fuck off West Brom (and Birmingham)
Fuck off West Brom (and Birmingham)
(Tune: obvious...!)

This one, perhaps with the omission of the *"and Birmingham"* bit, has now become standard fare wherever the Baggies play, but Wolves claim to be the motivating force behind its inception, which seems wholly reasonable. Next, another "uniquely Wolves" song, in as much as the Molineux version is just that bit longer than when supporters of other clubs have a go. Mary Hopkins' breast(s) must swell with pride when she catches The Central Match on a Sunday afternoon and her living room is filled with the strains of....

> *Once upon a time there was a tavern,*
> *Where we used to raise a glass or two (or three, or four)*
> *We used to while away the hours,*
> *Thinking of the things we used to do.*
> *Those were the days my friend,*
> *We thought they'd never end,*
> *We'd sing and dance forever and a day,*
> *We live the life we choose,*
> *We fight, we'd never lose,*
> *We are the Wolves, oh yes we are the Wolves.*

Yet another black and gold twist on a favourite theme crops us with the reworking of *Wandrin' Star*, the Lee Marvin effort, which tends to feature a particular terrace or stand when it appears elsewhere....

> *I was born under a Wanderers scarf,*
> *I was born under a Wanderers scarf,*
> *Do you know where hell is?*
> *Hell is at West Brom,*
> *Heaven is at Molineux,*
> *And that's where we come from.*
> *I was born under a Wanderers scarf,*
> *A Wanderers, Wanderers scarf.*

Variously dedicated to the home terraces at Hereford, Exeter and numerous other grounds, the closest approximation to this approach to the song comes from Ibrox with the *"I was born under a Union flag"* version - one of the few variants which extends along similar *"Do you know where hell is..."* lines.

West Brom's dismay at having allowed Steve Bull to make the short trip up the A457 has already been documented, and this must have seemed like an even more outrageous mistake at the end of the Black Country derby at the Hawthorns during 1989/90 when a late goal from the gentleman in question ensured that Wolves claimed all three points with a 2-1 win. Naturally, the Wolves contingent were not slow to spot the irony in this, and the departing Baggies must have been delighted to have filed out of the ground with *"Thank you very much for Stevie Bull, thank you very much, thank you very, very, very much...."* filling the air, to the tune of the Cadbury's Roses advert, more formerly known as *Thank U Very Much* by The Scaffold (*cf* Hartlepool United).

Back to the sixties, next, and one of post World Cup vintage. Similar efforts crop up elsewhere, notably Fulham, but as the Wolves fanzine on which ninety percent of this section is based had bothered to source the name of the original, it's their version which merits inclusion...

> Aye, aye, aye, aye, Parkes is better than Yashin,
> And Ernie is better than Eusebio,
> And we'll give the Baggies a thrashin'.

The Ernie in question is Ernie Hunt, a favourite at Molineux prior to his 1967 move to Everton; Phil Parkes was the Wolves keeper, here compared favourably to the famous Soviet custodian Lev Yashin, and the whole thing bounces along to the tune of some strange Italian aria by the name of *Cielito Lindo* - notice how this tune was used by the German and Spanish supporters at Euro '96 (not too sure what they were singing, though!).

From a similar era (the same, in fact!), there is yet another attempt to secure the "Longest Terrace Song in Football History" trophy with a litany of Wolves greatness based on *He's Got The Whole World In His Hands*. After an introductory burst of *"We've got the best team in the land"* (repeat four times for the full effect) the song proper started with....

> We've got Phil Parkes in our team,
> We've got Phil Parkes in our team,
> We've got Phil Parkes in our team,
> We've got the best team in the land.

....then on to Gerry Taylor, Bobby Thompson, and so on throughout the entire line-up (by way of Mike Bailey, Dave Woodfield, John Holsgrove, Terry Wharton, Ernie Hunt, Derek Dougan, Peter Knowles and Dave Wagstaff). Still from the late sixties, the chorus from the well known tune by The Monkees (a single and later the theme tune to their TV series) was suitably amended and gave rise to....

> Hey hey, we're the Wand'rers,
> Waggie's on the wing,
> Dougan's in the middle,
> And Bailey is the king.
>
> Hey hey, we're the Wand'rers,
> Taylor's young we know,
> But he'll be playing for England,
> Down in Mexico.

....see the preceding list for name checks on the players - Gerry Taylor did not, in fact, make it to the England squad for the 1970 World Cup (come to that, he never made the national side anywhere, at any time). Still firmly entrenched in the flower power era, and something which even the Wolves' fans of the day found difficult to explain - so we needn't bother even trying to fathom the reasoning behind it. In quieter moments on the North Bank (very few and far between, one would imagine) the following odd chant would start up....

Goodbye horse, goodbye horse,
He was saying goodbye to his horse,
And as he was saying goodbye to his horse,
He was saying goodbye to his horse
(repeat ad infinitum)

Basically to the tune of *Bless 'em All*, our source suggests that this song was used for the most part to "puzzle and bemuse" visiting supporters - sort of an "in joke" to which the North Bank was party - which, in fact, none of them actually were. Its purpose was always a bit of a moot point but on one occasion, with an impending riot about to kick off when Leeds United were the visitors, a swift chorus of *Horse* served to introduce such a surreal air to proceedings that a potentially nasty situation was diffused without blood being spilt. Latterly (during 95/6), although the song has long since disappeared from Molineux, rumour has it that Charlton Athletic supporters have begun to sing it - though they are no more able to understand exactly why they do so than were their Black Country counterparts of some thirty years ago.

Finally, putting contenders for The Extremely Long Song award on the back burner, there is an entry for the Extremely Old Song title - one of the earliest we've come across and which dates back to Wolves' F A Cup run of 1939. In praise of Dennis Westcott, a ridiculously prolific goalscorer who chipped in with the paltry total of eleven goals in the six match run to Wembley, and simply to the tune of *The Lambeth Walk*, we have....

When you go down Wembley way,
On the great Cup Final day,
You'll find them all,
Doing the Wescott Walk;
Goal...!

They play so free and easy,
They'll do as they damn well pleasy,
Why don't you make your way there,
Go there - stay there.

When you go down Wembley Way
On that great Cup Final day,
You'll find the Wolves,
Doing the Westcott Walk,
Goal...!

And that, rather appropriately, ends this abbreviated ramble through the Wolves song book which in its unadulterated form totals a staggering eighty five different songs and chants (and that figure is only based on the limited contributions which we received). Although there are a number of these which are merely the Wolves version of popular bits and pieces which crop up everywhere (we go!) there are certainly enough unique efforts to ensure that Molineux is the home of the most extensive library of ditties anywhere in Britain, and by implication, the world - unless, of course, someone now intends to write in and catalogue the vast array of chants which are peculiar to the supporters of some obscure Paraguayan team....*Dear Dicks Out!, I am a supporter of one of Paraguay's foremost club sides, Atletico Colléges de Luqûano, and we have nine hundred and four different songs which I now list for you pleasure.......*

Section Twelve

Wales and The West Country

Bristol City

Bristol Rovers

Cardiff City

Exeter City

Plymouth Argyle

Swansea City

Torquay United

Wales & The West Country

A really rather good selection of songs is the somewhat surprising result of our investigations on either side of the Bristol Channel - with the inventiveness, not to say the passion, of the supporters in the region being at odds with the image of the West Country as being a bit of a cultural backwater.

The most notable aspect of the material is that the followers of each club (with the exception of the two relatively low-profile outfits at Exeter and Torquay) have made a point of asserting their identity by some sort of theme song or - in the case of Cardiff City where there is no real definitive anthem - by way of one of the country's leading terrace dances.

All the clubs can command reasonable attendances when things are going well, and the Bristol and South Wales derby matches are always the high point of the season for the participating teams, with the depth of feeling involved often manifesting itself in some sort of crowd trouble. This sort of environment can be virtually guaranteed to produce some impassioned singing, and whilst Swansea City excel themselves with their catalogue of abuse aimed at Cardiff, the Bristol clubs also make a point of putting down their neighbours in no uncertain terms whenever their paths cross.

Plymouth are a slightly different kettle of fish, in that many of their songs seem intended to assert an identity borne of the relative isolation in which they find themselves. Naturally, Exeter are dealt some pretty caustic treatment when the occasion demands, but Argyle supporters seem to be more disposed toward proclaiming loyalty to club and county on their marathon trips around the rest of England - hence the peculiar *Oggie Song*.

St James Park has shown itself to be the home of a terrace choir which has undoubted potential but which seems a bit hamstrung by the constant underachievement of the team, whilst at Plainmoor, well, we find perhaps the archetypal collection from a club which has endured some pretty lean times of late, and which hasn't managed to whip up the sort of "let's have a laugh regardless" attitude which so often produces quality songs at other similar outfits.

Out on their own in more ways than one are Wrexham. Somewhat marooned in geographical terms and subsequently without a real local rival on which to sharpen their wit, energies have been expended on amending some of Wales's national themes. This has resulted in the high quality rehash of *Men Of Harlech* which - alongside the singularly impressive version of *Dirty Old Town* - sees The Racecourse blessed with two of the best songs from any part of the U K, let alone just Wales.

Bristol City

One of the few grounds currently in the lower divisions which would not look out of place in the Premier League, Ashton Gate - perversely - is not known as one of the most vehement cauldrons of noise. Once lamented by a club fanzine as being like *"Clifton Cathedral on the choir's day off"*, the East End of the Enclosure (alternatively known as the Chicken Run) has certainly become less boisterous in recent years, already on the road to oblivion before the seats finished it off for good and City's erstwhile singers moved into the shiny new John Atyeo Stand which replaced the old open terrace at the north end of the ground. It seems that the club's supporters now reserve their more effervescent performances for away matches, at which it is almost certain that this old favourite will make an appearance....

> *Drink up thee cider, drink up thee cider,*
> *For tonight we'll merry, merry be,*
> *We went down the Rovers,*
> *To do the bastards over,*
> *So drink up thee cider in the jar.*

Obviously, the Rovers in question are City's local rivals. This song was based on a single released by Adge Cutler in December 1966 - a best seller in Bristol for ten weeks after it hit the shops. Plymouth Argyle and - more distastefully for City supporters - Bristol Rovers have both tried to lay claim to the song as their own over the last thirty years, but the sleeve notes to Cutler's follow up album in 1967 assert that *"Drink up thee Cider has been adopted by City as their song"*, and it must, therefore, be considered as the sole preserve of the red and whites. The demise of Rovers' Eastville ground in the late eighties saw the "Tesco's Remix" of this song make an appearance, the supermarket's acquisition and subsequent partial demolition of the ground being celebrated with the lines *"Tesco's went down the Rovers, to take old Eastville over, and there's no Tote End any more"*. On the subject of Rovers' grounds, both Eastville and their subsequent home of Twerton Park have had stands destroyed by fire (the former, in 1980, possibly the work of City supporters, the latter ten years later definitely so) and, ever keen to delight in the misfortunes of their rivals, City were more or less obliged to start singing *"What shall we do with Bastard Rovers, What shall we do with Bastard Rovers, What shall we do with Bastard Rovers earlye in the morning - burn, burn, burn the bastards....."* to the ubiquitous *Drunken Sailor* tune (*cf* Derby County).

The first derby game to be played at Twerton following the fire also happened to coincide with the Gulf War and, equating the fire damaged ground with television pictures of Saddam Hussein's capital city after the U S Airforce had done a bit of landscaping, *"Is this Baghdad in disguise?"* was as predictable a chant as you're likely to hear anywhere (to the *Bread of Heaven* rhythm). This was, naturally, joined by the other popular *Conga*-based derby chant of *"We all shop at Tesco's, We all shop at Tesco's"*

Something which will always haunt City supporters is the pre-match entertainment laid on at the Gate in the late seventies and early eighties which - as well as the notorious dancing girls - saw the equally notorious Wurzels drag the name of the club through the mud. If anything was guaranteed to endorse the stereotyped view of West Country dwellers to the hilarity of visiting supporters, then the besmocked renditions of *I've Got A Brand New Combine Harvester* and the like was it, but surprisingly one of the Wurzels songs became what City fanzine *The Bountyhunter* has since described as "a magnificent terrace anthem". A traditional folk song, also numbered amongst the repertoire of such luminaries as The Yetties, it is something along the lines of....

> *It's one for the Bristol City,*
> *Two for the boys in red,*
> *Three for the lads down Ashton Gate,*
> *We'll follow 'em 'til we're dead, me boys,*
> *We'll follow 'em 'til we're dead.*

On a less parochial level, adherents to the City cause number anyone from Wales as being amongst the lowest forms of life it is possible to encounter, and although there might now be a couple of traffic-carrying bridges across the River Severn, there is little sign of any metaphorical bridge-building between City supporters and those of Cardiff and Swansea. Trips to the Vetch Field and Ninian Park inevitably prompt a few choruses of....

> *The Welsh are fucking shit!*
> *The Welsh are fucking shit!*
> *And now you're going to believe us,*
> *The Welsh are fucking shit!*

....to the *For He's a Jolly Good Fellow* tune. First used during a 5-0 thrashing of Swansea in the principality at the start of 1990/91, this has now become a more general appreciation of the merits of either of the Welsh Cities. Strangely, these two clubs seem rather less enthusiastic about the enmity which Robins' supporters like to think extends across the national boundary - they seem far too involved in their own internecine loathing to waste much energy cultivating any hatred towards Avon's finest (although Swansea have been moved to respond in some small way to the taunts from Ashton Gate).

There is one last contribution of note from Ashton Gate in that they can lay claim to be the first supporters in the country to have used the noble chant of *"Dicks Out!"*. Reputedly, this surfaced in the early days of the 1980/81 season when relegation from Division One was followed by a less than auspicious start to life in Division Two while the team was still under the guiding hand of manager Alan Dicks (the same Alan Dicks who incurred the wrath of Fulham supporters during an F A Cup defeat by Hayes, at which it was erroneously thought that *"Dicks Out!"* first came to light). So, not only have City supporters come up with one or two decent songs in their time, it looks as if a damn fine book title is down to them as well!

Bristol Rovers

Rovers' return to a ground in the City of Bristol during the 96/97 season (they now share the facilities at the Memorial Ground with the Rugby Union club) has recently seen an end to their nine year stay at Twerton Park, and will perhaps inspire some much needed creativity in a repertoire which has thus far been far too dependent on just one song of note. Obligatory copy for any newspaper report of Rovers' games over recent years has been the inclusion of a mention of the *Goodnight Irene* song which has become the club's theme over recent years, but which has reputedly been "bubbling under" for some little time....

> *Irene, goodnight, Irene goodnight,*
> *Goodnight, Irene, goodnight Irene*
> *I'll see you in my dreams*

....this is the chorus of an old dance hall song, written in the 1940's by American folk singer Huddie "Leadbelly" Ledbetter. The relevance to Rovers has two possible origins; in the (rather uninspiring) first instance, rumour has it that the song was pinched off Plymouth Argyle, and secondly, it is said to have been popular at the time of Rovers' 4-0 F A Cup cuffing of Man United in 1955/56, and has been sung since to commemorate the match. Whatever the real reason for its adoption by the Gasheads, the tune remains a bit of a mystery to anyone who is not wont to sport a blue and white quartered shirt of a Saturday, but if you're really itching to know how it goes, Ry Cooder recorded a version on his album *Chicken Skin Music* (Warner Brothers - cat. K54083).

The heartfelt hatred of all things from Ashton Gate, surprisingly, only came through in one song and, as our contributor stated, *"Me and a few mates came up with this in the pub, and we're having a hard time trying to get everyone to join in at matches"*. However, it is a noble effort nonetheless and merits inclusion even though only half a dozen or so Rovers supporters would appear to know all the words....

> *We are the Eastville Tote, decked out in Blue and White,*
> *We're off the Ashton Gate to slap the City Shite,*
> *And on last derby-day we saw the Rovers win,*
> *We laughed our bollocks off when Carlo banged it in.*
> *Ha ha ha ha ha ha, ha ha ha ha ha ha-ah,*
> *Ha ha ha ha ha ha, ha ha ha ha ha ha-ah...!*

....to the tune of *Paint it Black* by the Rolling Stones, which was placed in the (albeit somewhat bleary) public eye once again when it was used as the theme tune to that most sanitised of Vietnam war programmes, *Tour of Duty* (a favourite "filler" for those who compile the late-night viewing schedules). The *Eastville Tote* referred to in the above was the old home terrace at Eastville (surprise), presumably inhabited by Rovers' less savoury supporters before its 1987 conversion to the cold meats and delicatessen counter of a new Tesco superstore (hence the move to Bath). The inception of this song can be traced to sometime in the Winter of 1991, as it is imagined that *"Carlo"* is Carl Saunders who scored the winning goal in a Twerton Park derby in late January after Rovers had thrown away an early two goal lead and allowed City to draw level - before Saunders' sixtieth minute intervention decided the match in their favour.

Away from the singing side of things, but still on an admirably silly tack, Rovers' supporters became the latest to jump on the football/food bandwagon - an away game at Shrewsbury in 95/6 giving rise to the lunacy that follows. Having commendably imbibed a good few pre-match beers, it was perceived by a number of Rovers devotees to be a very splendid idea indeed to purchase some boxes of Weetabix and, having assumed their positions on the Gay Meadow terraces, to start lobbing said cereal items about in a good natured manner. Here the story gets a bit vague, but either on the way home from Shrewsbury, or on route to the next away match, a Rovers supporters' coach was stopped by the jolly old constabulary and actually searched for Weetabix - a large number (up to eighty from one coach, so the story goes) of these potentially highly dangerous items were found and subsequently taken away for questioning - nice to know that the good old British Bobby's sense of humour is alive and well! The episode, disappointingly, did not give rise to any songs (unlike Doncaster Rovers cream bun experience at Burnley, or any of the unseemly food-related nonsense at Orient).

Lastly, devotees of the Rovers' cause have always harboured a grudge against local TV commentator Roger Malone for a perceived pro-City bias which is all too apparent in his efforts - inevitably, this has resulted in a determined knot of Rovers fans taking it upon themselves to stand under the commentary box at matches and sing *"We all agree, Roger Malone is a wanker"* throughout the entire course of the game which, if nothing else, makes life extremely trying for the people editing the sound track for matches before it can be considered fit for broadcast - thoroughly juvenile, but exactly the sort of thing which needs to be encouraged.

Cardiff City

So the Welsh valleys are full of song are they...? Well, they're certainly not down Cardiff way, if the meagre contributions received from City supporters are anything to go by. Evidently the stress of following a club which has been teetering on the edge of extinction for the last few years has rendered those lusty Bluebird voices virtually silent, and Ninian Park's decline from national stadium to ramshackle tip has mirrored the fortunes of the club and its increasingly torpid supporters. The demise of the Bob Bank (submerged under a sea of seats in 1992) looks to have been the final nail in the coffin, and even the sudden burst of early nineties creativity based on the songs of Tom Jones has been unable to prompt anything of much note from the banks of the River Taff (whereas Staffordshire has become little short of a temple to the gyrating songsmith). Equally, the existence of a local rivalry with Swansea which remains the game's last bastion of regular, serious crowd trouble has failed to inspire larynxes to quiver in the Bluebird cause, and we are left with the rather lacklustre fare which follows. A half-hearted effort to abuse the residents of the Vetch Field has bequeathed....

> *He's a Swansea Jack, He's a Swansea Jack,*
> *He wears Black and White like he's some sort of queer,*
> *He can't handle women and he can't handle beer,*
> *He's a Swansea Jack*

....to the nation, sung to the tune of *My Liverpool Home*, but it seems that past deeds of greatness are all that are left to stir the emotions in South Glamorgan (or possibly in Mid Glamorgan!). In the fairly recent past, Jimmy Gilligan was accorded folk-hero status by the City supporters on the back of a (really rather unimpressive) record of thirty five goals in just short of a hundred games for the club. Prior to his departure for Portsmouth in October 1989, the adoration took on near biblical proportions with....

> *God said "Cardiff are the best"*
> *As he spoke to Joseph in his old string vest,*
> *The Virgin Mary said "I've been done,*
> *'cos I never had a son called Gilligan"*

....the tune to which is lost in the mists of time. Yet further back into the murky past, we come across Cardiff's one real claim to fame with their 1927 F A Cup win over Arsenal (*first team to take the Cup out of England, blah, blah, blah...*). With little else to brighten the intervening years, this noble feat is still celebrated with....

> *In 1927 in the merry month of May*
> *The Arsenal went to Wembley,*
> *They walked the Wembley Way,*
> *They thought they'd do the double,*
> *They thought they'd lift the Cup,*
> *But along came Cardiff City,*
> *To fuck the bastards up.*
>
> *Who's that team they call the Cardiff,*
> *Who's that team they all adore,*
> *We're the boys in Blue and White,*
> *Pissed and looking for a fight,*
> *And we'll hate the Swansea bastards evermore.*

The first section of this follows the oft-heard melody of *John Brown's Body*, with the second part switching to that of *Ally's Tartan Army*, and is none the worse for this swift change of tune in mid-flow. However paltry the vocal offerings from Ninian Park may be though, City supporters can still rightfully claim a place in the snappily-titled Terrace Goings On Hall of Fame by being members of the relatively exclusive group of supporters who have enlivened matches with something that can loosely be described as a dance at some time or another. Joining the followers of Crewe Alexandra, Grimsby Town, Cliftonville and the like - all of whom have found it necessary to leap about stupidly in order to proclaim allegiance to their team, City for their part have come up with something known as *The Ayatollah*. To really appreciate what this involves, you need to be an astute follower of world news, and to have caught sight on television of scenes of mass public mourning in a Middle Eastern country. The incident which lent its name to the merry jig was, in fact, the death of Iranian despot Ayatollah Khomenei (in 1989, I believe) which saw the streets of Tehran and the like swarming with people, all of whom were jumping up and down on the spot while beating themselves on the head with both hands - actions later to be precisely mimicked by City supporters. Quite why this was deemed suitable for transference onto the terraces of a struggling Welsh football club is beyond comprehension - unless the sorry state of the team was considered to be at least as grave a situation as the death of a world leader, if not more so. Performances of *The Ayatollah* were further embellished (as if any sort of improvement were needed) with a sort of anguished wailing noise, which was supposed to approximate the cries of the distraught mourners - absolutely top quality stuff.

Exeter City

Contrary to the idea put forward in the first edition that only one of the country's two St James' Parks is a cauldron of white noise, the Devon equivalent of Sir John Hall's luxurious playpen can now be confirmed as being at least the equal of its more illustrious namesake. First up, we find that the North East is again mirrored way down south with Hartlepool's "nasty" song having a counterpart in far off Exeter....

> *My brother's in borstal, my mother's got pox,*
> *My sister's a whore down in Devonport Docks,*
> *My uncle's a pervert, my aunty's gone mad,*
> *And Jack the Ripper's my dad.*
> *La la la, la la la la la, la la la la la...etc*
> *(Tune: Just One Of Those Songs)*

As with the other clubs where this makes an appearance, no-one actually seems to know why it was adopted at all! Altogether more obvious is the seasonal offering which is....

> *We wish you a merry Christmas,*
> *We wish you a merry Christmas,*
> *We wish you a merry Christmas,*
> *Now fuck off Argyle...!*

....a straightforward expression of ill-will towards nearby Plymouth, which is alternatively climaxed with *"....We wish you a merry Christmas and a Happy New Year - we hate Argyle and we hate Argyle..."* as a replacement for the distinctly non-festive last line.

The thoroughly stereotypical country bumpkin image of the South West then makes an unscheduled appearance via City's performances of *"Give us an ooooh... give us an aaaaaar...what's that spell - OOOH AAAAAR...!"*, and the usual *"....we can drive a tractor"* effort (as detailed under Plymouth's section over the page). More regularly used to take the piss out of residents of an area perceived as even remotely pastoral, these are used by the Grecians' supporters as sort of pre-emptive strikes - getting in with 'em a bit sharpish before the opposing supporters can start to use them for their own abusive ends - a bit of psychology on the terraces...!

Lee Marvin's omnipresent *Wanderin' Star* song (*cf* Lincoln City, Rangers *et al*) is another which has been adapted for use at St James' Park, with the undeniably quaint assertion that *"I was born under the Tea Stand End"* being made in the relevant place - there is surely room for expansion here, what with Devon being the epicentre of the multi-billion pound "quaint thatched tea-room" trade, perhaps a few lines extolling the virtues of scones, clotted cream and strawberry jam are what is needed?

On a less indulgent note, City appear to have entered the *Always Look On The Bright Side Of Life* fray - and not, it would seem, without some justification. Attributed elsewhere to (variously) Fulham, Sheff Wednesday and the mob from Old Trafford, Exeter have come up with documentary evidence to back up claims of having performed the song back in the late 1980's, in that the cover of club fanzine *The Exe Directory* comes complete with the strapline *"Looking on the bright side with Exeter City"*. Definitely in position for an issue dated Feb/March 1990, this seems to be the earliest mention of the song in a footballing context, a full year in advance of United's Cup Winners' Cup run which saw the song first come to nationwide prominence. Similarly, the very extensive catalogue of Fulham songs on which their entry in this book is based dates from December 1989, and contains no mention of *Bright Side* whatsoever. So, with Sheffield Wednesday's involvement being no more than unsubstantiated hearsay at the very best, it looks as if this long running dispute of national importance can finally be laid to rest with the proclamation that Monty Python's song made its debut as a football anthem on the terraces of St James' Park, Exeter which, for an otherwise nondescript club, is a pretty impressive thing!

Plymouth Argyle

The Argyle Songbook is one which is strong on reputation but, unfortunately, a bit thin on actual substance. Rumours have reached the *Dicks Out!* offices of a fairly extensive catalogue of largely traditional songs which were, in the not too distant past, performed by the Home Park throng. However, stirring renditions of *To Be A Pilgrim* (the hymn by John Bunyan), *Going Up Cambourne Hill* and a particularly fine version of *You Are My Sunshine* can be catalogued as no more than unsubstantiated claims to greatness as the definitive lyrics have not been made available. Argyle's attempts to embrace Bristol City's *Drink Up Thee Cider* as their own are both recorded and dismissed elsewhere, but it is not all doom and gloom for the Devonport End choral society, as the splendidly named *Oggie Song* is as fine a club anthem as you will find anywhere. Initially, this takes a similar self-depreciatory approach to that mirrored in some of Exeter City's efforts with the pre-emptive appearance of some agrarian lyrics, but it then veers sharply towards the surreal end of the football song kaleidoscope and becomes, most definitely, unique to Argyle....

244

I can't read, and I can't write,
But that don't really matter,
'cos I come from the West country,
And I can drive a tractor.

Oh how happy we shall be,
To get back to the West Country,
Where the oggies grow on trees,
Oh bugger janner!

And we'll all go back to oggie land,
To oggie land, to oggie land,
Yes we'll all go back to oggie land,
Where you can't tell sugar from tissue paper,
Tissue paper, marmalade or jam!

The tune to the first section of this is the "popular" one to which it is performed up and down the country, but the second and third verses are completely different and don't seem to conform to any well known metre. To partially clarify a couple of rather obscure words which make an appearance herein, an "oggie" is a West Country term for a Cornish pasty - so the whole thing disappointingly isn't sung in praise of Steve Ogrizovic after all - and "janner" is another word from the local dialect, which apparently means "someone from Plymouth" (or so we were informed by the very helpful young lady on the Argyle reception desk!). This definition, however, does not sit easily with the line in which the word appears, as *"Oh bugger someone from Plymouth"* seems a strange way to close out a song which is supposedly extolling the virtues of the place.

The next Argyle offering is no less confusing. A chant which came to the fore during the early 1980's as a precursor to a shout of *"Plymouth - Plymouth - Plymouth!"* (interspersed with three claps between each shout), we have....

Ooh ahh, ooh ahh ahh,
Ooh to be a Southerner.
Who's that man in the big fat nose?
The more he eats the more he grows
If he eats much more then he'll explode!

Strangely, it is claimed that chant was never used again after a game at Dean Court, Bournemouth in 1986, but our contributor was unable to shed any light as to why this was the case, and subsequent submissions from The Hoe have suggested that it did, indeed, remain in use after this date.

Glossing swiftly over two other chants which are unique to Argyle solely due to their singular preference for a shirt colour which mirrors the verdant sod on which they play (*"Come on you Greens"* and *"Green Army, Green Army"!*), we come to the refreshingly uncomplicated world of local rivalry. Exeter City are the team who are guaranteed to bring on apoplexy in any self respecting Argyle supporter, and The Grecians' relegation season of 1983/84 and the repeat performance of a decade later would have been celebrated to the south west of Dartmoor with....

> *City's going down, City's going down,*
> *On the beer we will go,*
> *Eeh aye eeh aye eeh aye oh!*

....*Knees Up Mother Brown* obviously being the inspiration for this one. A somewhat lengthier verbal assault on the residents of St James' Park comes by way of....

> *Who's that team they call the Exeter?*
> *Who's that team that never score?*
> *And they play in red and white,*
> *They're a fucking load of shite,*
> *And Terry Cooper's missus is a whore!*

....fairly standard fare based on *Ally's Tartan Army* from Scotland's 1978 World Cup excursion to Argentina, and something which many other clubs sing along similar lines, but Argyle must be classed as one of the foremost exponents as, when Alan Ball was in charge at City and his name therefore made an appearance in the last line (as does whoever happens to be the Exeter manager of the day), the whole thing was sung in a screeching high-pitched voice to reflect the said Mr Ball's less than dulcet tones.

On a less parochial tack, and before the 1996 play-off triumph over Darlington, Argyle had managed to exist through one hundred and ten years without getting any nearer to Wembley than their F A Cup semi-final defeat in 1984. Acknowledging this rather lamentable record in knock out competitions, and with due reverence to a small seaside resort just along the coast from Plymouth, Argyle's cup ties would generally be illuminated by renditions of either *"Wembury, Wembury, we've got our buckets and spades and we're off to Wembury"* or *"Wembury, Wembury, it's the greatest beach in Devon and it's just beside the sea"*, or possibly *"Que sera sera, what ever will be will, we're going to Wembury, que sera sera"* (or all three, come to that). All these three follow the same tunes as do the more popular versions sung by supporters who are bound for the twin towers, though the substitution of Wembury for its more famous counterpart suggests that Argyle fans have the sort of grasp on reality not normally associated with football supporters anticipating where they might find themselves come the end of the season!

Swansea City

Luckily, for the sake of the fine vocal reputation of the Welsh nation, Swansea have managed to conjure up a rather better selection than their despised neighbours from Ninian Park. Abuse of the Bluebirds features prominently in the Vetch Field songbook, and rarely will a derby between the two sides get under way without a good twenty minutes of the ultimate in succinct abuse which is the Swans' supporters non-stop chanting of *"Scum, scum, scum, scum, scum...."* at their opposite numbers (should, that is, the two sets of supporters actually occupy Ninian park or the Vetch at the same time, as the recent trend has been to ban supporters of the away team from the derby matches to try and avoid crowd trouble). This functional but uninspiring incantation will usually be augmented by a swift burst of *"You're scum and you know you are"* to the pandemic *Go West* rhythm. One of the contributory factors as to why the warring factions are now kept apart was an incident which took place after a game at the Vetch in the 1980's. A group of Cardiff fans were chased down to the seafront by a gang of Swansea supporters eager to make their acquaintance in the traditional manner. Deciding that the only way to avoid a real hiding was to continue their flight into the waters of Swansea Bay, the Cardiff fans dived in and swam off. Ever eager to make the most of this ignominious retreat by their arch-foes, whenever the two clubs have met subsequently, you will probably hear the Swansea supporters singing *"Swim-away, a swim-away, a swim-away, a swim-away"* in the style of the *"wim-away"* bit out of *The Lion Sleeps Tonight.* This initially rather bland effort is massively enriched by the associated actions, which involve making breast-stroke type swimming movements - quality piss taking of the highest order! This will, at some point, be followed by the rather more inventive reworking of *My Old Man's a Dustman* which begins....

> *Phil Stant is a wanker,*
> *He wears a wanker's hat,*
> *He plays for Cardiff City,*
> *And he's a fucking twat.*
> *He runs down the left wing,*
> *Then he runs down the right,*
> *And if he tried to score a goal,*
> *He'd take all fucking night.*
> *Ooooooooooohhhhhhh.....*
> *Carl Dale's a wanker,*
> *He wears a wanker's hat,*
> *He plays for Cardiff City.....*

....and so it goes on, in a rather Wolverhampton Wanderesque style, through the whole Cardiff team. The old Leeds United favourite to the *Que Sera Sera* tune is also a favourite at the Vetch, though obviously with *"Shall I be Swans, shall I be scum"* and *"...get your fathers' gun, and shoot all the Cardiff scum"* taking the place of the Chelsea references from the Elland Road version.

With regard to the deification of Swansea players, the North Bank has sought inspiration from far and wide. The Crystal Palace/Brighton/2 Unlimited influence has seen goalkeeper Roger Freestone become *"Roger, Roger Roger, Roger Roger, Roger Freestone"* (this *No Limits* offspring being accompanied by some suitably silly "rave" style hand waving), while Kwame Ampadu's surname has reaped the benefits of both the *Agadoo* and *Kumbaya* treatment in recent seasons (*cf* Watford and Ipswich Town). Jeremy Charles - a member of the Swans' team of the early 1980's - unusually had two entirely different songs dedicated to his name. The music from the British Airways adverts of the time prompted the inception of *"We'll take good care of you, Charlo, Charlo"*, while Erol Dunkley's *O K Fred* meant that *"O K Charlo, now you're a yagga-yagga"* was also prone to make an appearance or two.

English teams visiting the Vetch are generally guaranteed a frosty reception, and a wave of defiant Welsh nationalism usually leads to a performance of the *O Sole Mio/Red Flag* concoction in its Sheffield United incarnation, with *"The Welsh Flag"* being kept flying high, instead of one of an entirely red variety, by supporters who will *"never be mastered, by no English bastards"*. The cross-border rivalry which causes Bristol City supporters to be less than complimentary towards the inhabitants of the Vetch has inevitably lead to some sort of retort being put together in response to the Bristolian taunts. It takes the form of the usual song which suffices at many other clubs when a South Western team are in need of castigation, but has seen a rearrangement of the standard lyrics so that a more general summation of the qualities of City fans can be made in the last line....

> *I can't read and I can't write,*
> *But I can drive a tractor,*
> *I'm a Drizzle City fan,*
> *And I'm a fucking wanker!*

"Drizzle" is obviously supposed to be a piss take of the way in which the patrons of Ashton Gate pronounce the name of the city in which they live, so this brief four line effort actually contains a multiplicity of abuse for City supporters in that not only are they illiterate agrarian dullards, but they can't speak properly and are also *"fucking wankers"* - a triumphant exhibition of contumelious brevity, as the bloke with the gavel on *The Good Old Days* would have said!

Two other numbers have become de rigeur in Swansea since the craze for "non-football" songs first reared its rather irrelevant head in the early nineties.

In the first instance, the (original) Sunderland anthem, *Can't Help Falling In Love* has decamped to the Valleys, and reputedly enjoyed its finest hour when 20,000 Welsh voices gave it a Wembley airing at the 93/94 Autoglass Trophy final. Secondly, and far more impressively in that it appears to be a wholly unique Swans'-song, *Can't Take My Eyes Off You* by Andy Williams has mysteriously found its way into the Jacks' repertoire. Typically of this type of genre (blimey!), this contains absolutely no footballing references whatsoever, but neither do any of its equally popular counterparts *The Time Warp, Keep Right On, Delilah* and the like....

> *I love you baby, and if it's quite alright,*
> *I need you baby to warm the lonely nights,*
> *I love you baby, trust in me when I say,*
> *Oh pretty baby, don't bring me down when I pray,*
> *Oh pretty baby, now that I've found you, stay,*
> *And let me love you,*
> *Let me love yooooouuu...!*

The route by which this touching ballad has arrived on the Vetch's North Bank is sufficiently circuitous to defy a full and frank explanation, but the fact that it was recently released as a "B" side by the Manic Street Preachers (Welsh blokes!) may go some way towards providing an answer. If nothing else the song illustrates a pleasing versatility in those that lend their voices to the Swansea cause - it's difficult to imagine anything that could be much further removed from the opening *"Phil Stant's a wanker"* effort!

Can't Help Falling In Love featured at Swansea's most recent appearance at Wembley for the 96/7 Third Division play-off final (bit of a grim day, what with last minute free kicks and all) but the occasion was perhaps more notable for the outburst of national pride that was apparent. Both *Bread of Heaven* and *Land Of My Fathers* were given stirring performances during the game, but the real point of interest was another song which got an airing on Sky Sports' *Soccer A M* on the morning of the game. A group of Swansea supporters were guests of the programme and, on being introduced to the nation, they burst into a chorus of something which was subsequently reported to be a club song dating from the days of John Toshack's managership (from 1978 to 1984). The tune must have been commissioned especially for the club, as it does not bear much similarity to any other better known compositions....

> *Swansea, oh Swansea,*
> *Oh City said I,*
> *I'll stand there on the North bank,*
> *Until the day I die,*
> *Take me to the Vetch Field,*
> *Way down by the sea,*
> *Where I will follow Swansea - Swansea City!*

While the majority of the preceding Swansea songs and chants are all comparatively easy to explain with regard to their derivation, one strange chant - now seemingly redundant but very popular in its day - defies any sort of clarification at all. For no apparent reason, matches during the mid 1980's would be enlivened by endless repetitions of *"Jack and Danny, how's your fanny? How's your fanny, Jack and Danny?"* - the only possible connection with Swansea being the inclusion of the name *"Jack"* which, in the footballing fraternity, is a well known pseudonym for any City supporter. The reason for this particular name being utilised is an odd one, in that the lifeboat which used to service Swansea Bay (no doubt pressed into action in order to save fleeing Cardiff supporters on occasion!) numbered a dog by the name of Jack amongst its crew. It is not known when Jack the Dog donned his oilskins and sou'wester and took to the tempestuous sees to save drowning mariners, but evidently he became sufficiently well known for the name to have become widely associated with the town, and subsequently to have been applied to supporters of the football club - so now you know!

Torquay United

If ever any one incident in football history deserved to have been immortalised in song it was surely that memorable occasion when United's Football League status was preserved only by a goal scored against Crewe in injury time of the last game of the 1986/7 season, which had been made necessary when Bryn the Police Dog (as distinct from Jack the Lifeboat Dog!) ran on the pitch and bit Gulls' defender Jim McNichol on the leg, causing a gash that was to require seventeen stitches. The three or four minutes which were added enabled Torquay to equalise from being 1-2 down at the time of Bryn's intervention, and the point earned saw them finish level with Lincoln City who were relegated on goal difference. However, neither this nor the club's greatest triumph - promotion in 1991 via a win on penalties over Blackpool in a Wembley play-off - seem to have inspired the slightest vestige of creativity down on the English Riviera. Unfortunately, neither have The Gulls' recent struggles against adversity spawned the sort of bloody-minded "have a good laugh whatever' mentality which has given rise to so much lyrical greatness elsewhere, and we must look back to the 1960's to find anything of note which once uplifted the hearts of the Plainmoor faithful.

A godlike figure to the stout citizens of Torquay until 1968 (and probably beyond), Robin Stubbs plied his trade in the yellow and navy to such effect that his five years with the club brought him one hundred and twenty one goals in two hundred and fourteen appearances - a tidy record at the best of times, let alone for a United player. Sufficiently awestruck to have deemed a hymn of praise in order, Gulls' fans of the day looked to the theme music to Erol Flynn's *Robin Hood* film for the basis of their work, which thus gave the nation....

Robin Stubbs, Robin Stubbs, riding through the glen,
Robin Stubbs, Robin Stubbs, with his band of men,
Feared by the bad, loved by the good,
Robin Stubbs, Robin Stubbs, Robin Stubbs.

Simple it may have been, but this basic structure has survived the best part of thirty years and, sustained at the forefront of public consciousness through its use by the Monty Python team for their *Dennis Moor* song, it resurfaced in the 1990's in the more salubrious surroundings of Old Trafford as a paean of devotion to Ryan Giggs who was reckoned to *"running down the wing"* rather than being partial to any equestrian high jinks, and to be *"feared by the Blues, loved by the Reds"*, still, just goes to show how these songs persist. Obviously, Lee Sharpe must have brought the germ of this idea northwards, having made a few appearances for Torquay before his move to the other (far less impressive) United.

Those who performed the original Robin Stubbs version of this song must have done so in a particularly well-mannered way, as one of the football magazines of the day bestowed upon United's supporters the epithet "Best Behaved" in some sort of survey thing. Watching what was basically a shite side (alright, promotion in 1966 excepted) meant that even this small honour needed exploiting to the full, and thus *She'll Be Coming Round The Mountain* was amended to....

We're the best behaved supporters in the land,
We're the best behaved supporters in the land,
We're the best behaved supporters,
The best behaved supporters,
The best behaved supporters in the land,
Singing - I threw a bottle at the ref,
I threw a bottle at the ref....etc.

Impressively, this is another Torquay song which is still doing the rounds three decades after it first saw the light of day, having been adopted by supporters of several other clubs, albeit with some minor alterations. The 1990's remix has seen *"When we win"* inserted at the end of each line, and the bottle-throwing section replaced with *"But we're a right bunch of bastards when we lose"*, inferring that however mild-mannered the performers may be all the time they are enjoying the fruits of victory, defeat will prompt mayhem on a grand scale. All in all, therefore, Torquay may have what is basically a feeble selection of songs, but they have given the game two of its most enduring favourites, and must be praised accordingly (I still feel that *"How much is that doggy in the window, the one that bit Jim McNichols' arse"* really ought to have found its place at the forefront of Plainmoor's repertoire at some point, though!)

Wrexham

We have already touched on the relative (choral) merits of the two clubs in South Wales but, surprisingly, both Cardiff and Swansea must bow down and prostrate themselves meekly before the real songwriting greatness of the principality which is to be found on the terraces of the Racecourse Ground to the north. You will have noticed by now that we are not slow to enthuse about supporters from teams in the lower divisions who retain the ability to have a laugh in the face of adversity (F A Cup games against Arsenal and West Ham notwithstanding), and Wrexham certainly deserve any such plaudits. To see why, you need look no further than this first contribution, a version of *Men of Harlech* which must be right up there in the top ten of British Terrace Greats....

Here they come, our mighty champions,
Raise your voices to the anthem,
Marching like a mighty army,
Wrexham is the name.

See the Reds who fight together,
Speak their names with pride forever,
Marching like a mighty army,
Wrexham is the name.

Fearless in devotion, rising to promotion,
To the ranks of mighty heroes, fighting foes in every land.
History only tells a story, we are here to see your glory,
Stand aside, the Reds are coming, Wrexham is the name.

We have made the mighty humble,
We have made the mountains tumble,
Falling to our mighty army,
Wrexham is the name.

Down the wings the Reds are roaring,
To our greatest goal we're soaring
Destiny - we hear you calling,
Wrexham is the name.

Making no apologies at all for the mindless obscenity which follows, this really is fucking superb, and in my humble opinion, only Sheffield United's *Chip Butty Song* stands between this effort and the very pinnacle of football's lyrical pyramid.

Momentarily switching to something of less epic proportions, and a chant which originated in North Wales though which our contributor did not specifically label as a Wrexham song. It is one of many barbed comments which is aimed at Scousers, be they from Anfield, Goodison or, irritatingly for regulars of the dearly departed Cowshed, Tranmere. Appreciative of the reputation that residents of Merseyside have for being, err, ever alert for an opportunity to appropriate articles which may not strictly be freely available for acquisition, it seems that games in which said Liverpudlians make an appearance may present one of the very few occasions when a song from a West End musical transfers to the terraces. Lionel Bart's *Oliver* is the source for *"You've got to pick a pocket or two"*, which is used to draw a parallel between Fagin's gang of prepubescent dippers and cutpurses, and the alleged habits of those who reside in the shadow of the Liver Building.

Most definitely a Wrexham song, and one of more fulsome length, we find that The Pogues' *Dirty Old Town* has been reconstituted for use by the Reds' Mighty Army as....

I watch my team from the Crispin Lane,
Under the old Bushfield Stand,
Dirty old stand, dirty old stand,
In Wrexham town, it's a lovely old town.

Betty the tramp, she lives in a cave,
In Caergwrle, in Caergwrle,
She eats her chips off the King Street floor,
In Wrexham town, it's a lovely old town.

We go away in a transit van,
And drink loads of Wrexham lager,
We drink all day and we drink all night,
Then we come home defeated to that lovely old town.

Caergwrle is a small place a few miles to the north of Wrexham, but the troglodyte tendencies of Betty the Tramp have proved a little difficult to substantiate. Mention of Wrexham lager leads us onto another example of one of Wales' national songs having been adopted by supporters of the town club, with *Bread of Heaven* lending its tune to....

> *Wrexham lager, Wrexham lager,*
> *Feeeeeeed me 'til I want no more (want no more),*
> *Feed me 'til I want no more.*

Evidently a few beers is a fairly central part of the Wrexham Watching Experience which, it has to be said, is not wholly reprehensible (beer and footy - exactly what else is there to life, eh?). Disappointingly, it does not appear that the last of the triumvirate of Great Welsh Songs, *Sospan Fach*, has received the Wrexham treatment as yet, but it is to be hoped that this situation is rectified in the near future, as it's certain that the song would be improved should it become part of the Racecourse repertoire, as have the other two as detailed above.

Section Thirteen

Scotland

Aberdeen

Celtic

East Fife

Heart of Midlothian

Kilmarnock

Rangers

Scotland

If I were an accomplished enough writer to use words like "microcosm" in their correct context, then I would do so here, as the (sadly rather brief) section which follows encapsulates the entire range of football related songs. From the idiosyncratic oddities of East Fife, through the more conventional material of Kilmarnock and Hearts to the more serious end of the market with the Old Firm clubs, nothing is left out. This is perhaps because the structure of the game in Scotland extends from clubs that might be considered to be on a par with the semi-professional set-up in England at one end, to one or two of the genuine European superpowers at the other - with all points in between also being accommodated.

Obviously, the attitudes of supporters at these different sorts of club reflect the aspirations of the teams that they follow, hence the almost frivolous approach to things at the lower end of the scale, while much weightier matters are addressed the higher up the leagues you go.

The pinnacle of this more serious approach is obviously embodied by Rangers and Celtic, where the songs are dominated by the overbearing themes of religion, social division and the ongoing conflict in Northern Ireland. I have attempted to put forward some ideas as to why such matters have become such an integral part of the Old Firm rivalry, but if any aggrieved parties feel that I have either misconstrued or even trivialised the subject matter, please remember that my perspective is that of someone trying to make sense of things from an entirely objective and detached viewpoint, without any real access to more informed comment, and of attempting to relate everything back to the entirely facile game that is football.

As far as songs of a more immediately footy related nature go, it is probably fair to say that there is more diversity in the material submitted by the followers of the half dozen clubs featured than would be found in a similar selection from England. Each club has at least one song which is entirely the sole preserve of its supporters, and even when more recognisable tunes do turn up, they tend to have had some unique alterations made to them. It was, however, disappointing not to have received anything from the likes of Hibernian, either of the Dundee clubs or some of the "middle order" such as Morton, St Mirren and the like, so that a broader picture might have been presented. The quality of songs from the limited number of clubs actually covered would indicate that there are many other fine efforts which deserve to be made known to a wider audience - and perhaps the unduly put-upon Cowdenbeath fans would like to exercise their right to reply and furnish me with some concerted abuse directed at East Fife for future editions?

Aberdeen

As members of the "New Firm" which briefly held sway in the Scottish game during the early part of the 1980's, Aberdeen supporters have had more cause than most to have come up with a few decent songs - which has proved to be the case. First, though, something which smacks of being a long standing and traditional song which probably pre-dated the Dons successful spell under a certain Alex Ferguson - *The Northern Lights of Old Aberdeen*. The first section is obviously a bit contrived to make it relevant to the football club, but the second part has the look of a local song extolling the virtues of the city in more general terms, with reference to the meteorological/astronomical phenomenon which is the Northern Lights (vast shimmering lights in the night sky caused by ionised particles in the solar wind colliding with the earth's magnetic field - or something equally silly). The tune to the song - something which you might expect to have a noble and impenetrable metre of ancient Gaelic extraction - is in fact very similar to that used in the Cadbury's *Finger of Fudge* adverts (and must therefore be considered a close relative of those songs which bounce along to the Cadbury's *Roses* tune - *cf.* Wolves and Hartlepool United!):

> *When I was a lad, a tiny wee lad,*
> *My mother said to me,*
> *"Go see the Dons, the glorious Dons,*
> *Away down at Pittodrie",*
> *They call them the heavenly dancers,*
> *Superb in attack and defence,*
> *I'll never forget that wonderful sight,*
> *I've been a supporter since.*
>
> *The Northern Lights of Old Aberdeen,*
> *Are home sweet home to me,*
> *The Northern Lights of Old Aberdeen,*
> *Are where I long to be,*
> *I've been a wanderer all of my life,*
> *And many a sight I've seen,*
> *But God speed the day,*
> *When I'm on my way,*
> *To my home in Old Aberdeen.*

Having such obvious links with one specific club, it is almost inevitable that this song should be seized upon by the supporters of other teams and given some new and less complimentary words - in this instance it is Heart of Midlothian fans who have taken on this onerous task, and who have become the foremost exponents of the bastardised version (see the Hearts section!).

Players have proved a popular subject for song at Pittodrie over the years, with a former favourite who went on to become a star South of the border finding himself wooed by a corruption of The Ramblers ubiquitous *Sparrow* tune....

> There's only the one Gordon Strachan,
> And he is the king of them all,
> When he's on the ball,
> We all shout for goal,
> 'coz Gordon's the king of them all!

Three additional Dons' favourites are then lauded by something which seems to be based on *The Wild Rover* (but without recourse to any sort of chorus, it would appear)....

> And then there's Joe Harper who's king of the North,
> He plays at Pittodrie just up from Kincorth,
> He drinks all the whisky and Newcastle Brown,
> The Beach End boys are in town.
>
> And then Willie Miller came into the team,
> As a youngster in Bridgeton of scoring he dreamed,
> But it was as a defender in Aberdeen's red,
> That he lifted the Cup Winners Cup overhead.
>
> And then there's Drew Jarvie who's bald as a coot,
> He know how to head and he knows how to shoot,
> He scores on the ground and he scores in the air,
> So who the fuck needs hair?
> Drew Jarvie na, na, na, Drew Jarvie na, na, na.

Joe Harper plied his trade at Pittodrie during the 1970's, with Drew Jarvie following in his footsteps a little later. Somewhat out of place, the middle verse is about long serving Aberdeen stalwart Willie Miller, who enjoyed one of many highlights in an illustrious career when the Dons won the Cup Winners Cup in 1983, beating Real Madrid 2-1 in Gothenburg. All three made their mark in front of the old Beach End stand before it was replaced by the incongruous Richard Donald Stand which now towers about four times higher than the remainder of the ground.

Of more recent vintage the Danish player Henning Boel was also sufficiently impressive to merit his own song, but this took the form of a particularly sarcastic version of *The Quartermaster's Stores*....

> It's a goal, a goal, a goal for Henning Boel,
> It's a goal, it's a goal....!

....which derived its ironic touch from the fact that Boel managed just four goals during one hundred and fifty odd games for the Dons!

Apart from obviously trolling out a number of songs directed at their own players, Dons' supporters are also liable to aim a bit of abuse in the direction of any opponents who might incur their wrath. A particular target of such treatment has been Ian Durrant of Rangers, who for some reason has had most of the salient points of his career celebrated in song in the Granite City. A whole series of Durrant chants have enlivened Pittodrie over the years, with the fact that they all take the *Quartermaster's Stores* tune helping to bind them together into an ongoing narrative. The first example saw some fairly general abuse handed out with *"He's gay, he's bent, his arse is up for rent, Ian Durrant, Ian Durrant!"*, which could equally have been used to unjustifiably harangue any number of other players. Durrant then suffered a long term injury to a knee ligament which prompted *"He's gay, he's bent, he's got no ligament"* which swiftly became *"He's gay, he's queer, he's out for a year"* when it became apparent that the injury was going to rule Durrant out of first team action for quite some time. Then, one of those godsends for supporters who take pleasure in the misfortune of others when an evening out for Durrant ended in a fight which was writ large in Scotland's tabloid newspapers the following day - with the confrontation having taken place in a take-away food outlet, this incident was incorporated into the Durrant saga by way of *"He's gay, he's shite, he eats kebabs and fights!"*. No doubt, any subsequent misfortunes which befell the luckless Durrant were similarly treated, but the kebab episode is as far as our contributions have taken the story - with nothing ever having been sent in to say exactly why Durrant was singled out for this sort of treatment in the first place!

Finally, a parallel which can be drawn between supporters in the far North of Scotland with those in the South West of England. Both groups are constantly baited by supporters of other clubs with all manner of agrarian abuse in the case of the English clubs, and with constant references to sheep shagging directed at the Aberdonians. The supporters of Plymouth Argyle and Exeter City have already been recorded as pre-empting this sort of taunting by singing something along the lines of the *"....but we can drive a tractor"* song, and a similar degree of "early retaliation" is meted out by the Dons' supporters in a variety of ways. The succinct chant *"We fuck sheep! We fuck sheep"* is one such example, as is *Juantanamera*-lead song which is *"Sheep shagging bastards, we're only sheep shagging bastards, sheep shagging baaaaah-stards, we're only sheep shagging bastards"*. Most impressive of this type of Aberdeen ditty though are the performances of the club song, *The Northern Lights* in its entirety with all the words replaced by *"baaaah"'s*, which is just about as silly as football songs get, North or South of the border!

Celtic

A strange juxtaposition is apparent in the majority of Celtic songs, in that although the club is obviously one of the giants of Scottish football, drawing huge support from all parts of the country, it is from Ireland that much of their singing takes its inspiration. Obviously (and in terms of the utmost simplicity) this is as a result of the club's well documented Irish Catholic heritage - born of its foundation by Irish immigrants to Glasgow - with all the Republican ramifications that such a background entails. It is hard for an outsider to comprehend why the political (and by definition, religious) struggles in what amounts to a foreign country are so inextricably linked to something outwardly so inconsequential as a football team, but some appreciation of the role of the Celtic club in the lives of its supporters is needed before we can begin to understand why so many of the songs which follow have virtually nothing to do with football whatsoever. In the most basic of terms, the club have become something of a symbol of religious, social and cultural pride for those who pledge allegiance to the cause. Results are not simply a matter of points gained or lost, but are virtually a barometer by which the social standing of the club's supporters can be measured. Because of the historical links of the club with the Catholic church - and consequently with the struggles of the Catholic people - defeat means that rival supporters can not only simply deride the efforts of the eleven men in green and white who represent Celtic on the pitch, but that they can claim superiority over everything else that the Celtic Football Club and its supporters stand for. If ever the words of Bill Shankley's oft-quoted phrase about football being more important than a matter of life and death were true, then it is Celtic to whom they apply - and that, perhaps, is why the songs of the club's supporters so often avoid the comparatively mundane subject matter of twenty two blokes kicking a ball round a field.

Now, to the songs themselves, and the first instantly sets the tone for those that follow in that it is *The Soldier's Song* - the national anthem of the Republic of Ireland. Recently, it has become the vogue to sing this in its native Gaelic form, but as these words would be somewhat lost on about 99% of our readership, it is a translation which follows....

We're on the one road, maybe the wrong road,
We're on the road to God knows where,
We're on the one road, maybe the wrong road,
But we're together now - who cares?
North-men, South-men, comrades all,
Soon there'll be no Protestants at all,
We're on the one road, singing a song,
Singing a soldiers' song.

Soldiers are we, whose lives are pledged to Ireland,
Some have come from a land beyond the sea,
Sworn to be free, no more an ancient sire-land,
Shall shelter the despot or the slave,
Tonight we'll man the Bar-na-Boile,
In Erin's cause come woe nor weal,
'midst cannons' roar and rifles' peel,
We will chant a soldiers' song.

The nature of this song now leads us onto what is the predominant theme of the Celtic repertoire. With the Catholic sympathies already in place, it was only natural that the club's supporters should be supportive of the causes taken up by fellow adherents to the faith, and perhaps the most emotive such cause over the course of the twentieth century has been that of Irish independence. Obviously, this issue was also very much at the forefront of the Celtic supporters priorities given that with many of them being of Irish extraction, they would have had relatives directly involved in the conflict. The result of this in a footballing context has been that Celtic Park has been awash with Irish rebel songs - *The Merry Ploughboy* being a typical example of this sort of thing....

I am a merry ploughboy and I plough the fields by day,
'til a certain throughout came to my mind that I should run away,
Now I've always hated slavery since the day that I was born,
So I'm off to join the I R A and I'm off tomorrow morn',

Oh we're all off to Dublin in the green (fuck the Queen!),
Where our helmets glisten in the sun (fuck the sun!)
Where the bayonets flash and the rifles crash,
To the echo of the Thomson gun.

Of a very similar nature we have *The Boys Of The Old Brigade* which - with regard to its length, sees the Celtic supporters just beginning to get into their stride for some of the other prodigious songs which follow....

Oh father why are you so sad,
On this bright Easter morn'?
When Irishmen are proud and glad,
Of the land where they were born.
Oh son I see in memory's view,
A far off distant day,
When being just a boy like you,
I joined the I R A.

Where are the lads that stood with me,
When history was made,

Oh come with me, I long to see,
The boys of the Old Brigade.

On hills and farms the call to arms,
Was heard by one and all,
And from the glen came brave young men,
To answer Ireland's call,
But long ago we faced a foe,
The Old Brigade and me,
And by my side they fought and died,
So Ireland might be free.

Having thus celebrated a fictional freedom fighter and his colleagues, the focus now shifts to historical events in this next song *Sean South of Garryowen*. Just in case you may by now be thinking that these songs are far too long and far too obscure to ever have actually appeared at matches, I would point out that they've all been sent in by any number of different contributors, all of whom have made the point that the songs are still performed to this day - just listen carefully next time Celtic make an appearance on Sky...!

'twas on a dreary New Years Eve, the shades of night came down,
A lorry load of volunteers approached the border town,
There were men from Dublin and from Cork, Fermanagh and Tyrone,
But their leader was a Limerick man, Sean South of Garryowen,

And as they moved along the street up to the barrack door,
They scorned the danger they might meet, their fate that lay in store,
They were fighting for Old Ireland's cause to make their very own,
And the foremost of that gallant band was South from Garryowen.

But the sergeant spied their daring plan, he spied them at the door,
And the sten guns and the rifles heeled, a hail of death did pour,
And when that awful night was done, two men lay dead as stone,
There was one from near the border line and one from Garryowen.

No more will he hear the seagull cry on the lovely Shannon-side,
As he fell beneath the Northern sky, O'Hanlon by his side,
They've gone to join that gallant band of Plunkett, Pearsè and Tone,
A martyr for Old Ireland, Sean South of Garryowen.

One last genuine rebel song to consider, and one which stands out from the crowd due to its relative brevity....

Roaming in the gloaming
With a shamrock in my hand,
Roaming in the gloaming,

262

With St Patrick's Fenian band,
And when the music stops,
Fuck King Billy and John Knox,
Oh it's good to be a Roman Catholic!

This one is notable not only for the fact that it doesn't extend to eighteen verses, but because it is one of the few Celtic songs that is similar in attitude to those used across the city of Glasgow at Ibrox. Rangers supporters - who have a slightly different approach to the rivalry between the two clubs (see their own section for more on this) - are much more prone to abuse the Celtic traditions than to extol the virtues of their own beliefs, and as such they have proportionately more songs like the one listed above.

Now, putting matters of a more weighty nature to one side, it is obvious to all and sundry that Celtic have a long and illustrious history purely as a football club. They also have a long tradition of songs to go with this heritage - here's one that dates back over sixty years....

Sure you boast of your famous inventors,
And you sing of the land of the free,
But my song it concerns a centre,
Who plays for the Celtic F C.
Though he doesn't seem tall,
At chasing the ball,
And at playing the game,
He's ahead of them all.

James McGrory my boy,
You're our own pride and joy,
Your opponents, you make them look sad,
For with eight of the best,
McColl's record goes west,
Clever lad from the old Garngard,

To the tune of *Dear Little Town In The Old County Down*, this was a hymn of praise to Jimmy McGrory, Celtic's legendary goalscorer who bagged almost four hundred goals in a seventeen year career in the green and white between 1922 and 1939 - presumably eight of these goals must have come in one game, judging by line four of the second section.

One of Celtic's greatest triumphs in the eyes of their supporters was when they won the Coronation Cup in 1953 which, as its name suggests, was a tournament arranged to mark the Coronation of Queen Elizabeth II. The Queen however was an anathema to Celtic supporters, as she stood for everything that they despised - the Protestant Church, the Union that was constitutionally bound to oppose a united Ireland and - by association - Glasgow Rangers. It was, therefore, a glorious day in Celtic's history when not only did they reach the final of the competition, but they found themselves playing Hibernian (the Catholic club from Edinburgh) - a tournament which was supposed to be a celebration of the Union ended up being contested by two clubs with strong Republican sympathies! Many songs were written to commemorate this, but the following has proved to be the most enduring....

> Said Lizzie to Philip as they sat down to dine,
> I've just had a note from an old friend of mine,
> His name is George Young and he's loyal and true,
> And his big broken nose is a light shade of blue.
>
> He says that the Rangers are right on their game,
> And they're wanting a trophy to add to their fame,
> I'll send up some silver the Rangers can win,
> Said Philip - watch out or the Celts will step in.
>
> Said Lizzie to Philip "They don't stand a chance,
> I'll send up my Gunners to lead them a dance,
> With Celtic defeated the way will be clear,
> For Rangers to triumph in my crowning year.
>
> But alas for the hopes of our royal true blues,
> The Celts beat the Arsenal and Manchester too,
> Beat Hibs in the final - oh what a scene!
> All Hampden was covered in gold, white and green.
>
> Said Lizzie to Philip when she heard the news,
> "A blow has been struck to my loyal true blues,
> Please tell me dear Philip for you ought to know,
> How to beat Celtic and keep them below.
>
> Said Philip to Lizzie, "There's only one way,
> And I've known the secret for many a day,
> To beat Glasgow Celtic you'll have to deport,
> All the mad fighting Irish that give them support!"

So, with football now established as being the dominant subject matter for a while, time to look at another lengthy song - this time one which has been adopted in part by some clubs in England (Nottingham Forest, Spurs and Manchester United all having far less extensive renditions amongst their repertoires). Starts with the chorus, this one....

> Oh, over and over,
> We will follow you,
> Over and Over,

We will see it through,
We are Celtic supporters,
Faithful through and through,
And over and over,
We will follow you.

If you go to Germany,
You will see us there,
France or Spain, it's all the same,
We'll go anywhere,
We'll be there to cheer you,
As you travel round,
You can take us anywhere,
We won't let you down.

Repeat chorus

If you go to Lisbon,
We'll go once again,
In Zaire you'll find us there,
Calling out your name,
When you need supporting,
You will always know,
We'll be right there with you,
Everywhere you go.

Now, another of Celtic's songs which is rather better known down in England, and one which again crops up at a couple of clubs South of the border (Spurs again being one of these - curiously!). Unfortunately, the words to this one can only be based on these Anglicised versions, and on the limited exposure which the song has had on TV, as no-one from Celtic wrote in with the definitive lyrics. Suffice to say that the whole thing starts of with an ear-bursting four line chorus of *"Hail! Hail! The Celts are here!"* (plus some other words!) before continuing along the lines of....

Sure it's a grand old team to play for,
And it's a grand old team to see,
And if - you know - your history,
Then it's enough to make your heart go-ohh - ohhh - ohhh!
We don't care what the Rangers say.
What the hell do they know?
Oh we only know that there's going to be a show,
And the Glasgow Celtic will be there!

On the subject of songs which appear both at Celtic and at other venues, probably the most well known of this select band is *You'll Never Walk Alone*

265

- performed in Glasgow exactly as it is in Liverpool. There does not appear to be any particular reason for Celtic to have adopted this Anfield anthem - it's simply a case of one of the game's most devotional songs being picked up by some of the game's most devoted supporters.

Closing in on the present day, it has become apparent from some of the letters received in the course of researching this book that the atmosphere at Old Firm matches over the last two or three years seems to be considerably less bitter than it was previously. The hatred between the two sets of supporters is still deep and festering, but whereas in previous years the derby games would consist almost exclusively of an exchange of sectarian taunts of unbelievable venom, the last few matches between Celtic and Rangers have seen some chants which could easily be found at a "normal" derby game - and one song in particular is actually used by both sets of supporters. In the first instance, the very ordinary *Three Lions* song has found itself adopted by the Celtic support, but the sentiments are of a particularly antagonistic nature in that they refer to the marital problems of a certain Paul Gascoigne, which were all over the tabloid newspapers during 1996 and 1997 - short and to the point we have....

> *He beats his wife, he beats his wife,*
> *Gascoigne beats his wife!*

A very popular tune at Ibrox over the last couple of years has been Scott Joplin's *The Entertainer* - perhaps better known nowadays as being the tune from one of the Felix catfood adverts. Rangers supporters have used this with glee as their team closed in on Celtic's record of nine consecutive league titles, but over the course of 96/7 when the Celts were convinced that a Paolo di Canio inspired side was going to halt the Rangers run, a corresponding version took hold at Celtic Park....

> *Paolo di Canio says - "There'll never be nine in a row",*
> *Paolo di Canio says - "There'll never be nine in a row",*
> *You might think that you're great, just because you've won eight,*
> *But you'll never see nine in a row.*

This of course had a strictly limited shelf life, and won't be heard again for at least another nine years, if at all.

Two other songs were both to the forefront of the Celtic repertoire during 1996/7 - a traditional song by the title of *The Fields of Athenry* and a massively raucous and very popular reworking of *Winter Wonderland*, which seemed to start off along the lines of *"There's only one Jorge Cadete....",* unfortunately, I have not been able to establish the full words to either of these two in time to include them in this book - other than to say that the Rangers version of the Jorge Cadete song appears in their section.

East Fife

Newcomers to the *Dicks Out* experience, East Fife have soared straight to the very pinnacle of Scottish songwriting as a result of some of the stupidity which follows, and whilst not quite scaling the heights of greatness achieved by the previous holders, they are worthy successors to the crown once so nobly held by the lunatics who followed Meadowbank Thistle. As was the case when Thistle reigned supreme, many of the songs which follow have been popularised by the efforts of a superbly idiotic fanzine - the incomparable *AWOL* in Thistle's case, with the excellent *Away From The Numbers* taking on the role at Bayview. As with the majority of fanzines, abuse and derision by the bucket-load is poured on local rivals, and it is the other Fife teams who suffer more than most through East Fife's songs. A downturn in the club's fortunes in the late 1980's unfortunately meant that traditional rivals Raith Rovers and Dunfermline were able to look down on East Fife from above, but new targets for scorn were found in Cowdenbeath - previously lowly neighbours who now became regular opponents in local derbies.

The one abiding theme in the stream of invective aimed at Cowden was the perception that the town and its inhabitants were generally rather dirty - filthy in fact - though why this should be the case was not revealed. Anyway, putting such trivial matters as the accuracy or otherwise of these assertions, there were a couple of fine songs which made the point....

> *They come from near Lochgelly,*
> *They hav'nae got a telly,*
> *They're dirty and they're smelly,*
> *The Cowden Family*

....to the tune of *The Addams Family*, being the first. The bit about not having televisions was an added touch to illustrate the poverty in which the citizens of Cowdenbeath were believed to live. With the "dirt" theme more to the fore, comes this next song - a quality piece of work to the *Blackadder* theme....

> *Na na na, na na na, na na na na na na na,*
> *Na na na, na na na, na na na na na na naaaaaa,*
> *Black bastards,*
> *Black bastards,*
> *They come from Cowdenbeath,*
> *Black bastards,*
> *Black bastards,*
> *They're very black indeed!*

The "theme song" to the "Cowdenbeath and its inhabitants are rather grubby" movement was probably the least impressive of this short selection, but still

267

managed to lend its name to some rather fine elements of what became a high profile campaign - more if which a little later. The chant was one of many to the *Juantanamera* rhythm....

> *No soap in Cowden,*
> *Oh there's no soap in Cowden,*
> *No soap in Cowden.....*

And here *Away From The Numbers* takes centre stage. Having basically started the ball rolling, the fanzine (as is often the case) decided that there was considerable mileage to be got from the idea and, before too long, East Fife supporters were wandering around bedecked in T-shirts bearing the *"No Soap In Cowden"* slogan. With the movement gaining popularity, some posters also bearing the catchphrase were printed up and, on a daring raid into enemy territory, stuck up all over the centre of Cowdenbeath. More T-shirts with the words to *The Cowden Family* song then appeared - using illustrations from the cartoon strip of the same name which had already been running in the fanzine for some time. Unfortunately, we have no more news of the campaign following the inception of this burgeoning leisurewear industry, but it's a fair bet that the whole thing is still in full swing to this day.

As mentioned already, before Cowdenbeath took over the mantle of public enemy number one for the East Fife supporters, it was Raith Rovers who used to bear the brunt of the Bayview abuse. For the most part, it was two well established songs from England which were used to convey the ill feeling that existed with the Sheffield United *"arse of a crow"* song seeing the appropriately equipped East Fifers able to *"fly over Stark's Park tomorrow, and shit on the bastards below"*. The *Que Sera Sera* arrangement, popular with Leeds United supporters but also prevalent at Swansea and numerous other venues was also pressed into service, with the question *"Should I be Rovers, should I be Fife"* being posed in line three, and the response being that *"father's gun"* should be used to *"shoot all the Rovers scum"*. Less inventively but instead having the virtue of being strictly to the point, a one time (or two time come to that) Rovers' manager was also cheerily regaled with a chant which took the *"Barmy Army"* line - constant repetitions of *"Jimmy Nicholl - Irish bastard! Jimmy Nicholl - Irish bastard"* being quite the done thing in The Shed at Bayview.

The third of East Fife's local rivals, Dunfermline, are seemingly afforded less abuse in song than the other two, and what there is unfortunately cannot be reproduced because of the inevitable flood of complaints which would follow, Suffice to say that *She'll Be Coming Round The Mountain* is given a swift airing, with an assertion being made that it is better to be a member of a generally unpopular racial group than to be a Dunfermline supporter. I suppose the exclusion of this song on the grounds that it contains a racial element is little more than rank hypocrisy on my part given the unexpurgated nature of the Celtic and Rangers sections, but you have to draw the line somewhere!

In addition to these specifically targeted ditties, there are a vast number of more general East Fife songs, pledging allegiance to the club, the town and the region in which both are found or handing out random abuse to all and sundry. A few of these are certainly worthy of note, the first of which is a pretty unique reworking of *The Blaydon Races*....

> *Away the lads,*
> *You should have seen us coming,*
> *We're only here to drink your beer,*
> *And shag your fucking women,*
> *Away the lads and lassies,*
> *You should've seen their faces,*
> *Walking along the Wellesley Road,*
> *To see the Methil Aces.*

Wellesley Road runs along the back of the main stand at Bayview and Methill is the name of the town in which the ground can be found. Next, a traditional Scottish song which may or may not be called *The Bonny Bonny Banks Of Loch Lomond* finds itself debased beyond all common decency (!) and turned into one of football's inherently pointless "rather rude just for the sake of it" songs....

> *I love a lassie,*
> *A bonny, bonny lassie,*
> *She's as tight as the paper on the wall,*
> *She's got legs like a spider,*
> *I'd love to fucking ride her,*
> *Mary frae Methill*
> *Two - three - four...*
> *(then repeat the whole thing)*

Along similar lines, the now infamous Hartlepool "nasty" song gets a rare outing North of the border, with a number of substantial changes being made from its more usual format, though the tune is still *Just One Of Those Songs*....

> *Oh we're the boys on the Social,*
> *The boys on the dole,*
> *We're so fucking ugly,*
> *We can't get a hole,*
> *But we all go mental,*
> *When we score a goal,*
> *Oh the Bayview Boys are in town,*
> *Na, na, na - na na na na na, na na na na na....*

Briefly back to the animosity with Cowdenbeath, and it is a source of some vexation in Methill that the Central Park club have become known to all and sundry as *The Blue Brazil*, a name which I very hazily recall was coined during a time when Cowden were being even more inept than usual (probably during 1992/3 when they set new records for all manner of things such as most defeats in a season, most consecutive home defeats and generally being one of the most feeble sides in football, ever). The name - laden with irony - was given to the hopeless team (blue being the colour of their shirts), and they have been known by it since, as well as being surrounded by an air of generalised goodwill from all men (except East Fife) as is often the case with particularly useless outfits (Brighton, for instance!). As a reaction to all this, the Bayview supporters christened their team *The Methill Milan*, as nothing more than a piss-take of Cowden's affectionate nickname, and this is now intoned to the tune of *Blue Moon - "Milan - we are the Methill Milan; we are the Methill Milan"* - that sort of thing!

Lastly, the East Fife contribution to the ongoing collection of mainstream songs which transfer onto the terraces in their original format for no apparent reason. *The Lions Sleeps Tonight* (originally by The Tokens, covered by Dave Newman but probably best remembered for its 1982 release by Tight Fit - ooh, and *cf* Swansea City) was the choice, and it is the opening section with all manner of *"oooh - oooohs"* and *"wimaways"* which is popular - with the East Fife supporters if not with those who have to listen to their no doubt beery renditions!

Heart of Midlothian

In the wake of the oft trumpeted demise of Meadowbank Thistle, and in light of the continuing silence from Easter Road, Hearts can now be installed without a shadow of a doubt as Edinburgh's leading songsters. At the forefront of their (albeit unchallenged) progress to this illustrious position is the imaginatively title *Hearts Song* - now in its fifth decade as the acknowledged club anthem at Tynecastle. Conceived in the late 1950's by a certain Hector Nicol, the song was committed to vinyl in the 60's, alongside *Glory Glory To The Hibees* which was an Hibernian equivalent. Both songs are played before kick off at the respective grounds to this day, but with the lack of any information from Leith to the contrary, it is to be assumed that it was only the Hearts song which went on to become an enduring favourite with supporters. As far as the tune goes, it is basically an amalgamation of excerpts from the verse structure from *The Wild Rover* and some (possibly two) hymns, of which one of the latter forms the major part of the melody. Typically, I've no idea what the name of the relevant hymn might actually be, but it was on the sound track from the Eddie Murphy film *Coming To America* - being sung by the congregation at a church service which turned into some kind of beauty pageant half way through (!). Needless to say, it wasn't the words to the football song which were being used....

> *Away up in Gorgie at Tynecastle Park,*
> *There's a wee fitba' team that'll aye make its mark,*
> *They've won all the honours in footballing arts,*
> *And there's nae other team to compare with the Hearts*

> *chorus*

> *H - E - A - R - T - S*
> *If you cannae spell it then here's what it says:*
> *Hearts, Hearts glorious Hearts,*
> *It's down at Tynecastle they bide,*
> *The talk o' the toon are the boys in maroon,*
> *And Auld Reekie supports them with pride.*

> *For national caps we can always supply,*
> *Like Massie and Walker or Bauld and Mackay,*
> *If I had the time I could name dozens more,*
> *Who've helped in producing the old Hampden roar.*

> *repeat chorus*

> *This is our story, this is our song,*
> *Follow the Hearts and you can't go wrong,*
> *Some say that the Rangers and Celtic are grand,*
> *But the boys in maroon are the best in the land.*

> *We've won the league flag and we've won the league cup,*
> *Though sometimes we go down we'll aye come back up,*
> *Or forwards can score and it's no idle talk,*
> *Our defence is as strong as the Auld Castle Rock.*

Now, these words are the official version which was set out in one of the Hearts fanzines, but there was no explanation to the very odd structure of the song as it appears above. The first, second and fourth sections are all fairly straightforward, as they take the tune from the verses of The Wild Rover; the chorus is also standard fare, appearing twice in what seem to be sensible places, but the fly in the ointment is the third part which starts *"This is our story...."*, This is the part which is to the *Coming To America* tune (for want of a better name) and it is only this section which actually takes this tune, so this bit is sort of stuck in the middle on its own. Whatever, taken as a whole, it is a damn fine effort, and when I heard it belted out by the massed ranks of the Hearts supporters under the old covered end at Hampden Park during the 1986 Scottish Cup Final, it sounded as stirring and impressive as any other football song you may care to mention. The only problem here was that there seemed to be a number of alternative lines in use! The main difference from the recognised lyrics appeared to be in the second half of the chorus, which seemed to have been changed to something not too dissimilar from....

H - E - A - R - T - S,
If you cannae spell it then here's what it says:
Hearts, Hearts, glorious Hearts,
It's down at Tynecastle you'll find,
The world's greatest team and their loyal support,
Who all follow the Jam Tarts with pride.

In addition to this, the last line of the third section was something like *"But bollocks to them, we're the best in the land!"*. However, it must be recorded that having set out these amended versions in the first edition of *Dicks Out!* I received a very stern letter from a Hearts supporter of many years standing who said that the words to the song are never altered - so it is entirely possible that the last couple of paragraphs are completely spurious!

Another magnificent anthem next, which is based on *My Way* for the first two sections, before lapsing into the more common *Ally's Tartan Army* for the last bit. This was reputedly conceived en route to Czechoslovakia for a UEFA cup tie against Dukla Prague in 1986, but must have spent the next couple of years being honed to the finely polished finished article, as it is said that it was first performed in full at a game against Aberdeen at Pittodrie in October 1989 - it was certainly worth the wait....

And now, the end is near,
We've followed Hearts from Perth to Paisley,
We travelled far, by bus and car,
And other times we've gone by railway,
We've been - to Aberdeen,
We hate the Hibs,
They make us spew up,
So make a noise, the Gorgie boys,
Are going to Europe.

To see H M F C,
We'll even dig your Channel Tunnel,
Or go afloat on some big boat,
And tie our scarves around the funnel
We have no fear of other players,

Like Rossi, Boniek or Altobelli,
While overseas, the Hibs'll be,
In Porty-belly.

Bring on the Hibs, the Celts, the Rangers,
Bring on Spaniards by the score,
Barcelona, Real Madrid,
They will make a gallant bid,
For they only know the reason why we roar.

The end of the second section refers to Hibs staying at home (in the Portobello district of Edinburgh - hence Porty-belly) while Hearts are cavorting around Europe. By the same token, the references to "Gorgie" in several of the Hearts songs refers to the area of Edinburgh where most of the Jam Tart's support comes from.

Having made mention of Hibs a couple of times already, it's high time that some of the favourite songs from the Hearts contingent at the Edinburgh derby matches are considered. It has long been the tradition in Scotland for such games to be played on New Year's Day and, until recently, Hearts enjoyed such an extraordinary run of success in matches against the old enemy (something like twenty games unbeaten!) that a win over Hibs became virtually a traditional part of the festivities - it was certainly a regular enough occurrence to warrant a song....

Jingle bells, jingle bells,
Jingle all the way,
Oh what fun it is to fuck,
The Hibs on New Years Day

Another popular if uninspiring effort is to *She'll Be Coming Round The Mountain*, and is really just the Tynecastle incarnation of a theme which has cropped up at any number of other grounds over the years, with teams, supporters or individual players being the target (just substitute the relevant name for *"the fucking Hibees"* below). Now seems as good a time as any to illustrate it though, so it is the Hibs supporters who make an appearance in....

If you hate the fucking Hibees clap your hands (clap - clap!)
If you hate the fucking Hibees clap your hands (clap - clap!)
If you hate the fucking Hibees, hate the fucking Hibees,
Hate the fucking Hibees clap your hands (general clapping to fade....)

What is perhaps a lesser known element of these Edinburgh derby games (down in England at any rate) is that the two teams mirror the religious divide of the Old Firm in Glasgow - Hearts are the Protestant team and Hibs (as with Celtic, founded by Irish immigrants) are Catholic. However, whereas the Old

Firm games are played out to a ceaseless torrent of religious and sectarian abuse from both sides, these divisions are much less apparent when Hearts and Hibs square up. There only actually seem to be two of the Rangers' songs which have made the trip up the M8 to Edinburgh, and the first of these is merely the *Marching Through Georgia* piece which can also be heard in different guises at other grounds....

> *Hello, Hello, we are the Gorgie Boys,*
> *Hello, Hello, we are the Gorgie boys,*
> *We're up to our knees in Fenian blood,*
> *Surrender or you'll die,*
> *We are the Loyal Gorgie boys.*

In order to play down the sectarian element in this song *"Fenian blood"* can easily be replaced with the less emotive *"Hibee blood"*, but it seems that the Protestant suffix of *"Loyal"* remains intact in the last line whatever type of blood has been spilt. There is not, however, much that can be done to lessen the blast of religious intolerance in this next song - which is lifted straight from the pages of the Ibrox song book....

> *Oh, no Pope of Rome,*
> *No chapels to sadden my eyes,*
> *No nuns and no priests, fuck your rosary beads,*
> *Every day is the Twelfth of July.*

This is the basically the chorus only from a longer song (*cf* Rangers!), but the salient point is that July 12th is the anniversary of the Battle of the Boyne, fought in Ireland in 1690 and at which William of Orange (the Protestant William III of England) defeated the Catholic army of King James. (Go down the library for more on this subject and its implications - I'm not getting involved!).

The verses to this song (*No Pope of Rome*) take the tune of *Home On The Range*, and a similar American influence see this next Hearts offering follow *The Yellow Rose Of Texas* - it is another pointed reminder of the fact that Hibs' sorties onto the European stage are much less frequent than those of Hearts....

> *Hearts are going to Europe which no-one can deny,*
> *With players like Ferguson, John Colquhoun and Mackay,*
> *Everyone in Gorgie is always on a high,*
> *And Hibs just stayed in Leith because they couldnae qualify!*

Away from the petty sniping and low-key bigotry of rivalry in the city of Edinburgh, Hearts are not averse to dishing out abuse to any other teams that they happen to encounter. They have never got on particularly well with Aberdeen for some reason (the '86 Cup Final can't have helped!), and as a result the Aberdonian anthem *The Northern Lights Of Old Aberdeen* finds itself given a slightly new slant at the hands of the Tynecastle faithful (with the tune as per the original)....

> *The Northern Lights of Old Aberdeen,*
> *Mean sweet fuck all to me,*
> *The Northern lights of Old Aberdeen,*
> *Mean sweet fuck all to me,*
> *I've been a Hearts fan all my life,*
> *And many a sight I've seen,*
> *But the Northern lights of Old Aberdeen,*
> *Mean sweet fuck all to me.*

Finally, and just to show that two sides on the same side of Scotland's religious divide are capable of disliking each other just as much as if one were from the opposing camp, Hearts took great delight in taunting Rangers fans with the following after the massively controversial signing by the Light Blues of Mo Johnstone in 1989. Previously having been with Celtic, Johnstone was the first Catholic player for many a year to be welcomed into the Protestant stronghold of Ibrox and, in the eyes of the Hearts fans, this made the Glasgow club unworthy of their traditional values. Now, there are strictly protestant organisations throughout Scotland and Northern Ireland known as Loyal Orange Lodges, the members of which wear orange sashes when the occasion demands (*cf* Rangers' song *The Sash My Father Wore*) - and with Rangers now considered to have abandoned such traditions, the Hearts supporters weighed in with....

> *Glasgow Rangers, Glasgow Rangers,*
> *You're not fit to wear the Sash,*
> *You're not fit to wear the Sash!*

To the *Bread of Heaven* tune, this one really wound up the Rangers supporters who could normally be counted upon as the last people in the world to disavow their religious principles. The depth of feeling aroused at Ibrox by the signing of Johnstone can be gauged by the fact that some Rangers supporters have not watched their team since he was brought to the club - so you can imagine the reaction when Hearts fans started taking the piss out of them about the affair. Strangely, comments I have read by Rangers fans who walked out of Ibrox for good on July 10th 1989 when Johnstone put pen to paper have suggested that it was not the fact that he was either a Catholic or an ex-Celtic player that caused them to boycott the club they loved - it was simply because they thought that in many ways he just didn't measure up to the standards expected of someone who wore the Light Blue shirt - a bizarre concept for anyone trying to understand the Old Firm rivalry from the outside, but indicative of just how seriously the whole thing is taken by the fans in Glasgow.

Kilmarnock

With football currently enjoying a bit of a renaissance at Rugby Park, what with Scottish Cup wins and the like, Killie supporters are being given a chance to perform on the sort of stage that their undoubted talents deserve. Having plumbed the depths of the Second Division recently as 1990, it's perhaps surprising that such a wealth of songs exists, but - for whatever reason - there are certainly one or two worthy efforts down in Ayrshire. As with East Fife, the fact that what might be regarded as one of the lesser lights of Scottish football has a decent selection of songs is mirrored by there being a particularly fine fanzine on the scene - *Killie Ken* in this instance. There is obviously some mileage in the theory that supporters who possess the wit and wisdom to sustain a worthwhile fanzine are going to be more likely than most to come up with worthwhile songs as well. Anyway, enough of the pointless preamble and on to the Kilmarnock version of Rangers' *Copland Road* song to the tune of *We're No Awa' To Bide Awa'* (*cf* Rangers, obviously, and Burnley). This is another case of a song which has become synonymous with one club being picked up on to abusive ends by rival supporters, as has happened to *I'm Forever Blowing Bubbles* in London....

> *As I was walking down the Copland Road,*
> *I met a bunch of strangers,*
> *They said to me "Are you going to see,*
> *The famous Glasgow Rangers?"*
> *So we made our way to Ibrox Park,*
> *To see my Uncle Willie,*
> *And the boys in blue got fucked six - two,*
> *By the famous Ayrshire Killie*

The 6 - 2 scoreline obviously refers to a specific match, but no inkling was given as to which one - neither has it been possible to establish whether *"Uncle Willy"* was a purely fictional character (whose name conveniently rhymes with "Killie") or if he was based on a famous player from the past.

Next, a song which is something of a rarity in Scotland but which is one of the most common efforts down South, *The Halls Of Montezuma*. The Killie version follows the standard format of its English cousins....

> *From the banks of the River Irvine,*
> *To the shores of Sicily,*
> *We'll fight, fight, fight for the Killie,*
> *'til we win the Scottish League.*
> *To hell with Ayr United,*
> *To hell with Rangers too,*

> *We'll fight, fight, fight for the Killie,*
> *'til we win the Scottish League.*

Rather more extensive tinkering had been necessary before another common song was considered fit for consumption at Rugby Park with - apart from the obvious change in colour - *The Red Flag* undergoing some unique alterations to leave us with....

> *Flying high, up in the sky,*
> *We'll keep the blue flag flying high,*
> *Were e're we go, we'll fear no foe,*
> *We'll keep the blue flag flying high*
>
> *Flying high, up in the sky,*
> *We'll keep the blue flag flying high,*
> *Through dirt and muck we'll fight like fuck,*
> *To keep the blue flag flying high.*

With a persistent theme now beginning to develop, yet another song is imported from the home of the Sassenachs, but this time it's one of far less general usage as Killie become only the third (or possibly fourth) club to use Liverpool's *Poor Scouser Tommy/Red River Valley* as the basis for a song of their own....

> *As he lay on the battlefield dying,*
> *With the blood pouring out of his head,*
> *As he lay on the battle field dying,*
> *These are the last words he said:*
> *Kilmarnock, Kilmarnock!*
> *We are the champions.*

This would appear to retain the original tune over the opening four lines, but the last two deviate sharply from the Anfield original - that may in fact be no more than some sort of shouted climax to the abridged song.

Of far more appropriate Scottish roots, there is then one of the most coherent versions of *Ally's Tartan Army* to have manifested itself anywhere in the U K. Many club's supporters have taken short sections of the song and tacked them onto the end of other tunes, but the Killie version is probably the best example of the song as a stand-alone piece (with, as far as I can remember, lines three, four and five being lifted directly from Andy Cameron's original song)....

> *Who's this team we call the Killie,*
> *Who's this team we all adore,*
> *We're the boys in white and blue,*

And we're Scotland's gallant crew,
And we're out to show the world what we can do.
Bring on the Hibs, the Hearts, the Celtic,
Bring on Spaniards by the score,
Barcelona, Real Madrid,
We will make a gallant bid,
For Kilmarnock are the greatest team of all.

To something of a far less well defined structure next, and the Kilmarnock adaptation of *Land Of Hope And Glory*. There seem to have been (at least) two different versions doing the rounds, but as both are rather scrappy, it may have been better to have tried to lump them together into one decent song. Whatever, option one is....

Land of hope and glory,
Home of Kilmarnock F C,
We're from the West of Scotland,
Spreading Ayrshire fame.

Men like Jackie McGrory,
Boys like Tommy McLean,
The shall never be beaten,
On to victory.

Land of hope and glory,
Home of Kilmarnock F C,
We shall never be beaten,
On to victory.

Option two - equally nonsensical in my opinion - sees section three as above becoming section one, with lines three and four of the existing section one being tacked onto lines one and two of section two to become a new section two - very silly, although I'm sure there's a decent song in there somewhere if only someone can be bothered to look for it!

To one of football's most common anthems next - *Yellow Submarine*. Naturally, this oft-abused mode of underwater transport has become blue for its outing at Rugby Park, but it is the unique second part which should really be noted....

We all live in a blue submarine,
A blue submarine, a blue submarine,
We all live in a blue submarine,
A blue submarine.

And the boys, are all aboard,
Every one, a Killie fan,

Scarves of blue,
And scarves of white,
On our blue, submarine....

A couple of brief chants to consider now, the first of which seems to have been regarded as a particular Killie speciality in the late 1980's. Rather uninspiringly, though, it is no more than a standard interpretation of the Steam song *Na Na Hey Hey Kiss Him Goodbye* (re-released by Bananarama); *"Na na na na, na na na na, hey-ey, Ayrshire Killie!"* (repeated for, oooh, a very long time indeed). Then to one of a very few chants directed at neighbours Ayr United - a *Camptown Races* commentary on the parlous state of the architecture at Somerset Park - *"Who's the clown that built your stand - Lego, Lego! Who's the clown that built your stand, Lego, Legoland!"* This rather odd appreciation of structural engineering was aimed at the main stand - a decidedly unstable erection largely made up of bits of old weatherboarding held together with chicken wire which would probably have been made considerably safer by the addition of a couple of those square yellow bricks, and perhaps some of those long, flat white ones! In conclusion, one of the not insubstantial number of songs completely unrelated to football which have become woven into the fabric of the game after their essentially pointless adoption by various supporters. It was Marie Osmond who provided the inspiration for the Rugby Park irrelevance, with *Paper Roses* becoming a firm favourite on the terraces as well as lending it's name to a club fanzine....

I realise the way your eyes deceive me,
With tender looks that I mistook for love,
So take away the flowers that you gave me,
And send the kind that you remind me of -
Paper roses, paper roses,
Oh how sweet those roses seemed to me,
But they're only, imitation,
Like your imitation love for me!

Rangers

For a book which is largely supposed to illustrate the degree of wit and good humour with which the game is viewed from the terraces, it is a bit of a shock to enter the world of Glasgow's Old Firm rivalry and, in particular, to look at the songs which illuminate Ibrox Park, home of Rangers. The songs from Celtic are passionate and narrow minded, sure, but the vast majority of them are songs of support for the club or traditional anthems brought over from Ireland (as is the case with some of the Rangers songs) that are supposed to lift the spirits, even if they are almost exclusively about the deeds of Irish Republican heroes that the supporters of other clubs would regard as no more than criminals. There are epic songs about the illustrious history of the club and its players, but at Ibrox, the whole thing takes on a far darker aspect. Hatred, pure and simple, is what a great many Rangers songs are all about. There is a hatred for Celtic on a national basis - an essentially Irish club that came to dominate the game in Scotland; there is hatred for the supporters - the immigrant workers who crossed the Irish Sea and poured in to Glasgow; there is hatred for the religion and beliefs that those supporters hold dear and there is hatred towards the team itself - the only other outfit which has consistently been able to challenge Rangers' supremacy over the years. And of course, there is the hatred borne out of the Northern Ireland situation, which has really come from the common detestation of the people of the Irish Republic which is shared by Rangers supporters and the Protestants in Ulster in spite of there being a lack of the sort of personal involvement which is evident at Parkhead.

You only have to consider the Rangers version of *Wandrin' Star* - Lee Marvin's song from *Paint Your Wagon* - to get an idea of some of the feelings that are set into the foundations of Ibrox....

> *I was born under a Union Jack,*
> *I was born under a Union Jack,*
> *Do you know where hell is?*
> *Hell is in The Falls,*
> *Heaven is in the Shankhill Road,*
> *And we'll guard Old Derry's walls,*
>
> *So, I was born under a Union Jack,*
> *I was born under a Union Jack,*
> *Chapels were made for burning,*
> *Catholics go to hell,*
> *Proddies go to heaven,*
> *And it's just as fucking well.*
> *I was born under a Union Jack,*
> *A Union, Union Jack.*

Full of Ulster references, this, with the Falls and the Shankhill Roads being areas of Belfast known as sectarian strongholds, and with *"Old Derry's walls"* being a reference to the siege of Londonderry, the story of which is told in this next song (called *Derry's Walls*, surprisingly). This is one of the more historically based songs - and it's worth comparing the viewpoint with that put forward in some of the Celtic sagas such as *Sean South of Garryowen*. For the most part it's only the second and third sections of *Derry's Wall's* which are sung, but the first part helps to set the scene a bit....

> The time has scarce gone by, boys,
> Three hundred years ago,
> When rebels on old Derry's walls,
> Their faces dare not show.
>
> When James and all his rebel scum
> Came up to Bishop's Gate,
> With heart and hand and sword and shield,
> We forced them to retreat,
>
> And the cry was "No surrender!
> Surrender or yell die, die, die!"
> With heart and hand and sword and shield,
> We'll guard old Derry's walls.

Of a more contemporary feel, there is the famous Rangers arrangement of *Marching Through Georgia* - also popular in a different format at Old Trafford - but this is the song which can always be heard being performed at extreme volume whenever Rangers are shown on T V....

> Hello, Hello, we are the Billy Boys!
> Hello, Hello, you'll know us by our noise,
> We're up to our knees in Fenian blood,
> Surrender or you'll die,
> We are the Bridgeton Derry boys

Known as the *"Billy Boys"* after King William of Orange (hero of the seventeenth century battles which saw the Irish Catholics under King James defeated), the Rangers fans seem to use this as sort of a rallying cry for the various factions that attend their games, as the name of any area or region can be substituted for *"Bridgeton"* in the last line.

Picking up on one of the few sectarian songs which Edinburgh's protestant club Hearts, use on occasion, we then have *No Pope Of Rome* which takes the tune of *Home, Home On the Range*, Needless to say, there are a couple of verses which are additional to the Tynecastle version....

> Oh give me a home where there's no Pope of Rome,
> Where there's nothing but Protestants stay,
> Where seldom is heard a discouraging word,
> And flute bands play "The Sash" every day.
>
> Oh, no Pope of Rome,
> No chapels to sadden my eyes,
> No nuns and no priests, fuck your rosary beads,
> Every day is the Twelfth of July.

Up a wee narrow close just by Bridgeton Cross,
It is there is the place we call home,
On the Twelfth there we join, to remember the Boyne,
And to pray "Let's have no Pope of Rome"

Line four of the first section of this last song leads us nicely to the next as *"The Sash"* is short for *The Sash My Father Wore* - a song which takes its title from the ceremonial sashes worn by the Orange Lodge members (*cf* Hearts and their *"You're not fit to wear the sash"* song). In this instance, it is the second half which is the more regularly aired section....

Sure I'm an Orange Ulsterman from Erin's Isle I came,
To see my British brethren all of honour and of fame,
And they tell them of my forefathers who fought in days of yore,
That I might have the right to wear the sash my father wore.

It is old but it is beautiful and its colours they are fine,
It was worn at Derry, Aughrim, Enniskillen and the Boyne,
My father wore it as a youth in bygone days of yore,
And it's on the Twelfth I love to wear the sash my father wore.

Another song steeped in the tradition of the Orange Orders is *The Old Orange Flute* - which has been condensed down from four lengthy verses to the much shorter version which follows. Anyone who has ever seen footage of the Loyalist marches in Northern Ireland must have noticed that there is always a pipe band in attendance, and it's from these bands that the song takes its general theme, with the story coming from the extended original....

I married a Fenian, her name was McGuire,
'twas her, not the flute, that I threw on the fire,
And as she was burning I heard a strange noise,
'twas the old flute playing "Protestant Boys"
Tooderloo - tooderloo - fuck the Pope!

Again on the cyclical theme in which many of the Rangers songs are linked together, this leads us on to *The Protestant Boys*. Yet another extensive arrangement, it's just the first verse which has made it onto the terraces....

The Protestant Boys they are loyal and true,
Stout hearted in battle and stout handed too,
The Protestant Boys they are true to the last,
And faithful and peaceful when danger has passed.
And oh! they bear, and oh! they proudly wear,
The colour that floated o'er many a fray,
Where cannons were flashing and sabres were clashing,
And Protestant Boys still carried the day

The tune to this one may not be a million miles away from *The Wild Rover* but, unfortunately, as was the case with many of these songs, this is a bit of a stab in the dark as the "proper" tunes were not named, and they are equally likely to be based on some obscure traditional melody.

Still exhibiting this extraordinary preoccupation with historical tales, there are now three songs which - in a direct comparison with the Celtic songs about the I R A - are all centred around the volunteers that fought for the Loyalist cause (the Ulster Freedom Fighters and the Ulster Volunteer Force). The first two would seem to follow the tune to popular songs which appear throughout the British Isles - *The Red Flag* being first up under the guise of *Ulster Freedom Fighters....*

> *Ulster Freedom Fighters we,*
> *Whose cause is life and liberty,*
> *We'll fight and die to keep her free,*
> *We are the sons of Ulster*
>
> *So raise the standards, raise them high,*
> *Unfurl the Red Hand, let it fly,*
> *Beneath its colours we'll fight and die,*
> *We'll fight and die for Ulster*
>
> *From Derry's ancient city walls,*
> *Armagh, Tyrone, Fermanagh's choice,*
> *With Down and Antrim's men rejoice,*
> *To be the Sons of Ulster.*

Now for *Glory, Glory Hallelujah*, which turns up at Ibrox as *The Heroes of the U V F....*

> *Now they chased King James and all his gang*
> *From the gates of Derry's walls,*
> *They chased the bastard I R A*
> *Up the Crumlin and the Falls,*
> *They'll rally round the Shankhill*
> *When the voice of Ulster calls,*
> *The heroes of the U V F!*
>
> *Glory, Glory to the red hand,*
> *Glory, Glory to our homeland,*
> *Glory, Glory to that gallant band,*
> *The heroes of the U V F*

The last of this particular trio is *Here Lies A Soldier*, of which one verse and the chorus have been co-opted into regular use by the Rangers supporters (with a further two verses not seeming to be so readily used). As far as the tune goes, this is one which I have not been able to unravel....

> Don't bury me in Erin's Fenian valley,
> Take me home to Ulster, let me rest,
> And on my gravestone carve this simple message,
> Here lies a soldier of the U V F

> Here lies a soldier, here lies a soldier,
> Who fought and died for all he loved the best,
> Here lies a soldier, here lies a soldier,
> Here lies a soldier of the U V F.

And with that, we have now reached the end of this selection of wholly sectarian songs, but there are two more which need mentioning for the peculiar fact that they are both Rangers versions of Celtic songs (or vice versa). The Parkhead anthem *The Boys Of The Old Brigade* appears in Rangers colours as *The Y C V Brigade*, and *The Merry Ploughboy* also has a counterpart through *A Loyal Orangeman*. In both cases, the songs in each pair share a common tune and have very similar words, but are these are obviously altered to make them appropriate to one side of the religious divide or the other.

Phew - at last it's time for the matter of the game itself to be addressed, but in this first example, there is an alternative version which harks back to the same sentiments as are so prevalent in the songs listed above. This one is called simply *Follow, Follow*, and is recognised as the real anthem of Glasgow Rangers....

> Though the street be broad or narrow,
> We'll follow we will, follow we will, follow we will,
> Though the street be broad or narrow,
> We'll follow we will, we'll follow in the footsteps of our team,
> God bless them!

> Follow, follow, we will follow Rangers,
> Anywhere, everywhere, we will follow on,
> Follow, follow, we will follow Rangers,
> If they go to Dublin, we will follow on.

> There's not a team like the Glasgow Rangers,
> No, not one, and there never will be one,
> The Celtic know all about their troubles,
> We will fight 'til the day is won,
> There's not a team like the Glasgow Rangers,
> No, not one, and there never will be one.

This is the "respectable" version, for family consumption - it is the second section which is open to change should it be felt that the more forthright True Blue sentiments need to be expressed....

Follow, follow, we will follow Rangers,
Up the Falls, Derry's walls, we will follow on,
Dundee and Hamilton, fuck the Pope and the Vatican,
If they go to Dublin, we will follow on.

Back onto the footballing side of things, and another song which has become established as one of the main themes you'll hear at Ibrox. Called simply *Rangers* or *The Copland Road*, this is the song from which Kilmarnock and Burnley have taken inspiration, in spite of the fact that the tune is that of the peculiarly named *We're No Awa' To Bide Awa'*....

As I was walking down Copland Road I met a crowd of strangers,
Said they to me "Where can we see, the famous Glasgow Rangers?"
So I took them o'er to Ibrox Park, to see a great eleven,
Said I "It isnae paradise, but man, it's my blue heaven".
Some people write their songs about the land that they adore,
And some of how they fought and won their country's greatest war,
And others still seem quite content to use another theme,
But I've turned out a song about my favourite football team,
For there's no' a team in this whole wide world.
From the Real Madrid to the Hotspurs,
Could ever be as dear to me as the famous Glasgow Rangers.

Naturally, being a Rangers song, there has to be at least one other version of this, but it's only lines three and four which have alternative lyrics, which are....

So I took them o'er to Ibrox Park to see the flags unfurled,
After that display they had to say "You're the champions of the world!"

Now to the Rangers versions of what may considered far more ordinary football songs - no ancient Irish heritage in these ones! A taste of Molineux is brought to Glasgow with a short version of *Everywhere We Go*, which has an equally common bit tacked on the end (to the tune of *Mammie*)....

Everywhere we go - everywhere we go!
People want to know - people want to know!
Who the fucking hell we are - who the fucking hell we are!
So we tell 'em - so we tell 'em!
We're the boys in blue and white - we're the boys in blue and white!
We love to sing, we love to fight - we love to sing we love to fight!

> *Oh - oh - oh, Rangers, Rangers,*
> *Fuck the I R A!*
> *Oh - oh - oh Rangers, Rangers,*
> *I'd walk a million miles,*
> *For one of your goals,*
> *Oh Rangers!*

Not too sure whether Al Jolson's version had a second line similar to this particular interpretation of his song or not! Then, it's either Rod Stewart's *Sailing* or possibly *My Darling Clementine* which makes an appearance, with the last two lines fitting the rhythm of the latter, but the first two obviously taken from the standard terrace version of the former....

> *We are Rangers, we are Rangers,*
> *No one likes us, we don't care,*
> *We hate Celtic - Fenian bastards!*
> *And we'll chase them everywhere.*

There are then some fairly standard chants which add some (not entirely necessary) bulk to the Ibrox selection. The first is sort of along the lines of the *"Olé, Olé, Olé, Olé"* chant, so popular with the Republic of Ireland national team's supporters, but with an additional comment that would not be particularly well received by these same fans - *"Howay, Howay, Howay, Howay - Fuck the Pope and the I R A!"*. Of a very similar nature there is *"U D A, all the way - Fuck the Pope and the I R A"*, with the U D A being the Ulster Defence Association (another Loyalist paramilitary organisation) and lastly there is the very strange *"We are the people - clap - clap - clap - clap - clap!"* which is repeated twice, but which doesn't seem to fit any established pattern at all.

Two final songs to finish, both of which have come to prominence in the last couple of years, and both of which are used by Celtic supporters in a slightly altered format. With successive championships piling up by the bucket-load, a retort was prompted from Parkhead by the adoption of Scott Joplin's *The Entertainer* in the Ibrox stands - this one will continue to evolve as long as Rangers keep winning, having first been heard after the seventh of their current run of titles....

> *Oh it's seven in a row,*
> *Oh it's se-e-even in a row,*
> *And it's gonna be eight,*
> *And it's gonna be nine,*
> *And it's gonna be ten in a row!*

Although this was later copied by Celtic supporters, the boot seems to have been on the other foot for this last effort, with the *Jorge Cadete/Winter*

Wonderland song started by those of a green and white persuasion then being adapted by supporters who favour the light blues....

> *There's only one Jorge Cadete,*
> *He's got hair like spaghetti,*
> *He's Portuguese,*
> *He's one of these!*
> *Walking in a Laudrup wonderland.*

Obviously, Rangers' own Brian Laudrup takes his place in the last line, but the preceding phrase poses rather more of a conundrum - it can only be assumed that it is accompanied by frenzied "wanker" gestures from the performers, or something equally derogatory!

Section Fourteen

Northern Ireland

Cliftonville

Coleraine

Glentoran

Larne

Linfield

Northern Ireland

Unsurprisingly, there are a number of songs from the Province which reflect the deep social divisions which are such a feature of everyday life there, but there is a point of no little interest to be recorded in that Cliftonville - the club with the most ardent Republican following - have one of the largest collections of songs which can best be categorised as just plain silly. Crowd trouble seems to be a regular feature at games involving The Wee Reds, but when relative calm does descend on the terraces, you are likely to hear any number of songs which seem entirely out of place in so combustible an environment.

The same sectarian anthems which feature so strongly in the songbooks of Glasgow's Old Firm are common to more or less all the clubs in the Smirnoff League, but it was noticeable that these were offset by some excursions into rank silliness which number amongst the best in the British Isles - you need look no further than Larne and their *Mary Had A Little Lamb* effort for a wholly splendid example.

Common themes abound, with several songs being more or less obligatory fare for all the clubs from whom contributions were received, which perhaps reflects the relatively small fan-base which follows the game in Ulster. What is more surprising is the lack of any real number of songs which are unique to the Province. It is, after all, entirely separate from the mainland, and it might have been reasonable to expect a good few tunes to have cropped up which were substantially different from the sort of thing which you hear in England or Scotland. Traditional Irish songs are also a fairly scarce commodity, with only Glentoran's *Hills Of Donegal* carrying the flag for locally-inspired numbers, although had research been expanded to take in the Irish Republic, I'm sure more songs of this nature would have been in evidence.

In essence, then, the songs of Northern Ireland are somewhat predictable when it comes to the staple football related fare on offer, but the catalogue is spiced up by one or two particularly noteworthy additions to the list of less conventional songs which do so much to enhance the wider appeal of the game.

Cliftonville

A strange set of affairs at Solitude, as you might have expected the songs of The Wee Reds to be solely the sort of Republican battle hymns which are favourites at Celtic matches, given the club's reputation for a rabid anti-Unionist stance, and that of its supporters for extensive crowd trouble seemingly every time one of the "bigger" Loyalist clubs are encountered - but you'd be wrong. Obviously, there are a fair sprinkling of sectarian songs, but supporters in The Cage ('villes home terrace) seem to have at least an equal amount of songs which are just plain silly, probably the finest example of which is a fascination with *The Time Warp* - an exceedingly daft affair taken from *The Rocky Horror Show* which was released as a single in 1989 by someone going by the name of Damian. An integral part of the song is the accompanying dance and this, too, has been warmly embraced by the Cliftonville supporters - the actions are taken directly from the lyrics....

It's just a jump to the left,
And a step to the right,
With your hands on your knees,
You bend you knees in time,
It's just the pelvic thrust,
That drives you insane,
Let's do the Time Warp again....

It's difficult to imagine anything further removed from the violence with which Cliftonville have unfortunately become associated than this ridiculous behaviour - other than, perhaps, the full scale renditions of *You've Lost That Loving Feeling* which are also prone to take place. The song is also popular on the Trent End at Nottingham Forest, but the East Midlander's single verse and chorus pale into insignificance when set alongside the full-blown orations at Solitude....

You never close your eyes any more when I kiss your lips,
There's no tenderness like before in your fingertips,
You're trying hard not to show it, baby,
But baby, baby I know it.

You've lost that loving feeling, wooaah that loving feeling,
You've lost that loving feeling, and it's gone, gone, gone....

Baby, baby, I'd get down on my knees for you,
If you would only love me like you used to do,
We had a love, a love you don't find every day,
So don't, don't, don't let it slip away.

You've lost that loving feeling, wooaah that loving feeling,
You've lost that loving feeling, and it's gone, gone, gone....

Now there's no tenderness in you arms when I reach for you,
And you're starting to criticise everything I do,
It makes me feel like crying, baby,
'cos baby, something beautiful's dying.

You've lost that loving feeling, wooaah that loving feeling,
You've lost that loving feeling, and it's gone, gone, gone....

...ooh, fair makes you well up with tears, doesn't it! And if this wasn't enough to have supporters around the ground reaching for the Kleenex, it may well have been enhanced by a similarly extensive performance of *I Can't Help Falling In Love With You* (cf Sunderland). Setting their stall out to be hailed as the champions of the non-football football song, the two efforts listed above were almost invariably followed by *Summer Nights* from Grease and this little lot went three quarters of the way towards completing a quartet of such songs which was finished off by *Do They Know It's Christmas?* (sung in its entirety with original lyrics intact as per the Band Aid version).

Inevitably, not everything at Solitude is sweetness and light, and the sectarian issue plays a big part in the Cliftonville repertoire. A fairly mild mannered song first, to the tune of *Bless 'em All* (cf Glentoran)....

Bless 'em all, bless 'em all,
The long and the short and the tall,
Bless all the forwards and bless all the backs,
Bless all the boys with the red on their backs,
For it's off to Windsor we go - what for?
To give the Linfield a show,
For we'll never be mastered.
By no orange bastard,
It's off to Linfield we go.

By way of clarification, Linfield (one of the leading Protestant clubs) play their home games at Windsor Park, Cliftonville play in red and white (hence *"red on their backs"*) and the *"orange"* in line eight is basically another word for Protestant (cf Heart of Midlothian and the sash story). A little more forthright is this next song which - somewhat perceptively - I reckon might take the tune of the hymn *Glory, Glory, Glory* !

Glory, glory, glory, what a hell of a way to die,
Glory, glory, glory, what a hell of a way to die,
Glory, glory, glory, what a hell of a way to die.
To die an orange bastard, a dirty orange bastard!

About as popular with the Cliftonville supporters as Linfield are Glentoran, another Protestant club who play their home games at a ground called The Oval. Not short of inspiration at the best of times, a name like that is meat and drink to the patrons of The Cage - remember the old adverts......?

> *We are the Ovalteenies,*
> *Orange girls and boys,*
> *Shit scared of the Red's supporters,*
> *We don't make no fucking noise.*
> *When the Redmen in their hundreds,*
> *Come to East Belfast,*
> *We'll all run back home to mummy,*
> *'cos we know they'll kick our arse.*

....interesting to note the touch of realism that dictates that Cliftonville anticipate taking *"hundreds"* of supporters to Glentoran - if this was an English song you can bet that this would have been thousands!

Just to prove that there is one theme that unites supporters in England, Scotland and Northern Ireland, there are one bunch of poor unfortunates in the Smirnoff League who (like Aberdeen, Leeds and anyone from Wales) are labelled "sheep shaggers". Ballymena United are the team in question, but the Cliftonville supporters have come up with a new tune, if not particularly edifying lyrics, to which the assertions of ovine abuse can be made - the hymn *Bringing In The Sheaves*....

> *Shagging all the sheep,*
> *Shagging all the sheep,*
> *Ballymena United,*
> *Shagging all the sheep!*

Equally as common as sheep shagging songs are versions of *Just One Of Those Songs*, and Solitude has its own arrangement - albeit a little shorter than most....

> *We are the Cliftonville, the pride of the North,*
> *We hate the Glentoran and Linfield of course,*
> *We drink all the cider and sing 'til we're hoarse,*
> *We are the Cliftonville boys.*

And that, with the added assumption that a good many Republican songs do actually appear in their standard Celtic format, is just about enough, apart from what has to rate as one of the briefest chants to have ever remained popular for long enough to merit inclusion - lacking any sort of hidden nuances at all, this is simply *"We are Cliftonville - fuck Linfield!"* which, if nothing else, is unlikely to be misunderstood!

Coleraine

An interesting selection from one of the new inductees into the wonderful and frightening world of *Dicks Out*, in that Coleraine songs for the most part are fairly standard renditions of fairly standard songs, but these are interspersed with a couple of far more worthy efforts.

A bit of controversy first, and an indication of just how much importance can be attached to something so outwardly simple as a song in the volatile world of football in Northern Ireland. To an outsider, Coleraine appear to be one of the more moderate clubs in the province when it comes to sectarian attitudes - a club with Loyalist sympathies without doubt, but nothing to compare with the rabid fervour of some of the other clubs. There was, however, a bit of a furore when the fanzine which sent us all the following material was first published under the name of *For It's A Grand Old Team* - a line from a song which had reputedly been sung by Coleraine supporters in the past, but a song which is generally known as being a Celtic anthem (*cf* Celtic and Linfield) and of therefore having very definite Republican leanings. Although the fanzine's editors tried to make the point that they were merely taking inspiration from a harmless song, so many supporters of the club were wary of being tarred with the Republican brush as a result of the adoption of the name that it was eventually decided that it had to be changed. The new title was *Along The Bannside or Killowen* which was taken from the Coleraine version of *Show Me The Way To Go Home*, a favourite in Ulster which had been associated with the club much longer than *For It's A....*, and without any sectarian leanings (real or perceived) to boot. Compare this with the Glentoran version, as well as with those from Liverpool and Spurs....

> *Show me the way to go home,*
> *I'm tired and I want to go to bed,*
> *I had a little drink about an hour ago,*
> *And it's gone right to my head,*
> *No matter where I roam,*
> *Along the Bannside or Killowen,*
> *You will always hear me singing this song,*
> *Show me the way to go home.*

"The Bannside" refers to the River Bann which flows through Coleraine, but I've no idea who or what *"Killowen"* might be.

Next to a rather fine reworking of the Torquay United *Robin Stubbs* song, to the tune of the *Robin Hood* theme - this time in praise of a Showgrounds legend by the name of Derek Cook. Presumably the gentleman in question was possessed of a fine head of ginger hair....

Derek Cook, Derek Cook,
Rising through the air,
Derek Cook, Derek Cook,
With his orange hair,
Gets to the ball,
Misses fuck all,
Derek Cook, Derek Cook, Derek Cook!

Mr Cook is also feted by way of a Brian Dean-esque version of *The Banana Boat Song* (*cf* Sheffield United, with "Cookie" replacing "Deano" throughout) and in a singularly narrative version of *The Red Flag* which is....

Oh Robbie Beck now he did fall,
Never saw where Cookie put the ball,
He ball the ball right in the net,
And poor old Robbie stood and wept.
He looked up high, up in the sky,
He saw the blue flags flying high,
Wherever we go, we'll fear no foe,
We'll keep the blue flag flying high.

With the last couple of lines harking back to the original lyrics, it is the first part of the above which alludes to one of Cook's more significant goals - but I'm unable to shed any light on the circumstances other than to say that it was scored in spite of the efforts of Glenavon goalkeeper Robbie Beck.

On to a couple of songs imported from London - the first being not a million miles removed from the West Ham version of The Ramblers *Sparrow* song....

He's only a poor little Bannsider,
His colours they are white and blue,
And some day this season,
For no fucking reason,
He's going to kick the shite out of you!

....and the second being based on *Just One Of Those Songs*, and revealing where the true loyalties of the Showgrounds' supporters lie....

We are the pride of all Ulster,
The cock of the North,
We hate the Jamesies,
They're bastards of course,
We're the Bannsiders,
Without any doubt,
We are the Coleraine boys,
Na na na, na na na na na, na na na na na....

The *"bastards"* to which this song refers are *"Jamesies"* - the (descendents of) the Catholic followers of King James.

Some of the more run of the mill Coleraine songs include a derivation of Manchester United's *Lord Of The Dance* with the Irish Cup being the sought after trophy, Kilmarnock's *"Legoland"* song - directed at the majority of other clubs in the Irish League, most of whom are purported to have pretty ramshackle stadia, and *My Liverpool Home* (*cf* Portsmouth) which has become *In Your Belfast Slums* and must therefore be directed mainly at the followers of Linfield, Glentoran and Cliftonville (although it could equally apply to Crusaders and Distillery supporters). All in all then, a pretty diverse selection of songs from the North of County Londonderry - and one which is more than worthy of its place in these pages.

Glentoran

One of Northern Ireland's traditional footballing powers, The Glens (odd how the team from The Oval have become known as this, while Glenavon haven't!) have developed a considerable rivalry with the other half of the old duopoly, Linfield. Interestingly in the context of Irish football, this is purely a football-based feud, with both sides coming from the same (Loyalist) side of the sectarian divide, but the animosity seems none the less intense for that.

A cheery refrain with which to begin, laden with anti-Linfield sentiment, and taking the form of the Wolverhampton Wanderers epic (without, of course, ever approaching the pre-eminence of the Molineux saga in the field of repetition-based songs)....

> *Oh here we go - oh here we go!*
> *We're at it again - we're at it again!*
> *We're moving up - we're moving up!*
> *We're moving in - we're moving in!*
> *We are the lads - we are the lads!*
> *From East Belfast - from East Belfast!*
> *We are the best - we are the best!*
> *So fuck the rest - so fuck the rest!*
> *There was a bird - there was a bird!*
> *A Linfield bird - a Linfield bird!*
> *It landed on - it landed on!*
> *My window sill - my window sill!*

I coaxed it in - I coaxed it in!
With a piece of bread - with a piece of bread!
And then I crushed - and then I crushed!
The birdies head - the birdies head!
Glentoran! - Glentoran!

The loathing of all things connected with the Windsor Park outfit may not have done much for the cause of tolerance and harmony in the game, but it has thrown up one of the finest examples of abuse aimed at a single player that football has ever seen. The fellow in question was one Lindsay McKeown - a Linfield player renowned for his gross ugliness (so we are told). With John Hurt's portrayal of the hideously disfigured John Merrick still fresh in the minds of those on the terraces of The Oval, McKeown was roundly abused by a short piece which took the tune of *Tom Hark* by The Piranhas....

Lindsay McKeown, the Elephant Man!
Lindsay McKeown, the Elephant Man!
Da da da da - oooh, da da da da oooh!
D-da d-da da - oooh, da da da da - oooh!

Now, not only is this a fine song in its own right, but it simply has to be mentioned that the band which originally released it in 1958 were the superbly named Elias And His Zig-Zag Jive Flutes - probably the finest title ever taken by any musical ensemble, ever. Not only did McKeown find himself regaled with abuse by way of the above, he also had the singular honour of a dance being conceived in his honour. Following on from the *Elephant Man* theme, it will be necessary for you to conjure up images of *Play School* presenters pretending to be elephants (arm flopping around in front of face in a trunk-like manner) for you to be able to get any sort of realistic idea of what was going on while the Glentoran supporters were chanting *"Let's all do the Lindsay, Let's all do the Lindsay!"* to the Conga rhythm - cruel but strangely laudable behaviour nonetheless! There is also another Glentoran dance along very similar lines which again takes the Conga approach and is *"Let's all do the bouncy, let's all do the bouncy!"* - presumably this is a manifestation of nothing more than sheer silliness, and the dance itself, well, must be just bouncing up and down, mustn't it? (ooh - *cf* Bolton Wanderers!).

Away from the sadistic world of McKeown-baiting, we come to the Glentoran versions of two seemingly compulsory Northern Irish songs - the first of which is *The Red Flag*....

Forever and ever, we'll follow the Glens,
Glentoran for ever, we'll follow you,
We'll capture the Gold Cup, the City Cup too,
If we don't win the league, the Irish Cup'll do,
So let Linfield be bastards forever!

Not, it has to be said, one of the more coherent of the many versions of this classic football anthem (close to being nonsensical drivel, to be honest!). However, *Bless 'em All* get's far more sensible treatment, although either this or the Cliftonville version is no more than shameless plagiarism as both are more or less identical in all but the most elementary of ways....

> *Bless 'em all, bless 'em all,*
> *The long and the short and the tall,*
> *Bless all the forwards,*
> *And half backs and backs,*
> *Bless all the fellows in red, green and black,*
> *For we're singing goodbye to them all,*
> *It's back to The Oval we go,*
> *For we'll not be mastered,*
> *By no Linfield bastard,*
> *So cheer on the lads, bless 'em all.*

Now, assertions in the first edition of this book that the following song had gravitated onto the terraces have been confirmed, as has the suggestion that a rather less gentlemanly version existed. The original, first, of a long standing club song to the tune of *The Hills Of Donegal*....

> *I am a grand wee Ulsterman,*
> *And Thompson is my name,*
> *I like a drink on Saturday,*
> *I like a football game,*
> *To Windsor Park I like to go,*
> *To see the Blues go down,*
> *'cos I support Glentoran,*
> *From the other side of town.*

> *I always wear my Glens scarf,*
> *No matter where I go,*
> *I always have it round my neck,*
> *no matter where I've been,*
> *A Blueman tried to strangle me,*
> *he pulled my scarf so tight,*
> *I only said "C'mon you Glens!"*
> *He wanted me to fight.*

The amended version - dating back to the mid 1970's - relates to the relationship that Glen's supporters had (and probably still have) with their cross-city rivals from Cliftonville - whose Republican sympathies have only served to fuel what would probably have been a lively local rivalry even without the sectarian element being in place....

I am a loyal Orangeman,
My scarf is red and green,
I pledge my life to Ulster,
To The Glens and to The Queen,
To North Belfast I like to go,
To fight the Fenian scum,
To chase them over Buirgéis Hill,
And back where they come from.

The obvious inference in this is that Cliftonville's Catholic supporters are going to be chased out of the city and back to the Republic where, in the minds of the Glentoran fans, they belong. Buirgéis Hill is to the South of the city of Belfast (on the way to the Republic!), but it seems odd that the traditional Gaelic name is used in what is otherwise such a plainly Loyalist song. Even more peculiarly, there does not appear to be such a "confrontational" version of this song referring to Linfield - towards whom the rest of the Glens' ire is directed.

Larne

Another club whose supporters fall under our spotlight for the first time, Larne's repertoire is - it has to be said - not massively inspirational, apart that is from one absolutely stupendous song, the likes of which are to be found nowhere else whatsoever. Quite clearly the finest football song in Northern Ireland, it is sort of *Mary Had A Little Lamb* with loads of extra bits thrown in for good measure, anyway, be amazed - be very amazed....

Mary had a little lamb,
It's fleece was white as snow,
Singing out the praises of the Larne boys!
And everywhere that Mary went,
The lamb was sure to go,
Singing out the praises of the Larne boys!
Hurray for Mary!
Hurrah for the lamb!
Hurrah for the Larne boys who never give a damn!
And everywhere that Mary went,
The lamb was sure to go,
Singing out the praises of the Larne boys!

> *Mary had a little lamb,*
> *She also had a duck,*
> *Singing out the praises of the Larne boys!*
> *And everywhere that Mary went,*
> *The duck was sure to go,*
> *Singing out the praises of the Larne boys!*
> *Hurrah for Mary!*
> *Hurrah for the duck!*
> *Hurrah for the Larne boys who never give a fuck!*
> *And everywhere that Mary went,*
> *The duck was sure to go,*
> *Singing out the praises of the Larne boys!*

I don't imagine that I was alone in having a vague idea of what was to follow after the initial revelation that Mary *"also had a duck"* - probably the most predictable rhyme in any song in this book! Nonetheless, this really is a spectacular song - one of the very best!

To be honest, there's not much that could stand comparison with such magnificence, but at least the sentiments of the following must be applauded, even if it is otherwise a very simple song....

> *The red and whites are on the piss again,*
> *On the piss again, on the piss again,*
> *The red and whites are on the piss again,*
> *We're all drunken bastards.*

The tune to this was not disclosed, but given that it is of fairly recent vintage, I wouldn't be surprised if it was along the lines of *Down By The Riverside*, as popularised by Manchester United supporters (well, it seems to fit reasonably well!).

Now, not only do Larne's supporters have a noble song of their own, but they seem to have been the first to have used Jackie Lee's *Rupert The Bear* tune which has subsequently gone on to wider fame at the hands of Newcastle United supporters in its *Philippe Albert* guise. A very similar contemporary of the original release in the early seventies was evidently *"Gerry, Gerry O'Kane - everyone knows his name!"*

Swiftly passing over both the honest appraisal of the team's talents which was *"We are red, we are white, we are Larne and we are shite"* (a derivation of the more popular *"We are red, we are white, we are fucking dynamite"* sort of thing) and the Larne contribution to religious tolerance which was *"We don't sing sectarian songs - fuck the Pope, fuck the Pope!"*, we come to what is seemingly the most popular pastime amongst football supporters in the province, regardless of who they support - abusing Ballymena United. As is the case with other clubs, all the "usual" sheep-shagging songs make an appearance, but there are one or two which seem to be exclusive to Larne. The first of these includes some more general agricultural abuse, and is to an entirely unknown tune....

> *Doing the shitkickers' waltz,*
> *You don't give two hoots,*
> *If you've got shit on your boots,*
> *Doing the shitkickers' waltz.*

> *Doing the sheepshaggers' waltz,*
> *You've got to get,*
> *Sheep's hooves in your boots,*
> *Doing the sheepshaggers' waltz!*

Another to take a wider swipe at the whole farming community reiterates the assertion that anyone who makes a living on the land is likely to have a certain aroma about them - the tune again might well be *Down By The Riverside*....

> *The Ballymena bells go dung-a-lung-a-lung,*
> *Dung-a-lung-a-lung, dung-a-lung-a-lung,*
> *The Ballymena bells go dung-a-lung-a-lung,*
> *For all you smelly bastards!*

And that's about it from Inver Park - but the Antrim coast is now firmly on the football map in the light of that superb version of *Mary Had A Little Lamb* - a very fine song indeed!

Linfield

A strangely uninventive repertoire from what is probably Northern Ireland's most fiercely Loyalist club - with inspiration being drawn from far and wide but with not much evidence of songs which are exclusive to Windsor Park. As mused upon in the Burnley section, there is a very strong link between Linfield and Glasgow Rangers, and as a result many of the songs which are popular at Ibrox also appear in Belfast. *The Sash My Father Wore, Old Derry's Walls* and even *Follow, Follow* have all surfaced in the Linfield cause, with the latter taking its lead from the more abusive of the two versions which are doing the rounds under the Rangers' banner....

Should the streets be broad or narrow,
We'll follow we will, follow we will, follow we will,
Should the streets be broad or narrow,
We'll follow we will, we'll follow in the footsteps of our team,
God bless them!

Follow, follow, we will follow Linfield,
Up the Falls, Derry's walls, we will follow on,
Cliftonville and Glentoran, fuck the Pope and the Vatican,
If they go to Dublin, we will follow on.

There's not a team like the Belfast Linfield,
No, not one, and there never will be one,
The Celts know all about their fucking troubles,
We will fight 'til the day is done,
There's not a team like the Belfast Linfield,
No, not one, and there never will be one.

Apart from the name changes, there are one or two very slight differences between this and the "proper" Rangers version, but it is to all intents and purposes a straight reproduction of the original.

The same confusion as was manifested at Coleraine then makes an appearance at Windsor Park, as Celtic's inherently Republican *For It's A Grand Old Team* is also a Linfield song, albeit with the salient line having been changed to *"Here, here, the Blues are here!"* Of a more exclusive nature, we then find a strange song which seems to be made up from the jumbled parts of about three other more standard compositions - this odd amalgamation gives us....

Glory, glory, glory,
Listen to our song,
We are the Belfast Linfield,
We're the best team in the land,
- two, three, four -
Bring on the Ballymena,
bring on the Crusaders too,
Bring on the shitey Glentoran,
And we'll show them what to do.

Glossing over the heartfelt but singularly obscene treatment given to leading members of the Catholic community in the Linfield version of Boney M's *Holi-Holiday*, and the equally contentious abuse levelled at Glentoran for the mere fact that there is a Catholic chapel a short distance from The Oval (you can gauge how nasty these two songs must be just by looking at one or two others which have managed to escape censorship!), we come to something which is either another statement of Loyalist sentiment, or perhaps just a bit of abject silliness. It would appear that *Jerusalem* has become part of the Linfield song book, with the original lyrics intact (as is the case with Doncaster Rovers!). Although it is difficult to imagine the song making an appearance at a football ground in anything other than the cause of the utmost stupidity, it's just possible that the same sentiments which have seen the song become a favourite with supporters of the English rugby union team have meant that it is in the Linfield repertoire for purely sectarian reasons....

> *And did those feet, in ancient time,*
> *Walk upon England's mountain green?*
> *And was the holy lamb of God,*
> *On England's pleasant pastures seen?*
> *And did the countenance divine,*
> *Shine forth upon our clouded hills?*
> *And was Jerusalem builded here,*
> *Among those dark satanic mills?*

And with that final piece of by now reassuringly familiar and rather half-baked research, that appears to be the end of the Linfield entry, the Northern Ireland section, and the book as a whole (apart from the frankly rather dull appendix and index), so thank you for your kind attention, and in the words of that immortal song (to the tune of *On Ilkley Moor Ba T'Hat*)...."*Why don't you fuck off, oh why don't you fuck off, oh why don't you fuck off...?*"

303

Appendix

The following is a list of songs which have been adopted on the terraces having first made an appearance in the charts in one guise or another. Hopefully, this will provide a handy reference if you're trying to track down a song to which you know the tune, but are not necessarily aware which particular terrace choir number it amongst their repertoires.

Song Title	Performer	Club(s)
A Little Respect	Erasure	Leyton Orient
Agadoo	Black Lace	Watford
American Pie	Don MacLean	Hereford United
Annie's Song	John Denver	Sheffield United
Banana Boat Song	Harry Belafonte	Sheffield United
		Ipswich Town
		West Bromwich Albion
Banana Splits Song	The Dickies	Manchester City
Batchelor Boy	Cliff Richard	Rotherham United
Beat on the Brat	The Ramones	Hereford United
		Wolverhampton Wanderers
Between The Wars	Billy Bragg	Cambridge United
Blue Moon	Bob Dylan	Crewe Alexandra
		Brighton & Hove Albion
		Barnsley
		Rotherham United
		Manchester City
		Shrewsbury Town
		East Fife
Boom Boom Boom	Outhere Brothers	Port Vale
Can't Help Falling In Love With You	Elvis Presley	Swindon Town
		Sunderland
		Swansea City
Can't Take My Eyes Off of You	Andy Williams	Swansea City
Caravan Of Love	Housemartins	Hull City
Centrefold	J Geils Band	Doncaster Rovers
Crazy Crazy Nights	Kiss	Bradford City
Da Do Ron Ron	The Crystals	Bradford City
Daydream Believer	The Monkees	Sunderland
Delilah	Tom Jones	Stoke City
		Stockport County
Dirty Old Town	The Pogues	Wrexham
Distant Drums	Jim Reeves	Millwall
		York City
Double Dutch	Malcolm Maclaren	Hull City
		Burnley
Down Down	Status Quo	Fulham

305

Give It Up	K C & The Sunshine Band	Hull City
Glad All Over	Dave Clark Five	Crystal Palace
Gold	Spandau Ballet	Barnet
Go West	Pet Shop Boys	Arsenal
		West Bromwich Albion
Hey Girl Don't Bother Me	The Tams	Middlesbrough
Hey Jude	The Beatles	Brentford
		Stockport County
Hey Luciani	The Fall	Barnsley
Hi Ho Silver Lining	Jeff Beck	Sheffield Wednesday
		Sheffield United
Hooray, Hooray, It's A Holi-holiday	Boney M	Charlton Athletic
Hot Hot Hot	Arrow	Arsenal
		Middlesbrough
		West Bromwich Albion
I Should Be So Lucky	Kylie Minogue	Reading
Israelites	Desmond Dekker	Norwich City
Jerusalem	Herb Alpert/The Fall	Linfield
		Doncaster Rovers
Just One Of Those Songs		Gillingham
		Bradford City
		Sheffield Wednesday
		Hartlepool United
		East Fife
		Manchester United
		Exeter City
		Cliftonville
		Coleraine
Karma Chameleon	Culture Club	Hull City
Let's Dance	Chris Montez	Chelsea
Lily The Pink	The Scaffold	Manchester United
Lola	The Kinks	Newcastle United
Long Haired Lover from Liverpool	Jimmy Osmond	Tranmere Rovers
Love Is Law	The Seahorses	Brighton & Hove Albion
Macarena	Los Del Rio	Liverpool
		Manchester United
Merry Christmas/War Is Over	John Lennon	Doncaster Rovers
Merry Ploughboy	Dermot O'Brien	Celtic
Merry Xmas Everybody	Slade	Wigan Athletic
Mighty Quinn	Manfred Mann	Millwall
		York City
Mrs Robinson	Simon & Garfunkel	A F C Bournemouth
		Southampton
		Brighton & Hove Albion
Mull Of Kintyre	Paul McCartney & Wings	Charlton Athletic
		Nottingham Forest
		Lincoln City
		Grimsby Town
My Ding-a-ling	Chuck Berry	Manchester United
My Way	Frank Sinatra	Heart of Midlothian
Na Na, Hey, Hey.......	Bananarama	Derby County
Nellie The Elephant	The Toy Dolls	Watford

Song	Artist	Club
New York, New York	Frank Sinatra	Aston Villa
No Limits	2 Unlimited	Brighton & Hove Albion
		Crystal Palace
		Burnley
		Swansea City
Oh Boy	Mud	Fulham
Oh What An Atmosphere	Russ Abbott	Crystal Palace
Oops Upside Your Head	The Gap Band	Leeds United
		Manchester United
Paint It Black	Rolling Stones	Bristol Rovers
Peek A Boo	New Vaudeville Band	Chelsea
Poing	Rotterdam Termination Source	West Bromwich Albion
		Crystal Palace
Prince Charming	Adam & The Ants	Sheffield United
		York City
Que Sera Sera	Geno Washington	Leeds United
		Scunthorpe United
		Bradford City
Raining In My Heart	Leo Sayer	Sheffield Wednesday
Riders In The Sky	The Ramrods	Charlton Athletic
Rupert The Bear	Jackie Lee	Newcastle United
		Larne
Sailing	Rod Stewart	Millwall
		Derby County
Save Your Kisses For Me	Brotherhood of Man	Preston North End
Scottish Soldier	Andy Stewart	Oldham Athletic
Singing The Blues	Tommy Steele	Reading
		Sheffield Wednesday
Son Of My Father	Chocory Tip	Notts County
		Manchester City
Stand Down Margaret	The Beat	Notts County
Streets of London	Ralph McTell	Stockport County
Teddy Boy Boogie	Crazy Cavan	Gillingham
Tennesse Wig Walk	Bonny Lou	A F C Bournemouth
		Fulham
		Northampton Town
		Scunthorpe United
Thank U Very Much	The Scaffold	Hartlepool United
		Wolverhampton Wanderers
The Entertainer	Scott Joplin	Celtic
		Rangers
The Happy Wanderer	Obernkirchen Childrens Choir	Newcastle United
The Lion Sleeps Tonight	Tight Fit	Swansea City
		East Fife
The Sparrow	The Ramblers	Ipswich Town
		West Ham United
		Coleraine
The Time Warp	Damian	Cliftonville
There's No-one Quite Like Grandma	St Winifreds School Choir	Manchester City
Those Were The Days	Mary Hopkins	Chelsea
		Huddersfield Town
		Wolverhampton Wanderers
Tom Hark	The Piranhas	Glentoran

Too Good To Be Forgotten	Amazulu	Northampton Town
Too Sexy	Right Said Fred	Stockport County
Twenty Four Hours From Tulsa	Gene Pitney	Portsmouth
Twist & Shout	The Beatles	Coventry City
Viva Bobby Joe	The Equals	Southampton
Wandrin' Star	Lee Marvin	Lincoln City
		Wolverhampton Wanderers
We'll Meet Again	Vera Lynn	Leeds United
		Exeter City
		Rangers
We Shall Overcome	Joan Baez	Middlesbrough
		Southampton
What's New Pussycat?	Tom Jones	Port Vale
White Christmas	Bing Crosby	Barnet
Wonder of You	Elvis Presley	Port Vale
Wonderwall	Oasis	Manchester City
Yellow Submarine	The Beatles	A F C Bournemouth
		Oxford United
		Reading
		Hull City
		Newcastle United
		Port Vale
You Need Hands	Max Bygraves	Chesterfield
You'll Never Walk Alone	Gerry Marsden	Liverpool
		Celtic
You've Lost That Loving Feeling	Righteous Brothers	Nottingham Forest
		Cliftonville
Young, Gifted and Black	Bob & Marcia	Hull City

Index

A F C Bournemouth
   27, 38, 51, 74,108,111, 171
Aberdeen   275
Adamson, Jimmy   126
Agana, Tony   133
Albert, Phillippe   154, 300
Andy Pandy   10
Archer, Bill   8
Arsenal   56, 174, 223
Ashford, Noel   29
Aston Villa   71, 220, 224
Ayr United   279
Babb, Phil   175
Baldwin, Tommy   44
Ball, Alan   179, 246
Ballymena United   293, 300
Banana Splits, The   177
Barnet   71, 109, 118, 162
Barnsley   89, 127
Bartlett, Kevin   225
Batch, Nigel   107
Bates, Chick   24
Baxter, Billy   70
Beauchamp, Joey   11
Beck, John   190
Behr, Danni   187
Bell, Derek   107
Bell, Willie   217
Bellotti, David   8
Bergara, Danny   133, 194
Berkovic, Eyal   16
Beverley Hillbillies   171
Birmingham City   49, 217, 227, 230
Bjornebye, Stig Inge   175
Blackburn Rovers   165, 167, 189
Blackheath Electrodrives   217
Blackpool   191, 195, 196
Blaydon Races   75, 151, 157, 269
Blue Moon   200
Blue Peter   125, 166
Bly, Billy   103
Boel, Henning   258
Bond, John   179
Borthwick, John   146
Bowry, Bobby   48
Bowyer, Ian   204
Bradford Park Avenue   117
Brentford   211
Brighton & Hove Albion   74, 87, 104,115

Bristol City   86, 166, 240, 248
Bristol Rovers   211, 237
Brock, Kevin   23
Bruce, Steve   28
Bryn the Police Dog   250
Buckley, Alan   101
Bull, Steve   224, 231
Bunn, Frank   106, 189
Burnley   105, 121, 161, 276, 285
Busby, Matt   182, 183
Butlin, Barry   134
Cadete, Jorge   286
Cantona, Eric   49, 127, 187, 206
Cardiff City   53, 203, 247
Carroll, Dave   30
Carter, Roy   24
Caveman Crew   5, 29
Celtic   56, 92, 280, 286, 294
Charles, Jeremy   248
Charlton Athletic   85, 93, 107, 233
Charlton, Bobby   182
Chelsea   49, 62, 88, 128, 166, 209, 226
Chester City   164, 200, 212
Chesterfield   90, 120
Chigley   125
Cliftonville   91, 298, 302
Clough, Brian   17, 209
Cockerill, John   100
Colchester United   18, 71, 78
Collymore, Stan   84
Cooper, Steve   115
Coventry City   68
Cowdenbeath   267, 270
Cox, Arthur   93
Crawford, Ray   70
Crewe Alexandra   175, 250
Crystal Palace   224
Cunningham, Tony   107
Cunnington, Shaun   100
Currie, David   115
Currie, Tony   128
Darlington   144, 146, 147
Deane, Brian   133
Deehan, John   77
Derby County   107, 166
di Canio, Paolo   266
Dicks, Alan   239
Doncaster Rovers   71, 83, 88, 90,103, 110,
      115, 138, 189, 303

Dunfermline Athletic   268
Durrant, Ian   259
Eustace, Peter   53
Everton   23, 108
Exeter City   146, 246
F C Utrecht   136
Fantasy Football League   35, 46, 54, 88
Ferdinand, Les   158
Festa, Gianluca   149
Fjortoft, Jan-Aage   134
Flashman, Stan   109
Ford, Andy   24
Ford, Tony   107
Franklin, Neil   71
Freestone, Roger   248
Fry, Barry   109
Fulham   74, 111, 239
Futcher, Ron   118
Gabbiadini, Marco   157
Gascoigne, Paul   266
Gates, Eric   77, 157
Giggs, Ryan   187, 251
Gilbert, Dave   100
Gilligan, Jimmy   241
Gillingham   28, 74
Ginola, David   154
Glenavon   295
Glentoran   292, 302
Goodman, Don   225
Graham, George   129
Greygoose, Dean   196
Grimsby Town   107
Gritt, Steve   8, 40
Hansbury, Roger   168
Harkouk, Rachid   48
Harper, Joe   258
Hartlepool United   104, 106, 118, 138, 144,
                     208, 231, 243, 269
Harvey, Joe   154
Heart of Midlothian   257, 282
Heath, Adrian   161
Hereford United   120
Hibernian   270, 273
Hill, Jimmy   33, 222
Hillyard, Ron   28
Hong Kong Phooey   168
Horner, Billy   144
Howe, Don   33
Hudson, Alan   50
Hull City   100, 145, 168
Hunt, Andy   225
Hunt, Roger   43
Ipswich Town   63, 133, 148, 248
Jarvie, Drew   258

John, Elton   60
Johnson, Peter   212
Juninho   149
Kamara, Chris   24
Keane, Roy   187
Kendall, Howard   177
Khomenei, Ayatollah   242
Kilmarnock   167, 285
Kinkladze, Georgiou   180
Kiwomya, Chris   73
Knight, Ian   102
Law, Denis   186
Lawrence, Jamie   88
Lawson, Alan   189
Lee, Gordon   192
Lee, Jason   46, 88, 92
Lee, Sammy   6
Leeds United   39, 115, 117, 173,186,
                233, 247
Leicester City   51
Lewis, Russell   24
Leyton Orient   24
Lincoln City   102, 171, 243, 250
Lindsay, Alec   195
Linfield   167, 296
Little, Alan   131
Liverpool   43, 48, 125, 169, 184, 266, 277
Lowndes, Steve   115
Luton Town   58
Lydon, Joe   195
Macari, Lou   210
Machin, Mel   4
Macmanaman, Steve   175, 184
Maidstone United   25, 121
Manchester City   78, 122, 130, 185, 200
Manchester United 43, 46, 60, 106, 118,
                   127, 163, 177, 281, 300
Mansfield Town   120
Mariner, Paul   77
Marples, Chris   83
Marriot, Andrew   167
Maskell, Craig   26
Maxwell, Robert   86, 93
McAteer, Jason   175, 184
McClair, Brian   6
McGarry, Bill   71
McGhee, Mark   88
McGrath, Paul   128
McGrory, Jimmy   263
McHale, Ray   24
McKechnie, Ian   103
McKeown, Lindsay   297
McMenemy, Lawrie   15
McNichol, Jim   250

Meadowbank Thistle 52, 125, 226, 267
Mee, Bertie 51
Megson, Gary 191
Mercer, Joe 178
Middlesbrough 15, 35, 68, 128, 164
Miller, Willie 258
Millwall 105, 139
Milne, Ralph 187
Minogue, Kylie 25
Monty Python 183, 199, 244, 251
Moore, Darren 122
Morrow, Steve 26
Murphy, Colin 96
Nayim 57
Nellie The Elephant 58
Newcastle United 111, 147, 148, 157, 300
Nicholl, Jimmy 268
Nogan, Kurt 7, 167
Northampton Town 111
Nottingham Forest 56, 84, 162, 264, 291
Notts County 86, 178, 226
Ogley, Alan 144
Onuora, Iffy 10
Oxford United 78
Oyston, Owen 191
Pennyfather, Glenn 73
Pepper, Nigel 140
Peterborough United 23
Phillips, Gary 26
Pickering, Fred 171
Play School 297
Pleat, David 34, 58, 185
Plymouth Argyle 237, 239, 243
Port Vale 210, 227
Portsmouth 23, 203
Preston North End 196
Raith Rovers 268
Rangers 167, 188, 231, 243, 259, 264,
        274, 275, 276, 301
Ravanelli, Fabrizio 150
Reading 89, 162
Reid, Peter 153, 155
Rice, Brian 92
Richard, Cliff 129
Rioch, Bruce 85
Robinson, Michael 5, 7
Robinson, Steve 5
Robson, Bryan 4, 170
Rotherham United 23, 122
Rowland, Andy 24
Rupert The Bear 154, 300
Saunders, Carl 240
Scarborough 153, 230
Scunthorpe United 74, 122, 154

Senior, Trevor 26
Shankly, Bill 51
Shearer, Alan 158, 162
Sheffield United 85, 104, 115, 139, 152,
        194, 226, 268, 295
Sheffield Wednesday 146, 169
Sherwood, Steve 101
Shipperley, Neil 5, 16
Shrewsbury Town 95, 147, 240
Silkman, Barry 48
Slough Town 29
Southampton 62
St John, Ian 169
Stannard, Jim 10
Stiles, Nobby 187
Stockport County 39, 210
Stoke City 189, 192, 206
Stokes, Bobby 15, 16
Strachan, Gordon 258
Stubbs, Robin 250
Sunderland 27, 111, 148, 152, 249, 292
Swansea City 85, 163, 225, 241, 270
Swindon Town 24
Tait, Paul 220
Taylor, Graham 60
Telford United 208
Three Lions 131, 191, 266
Torquay United 122, 202, 294
Tottenham Hotspur 143, 265
Tranmere Rovers 208
Waltzing Matilda 124
Walwyn, Keith 139
Ward, Peter 6
Wark, John 73
Watford 248
West Bromwich Albion 29, 35, 48, 85, 230
West Ham United 46, 111, 180, 295
Westcott, Dennis 233
Wigan Athletic 87
Winstanley, Eric 116
Winstanley, Mark 116
WolverhamptonWanderers 24, 89, 103,
        120, 146, 205, 247, 285, 296
Wright, Ian 35, 47, 149
Wycombe Rhubarbs 29
Wycombe Wanderers 23, 140
Yallop, Frank 73
Yeats, Ron 169
Yogi Bear 230
Yorke, Dwight 218
Youds, Eddie 73
Zulu Warriors 220

Acknowledgements

Obviously, a book of this nature would never have got off the ground without the assistance of the many people who have sent in contributions over the last few years, but these are now far too numerous to list individually, so I will just record a general thank you to everyone who has bothered to write in with the details of songs (or who has put up with my interminable 'phone calls, asking them to sing things to me!)

More specifically, thanks to Dave and Judi at Red Card for their (probably entirely ill-conceived) faith in the book, to everyone involved in the production, to all the girls at the Crazy Horse Bureau for giving me the benefit of their extensive knowledge of early 1970's song titles (showing your age!) and - I suppose - to the Lovely Linda for putting up with all the late nights and the obscene outbursts directed at failing computer systems, and for knocking up various sandwiches as and when required.